The Illustrated Encyclopedia of the World's
MODERN LOCOMOTIVES

A technical directory of major international diesel, electric and gas-turbine locomotives from 1879 to the present day

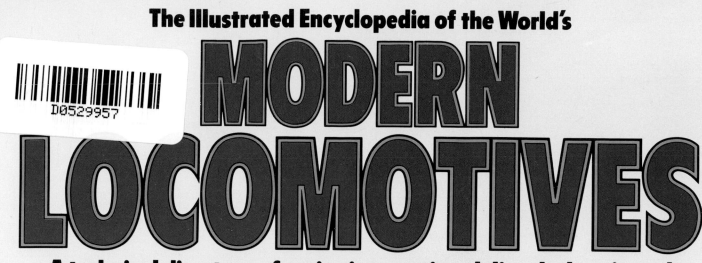

A Salamander Book

All correspondence concerning the content of this volume should be addressed to Salamander Books Ltd., Salamander House, 27 Old Gloucester Street, London WC1N 3AF, United Kingdom.

This book may not be sold outside the United States of America and Canada.

R
q 625.2
H

Credits

Editor: Ray Bonds

Designer: Philip Gorton

Color artwork: © Salamander Books Ltd.: David Palmer, Clifford and Wendy Meadway, Michael Roffe, Dick Eastland, Ray Hutchins, W.A. Conquy.

Picture research: Diane and John Moore *(full picture credits are given at the back of the book)*

Filmset: Modern Text Ltd.

Color and monochrome reproduction: Rodney Howe Ltd. and Bantam Litho Ltd.

Printed in Belgium by Henri Proost et Cie.

The Authors

BRIAN HOLLINGSWORTH, M.A., M.I.C.E.

Brian Hollingsworth has had an extravagant passion for railways ever since he can remember. After qualifying in engineering at Cambridge University, and after a brief excursion into the world of flying machines, he joined the Great Western Railway in 1946 as a civil engineer. Later, his mathematical background led him into British Rail's computers and also to a heavy involvement with BR's TOPS wagon and train control system.

He left British Rail in 1974 to take up writing and has published eleven major books on various aspects of railways and locomotives (including one on how to drive a loco), including Salamander's 'The Illustrated Encyclopedia of the World's Steam Passenger Locomotives', besides contributing to technical railway periodicals.

He is director of the Romney, Hythe and Dymchurch Railway and civil engineering adviser to the Festiniog Railway. He has a fleet of one-fifth full size locomotives which run on his private railway in his own 'back garden' (actually a portion of a Welsh mountain!), and he actually owns the full-size LMS 'Black Five' Class 4-6-0 No. 5428 *Eric Treacy*, which operates as a working locomotive on the North Yorkshire Moors Railway for tourists and rail enthusiasts.

ARTHUR F. COOK, M.A., M.I. Mech. E.

A lifelong railways enthusiast, Arthur Cook was born in the famous English railway town of Doncaster, Yorkshire. He read Engineering at Cambridge University, and stayed on as a research student. After obtaining his degree he subsequently taught at Southampton University, was Principal of the Macclesfield Technical College, and was Administrator at the County Education Headquarters at Chester. He recently retired from British Rail after many years of service. Mr. Cook has written many technical articles on trains and railway systems, particularly modern rail power, and contributed to Salamander's 'Illustrated Encyclopedia of the World's Steam Passenger Locomotives'.

Acknowledgements

The publishers and authors express their thanks to Christopher Bushell, who checked the manuscript, making many valuable suggestions, as well as to Margot Cooper and Llinos Black who undertook the typing.

As regards all the wonderful artwork and often rare photographs in the book, we also pay tribute to the team of artists, in particular David Palmer, to Diana and John Moore, and to all those people and institutions who have scoured their archives and photo collections to help make the book one of the best illustrated on locomotives and self-propelled trains.

ning between Reading and Swindon and, more impressive, ran from London to Leicester (99 miles — 158km) in just under the hour. These favourable experiences led to the authorising of three 14-car "production prototype" trains, the two central cars of each train being non-tilting and non-driving power cars, providing 8,000hp (5,970kW) for traction. The two halves of the train were isolated from one another and each had to have its own buffet/restaurant car; 72 first-class and 195 second-class seats were provided in each half.

Electric propulsion was chosen because there was no diesel engine available with a suitable power-to-weight ratio, and a gas turbine was now considered too extravagant in fuel consumption after the recent trebling in price of oil. Moreover, the envisaged first use for APT trains was now on the longer electric journeys out of Euston to Glasgow, Liverpool and Manchester. One innovation was the solution to the problem of braking from very high speeds above 155mph (250km/h). The hydro-kinetic (water turbine) brake was adopted, giving a reasonable braking distance of 2,500yd (2,290m) from full speed, with 2,000yd (1,830m) possible in emergency. Disc brakes provided braking force at speeds too low for the hydro-kinetic brakes to be effective.

The first APT-P train was completed in 1978, but there was a series of tiresome small defects including one that caused a derailment at over 100mph (160km/h).

This meant that, although the 4hr 15min Glasgow to London service (average speed 94mph — 151km/h), which it was intended to provide at first, had been printed in the public timetables for several years, it was not until late-1981 that public service actually began. Even then, only one complete Glasgow-to-London and back public run was made. A combination of further small defects, unprecedently severe weather and impending serious industrial action, led BR to take the train out of public service, although tests continue. It all happened in a blaze of unfortunate publicity, which mattered less than the fact that authorisation by the government of a series-production version (APT-S) was deferred indefinitely.

A series of options now presented themselves. Because it was not economic to provide continuous cab signalling, the APT trains were in the end limited to the speed of the HST already described. Accordingly, one might envisage an electric version of the latter train, very simply obtained by replacing diesel alternator sets with the necessary electrical equipment. Some faster running round curves might well be possible without any of the complications of tilting, but it is the tilting and riding mechanism of the APT which has been its most successful feature. An alternative proposal is a simpler or "utility" 125mph APT (APT-U) with no 150mph capability, no articulation (which saves money on maintenance facilities), and no hydro-kinetic brake.

Above: *An Advanced Passenger Train propelled by a diesel locomotive is shown to the crowds watching the cavalcade of railway motive power at Rainhill in May 1979.*

Below: *British Railways' Advanced Passenger Train demonstrates its tilting capability during a high-speed test run on the London-Glasgow West Coast main line in 1981.*

Index

Bold figures refer to subjects mentioned in captions to illustrations

Picture Credits

The publishers wish to thank the following organisations and individuals who have supplied photographs for this book. Photographs have been credited by page number. Some references have, for reasons of space alone, been abbreviated as follows:

AC = Arthur Cook. BBC = BBC Hulton Picture Library. BH = Brian Hollingsworth. BS = Brian Stephenson. CG = C Gammell. CV = Colourviews, Birmingham. JJ = Jim Jarvis. HB = Hugh Ballantyne.

Back cover: Italian State Railways. **Page 6:** J Winkley. **7:** top, South African Railways; bottom left, P Robinson; right, GFA. **8:** General Electric. **9:** top, BH; bottom left, Victorian Government Railways; bottom right, DB. **10:** top, CG; bottom, R Barton. **11:** top, P Robinson; bottom left, Swedish State Railways; bottom right, K Yoshitani. **12:** Union Pacific. **12-13:** SNCF. **13:** bottom left, JJ; bottom right, J Winkley. **14:** Panama Canal Company. **14-15:** SNCF. **15:** top right, P Robinson; bottom, BS. **19:** SNCF. **20:** R Barton. **21:** J Winkley. **22:** top, BBC; bottom, J Winkley. **23:** top, Deutsches Museum, Munich; bottom, JJ. **26-27:** Gornergratbahn. **29:** J Winkley. **31:** via MARS. **32:** JJ. **33:** top, Panama Canal Company, BH. **34:** Colour-rail. **36:** top, J Winkley; bottom, BBC. **36:** BH. **38:** JJ. **39:** J Winkley. **40:** Colour-rail. **41:** BS. **42:** BS. **43:** R. Bastin. **44:** Swiss Federal Railways. **45:** Top, Swiss Federal Railways, bottom. **47:** BH. **48:** LG Marshall. **49:** JJ. **50:** Swedish State Railways. **51:** top, JJ; bottom, Post Office. **53:** National Railway Museum. **54-55:** JJ. **56-57:** AC. **58:** top, CG; bottom, CV. **59:** AC. **61:** BH. **62:** top, Colour-rail; bottom, Oxford Publishing Co. **63:** top, BS; bottom, Oxford Publishing Co. **64:** top, J Winkley; bottom, Union Pacific RR. **65:** top, JJ; bottom, Union Pacific RR. **66:** Italian State Railways. **67:** top, Italian State Railways; bottom, Danish State Railways. **68:** AC. **69:** GFA. **71:** BS. **72:** CG. **73:** CG. **74:** top, AMTRAK; bottom, BH. **75:** AMTRAK. **76:** BS. **77:** BS. **78:** CG. **79:** top, AT&SF. **80:** Emery Gulash. **81:** top, J Winkley; bottom, CG. **82:** top, BS; bottom, CG. **83:** J Whiteley. **84:** BLS. **85:** R Bastin. **86-87:** AT&SF. **88-89:** JJ. **90:** Burlington Northern RR. **90:** top, GFA; centre, Burlington Northern RR; bottom, Burlington Northern RR. **92:** top, CV; bottom, CG. **93:** top, Oxford Publishing Co; bottom, JJ. **94:** BH. **95:** J Winkley. **96:** BS. **97:** SNCF. **98:** D Cross. **99:** Colour-rail. **100:** top, CV; bottom, via MARS. **101:** top, NZGR; bottom, J Winkley. **102-103:** Italian State Railways. **104:** BH. **105:** Fairbanks-Morse. **106:** SNCF. **107:** R Bastin. **108:** BS. **109:** top, Colour-rail; bottom, SAR. **110:** SNCF. **112:** Danish State Railways. **113:** J Winkley. **114:** BS. **115:** top, BS; centre, J Whiteley; bottom, J Westwood. **116:** top, D Cross; bottom, M Kashima. **117:** top, BS; bottom, M Kashima. **118:** top, J Winkley; bottom, P Robinson. **119:** top, P Robinson; bottom, D Cross. **120-112:** top, P Robinson; bottom, J Westwood. **122:** J Westwood. **123:** top left, J Winkley; top right, Romanian State Railways; bottom, P Robinson. **124-125:** BS. **125:** Swedish State Railways. **127:** top, ASEA; bottom, JJ. **128:** J Winkley. **129:** BH. **130:** top, HB; bottom, P Robinson. **131:** left, HB; right, CG. **132:** Southern Pacific RR. **133:** Denver & Rio Grande RR. **134:** top, Colour-rail; bottom, JJ. **135:** Colour-rail. **136:** R Robinson. **137:** top, CV; bottom, BS. **138:** top, D Cross; bottom, BS. **139:** R Bastin. **140:** J Westwood. **141:** top, SNCF; bottom, MARS. **142:** top, P Cook; bottom, Koyusha. **143:** top, P Cook; centre, Japanese Information Service; bottom, K Yoshitani. **144:** JJ. **145:** BS. **146:** Dr Hedley. **147:** J Winkley. **148:** DB. **149:** J Westwood. **150-151:** top, BR; bottom, BS. **152:** top, SNCF; bottom, BS. **153:** top, SNCF; bottom, CG. **154:** AMTRAK. **155:** top, J Winkley; centre & bottom, AMTRAK. **156:** H Kawai. **157:** CV. **158:** top, Union Pacific RR; bottom, J Winkley. **159:** Union Pacific RR. **160:** J Winkley. **161:** top, HB; bottom, London Transport. **162-163:** top, SNCF; bottom, BS. **164:** R Bastin. **165:** SNCF. **166-167:** BS. **168:** J Winkley. **169:** CV. **170:** NZGR. **171:** top, NZGR; bottom, DB. **172:** top, R Bastin; bottom, HB. **174:** top, K Yoshitani; bottom, H Kawai. **175:** top, H Kawai; bottom, Kazunori. **176:** CV. **177:** AMTRAK. **178:** top, HB; bottom, Queensland Government Railways. **179:** top, Victorian Government Railways; bottom, Queensland Government Railways. **180:** top, CG; bottom, JJ. **181:** top, Finnish State Railways; bottom, CG. **182-183:** South African Railways. **184:** top, CV; bottom, CV. **185:** J Winkley. **185:** top & centre, J Whiteley; bottom, Romney, Hythe & Dymchurch Railway. **187:** top, Austrian State Railways. **188:** top, RH&DR. **188:** FOB. **189:** AC. **190:** R Bastin. **191:** BS. **192-193:** DB. **194-195:** Via Rail. **196:** NSW Railways. **197:** top, J Dunn; bottom, N Gurley. **198:** HB. **199:** top, SAR; bottom, Colour-rail. **200-201:** SNCF. **201:** CV. **202:** top, Italian State Railways; bottom, BR. **204-205:** BR.

Above: *20,000-tonnes-plus in a single load: three Class 9E electric locos haul an iron ore train to Saldanha Bay, South Africa.*

Below: *At 77.4mph (124.6km/h) from Berlin to Hamburg the "Flying Hamburger" was the world's fastest train before World War II.*

at only a few horsepower output. Indeed, often they replaced literal "horsepower" rather than steam. It was very early on that electric railway carriages began to incorporate motive power within themselves and so do away not only with steam locomotives but with locomotives altogether. Now, a hundred years later, people travelling from Paris to Marseilles, London to Cardiff or Edinburgh, and Tokyo to Hiroshima, for example, no longer go to the head of the train to look at the locomotive—for one very good reason: it hasn't got one.

An early line—at Portrush, in what is now called Northern Ireland—began in 1883 to use "white coal", that is, electricity generated by water power, and 1890 saw the application of electric traction to the world's

first electric underground railway or subway. This was the City & South London Railway, nowadays part of London Transport's Northern line. By now, the principles of electric traction were well established, although all the applications were for relatively light railway operations.

In 1895 came the first successful "heavy" application of electric power, on the Baltimore & Ohio Railroad's new line, mainly in tunnel, serving a new station in the centre of Baltimore. This was a very bold step into the unknown, because the haulage power of the locomotives was increased by a factor of several times over that of those then existing in regular service. The installation was completely successful and opened the door to a whole new field of heavy-duty electric-railroading.

Three further significant steps were taken close to the turn of the century. A German consortium of electrical suppliers, with the co-operation of the government, carried out some trials with large, heavyweight, streamlined motor-coaches, as well as a locomotive. Speeds over 100mph (160km/h) were attained in 1901, and two years later these were raised to an amazing 130½mph (210km/h), using one of the motor coaches. For Germany, this record stood for over 70 years.

Then in 1906 came the electrification of the Giovi incline, connecting the Italian port of Genoa with its hinterland. This put some of the elements together to show that a line which was impossible to run satisfactorily with steam locomotives—because of a combination of heavy traffic, extreme gradients and smoky tunnels—presented no difficulty for electric traction.

Lastly, in 1907, the New York, New Haven & Hartford Railroad electrified a section of its main line using single-phase alternating current overhead catenary current supply with simple double-bogie (Bo-Bo) locomotives and self-propelled passenger trains—just the way railways do it now.

In just over a quarter of a century, electric traction had demonstrated superiority over steam in power, speed, absence of pollution, convenience—all the qualities needed or desirable in the running of a railway, in fact. It had demonstrated a quite remarkable reliability and ease of maintenance and servicing. So why did not its tide come in like a flood?

The reason, of course, was the great expense involved. Compared with steam, electric locomotives were more expensive by a factor of two or three and, in addition, there was also the cost of the conductor rails or wires, transmission lines and sub-stations and often the power stations themselves to be added. In general terms (and greatly over-simplifying the considerations involved), one could talk of the cost of equipping an electric railway costing four to six times the amount needed to equip a steam railway for the same traffic. So no wonder electrification was then seldom resorted to except when there was really no alternative.

Diesel Traction

The diesel engine in the form in which it is now universally used is much less the work of Doctor Rudolph Diesel, of Germany, than of a Briton called Ackroyd-Stuart. In the 1880s he demonstrated an internal combustion engine in which the fuel was injected into the cylinder at the end of the piston stroke. This engine was turned into a practical proposition by Richard Hornsby & Co., of Grantham, England, later Ruston & Hornsby. Dr. Diesel's engine, demonstrated in 1898, used a high compression ratio typical of present day engines to

Above: *Electric locomotive building at General Electric's plant at Erie, USA. Note running gear ready to receive the bodyshell.*

Below: *A giant Great Northern Railway Class W1 electric locomotive nearing completion by General Electric in 1946.*

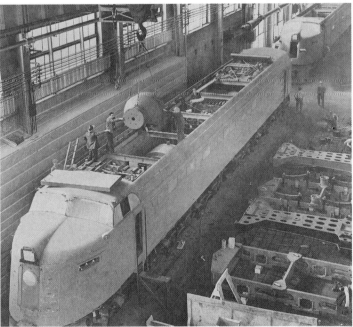

obtain a big increase in thermal efficiency, but the fuel had to be injected by a blast of compressed air at some 1,000psi (65kg/cm²). This involved heavy ancillary equipment.

In 1896 a small diesel locomotive, the first in the world and which one might more reasonably call an Ackroyd-Stuart locomotive, was built at Hornsbys. It was used for shunting purposes in the works. The first recorded use of a compression-ignition locomotive in public service seems to have occurred in Sweden, when a small railcar with a 75bhp (56kW) engine and electrical transmission was put into service on the Mellersta & Södermanlands Railway in 1913. Of course, this was hardly a greater output than would nowadays be installed in a medium-sized family car,

Introduction

THE MOTIVE power of a modern railway is almost always diesel or electric. Considerable numbers of steam locomotives also exist, as well as some trains driven by gas-turbines, while trains that are moved by petrol engines, cables, sail-power or even flesh-and-blood horses can also still occasionally be found. After iron horses such as *Puffing Billy* and his like took over from the hay-burners on the world's railways—such as they were—in the early 1800s, steam power ruled effectively, but not unchallenged, for more than a century.

The first serious challenge came in early Victorian times from the atmospheric system. Lineside pumping stations evacuated the air from pipes placed along the centre of the tracks. Trains hauled by piston carriages were thus sucked along, the pistons inside the pipes being attached to the carriages by arms which passed through a longitudinal valve.

The most celebrated installation was that of Isambard Kingdom Brunel along the south Devon coast between Exeter and Newton Abbot, but it only lasted in public service a few months. The least unsuccessful was a less ambitious project installed in Ireland between Kingstown (now Dun Laoghaire) and Dalkey, and this lasted from 1844 to 1854. It could be argued that atmospheric railways were also steam railways in the sense that they depended on steam-driven engines generating the power, but of course that also applies to the majority of electric railways today. Even nuclear power stations are also steam-driven!

Electric Traction

Experiments in true electric traction began in 1835, a bare six years after *Rocket* took to the rails, notably by a blacksmith called Thomas Davenport who came from Vermont, USA. He patented his electric motor as early as 1835, although others—Daniel Gooch of Britain's Great Western Railway was one—also constructed small demonstration motors powered by electricity. Davenport built a model electric railway which still survives.

In 1842 a Scotsman called Robert Davidson built a full-size electric locomotive which actually ran slowly but successfully when tried on the metals of the Edinburgh & Glasgow Railway, although it was clearly not a practical means of traction. The problem really was to find an adequate source of power.

Wet primary batteries such as Leclanché cells were totally inadequate for the purpose and the tale of the modern locomotive really begins with an Italian called Antonio Pacinotti who in 1860 built the first dynamo. Pacinotti's machine could also be used as an electric motor and his creation is the basis of the vast majority of locomotives and trains today.

So our book begins in 1879, appropriately with the first electric locomotive in public service. Incidentally, even the majority of diesel locomotives are more pedantically but correctly described as electric locomotives of the self-generating type.

As readers will see from the history of development portrayed in the pages which follow, it was many years before the kind of current to be used was settled. The trouble was that, while direct current (dc) was best

Above: *Typical North American railroading ... a pair of standard diesel-electric road-switcher units head a Canadian Pacific freight.*

Right: *With 125mph (200km/h) capability, Britain's HST 125s are the world's fastest diesel trains. This is today's "Flying Scotsman".*

for traction motors, alternating current (ac) was better for transmission. Some railways preferred expense and complications on the locomotives; others preferred to have them in the supply system. Many lines compromised by using special alternating current of such a low frequency that it was almost dc. In the last few years, however, the question has been resolved by the development of simple ways of conversion on the locomotives, so that the supply systems can be ac and the motors dc.

In those early days, long before electricity supply networks came into existence, electric railways used direct current supplied from their own power stations. Most of them were closely related to street tramway lines and were low-key operations using vehicles rated

Contents

Above: *Steam for the future? South African Railways' Class 26 "steam" locomotive with gas-generator firebed, in August 1981.*

Below: *General Motors' dominance of the diesel market is illustrated by this Class X45 locomotive in Victoria, Australia.*

Above: *It is a sign of the times that the number of this German locomotive has an extra figure for assisting in computer entries.*

and went no distance towards proving the diesel engine as suitable for rail traction.

As we all know from our motor cars, the problem of using internal combustion engines for traction is — in lay terms — that they need to be going before they will go. This is in contrast to steam engines and electric motors which can produce a force while still at rest. For low powers, the familiar gear-box and clutch in the motor car can be used, but for hundreds — and certainly for thousands — of horsepower something more sophisticated is needed.

Experiments with a diesel engine driving an air compressor and feeding compressed air to a normal steam locomotive engine and chassis were not successful, although the scheme was a simple one. The use of

hydraulic fluid as a transmission medium has been reasonably satisfactory, but by far the majority of diesel locomotives ever built have, and have had, electric transmissions. A diesel engine drives an electric generator or alternator which feeds current to the motors of what amounts to an electric locomotive.

The story of compression-ignition power in this book begins therefore with the first diesel-electric locomotive of more than very modest power to run successfully in commercial service. It was put into service by the Ingersoll-Rand, the General Electric and the American Locomotive companies in 1924, and it is a pleasure to write that GE at least still supplies diesel locomotives to the world from its plant in Erie, Pennsylvania.

Because the concept of this first commercially-successful diesel locomotive involved building, to start with, an electric locomotive complete with traction motors and control gear, and then adding to that a diesel-driven generator to supply current for the electric locomotive, it was not only expensive but complex. Furthermore, electrical equipment is not happy living in close company with the vibration and oil-mist which surrounds even the best-maintained diesel engines. Accordingly, in most places and for many years, diesel locomotives—however economical they might be as regards fuel consumption and however efficient operationally—led rather unfulfilled and unhappy lives.

The key to what amounted almost to a complete take-over of the un-electrified railways of the world was the entry into the locomotive field in the 1930s of US General Motors, the world's greatest road vehicle manufacturers. They did not solicit orders until they had a product upon which they could rely and which was sold, complete with a spare parts and repair service—just like one of their motor cars, in fact. Also, just as it was with their motor cars, customers had to buy the models offered, not the ones they thought they wanted.

In this way mass-production and standardisation were able to reduce the cost of a diesel-electric locomotive to a reasonable level. Furthermore (and unlike anybody's motor car) all GM's diesel units were intended to be used on a building-block basis: couple up four units to make a super-power loco, then three, two or perhaps only one for lighter duties, only one crew being needed because of the remote-control facilities (known in railroad parlance as "multiple-unit" working). Individual units were compact enough and light enough to go anywhere a freight car could go and this did away with any need for special types of locomotive for special duties.

It is only a slight exaggeration to say that to take charge of a railroad's motive power procurement at that time it was not necessary to be an expert in the niceties of locomotive design, so long as one could read a manufacturer's catalogue. The policies adopted added up to a stupendous story of success, as the pages which follow reveal.

The following pages also reveal the converse. Those railways—British Railways being perhaps the most notorious example—which were unable to ditch habits of motive power acquisition formed in steam days (that is, of ordering separate custom-built designs for the different duties) found the going exceedingly hard for many years. In some ways, also, the one nation which applied some of General Motors' diesel thinking to steam finds the end result now entirely to their satisfaction, although the Chinese could not have fore-

Above: *A Chinese-built BJ "Beijing" diesel-hydraulic locomotive for passenger train haulage, seen when brand new in 1980.*

Below: *The driver's view: an AMTRAK engineer at the controls of a diesel-electric passenger locomotive at Ogden, Utah, USA, in 1980.*

seen the big change in the cost of oil relative to coal on the world markets to which this satisfaction is due.

Other Forms of Traction

Gas-turbine locomotives are wholly practical, even with direct drive, but suffer from the fact that their efficiency falls off badly when running at any power output different from their rated one. Trains make highly variable demands on their motive power so it is not surprising that this form has not become common, although there have been sufficient successful applications to justify the inclusion of several turbine-driven entries in this book.

The authors in no way accept the notion that the

Above: *A British Railways standard Class 87 Bo-Bo electric locomotive hauls a passenger train through the northern hills.*

Left: *An all-purpose loco, Swedish State Railways' Class Rc4 electric unit by ASEA, seen in a typical Scandinavian setting.*

Above: *These Japanese high speed "Bullet" trains were the first in the world to offer 100mph (160km/h) start-to-stop average speeds.*

terms "steam" and "modern" are mutually exclusive, and accordingly a sprinkling of steam locomotives which look towards the future, in spite of being steam, have been included. There is even a prospect of steam traction making a come-back in certain countries in the not too distant future.

Of other forms of modern power successfully applied to rail transport over the years, steam-turbine-electric traction is noted in one entry and so is movement dependent on energy stored in a heavy rotating fly-wheel. Gas-generator machines with free pistons driving turbines or reciprocating engines have been tried but have hardly succeeded. Rail movement by muscle power (animal and human) or cable traction is excluded, although a few examples of the former and

a great many of the latter can be found. Wind-and-sail power, on the other hand, really has disappeared from the serious railways of the world, and accordingly has (with great regret) no place in this book.

High Speeds

To some, the eclipse of steam traction in recent years has made railways a whole lot less exciting, but this has been amply compensated for by the really startling speeds now being run. The promise of those high-speed trials of 1903 in Germany was at last fulfilled with the electric "Bullet" trains in Japan in 1966 and the diesel-electric HST125 trains in Britain in 1978, as well as more isolated runs in France, Germany and elsewhere. City-to-city speeds of 100mph (160km/h) and running speeds up to 125mph (200km/h) have now become commonplace.

The French have just gone a further stage ahead with a new Paris to Lyons railway, purpose-built for very high speeds indeed. The electric TGV (*Train à Grande Vitesse*) trains used on this line run at up to 162mph (260km/h) to provide a frequent service between these two great cities of France in two hours only for the 266 miles (426km). Hardly time for a meal, at least not a French one!

Other railways, unable to afford new lines, have attempted to build trains which would negotiate the curves of a steam-age railway at these electric-age speeds. It is no disgrace that British Railways found its 150mph (240km/h) Advanced Passenger Train, which tilted to provide built-in super-elevation or banking, just a little bit too difficult. The Italians, the Spanish, the Canadians, the Germans, the Swiss, as well as others, have also encountered problems with this promising idea. The Japanese, on the other hand, have successfully put tilting trains into service, but these have not been for running, say, 150mph (240km/h) trains on 75mph (120km/h) alignments but for having 80mph trains (128km/h) on 40mph (64km/h) alignments on mountain routes. In this way Japan has been able to solve its tilting problems in isolation from the high speed ones.

With 162mph (260km/h) trains in service, one can ask whether rail travel could go even faster. There do seem to be indications that the speed is near the limit possible in practice for flanged steel wheels running on steel rails. While higher speeds might be possible with hover-trains or a magnetic levitation system, this would almost certainly preclude through running on to conventional railway tracks.

For example, the TGV trains enter and leave central Paris on conventional tracks (with a different system of electrification) and extend their runs to Marseilles and into Switzerland (with yet another electrification system) without any special provision other than relatively simple current conversion equipment installed on the trains themselves.

What might happen is that TGV-type railways should appear elsewhere. Some are contemplated in France, of course, but many other countries could find suitable routes. The long-heralded extinction of oil supplies will give a significant uplift to the prospects of new electric railways and it does seem that the excellent hardware described in the later pages of this book will be available when the call finally comes.

It is an illustration of how quickly information concerning railway development can be over-shadowed that since most of this book went to press, the speed limit of the French TGV trains has been raised from 162mph (260km/h) to 168mph (270km/h).

Below: *The Chicago to Los Angeles "City of Los Angeles" diesel-electric streamliner on its inaugural run, May 1936.*

The Descriptions

The main body of this book consists of descriptions of individual locomotives or trains, arranged (in general) chronologically. The items have been chosen in order to tell the story of modern railway motive power consecutively from its beginnings right up to the present day. To achieve this, the first consideration has been to mark in chronological order the major milestones of progress. The second objective has been to put in as much technical variety as possible, including a fair number of interesting "might-have-beens". The criterion for their inclusion is that they should have got at least as far as hauling fare-paying traffic. Lastly an attempt has been made to give reasonable world-wide geog-

Below: *Indian Railways' WDM Class Co-Co diesel-electric loco No. 17521 brings the "Andhra Pradesh Express" through Dhaulpur.*

Above: *A French National Railways Class 15000 Bo-Bo electric locomotive heads the Paris-Strasbourg rapide "Le Stanislas".*

Below: *A newly rebuilt GP9 general purpose locomotive of the Atchison, Topeka & Santa Fe Railway, in Cleburne Shops, 1979.*

raphical coverage, assisted by the fact that modern motive power now originates in far fewer countries than did steam-powered locomotives.

Whilst coverage of the subject is adequate when it comes to main line railroading, the treatment of motive power for other important facets of railway working has had to be less thorough, for reasons of space. For example, only two entries cover the subject of rapid-transit or city railways, for which a whole book would be needed. The same applies to locomotives for switching or shunting. Another gap concerns the few steam locomotives included on the grounds of their modernity—for the origins of these, readers are referred to the companion volume *The Illustrated Encyclopedia of Steam Passenger Locomotives.*

Each description is headed by the appropriate class, name or number followed by its wheel arrangement code. An illustrated explanation of the meanings of these codes is given separately. The country concerned and the name of the railway (or, in some cases, the suppliers) comes next, followed by the date of construction.

The actual text begins with tabulated details as follows....

Type: The purpose and kind of locomotive or train under discussion.

Gauge: The distance between the inner edges of the rails, given in feet and inches and in millimetres.

Propulsion: A brief *resumé* of what makes the wheels go round. The power output is usually included here; the one-hour value is specified in horsepower and kilowatts.

Weight(s): Both the adhesive and the total weight of the locomotive in running order, are specified in pounds and in tonnes. If the adhesive weight equals the total weight, one pair of figures only is given.

Max. axleload: This is the heaviest weight carried by any individual axle and again is specified in pounds and tonnes.

Overall length: This is the length of the locomotive or train measured between buffer or coupler faces, specified in feet and inches and millimetres.

Tractive effort: This is the maximum theoretical drawbar pull which a locomotive can exert, specified in pounds and kilo-Newtons. This entry is omitted as inappropriate in the case of a self-propelled train.

Max. speed: An arbitarily specified speed limit applied to the locomotive or train in question, for safety reasons, specified in miles per hour and kilometres per hour.

As regards the text itself, more emphasis is placed on differences from the norm than on similarities. The reader is also warned that, although the information given is carefully researched and set down in good faith, the figures must be interpreted with reserve. For example, the performance of an electric locomotive depends directly on the voltage of the supply and this can vary within wide limits according to the currents being drawn from the system at any particular moment. Weights can vary quite considerably from those in specifications—and only the honest Chinese admit that they do! The power output of diesel engines can vary according to the precise adjustment of fuel pumps and so on. Even the track gauge is not entirely reliable, for spikes sometimes work loose on even the best regulated railways.

The following abbreviations are used in the tables and text....

ac = alternating current; **ch** = chains (of 66 feet/ 20,117mm); **dc** = direct current; **ft** = feet; **hp** = horsepower; **Hz** = hertz or frequency per second; **in** = inches; **km** = kilometres (km/h = kilometres per hour); **kN** = kilo-Newtons (1kN = 225lb/147kg force)*;

Below: *Ship-hauling locomotives prepare to take a US ambulance ship through the canal locks, Pedro Miguel, Panama, June 1919.*

kW = kiloWatts; **lb** = pounds; **m** = metres; **max** = maximum; **mm** = millimetres; **mph** = miles per hour; **t** = tonnes **V** = volts

*Note: the only one of these terms not in lay use is the kilo-Newton. Although we may be content to measure both a force and a mass in the same units, pounds or kilograms as convenient, a purist is not content with this, as it takes no account of any possible variation in the force of gravity, which is the connection between a mass and the force it can exert. Hence the Newton, appropriately named after the discoverer of the laws of motion. For our purposes, 1,000 Newtons or one kilo-Newton can be taken to be 225lb (147kg)—but when we come to build railways on the Moon a different conversion value will apply!

Above: *A British cross-country express from Newcastle to Cardiff passes Ousdon Junction, Co. Durham, with a Class 45 diesel-electric.*

Above: *Today's fastest! A French Train à Grande Vitesse, or TGV, set now permitted to run at 168mph (270km/h).*

Below: *German Federal Railway Class ET 403 high-speed four-car electric train now used on airport-city-airport link service.*

Wheel Arrangements

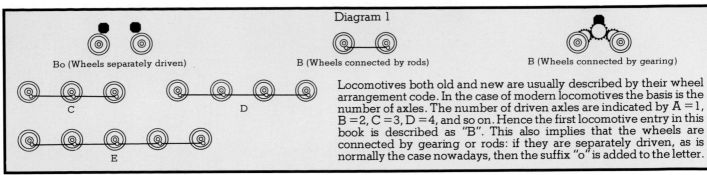

Diagram 1

Bo (Wheels separately driven)

B (Wheels connected by rods)

B (Wheels connected by gearing)

C

D

E

Locomotives both old and new are usually described by their wheel arrangement code. In the case of modern locomotives the basis is the number of axles. The number of driven axles are indicated by A = 1, B = 2, C = 3, D = 4, and so on. Hence the first locomotive entry in this book is described as "B". This also implies that the wheels are connected by gearing or rods: if they are separately driven, as is normally the case nowadays, then the suffix "o" is added to the letter.

Diagram 2

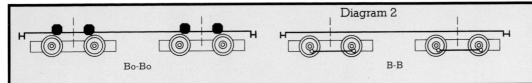

Bo-Bo

B-B

Three-quarters of all modern locomotives and almost all the power cars of self-propelled trains are of the arrangement shown in the left-hand figure, consisting of two two-axle "bogies" or "trucks".

Diagram 3

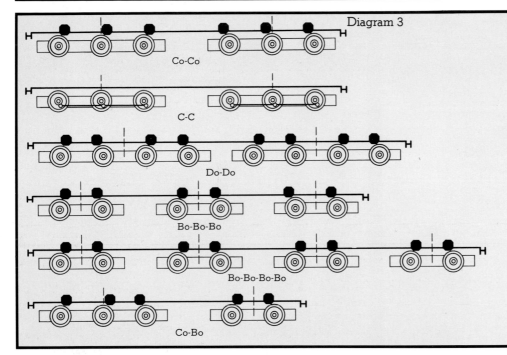

Co-Co

C-C

Do-Do

Bo-Bo-Bo

Bo-Bo-Bo-Bo

Co-Bo

The bogie arrangement is often extended to include three-axle and four-axle bogies. More than two bogies are occasionally used and unsymmetrical combinatons can also be found in rare cases. Bogie locomotives having wheels connected with rods are nowadays never built and rarely found, but the arrangement with bogie wheels connected by gearing is reasonably common. Even so, the fact that the overwhelming majority of locomotives, both diesel and electric, have axles individually driven by separate electric motors means that the suffix "o" and even the hyphen can be dropped. A Bo-Bo becomes therefore and BB. Whatever the wheel arrangement used, though, the principle involved is that each bogey is separately described as in diagram 1 above, and then combined with hyphens.

Diagram 4

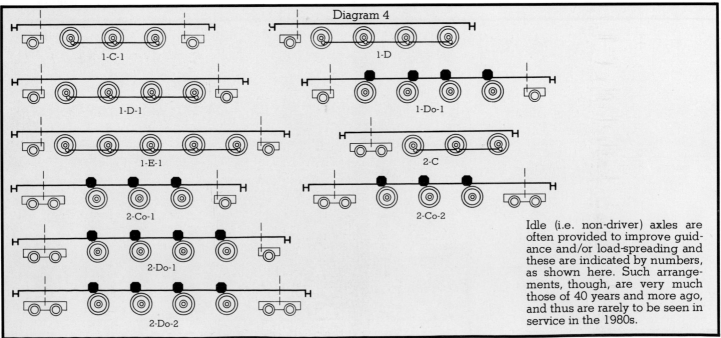

1-C-1

1-D

1-D-1

1-Do-1

1-E-1

2-C

2-Co-1

2-Co-2

2-Do-1

2-Do-2

Idle (i.e. non-driver) axles are often provided to improve guidance and/or load-spreading and these are indicated by numbers, as shown here. Such arrangements, though, are very much those of 40 years and more ago, and thus are rarely to be seen in service in the 1980s.

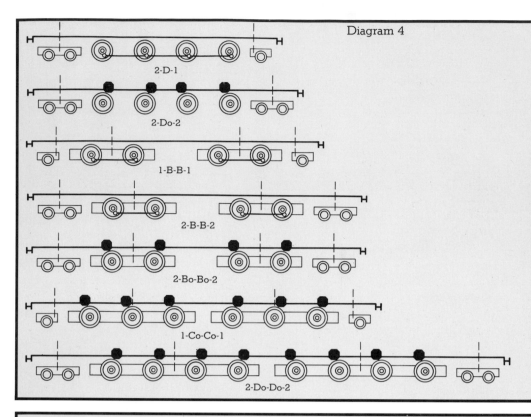

Diagram 4

2-D-1

2-Do-2

1-B-B-1

2-B-B-2

2-Bo-Bo-2

1-Co-Co-1

2-Do-Do-2

It is also a point that this notation can be used (and often was, particularly by the countries of continental Europe) to describe steam locomotives, as well as diesel and electric ones. Such steam locomotives as appear in this book are here delineated in this manner.

The power of cars of self-propelled trains, which play such a large part in modern railway operation, are not usually described in this way. Almost without exception they are of the Bo-Bo, BB, Bo-2 or B-2 wheel arrangement and therefore need only to be described by stating whether there are one of two motored bogies in the layout.

In contrast and in days gone by, electric locomotive wheel arrangements were often extremely complicated, as shown here and below. It was really for this reason that the simpler Whyte system (used traditionally for steam traction, whereby, for example, a 2-D-1 was described as a 4-8-2) was found inadequate.

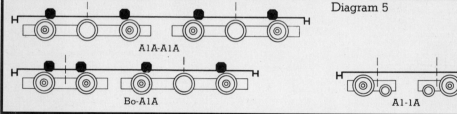

Diagram 5

A1A-A1A

Bo-A1A

A1-1A

Driven and non-driven wheels are sometimes included in the same bogie or main frame, as shown here, usually to provide better load-spreading rather than guidance.

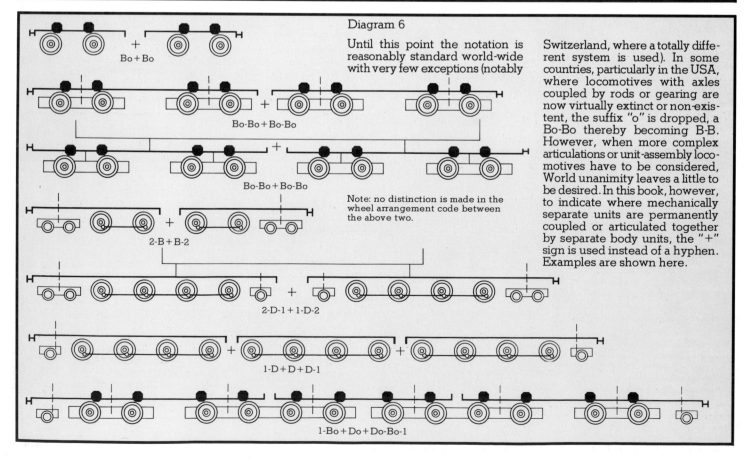

Diagram 6

Until this point the notation is reasonably standard world-wide with very few exceptions (notably Switzerland, where a totally different system is used). In some countries, particularly in the USA, where locomotives with axles coupled by rods or gearing are now virtually extinct or non-existent, the suffix "o" is dropped, a Bo-Bo thereby becoming B-B. However, when more complex articulations or unit-assembly locomotives have to be considered, World unanimity leaves a little to be desired. In this book, however, to indicate where mechanically separate units are permanently coupled or articulated together by separate body units, the "+" sign is used instead of a hyphen. Examples are shown here.

Bo + Bo

Bo-Bo + Bo-Bo

Bo-Bo + Bo-Bo

Note: no distinction is made in the wheel arrangement code between the above two.

2-B + B-2

2-D-1 + 1-D-2

1-D + D + D-1

1-Bo + Do + Do-Bo-1

Glossary

Adhesion—the frictional grip between wheel and rail.

Adhesive weight—the sum of driving wheel loads.

Air brake—power braking system with compressed air as the operating medium.

Air cushion—type of spring used in some modern carriage suspension systems with air as the operating medium.

Alternating current (ac)—electric current which reverses its direction flow at rapid and regular intervals.

Alternator—a machine which converts mechanical energy to electrical energy and generates alternating current.

Anti-slide/skid—a device for detecting and automatically correcting wheel slide or skid during braking by a momentary reduction of braking force.

Anti-slip—electrical circuit which detects driving wheel slip on diesel and electric locomotives. The difference in current taken by a particular traction motor when wheel slip occurs causes an illuminated warning to be given to the driver. In addition, an automatic reduction in engine power and/or partial application of the locomotive brakes may be effected.

Armature—the rotating part of a direct current electric motor or generator. Contains a number of coils, or windings, which rotate in a magnetic field and are connected to the commutator.

Articulation—the sharing of one bogie by adjacent ends of two vehicles.

Asynchronous—an alternating current electric motor whose speed varies with load and has no fixed relation to the frequency of the supply.

Axlebox—box-shaped casting of steel, bronze or cast iron, housing the axle bearing and its associated lubrication system. Working in vertical guides attached to the main frame, it transmits the weight of the vehicle to the axle via the springs.

Baggage car—American term for luggage van.

Ballast—material placed between the sleepers and formation of railway track to distribute the load of passing traffic, prevent lateral and longitudinal movement of the track, provide effective drainage and a convenient medium for maintaining level and gradient.

Banking—assisting the working of a train, usually when ascending a gradient, by attaching one or more locomotives to the rear.

Bearings—the bushing or metal block of anti-friction material which transmits the load via an oil film to a journal.

Bellows—flexible ducting used for conveying cooling air to traction motors mounted on the bogie of an electric or diesel-electric locomotive.

Berne gauge—standard loading gauge for main line railways on continent of Europe.

Berth—bed in sleeping carriage.

Bi-current locomotive—designed to operate on two different electric current frequency systems.

Body shell—basic body section of a vehicle without internal fittings.

Bogie (American, truck)—independent short wheel base truck with four or six wheels, capable of pivoting about the centre at which it is attached to the underframe of long vehicles.

Boiler—steam producing unit. Locomotive type consists essentially of a fire box surrounded by a water space in which the combustion of fuel takes place, and barrel containing the flue tubes surrounded by water.

Bolster—transverse floating beam member of bogie suspension system supporting the weight of vehicle body.

Brush conductor—usually of carbon providing electrical contact with a sliding surface moving relative to it such as the commutator of a direct current machine.

Buffet car—carriage equipped for serving light refreshments to passengers.

Cam—reciprocating, oscillating or rotating body which imparts motion to another body known as a follower, with which it is in contact.

Camshaft—a shaft which carries a series of cams for operating the inlet valves and exhaust valves of a diesel engine, and contactors in some electric traction control gear systems.

Cant—amount by which one rail of a curved track is raised above the other. Cant is "positive" when the outer rail is higher than the inner rail and "negative" when the inner rail is higher than the outer.

Cant deficiency—the difference between the amount of cant provided and the amount of cant required to negotiate the curve at the maximum permitted speed without wheel flange to rail contact.

Car—American term for a carriage or wagon.

Carriage—passenger-carrying railway vehicle.

Catenary—supporting cable for the contact or conductor wire of an overhead electrification system.

Circuit breaker—automatic switch for making and breaking an electrical circuit under normal or fault conditions.

Cog wheel—toothed wheel or pinion which engages with the rack laid between the running rails of a rack and pinion system mountain railway.

Coil—one or more convolutions of bare or insulated wire which produce a magnetic force when subjected to an electrical current.

Collector shoe—metal block in contact with conductor rail for collecting current from third rail electrification system.

Common carrier—a transport organization which is not permitted to be selective in the freight accepted for conveyance. Required by law to carry, with very few exceptions, all traffic offered.

Commutator—part of the armature of a direct current electrical machine upon which the brushes bear. Cylindrical assembly of copper segmented bars insulated from each other and connected to the coils of the armature winding.

Commuter—holder of railway season ticket. Term now generally applied to a person who travels by public or private transport daily between residence and place of work.

Composite coach/carriage—vehicle with accommodation for more than one class of passenger.

Compression stroke—second piston stroke of four-stroke cycle diesel engine during which air charge in cylinder is compressed and heated by piston movement.

Compressor—machine for raising the pressure of air above atmospheric. Provides compressed air for operation of brakes, auxiliaries and so on.

Conductor—see guard.

Consist—composition or make-up of a train.

Contactor—remotely controlled switch used for frequently making and breaking electrical power circuits on load.

Converter—machine for converting electric power for alternating current to direct current or vice versa.

Core—iron section around which is wound the coil or wire through which an electric current is passed to produce a magnetic force in an electro-magnet.

Coupling (American, coupler)—device for connecting vehicles together. Many types in common use, ranging from simple three link to automatic which may also provide electrical and air services connections.

Crank—device for converting rotary to reciprocating motion or vice versa. Consists of an arm, one end of which is fixed to a shaft and the other free to rotate about the axis of the shaft.

Current—rate of flow of electricity round a circuit.

Cycle—series of events repeated in a regular sequence. Diesel engines operate on a two or four stroke cycle.

Dead-man's handle—device for cutting off power and applying the brakes in the of the driver becoming incapacitated whilst driving.

Dead section—length of conductor in an electrified railway system which is not energised.

Deck—see footplate.

Diesel—compression ignition, internal combustion engine.

Direct current (dc)—electrical current which flows in one direction continuously.

Direct drive—direct mechanical connection between output end of prime mover and driving wheels of locomotive.

Disc brake—braking mechanism utilizing friction pads applied by caliper action to a disc secured to vehicle axle or wheel centre.

Double head—to attach a second locomotive to the front of a train.

Down—usually the line of track which carries trains in a direction away from the town or city in which the headquarters of the railway company are located.

Down grade—American term for falling gradient—downhill.

Drive—transmission of power.

Dual control—operated or controlled from two separate positions.

Dynamic braking—system of braking utilizing the braking characteristics of the engine compression, transmission or traction motors.

Dynamic loading—load applied to track or structure by vehicle in motion passing over it.

Dynamo—direct current electrical machine used for charging batteries and providing current for carriage lighting.

Dynamometer car—vehicle with equipment for measuring and recording draw-bar pull, horsepower, speed, and so on, of a locomotive under load.

Earth—electrical connection to complete a circuit.

Eccentric—disc, keyed to a shaft or axle, whose centre does not coincide with that of the axle. It rotates inside a ring, known as an eccentric strap, to which is attached the eccentric rod, and imparts reciprocating motion to a link for operating the steam distribution valve to the cylinder.

Electric traction—haulage of vehicles by electric-motor-driven unit utilizing electric power obtained from batteries or an external source via conductor wire or rail.

Exhaust steam—emission of steam from the cylinder after completion of the working stroke.

Expansion of steam—increase in volume of steam in the cylinder after the supply has been cut off. The ability to take maximum advantage of the expansive qualities of steam results in economies in the consumption of fuel and water.

Express—fast train stopping at few intermediate stations.

Fairing—structure or cover to provide a smooth surface and reduce air resistance.

Feed—supply with fuel or water, electrical current or other power source.

Field—space around a magnet or a conductor carrying an electric current where magnetic lines of force may be detected.

Firebox—part of a steam locomotive boiler where combustion of the fuel takes place.

Flange—projecting edge or rim on the periphery of a wheel or rail.

Footplate (American, deck)—cab floor or operating platform of locomotive.

Formation—make-up of a train of vehicles.

Four-foot way—space between running rails of standard gauge 4ft 8½in (1,435mm) track.

Frame—foundation or chassis upon which a locomotive is built.

Frequency—number of times a second an alternating electric current reverses its direction of flow.

Gap—break in continuity of conductor rail.

Gas turbine—rotary internal combustion machine which is driven by gas flow thus causing varied disc(s) mounted on common shaft to turn at high speed.

Gauge—standard measure; the distance between running edges or inner faces of the rails of railway track.

Generator—electrical machine which changes mechanical energy into electrical energy. Term generally applied to one which produces direct current.

Generator—automatic oil-fired steam producer fitted to diesel locomotives where there is a requirement for passenger vehicles to be steam heated.

Governor—device for maintaining as closely as possible a constant engine crankshaft speed over long periods during which the load on the engine may vary.

Grade/gradient—slope or inclination to the horizontal of a railway. Expressed in degrees from the horizontal, as a percentage, or unit rise or fall to the horizontal or slope length.

Gross weight—total weight of train including payload.

Guard, (American conductor)—person in charge of a train.

Handbrake—means of applying the brake blocks to the wheel treads without power assistance. Usually in the form of a screwed shaft with a running nut, attached to the brake gearing.

Headstock—main lateral end member of a carriage or wagon underframe to which the buffers and drawgear may be attached.

Heating of trains—usually effected by one of three methods: steam-fed radiators, electric-resistance heaters, or hot-air circulation from oil-fired combustion heaters.

Heating surface—areas of locomotive boiler exposed to heat on one side and available for water evaporation on other.

Horsepower—a unit of power equal to 75kg metres per sec, 33,000ft per lb per min, or 746 watts.

Hot box—an overheated vehicle axlebox bearing resulting from breakdown of lubricating film between bearing and journal.

Induction—production of an electric current by change of magnetic field.

Injector—device for forcing water into the boiler of a steam locomotive; also device for feeding atomized fuel oil to cylinder or combustion chamber of a diesel engine.

Insulate—isolate an electrical conductor by the inter-position of a non-conductor to restrict the current flow to a definite path.

Integral construction—carriage construction where the body and underframe form one stress and load carrying structure.

Journal—area of a shaft or axle supported by a bearing.

Light engine—locomotive running without a train.

Lighting of carriages—by axle driven dynamo, capable of generating when rotated in either direction. Also charges the batteries which supply lighting power when the train is stationary or running slowly.

Live rail—electrical conductor for transmitting power to locomotives or train on third-rail electrified lines.

Load factor—the ratio of actual train loading to maximum capacity.

Loading gauge—the limiting dimensions of height and width of rolling stock and loads carried to ensure adequate clearance with lineside structures.

Mercury arc—static device employing a mercury pool cathode for converting alternating to direct current.

Metro—underground railway system for mass conveyance of short journey passengers.

Monocoque—vehicle structure with underframe and body designed to form a single unit on aircraft construction principles.

Monorail—railway system where the track consists of a single rail.

Motion—movement; a moving

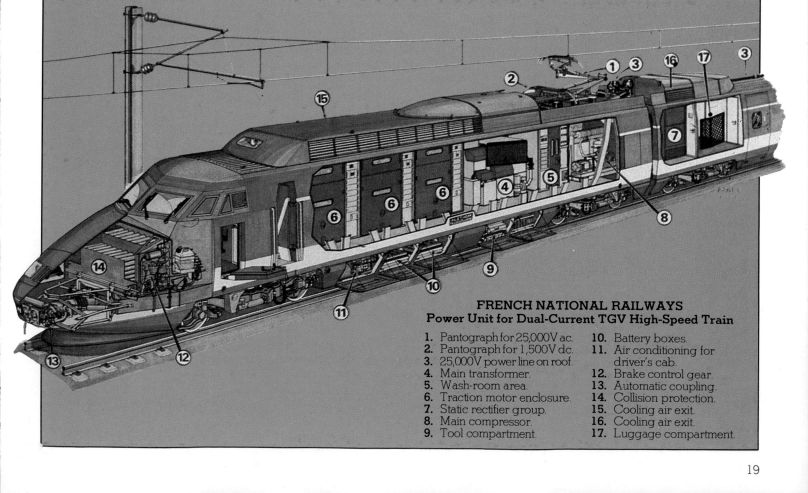

FRENCH NATIONAL RAILWAYS
Power Unit for Dual-Current TGV High-Speed Train

1. Pantograph for 25,000V ac.
2. Pantograph for 1,500V dc.
3. 25,000V power line on roof.
4. Main transformer.
5. Wash-room area.
6. Traction motor enclosure.
7. Static rectifier group.
8. Main compressor.
9. Tool compartment.
10. Battery boxes.
11. Air conditioning for driver's cab.
12. Brake control gear.
13. Automatic coupling.
14. Collision protection.
15. Cooling air exit.
16. Cooling air exit.
17. Luggage compartment.

mechanism; the valve gear of a steam locomotive.

Motor bogie — bogie having driving wheels or motored axles.

Motor generator set — electric motor and generator mechanically coupled for the purpose of converting direct current from one voltage to another.

Motorman — driver of an electric tram, railcar or multiple-unit train.

Multi-system or voltage locomotive — locomotive designed to operate on more than one electrical system.

Multiple unit — two or more locomotives or powered vehicles coupled together, or in a train, operated by only one driver.

Narrow gauge — railway track of less than the standard gauge.

Nominal rating — full load output of machine capable of being sustained for continous period of 12 hours without distress.

Nose-suspended motor — traction motor mounted on bearings on axle being driven, with a "nose" resiliently fixed to a bogie cross member to prevent rotation round axle. Gear on axle is in constant mesh with pinion on armature shaft.

Notch — intermediate position of electric traction power controller; indentation in manual signal box lever frame to hold lever in position.

Observation car — passenger-carrying vehicle, usually at rear of train, with windows and seating arranged to give maximum view of passing scenery.

One-hour rating — 10 per cent above nominal rating which machine should be able to sustain for continous period of up to one hour without distress.

Out-of-gauge — vehicle or load which exceeds the loading gauge limits.

Overhead — catenary and contact wire of a suspended electrical distribution system.

Over-ride — take precedence over; manual control over a normally automatic operation.

Over-speed trip — mechanism for stopping a diesel engine in event of excessive crankshaft rotational speed.

Packing — oil absorbing material used to assist the lubrication of an axle bearing; also material placed in the gland to maintain a leak free joint when subjected to pressure.

Pantograph — link between overhead contact system and power circuit of an electric locomotive or multiple unit through which the power required is transmitted. Simplest form is spring loaded pivoted diamond frame with copper or carbon contact strip.

Parlor car — American term for luxuriously fitted railway carriage.

Parallel connection — electrical conductors or circuits so connected that the sum of the currents in the individual conductors or circuits is equal to the total current supplied.

Payload — that part of the total weight of the train which is revenue earning; excluding weight of empty vehicles and locomotive.

Peak hour — period of time when traffic levels are greatest.

Pendular suspension — carriage suspension allowing body to tilt to compensate for fast running round curves.

Pony truck — two-wheel pivoted truck to assist the guidance of a locomotive around curves.

Pullman car — railway carriage providing a higher standard of service and comfort than normal and for which a supplementary fare is exacted.

Push-pull — method of operating whereby the locomotive may be other than at the head of the train, although controlled from there.

Rack railway — system used on mountain railways (and occasionally elsewhere) where gradients exist too steep for the normal adhesion between wheel and rail to be effective. A pinion on the locomotive engages in a rack fixed to the track. The rack can consist either of a longitudinal series of steel teeth or of rungs of gear-tooth profile fixed to side members like the rungs of a ladder.

Railcar — self-propelled passenger-carrying vehicle.

Railroad — American term for a railway.

Rapid transit — system for high-speed urban mass transport.

Rectifier — a device for converting alternating electric current to direct current.

Regenerative brake — electrical braking system whereby the traction motors of direct current electric locomotives work as generators and feed electrical energy back into supply system.

Registration arm — cantilever which gives contact wire an offset in relation to track centre line in overhead electrification system.

Relay — remotely controlled electromagnetic switch for low electrical currents. Used to make and break circuits which in turn may operate power circuits, other relays and so forth.

Resilient baseplate — pad of resilient material such as rubber

bonded cork, inserted between foot of flat bottom rail and sleeper or paved continuous track bed.

Resistance — force, opposing motion; that which opposes the flow of current in an electric circuit, measured in ohms. Used to dissipate surplus electrical energy in form of heat.

Reversing station — point where train reverses direction of travel during course of journey. May be at normal dead-end or terminal station layout or on zig-zag section of steeply graded line.

Rheostat — variable resistance for regulating the flow of electric current.

Rheostatic braking — electrical braking system whereby the traction motors work as generators, the resultant electrical energy being dissipated as heat in resistances.

Rigid wheel base — horizontal distance between the centres of the first and last axles held rigidly in alignment with each other; the coupled wheels of a steam locomotive.

Roller bearing — hardened steel cylinders located in a cage which revolve in contact with inner and outer races.

Rolling stock — carriages and wagons; railway vehicles.

Rotor — rotating part of an electrical (usually alternating current) machine.

Round house — engine shed in which the locomotive stabling tracks radiate from a turntable.

Ruling gradient — limiting gradient (and therefore trainload) for traction and braking capacities.

Running gear — term generally applied to the wheels, axles, axleboxes, springs, frames of a railway vehicle.

Running light — locomotive movement without a train attached.

Safe load — maximum load which may be applied without undue risk.

Safety valve — directly connected to the steam space of all boilers and set to operate automatically

Below: *A British Railways driver demonstrates the use of the "dead-man's handle".*

at a pre-determined pressure to release excess steam.

Scavenge — to remove the products of combustion from an internal combustion engine cylinder by a regulated flow of air.

Secondary winding — output side of a transformer.

Semi-conductor — material used in electric traction rectifiers, whose electrical resistance depends on the direction of the applied voltage. Germanium and silicon are typical examples.

Series connection — electrical conductors or circuits so connected that the same current flows in each conductor or circuit.

Series-parallel connection — method of connecting traction motors whereby individual motors are connected in series to form groups and each group then connected in parallel.

Series motor — direct current electrical machine with ideal traction characteristics. Produces a high torque when the vehicle is started and as the load increases the speed drops.

Service coach — carriage used for railway departmental purposes, not in public use.

Service life — expected working life of a component before replacement required.

Servo — control system whereby a small amount of effort is augmented to do a large amount of work.

Shock absorber — telescopic hydraulic device for damping spring suspensions.

Shoe brake — simple arrangement for applying a retarding or braking force to the periphery of a rotating drum or wheel, by pressure of a block of wood, metal or friction material against it.

Short circuit — point of very low resistance in an electrical circuit usually, if accidentally resulting from insulation failure.

Shunt — direct onto a minor track; marshal vehicles into a particular order.

Shuttle — train which gives a frequent return service over a short route.

Side corridor — passenger carrying vehicle with connecting corridor between compartments along one side.

Single-phase — single alternating electric current. One phase of three-phase supply.

Sleeper — steel, wood or precast concrete beam for holding the rails to correct gauge and distributing to the ballast the load imposed by passing trains.

Slip — loss of adhesion between driving wheel and rail causing wheels to spin; also short curved connecting line joining lines which cross one another on the level; also driving member rotating at a higher speed than driven in a fluid coupling.

Smoke box — extension to barrel at the front end of a locomotive boiler housing the main steam pipes to cylinders, blast pipe, blower ring and chimney. Other fittings may include superheater header, regulator, spark arrester.

Soleplate — longitudinal main frame member of fabricated or built up carriage bogie, usually of standard rolled steel section or pressings. Also a plate inserted between the chairs and the sleeper at a pair of points to maintain the correct gauge and prevent any spreading of the gauge that might occur from the gradual enlargement of the spike holes in the wooden sleepers.

Stall — to come to a stand under power. Occurs when train resistance exceeds tractive power.

Standard gauge — 4ft 8½ (1,435 mm), between rails in a country.

Stephenson valve gear or link motion — for each valve there are two eccentrics fitted to the crank axle, which impart a reciprocating motion through eccentric rods to a slotted expansion link. The fore-gear eccentric rod is coupled to the top, and back gear to the bottom of the expansion link, which in turn is suspended by lifting links from the reversing shaft. In the slot of the expansion link is a die block which is connected to the valve spindle by an intermediate valve rod. Operation of the reversing gear in the cab lowers or raises the expansion link which, in turn, transfers the movement of fore or back gear eccentric rods to the valve. In the mid-gear position the link oscillates about the die block and imparts a reciprocating movement to the valve equal to twice the steam lap plus twice the steam lead. A feature of the Stephenson valve gear is that the steam lead is greatest at mid-gear and minimum at full forward or backward gear.

Streamlining — special shaping of vehicles to minimize air resistance.

Streetcar — see tramcar.

Stub axle — short non-revolving axle which supports only one wheel.

Sub-station — point in electricity distribution system where supply is converted or transformed to suit needs of user.

Sub-way — underground passage to give access to platforms. American term for underground railway.

Supercharge — supply air to the inlet valves of a diesel engine at above atmospheric pressure.

Superelevation — see cant.

Superheating — increasing the temperature and volume of steam after leaving the boiler barrel by application of additional heat.

Suspension — connecting system, including springs, between vehicle wheel and body, designed to give best possible riding qualities by keeping unsprung weights to a minimum and reducing shock loadings on track.

Swing link — metal bar pivoted at each end. Part of suspension system of many bogies and trucks.

Switch — device for opening and closing an electrical circuit.

Switch — American term for points.

Synchronous — electric motor whose speed varies in direct proportion to the frequency of the supply.

Tachometer — instrument giving

a continuous indication of rotational speed of diesel engine crankshaft and so on.

Tank locomotive — one which carries its fuel and water supplies on its own main frames.

Tap — intermediate connection between the main connections of an electrical circuit or component.

Tender locomotive — one which carries its fuel and/or water supplies in a separate semi-permanently coupled vehicle.

Third rail — non-running rail carrying electrical current to electric locomotive or train.

Three-phase — simultaneous supply or use of three electrical currents of same voltage, each differing by a third in frequency cycle.

Throttle — American term for regulator. Valve controlling flow of fuel to diesel engine.

Track circuit — section of running line insulated from adjoining sections, into one end of which is fed a low-voltage electrical current with a relay connected across the rails at the other end. When the track section is unoccupied the relay is energised, but the wheel sets of a passing train produce a short circuit which leaves the relay without current. Consequent movement of the relay arm is used to make or break other electrical circuits connected to associated signalling equipment, including illuminated track diagrams, point and signal interlocking automatic colour-light signals.

Tail lamp — lamp affixed to, or illuminated if an integral part of, the rear end of the last vehicle, to indicate the train is complete.

Train-pipe — continuous air or vacuum brake pipe, with flexible connections between vehicles, through which operation of the train brake is controlled.

Tramway — light railway or rails for tramcars.

Tramcar (American, street-car) — electrically operated public service passenger vehicle on rails in the street.

TEE (Trans Europ Express) — international European luxury express passenger service conveying

Above: *A "multiple unit", with four Denver & Rio Grande Western RR units hauling coal in Rockies.*

only first class passengers at a supplementary fare.

Transformer — device which by electromagnetic induction converts one voltage of alternating current to another.

Transmission — mechanical, hydraulic or electrical arrangement necessary with diesel traction to enable diesel engine to be run whilst locomotive is stationary and provide the necessary torque multiplication at starting. Mechanical transmission usually consists of clutch or fluid coupling, gearbox and final drive/reversing unit. Hydraulic transmissions include one or more torque convertors which may incorporate an automatic gearbox. Electric transmission consists of an alternator or generator directly coupled to the diesel engine which supplies electric current to one or more traction motors driving the locomotive wheels.

Trip — means of release by knocking aside a catch.

Trolley — pole mounted on roof of electric vehicle with wheel attached to outer end to pick up electric current from overhead contact wire.

Truck — open railway wagon. American term for bogie on a locomotive or wagon.

Trunk — main route or line of railway from which branch or feeder lines diverge.

Tube — underground railway running in a tunnel, excavated by mining methods.

Turbine — rotary machine consisting of one or more sets of blades attached to a shaft; driven by steam or gas flow in railway applications.

Turbo-charger — turbine, driven by the flow of exhaust gases from a diesel engine coupled to a rotary compressor which supplies air at above atmospheric pressure to the engine-inlet valves.

Tyre (American tire) — steel band forming the periphery of a

wheel on which the flange and tread profile is formed.

Underframe — framework or structure which supports the body of a carriage or wagon.

Underground — beneath the surface of the ground. Railway built below street level in large cities to avoid congestion.

Up line — line over which trains normally travel towards the headquarters of the railway company concerned.

Up train — one which travels on or in the direction of the up line.

Vacuum — space from which air has been exhausted.

Vacuum brake — braking system with atmospheric air pressure as operating medium.

Valve gear — mechanism which controls the operation of the steam distribution valve in the steam chest of a locomotive cylinder.

Valve — device for controlling the flow of a liquid or gas.

Van — covered vehicle for conveyance of luggage, goods or use of guard.

Variable gauge — vehicle or wheelset with facility for operating on more than one track gauge. Achieved by sliding wheel along axle and locking in appropriate position to suit required gauge.

Vestibule — covered gangway giving access between vehicles.

Vigilance device — ensures the continued vigilance or alertness of the driver by requiring him to make a positive action at frequent intervals. Failure to do so results in power being cut off and the brakes applied.

Voltage — electromotive force measured in volts.

Wagon — railway vehicle for the conveyance of goods.

Walschaerts valve gear — movement of the valve is obtained from two sources, a single eccentric or return crank and the piston crosshead. The eccentric rod is coupled to the bottom of the expansion link which pivots on trunnions at its centre. A die block slides in the link and is coupled to one end of the radius rod which is attached at the other end to the combination lever, above or below the valve spindle depending on whether inside or outside admission. Operation of the reversing gear causes the rear end of the radius rod, and therefore the die block in the expansion link, to be raised or lowered, varying the cut-off and direction of locomotive travel. The lower end of the combination lever is attached to the crosshead via a union link and provides movement of the valve equal to twice the lap plus twice the lead. Unlike Stephenson gear the lead is constant whatever the position of the reversing gear.

Working timetable — timetable including all trains running over a particular route or area.

Yard — group of lines or sidings where auxiliary operations to train working are undertaken.

Siemens' Original B

Type: Demonstration electric locomotive.
Gauge: 1ft 5¾in (450mm).
Propulsion: Direct current fed at 150V via a raised centre conductor rail and liquid control resistance to a 5hp (3.75kW) motor connected by gearing to the driving wheels.
Overall length: 5ft 2in (1,570mm).
Max. speed: 8mph (13km/h).

This little tractor represented the first successful use of electric power for the haulage of a train on a public railway. Accounts vary as to its length, but it seems the railway was only about ¼ mile (0.4km) long and in the form of a circle. It was first laid as a demonstration line at the Berlin Trades Fair of 1879 (the outfit was also demonstrated elsewhere), but its use led directly to a second public electric line in a Berlin suburb soon after the exhibition closed. (In fact, it was a tramway and so outside the scope of this book.) The Siemens locomotive was successful and in this way, on May 31, 1879, came into being the future method of traction of many of the world's most important railways.

Attempts had been made to produce an electric locomotive even before the dynamo had been developed during the 1860s, but the problem of producing sufficient current was not easily solved by such means as batteries of primary cells. A Scotsman called Robert Davidson demonstrated a crude battery tractor on the railway between Edinburgh and Glasgow in 1842. The "motors" consisted of wooden cylinders mounted on the axles to which iron bars were fixed. Electromagnets were switched on and off to attract these bars in such a way as to produce rotation. Although the locomotive worked, it was clearly not a practical proposition. In spite of many other attempts, 35 years were to elapse before success was achieved.

It was the dynamo, used to generate current and also adapted as a motor to produce torque, that gave Werner von Siemens this success in Berlin. A small steam-driven power station produced direct current at 150V. The locomotive was started and controlled by a liquid resistance (*see glossary*). Current was collected from a central third rail, its return

Below: *The world's first electric train carrying a load of passengers on a short circular track at the Berlin Trades Fair, May 1879.*

Siemens' Single railcar

Type: Electric railcar.
Gauge: 2ft 8½in (825mm).
Propulsion: Direct current at 460V fed via a central third rail and rheostatic control to two 8hp (6kW) motors with link-belt drive to the wheels.
Weight: 14,326lb (6.5t).
Overall length: 30ft 0in (9,144mm).
Max. speed: 10mph (16km/h).

August 3, 1883 was the day when a short electric pleasure railway was opened along the seafront at Brighton and the date is notable in two ways. This little railway was the first electric line in the world to achieve any sort of permanent existence, for it still runs today having carried some 60 million passengers. Furthermore, it was a pointer to the situation a century later when most electric passenger trains would be self-propelled and no longer need locomotives. It was also the first electric railway in Britain, although another in what is now called Northern Ireland was to open five weeks later. This was the Giant's Causeway Tramway at Portrush, the first railway in the world to run on hydro-electricity, using its own power station.

The Brighton line also originally had its own generating station but using a gas engine as the source of power. Later, power was taken in a way much more typical of the future, from Brighton Corporation's public supply via a substation, an arrangement that was facilitated by the fact that Magnus Volk, who promoted the line, was also the Corporation's electrical engineer. Volk has given his name to the railway.

The scale of the initial operation can be judged from the fact that the original temporary car was built, a ¼-mile (0.4km) of 2ft (610mm) gauge track laid and the generating plant installed all within three weeks. The first season's operation was in the nature of an experiment and by April 1884 the line, which originally ran only from Aquarium Station to the Old Chain Pier, was extended and rebuilt to run from the Palace Pier to Black Rock, a distance of 1¼ miles (2km). The gauge was also altered to 2ft 8½in (825mm), an apparently peculiar figure no doubt chosen because it was exactly two English feet less than standard gauge. The details of the cars built for the permanent line are those given above.

Currently, the line is operated during the summer season by nine 32-seat cars, seven of which are indigenous, the other two having come recently from the now closed Southend Pier Tramway. It is still as popular as ever, and traffic is not discouraged by the fact that an excellent view of Brighton's famous nude bathing beach is available from the cars. A further extension along the beach to Rottingdean laid with a four-rail track to 18ft 0in (5,486mm) overall gauge, on which a car on stilts ran through the sea at high tide, did not last very long.

Left and right: *Views of single electric cars of Volk's Electric Railway at Brighton, England, the oldest existing electric railway in the world, which in 1983 celebrated its centenary. The line is now run by the Brighton Corporation.*

path being via the wheels and running rails.

The train could carry some 30 passengers seated back to back on three four-wheel cars at a speed of 4mph (6.5km/h). The mechanical design of the locomotive was quite complex by present day standards. The armature shaft was mounted longitudinally under the driver's seat, while the field windings protruded each side above the wheels.

The motor was enormous compared with the size of one of similar power today. Torque was transmitted via three spur gears (with an intermediate shaft!) to the longitudinal driving shaft between the wheels, thence via bevel gears to a transverse shaft. There were two pairs of bevel gears arranged so that either pair could be put into mesh by means of an external handle—requiring the driver to dismount—to give forward and reverse. The two driving axles were turned by further spur gears meshing with a gear wheel on the transverse shaft.

The locomotive can be seen today in the Deutsches Museum, Munich, West Germany.

Right: *Werner von Siemens' pioneer electric locomotive demonstrated in Berlin, Germany, in May 1879.*

Nos. 1-3 B₀+B₀

USA: Baltimore & Ohio RR (B&O), 1895

Type: Main line electric locomotive.
Gauge: 4ft 8½in (1,435mm).
Propulsion: Direct current at 675V fed via a rigid overhead conductor to four gearless motors of 360hp (270kW) each.
Weight: 192,000lb (87t).
Max. axleload: 48,488lb (22t).
Overall length: 27ft 1½in (8,268mm).
Tractive effort: 45,000lb (201kN).
Max speed: 60mph (96.5km).

The world's first main line electrification was installed on this section of the first public railway in America; it ran through the city of Baltimore and in particular through the 1¼-mile (2km) Howard Street tunnel, adjacent to a new main passenger station at Mount Royal. The tunnel was on a gradient of 1-in-125 (0.8 per cent) and trouble with smoke and steam therein was anticipated. The solution adopted was electrification carried out by General Electric of Schenectady, New York State.

More remarkable than anything was the boldness of the decision —these B&O locomotives were over nine times heavier and nine times more powerful than their nearest rivals. It was upon such an enormous leap forward as this

that the success of the whole vast investment in the new line was dependent, because a very different construction would have been necessary for steam traction.

Gearless motors were again used, but not mounted direct on the axle, although concentric with it. Torque was transmitted to the wheels through rubber blocks; this flexible drive was yet another feature many years ahead of its time. Each four-wheeled tractor unit was mechanically quite separate, although two were permanently coupled to form one locomotive. There were three double locomotives in all.

The locomotives were quite successful and had no problems

hauling 1,630t (1,800 US tons) trains up the gradient. The load including the train's steam engine, which did no work in the tunnel. Trouble was encountered with corrosion of the unusual conductor arrangements; a brass shuttle ran along a Z-section overhead rail, the shuttle being connected to the locomotive by a one-sided tilted pantograph. A conventional third rail mounted outside the running rails replaced this amazing overhead system in 1902.

These locomotives stopped work in 1912, but one was laid aside for many years—in fact, until B&O's centennial "Fair of the Iron Horse" in 1927, at which it was exhibited. Alas, scrapping followed and so the first-ever main-line electric locomotive is no longer to be seen. Electric traction continued in use on the B&O using more modern power until 1952 when electric locomotives of the self-generating type—that is, the all too familiar diesel—took over.

Nos. 1-16 B

Type: Underground railway electric locomotive.
Gauge: 4ft 8½in (1,435mm).
Propulsion: Direct current at 500V fed via a central conductor rail to two 50hp (37.3kW) gearless motors with axle-mounted armatures.
Weight: 20,700lb (9.4t).
Overall length: 14ft 0in (4,267mm).
Max. speed: 25mph (40km/h).

The first electric underground railway in the world was the City & South London line, opened on December 18, 1880. Sixteen locomotives were constructed by Beyer Peacock of Manchester, with electrical equipment supplied by Mather & Platt, also of Manchester, and Siemens of Berlin, for the 3½-mile (5.6km) line, which ran from King William Street Station in the "city" area of London to Stockwell south of the Thames.

The locomotives were completely satisfactory and operated the line for more than 30 years until it was reconstructed in the early 1920s. It now forms part of London Transport's Northern Line, and all except the final few yards at the city end is included in 17¼ miles (27.8km) of continuous tunnel which was for very many years the longest railway tunnel in the world.

Above: *City & South London Railway four-wheeled electric locomotive, as built in 1880.*

In contrast to the Siemens locomotive of 1879, these machines were very simple. The armatures were wound direct on the axles —no gearing or other complications. The braking system also had a simplicity never achieved later. Westinghouse air brakes were used, but there was no compressor. Instead a reservoir was provided and this could be recharged from compressed air supplies provided at the terminal stations.

Another interesting feature (which in contrast, was unnecessarily complex) was the conductor rail mounted on glass insulators. The top of this rail was *below* the level of the running rails, and at points and crossings a ramp was provided to lift the collecting shoes clear of the running rails. This also lasted until reconstruction in 1920, when the usual third and fourth conductor rail arrangement was provided.

One of these locomotives (No.1) is on display at the Science Museum in South Kensington, London, while one of the strange little windowless cars it hauled can be seen at London Transport's museum at Covent Garden.

Left: *Pioneer electric main-line locomotive, put into service on the Baltimore & Ohio RR in 1895.*

Nos. 1-4 He 2/2 Switzerland:
Gornergrat Railway (GGB), 1898

Type: Rack-and-pinion mountain railway locomotive.
Gauge: 3ft 3⅜in (1,000mm).
Propulsion: Three-phase current at 550V 40Hz fed via twin conductors and the running rails to two 90hp (68kW) motors geared to the driving pinions.
Weight: 25,356lb (11.5t).
Length: 13ft 6½in (4,130mm).
Tractive effort: 17,632lb (78kN).
Max. speed: 5mph (8km/h).

Electric traction came very early to the pleasure railways of the world—in those days smoke and steam were not thought of in terms of enjoyment—and mountain lines were particularly suitable for electrification. Enabling geriatrics as well as athletes to enjoy the glories of the Alps had long been a possibility under steam power, but when it came to climbing up from Zermatt to see the Matterhorn from that great belvedere the Gornergrat, three-phase electric traction was chosen.

At this time, several railways in Europe and North America were already operated by dc traction, and as Switzerland had no coal

but an abundance of water power there was considerable interest there in the new mode of traction. In particular two engineers, C.E.L. Brown and W. Boveri, seeking to improve on the low efficiency of early dc schemes, applied themselves to the problems of three-phase traction. This offered the possibility of eliminating commutators, reducing weight, and allowing braking by regeneration on down gradients.

In 1895 a tram driven by a motor of their design, and manufactured by the newly-formed Brown Boveri Company, was tested successfully between Lugano and Paradiso. This system required two overhead wires with separate current collectors, whilst the third line of supply was taken through the running rails. Encouraged by this success, the engineers offered to produce three-phase rack locomotives for the Gornergrat line and a railway proposed to carry tourists to the top of the Jungfrau.

Left: *Gornergrat Railway train with original-type locomotive, leaving Riffleberg for Zermatt. The Matterhorn in background.*

AEG Single railcar Germany:
Study Group for Electric High Speed Railways (StES), 1901

Type: High-speed experimental railcar.
Gauge: 4ft 8½in (1,435mm).
Propulsion: Three-phase current at a voltage variable between 10,000 and 14,000 and a frequency variable between 38 and 48Hz, fed via a triple overhead side-contact wire and a step-down transformer to six gearless synchronous motors each capable of 750hp (560kW) for short periods.
Weight: 132,250lb (60t).
Max. axleload: 13,225lb (10t).
Overall length: 72ft 6in (22,100mm).
Max. speed: 130.85mph (210km/h).

Around the turn of the century the two principal German electrical contracting firms, Siemens & Halske and Allgemeine Elektrische Gesellschaft (AEG) formed, with the support of the Prussian government and various banks, a consortium known as the Studiengesellschaft fur Elektrische Schnellbahnen (Study Group for Electric High-speed Railways).

In 1901, the use of a 14.5 mile (23km) military railway near Berlin was obtained and triple overhead contact wires erected at the side of the track. A railcar built by Siemens was the first test vehicle to be tried out, but the light rail (65lb/yd—32.5kg/m) and shallow ballasting proved inadequate. The swaying and pitching was alarming and finally a derailment occurred at a speed of 100mph (160km/h), putting an end to the trials for the time being. The track was then relaid and strengthened with 85lb/yd (42kg/m) rail, new

closely-spaced sleepers and deep ballasting. The minimum curve was eased to 100 chains (2,000m) radius, while the wheelbase of the six-wheel bogies of the cars was increased from 12ft 6in (3,800mm) to 16ft 5in (5,000mm) to improve stability. An interesting point was that the speed to be reached on any particular run was set by arrangement beforehand, as it

would depend on the frequency of the supply controlled from the power station.

In 1903, after all this had been

done, further attempts were made and 130.5mph (210km/h) was reached smoothly, demonstrating the practicability—only recently

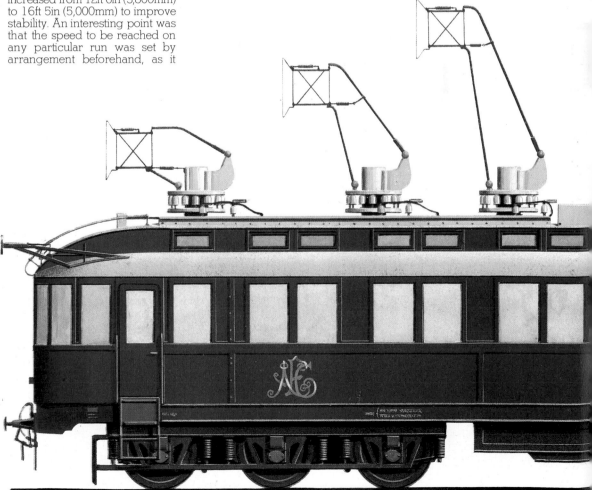

In a distance of 5.8 miles (9.3km) the Gornergrat line rises 4,872ft (1,485m) to an upper terminus at 10,134ft (3,089m), and the maximum gradient is 1-in-5 (20 per cent). Construction began in 1896 and on November 24, 1897 the first trial was made with the world's pioneer three-phase locomotive. Initial tests were successful, and the railway opened in 1898 with three trains, a fourth being added in 1902. The same stock was still in use in 1930, when the locomotives were converted to operate on the standard frequency of 50Hz at 755V.

Choice of three-phase traction had overwhelming advantages for such a railway. Most significant was the fact that as long as the motors remained connected their speed of rotation was governed wholly by the frequency of supply. This automatically governed train speed, a feature that was most important on the descent. By contrast, the complications associated with the need for two independent overhead conductors were not significant on the simple track layouts of a rack-and-pinion line. Special arrangements could be made for a situation when—typi-

Above: *Propelling skiers up to the Gornergrat. Note the wagon for skis at the head of the train.*

cally in the late afternoon—all the trains were descending and pumping electricity back into the power station.

The Gornergrat locomotives are *true* rack engines; that is to say the drive is only on the cog wheels, the rail wheels being idlers. The rack system used was Abt's, with a pair of cog-wheels meshing with a double rack on the ground. The teeth on one side were out-of-phase with those on the other, as this smoothed out

the thrust. Power came from a hydro-electric plant generating at 5,400V 40Hz, which was transformed to 550V for traction.

These machines originally belonged to that select club of timber-built locomotives. They had two motors of 90hp mounted on the body, each connected to a rack wheel through gearing. Two

sets of double pantographs were mounted on the roof. Like most Swiss locomotives, the mechanical parts were made at the Swiss Locomotive Works at Winterthur, while electrical equipment was naturally by Brown Boveri. One end of a coach rested on the frame of the locomotive, and the other end was supported on a bogie. This combination normally propelled a second coach with four wheels; the whole assembly carrying 110 passengers.

The slow walking pace of these trains was just right for summer sightseers; but when Zermatt developed as a winter resort after World War II, the vast commuting crowds of skiers found these repetitive journeys painfully slow. The first of a new series of motor coaches arrived in 1947, halving the journey time, and soon took over all passenger workings. Even so, three out of the four original locomotives survive, much rebuilt and renumbered 3001-3. It is remarkable that these octogenarians—the world's first three-phase locomotives—should have had such long lives, outliving most of the later three-phase main line systems.

become a reality—of really fast self-propelled electric express trains. Writing 30 years later Dr-Eng Walter Reichel (who part-

icipated in the trials) commented dryly "It is probable that 230km/h (143mph) could have been reached had not caution out-

weighed a thirst for knowledge."

In addition to this AEG railcar, Siemens & Halske ran both a high-speed railcar which reached

128.5mph (207km/h) and a locomotive which with a train was able to achieve 81mph (130km/h).

Left: *The high-speed experimental railcar constructed by the German General Electric Co., which reached 130½mph (210km/h) in 1903. Note the separate current-collecting bows for each end and each contact wire.*

St. E. S

Class S 1-D₀-1

Type: Electric passenger locomotive.

Gauge: 4ft 8½in (1,435mm).

Propulsion: 660V direct current collected from under-contact third rail supplying four 550hp (410kW) frame-mounted gearless traction motors with armatures on the axles.

Weight: 142,000lb (64.4t) adhesive, 200,500lb (91t) total.

Max. axleload: 35,500lb (16.1t).

Overall length: 37ft 0in (11,277mm).

Tractive effort: 32,000lb (145kN).

Max. speed: 70mph (113km/h).

A major development in electric traction occasioned by a collision between two steam trains—such was the electrification of New York Central's Grand Central terminal in New York and the surrounding lines. The smoke nuisance in this major city location had long brought criticism upon the railway, but it was the 2-mile Park Avenue tunnel on the approach lines which constituted an operating hazard. At busy times the tunnel was choked with smoke, and sighting of signals was impeded. After several collisions in the tunnel, the climax came in January 1902, when a train ran past a red signal and collided with a stationary train, causing 15 deaths.

The New York Legislature thereupon passed an act prohibiting the use of steam south of the Harlem River after July 1, 1908. Since 1895 the Baltimore & Ohio had operated the Baltimore Belt line with electric traction, including the Howard Street tunnel, so the legislation was not unreasonable, but it had the additional effect of forcing the issue of a major rebuilding of the terminal station.

The railroad adopted the third-rail system at 660V dc with under-contact current collection, and General Electric was appointed contractor. The great pioneer of electric traction, Frank Sprague, was one of the engineers to the project, and for commuter services on the electrified lines Sprague's multiple-unit system of control was applied to 180 cars. For haulage of long-distance trains, GE's engineer Asa Batchelder designed a 1-Do-1 locomotive of massive proportions, which incorporated a number of novelties of his devising. The principal feature of the design was the use of bi-polar motors, with the armature mounted on the axle and the two poles hung from the locomotive frame. The continuous rating was 2,200hp, and the short-term rating of 3,000hp gave a starting tractive effort of 32,000lb (145kN), which enabled the locomotive to accelerate a train of 800 US tons at 1 mile per second per second (0.45m/s²), and maintain 60mph (97km/h) with 500 tons. The locomotives were fitted with Sprague's multiple-unit control, so that they could operate in pairs with one driver, and they were the first locomotives to be so equipped.

The frames were outside the wheels to allow room for the armatures. The body had a central cab with a good all-round view, and with little more than the air compressors above floor level, the cab was very roomy. Other equipment was housed in the end hoods, including an oil-fired train-heating boiler.

The prototype locomotive, No. 6000, was completed late in 1904, and was tested exhaustively on a 6-mile (9.6km) stretch of the NYC main line near the GE works at Schenectady, which was electrified for the purpose. The test included side-by-side comparative runs with the latest steam engines, in which the steam engine usually gained an early lead, but was then overtaken and handsomely beaten by the electric.

The success of No. 6000 was followed by orders for 34 similar locomotives, classified "T", which were delivered in 1906. One of them hauled the first electrically-worked train from the partially-completed Grand Central Station in September 1906. Full electric

Below: *The prototype 1-Do-1 electric locomotive, as built for the New York Central & Hudson River Railroad in 1904.*

working was instituted in 1907, but unfortunately three days later a train hauled by two "T" class locomotives derailed on a curve, causing 23 deaths. Although the cause of the derailment was not established definitely, the locomotives were rebuilt with end bogies, thus becoming 2-Do-2, and they were reclassified "S".

In regular service the electric locomotives showed savings in operating and maintenance costs compared with steam varying between 12 per cent in transfer service to 27 per cent in road service. In 1908-09 a further 12 locomotives were delivered. The entire class survived through half-a-century of service, ending their days on switching and empty coaching stock working. No. 6000 went to a museum after 61 years' service. Some of the class were still at work for Penn Central in the 1970s.

Left: *After rebuilding as a 2-Do-2 and more than 70 years service Class S No. 113 is on show at the St Louis Transport Museum.*

Class E550 E

Type: Electric mountain locomotive.
Gauge: 4ft 8½in (1,435mm).
Propulsion: Three-phase current at 3,400V 15Hz fed via twin overhead wires and the running wheels to two 1,000hp (750kW) motors connected to the wheels by jackshafts and coupling rods. Control by liquid resistances.
Weight: 138,850lb (63t).
Axleload: 27,990lb (12.7t).
Overall length: 31ft 2in (9,500mm).
Tractive effort: 22,040lb (100kN).
Max. speed: 31mph (50km/h).

Being a land possessing no supplies of coal but having ample areas of mountainous country, Italy was a natural possibility for electric traction. As regards expertise, it perhaps says enough that Volta of the volt was an Italian, while the maker of the world's first dynamo/electric motor was another, Pacinotti by name. It is then no surprise that, as regards electrification, Italian railways came in early and have progressed further and more quickly than most others.

In 1901 a local railway north of Milan, running 16 miles (26km) from Colico to Chiavenna, had been electrified experimentally, the work being done free of charge by Ganz & Co of Budapest, of whom more will be heard later. The three-phase system used had twin overhead wires which, together with the running rails, gave the three conductors necessary. The supply was at 3,400V 15.8Hz. The trials were successful and in 1902 the system was extended to the 50-mile (80km) Lecco-Colico-Sondrio line on a permanent basis. So Italian electrification became established on a line with light traffic.

A particularly difficult line to work by steam, because of its gradients, its heavy traffic and its tunnels, was the Giovi incline which connected the port of Genoa with its hinterland. The original line, built in 1853, involved a climb of 4½ miles (7.2km) at 1-in-28½ (3.5 per cent) followed by a 2-mile (3.2km) tunnel. A diver-

sion with easier grades of 1-in-62 (1.6 per cent) and a 4-mile summit tunnel was opened in 1889, but by 1905, when Italian State Railways (FS) was formed, the traffic offering was such that the combined capacity of both the old and the new lines was insufficient.

The experience gained on the Lecco-Colico-Sondrio line gave the infant FS enough confidence to tackle the Giovi line using the same principles, the work being completed in 1908. The locomotives supplied were these ten-coupled tractors, capable of taking 400t (440 US tons) up the 1-in-28 (3.5 per cent) gradient, at their fixed top speed of 31mph (50km/h). An alternative fixed speed of 14mph could be obtained by connecting the motors in cascade. The reason for the low-frequency supply lay in the fact that designers were unhappy about transmitting the heavy forces involved through such

Class 1099 C-C

Type: Electric mountain locomotive.
Gauge: 2ft 6in (760mm).
Propulsion: Single-phase medium-frequency current at 6,500V 25Hz, fed via overhead wire and step-down variable transformer to two 300hp (225kW) motors, one on each bogie, connected to the driving wheels by jackshafts and coupling rods.
Weight: 103,590lb (47t).
Max. axleload: 17,632lb (8t).
Length: 36ft 2in (11,020mm).
Tractive effort: 10,150lb (45kN).
Max. speed: 31mph (50km/h).

73 years young and still no successors in sight! These fine early examples of the electric loco-motive-builder's art have worked virtually all the services on what is now Austrian Federal Railways' narrow-gauge branch from St Pölten—on the Vienna to Salzburg main line—south through the mountains a distance of 56 miles (91km) to Mariazell and Gusswerk ever since electrification was completed in 1911. The line was built in 1898 by the local provincial authority as the Lower Austria Council Railway (*Niederoester-reichische Landesbahn*—NOLB), which was also responsible for

the electrification. In 1921 the NOLB system was absorbed into Austrian Federal Railways.

Simplicity was the keynote of the locomotives' design and this has no doubt contributed much to their exceptional longevity. For example, in spite of the long and steep gradients, electric braking is not provided. Some complexity is involved, however, in the draw-gear which is mounted on the bogies. This comprises combined central buffer and link-and-pin couplings as well as screw couplings on each side. A single pantograph now replaces the two unusual current collectors orig-

inally provided, each consisting of a small pantograph mounted on what for all the world looked like the frame of a step-ladder.

It is quite common to find ancient locomotives looking more or less the same as they did when they left the builders' works, but which have been fundamentally re-equipped as regards their working parts. The Class "1099s" are the opposite—internally they are virtually the same, but brightly-painted modern bodywork has replaced the original drab brown box-like exterior. In spite of wars, economic troubles and various foreign occupations, all 16 still

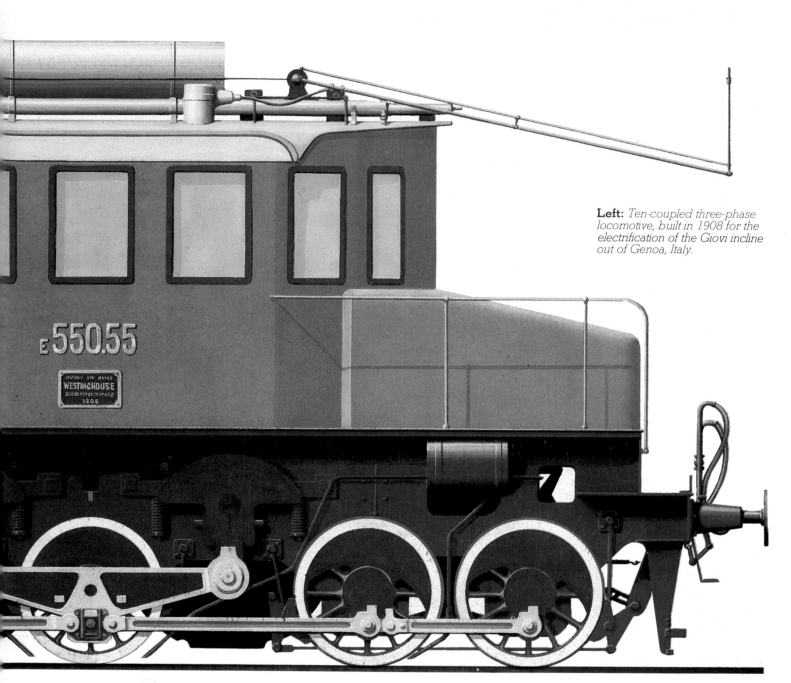

Left: *Ten-coupled three-phase locomotive, built in 1908 for the electrification of the Giovi incline out of Genoa, Italy.*

gearing as was then available. Low-frequency synchronous motors can conveniently have a suitably low corresponding rate of revolution, thereby doing away with the need for gearing.

Incidentally the designation "E550" has the following significance: "E" = electric, first "5" = 5 driving axles, second "5" = the service on which the locomotive is to be used (in this case heavy freight), and the final "0" is the sequential number of the class within the same type and service.

Success attended all the efforts made and the electrification was rapidly extended to other main lines in that part of Italy, the Mont Cenis tunnel and the French frontier being reached in 1912.

The fleet of "E550s" rose by leaps and bounds, and by 1921, when they were superseded by the similar but more powerful "E551" class, the total had reached 186. They were then by far the most numerous class of electric locomotive in the world. One of these famous machines survives in Milan, on display at the Leonardo da Vinci Museum of Science & Technology, as befits a class of locomotive that was the first to show that electricity could do what steam could not.

survive—Nos. 1099.01-16. The mechanical parts were built by Krauss Works at Linz, Austria, and the electrical equipment by Siemens-Schuckert of Nuremberg, West Germany.

Right: *Austrian Federal Railways' Class 1099 600hp (450kW) electric locomotive, built in 1910 for the metre-gauge Mariazellerbahn in Lower Austria, heads a train from St. Polten to Gusswerk. All 16 of these locomotives still miraculously survive, although new bodywork recently fitted to the whole Class gives them a changed appearance.*

Be 5/7 1-E-1

Type: Heavy-duty mixed-traffic electric locomotive.
Gauge: 4ft 8½in (1,435mm).
Propulsion: Single-phase current at 15,000V 16⅔Hz fed via overhead catenary and step-down transformer to two 1,250hp (933kW) motors connected to the wheels by gearing, jackshafts and coupling rods.
Weight: 172,353lb (78.2t) adhesive, 231,420lb (105t) total.
Max. axleload: 36,586lb (16.6t).
Overall length: 52ft 6in (16,000m).
Tractive effort: 39,670lb (176kN).
Max. speed: 47mph (75km/h).

When the Simplon tunnel route from Brig, Switzerland, to Domodossola was opened in 1906, businessmen in the Swiss capital Berne, found themselves a mere 52 miles (85km) away from the northern portal of this channel of trade, yet separated from it by the great mountains of the Bernese Oberland. As the Swiss Federal Railways system (then occupied in digesting its recently-absorbed component parts) offered no assistance, it was a case of self-help; with a commendable lack of delay, construction of the Berne-Lötschberg-Simplon Railway began in 1906.

The project was a bold one involving construction of a third major 'Swiss Alpine tunnel, the Lötschberg, 9.1 miles (14.6km) in length. There were long ascending ramps at 1-in-37 (2.7 per cent)

including many further bores, both spiral and otherwise. Whilst this combination of tunnelling and gradient was ideal for electric traction, it needed courage amounting almost to rashness to adopt it for a project of this magnitude at this time. But the engineers had a starting point. Three-phase electric traction had been used in the Simplon tunnel from its opening and, as we have seen, it had also been adopted in Italy for the Giovi and other lines. However, the Swiss electrical firm of Oerlikon realised (as it has turned out with remarkable foresight) that this form of electrification had limited potential for other than specialised lines.

Above: *Bern-Lötschberg-Simplon pioneer Be 5/7 electric locomotive of 1912 at Brig, July 1954.*

Accordingly, in 1905, Oerlikon went so far as to electrify at their own cost as a demonstration Swiss Federal Railways' 14 mile (22.5km) branch from Seebach to Wettingen. They used their own system of 15,000V 16⅔Hz single-phase low-frequency alternating current developed by their Chief Engineer Dr-Eng Huber-Stockar. By using a low frequency (so low that lamps lit by this current can be seen to flicker strongly), it was possible to overcome the difficulties of using alternating current in a variable-speed motor. At the same time, the current could be fed to the locomotives at high voltage, with a convenient step-down transformer to produce the much lower and variable voltage suitable for the driving motors. The electrification was a technical but not a commercial success and was dismantled after the demonstration was over.

So the first major main line to be built as an electric railway came into being, and to work it 13 of these handsome ten-coupled locomotives' were built — the most powerful in the world. The electrical equipment naturally came from Oerlikon, while equally naturally the mechanical parts came from the Swiss Locomotive Works at Winterthur. The locomotives achieved their objective by being

Right: *These giant locomotives of the Lötschberg Railway were the most powerful in the world in 1912.*

Nos. 1-67 HGe 2/2
Panama Canal Zone:
Panama Canal Company, 1912

Type: Rack-and-adhesion electric canal mule locomotive.
Gauge: 5ft 0in (1,524mm).
Propulsion: Three-phase current at 200V 25Hz fed via twin outside conductor rails to two 150hp (112kW) motors with pole-changing arrangements to give the fixed speeds. The rack pinions driven through gearing and the adhesive driving wheels via friction clutches.
Weight: 99,180lb (45t).
Overall length: 31ft 6½in (9,617mm).
Tractive effort: 28,600lb (127kN).
Max. speed: 5mph (8km/h).

Whilst handling ships passing through the Panama canal, these unique and fascinating machines for 50 years pulled heavier loads than any other railway locomotive

in the world (as do their somewhat similar successors). They also climbed the steepest gradient of 1-in-1 (100 per cent) on the steps abreast of the lock gates—but not under load, as ships would at that moment be stationary in the lock. Elsewhere the running lines are level; the trackage extends to 20¼ miles (32km) of which 12 miles (19.3km) is equipped with Riggenbach "ladder" rack of a specially heavy pattern.

The braking system also has sufficient force to deal with the massive inertia of an ocean-going ship as well as being able to stop the locomotive in 10ft when descending a 1-in-1 (100 per cent) gradient at 3mph (4.8km/h). Locomotive power has to be provided at each of the four "corners" of a ship and there is a complex control system for the winch set

between the cab units. Such is one of the most remarkable locomotive types ever built.

Above: *Flexibility is the name of the game: a Panama Canal ship-hauling electric loco.*

able to handle 300t (330 US ton) trains up the 1-in-37 (2.7 per cent) grade at 31.25mph (50km/h).

There were serious problems in the early days, both electrical and mechanical. Sudden surges of high voltage occurred under certain conditions and this damaged equipment. More serious was the harmonic vibration to the point of failure of the massive triangular connecting pieces joining the driving pins to the two drive shafts to those of the central driving wheel. Before long the causes of the problems were

identified and cures found, and it says enough that Norway, Sweden, Germany and Austria all adopted the same voltage and frequency for their main-line electrification, while the locomotives gave more than 40 years of good service. Today Lötschberg "Be 5/7" No.151 has a well-deserved place in the Swiss Transport Museum at Lucerne.

Above: *Ten-coupled electric locomotive No. 151 of the BLS Railway on test between Speiz and Brig, Switzerland, in 1912.*

HBERG   SIMPLON

Nos. 21-28 C

Type: Electric rack-and-adhesion locomotive.
Gauge: 3ft 3⅜in (1,000mm).
Propulsion: Direct current at 1,500V fed via twin contact wires to two 400hp (298kW) traction motors. One motor drives the railwheels via gearing, jackshaft and connecting rods; the other motor drives the rack pinion via gearing.
Weight: 80,445lb (36.5t).
Max. axleload: 27,550lb (12.5t).
Overall length: 27ft 0½in (8,240mm).
Tractive effort: 13,225lb (59kN) adhesion, 26,450lb (118kN) rack-and-adhesion.
Max. speed: 25mph (40km/h) on adhesion sections, 7.5mph (12km/h) on rack sections.

The little Bernese Oberland Railway (the "BOB" to its many loving British friends) is the first stage of an amazing Swiss mountain railway system which by two routes and two changes of gauge takes people to the Jungfraujoch, highest railway station in Europe. Since 1890, it has connected with the main line at Interlaken and served directly the resorts of Grindelwald and Lauterbrunnen. Included in the system are several rack-and-pinion sections equipped with the Riggenbach or ladder rack.

Everything was done by steam in the early days, but in 1914 the 14.7 mile (23.5km) system was electrified. For working the trains, these eight neat locomotives were supplied by Oerlikon and the Swiss Locomotive Works. Two identical motors were fitted, one driving the main cog-wheel for operation on the rack, and the other driving the rail wheels and used both on the rack and off it. On the wholly adhesion sections, 125t (137 US tons) can be hauled up the maximum grade of 1-in-40 (2.5 per cent) from Interlaken to the junction at Zweilütschinen, while the 1-in-8.3 (12 per cent) rack sections up to Grindelwald and 1-in-11.1 (9 per cent) up to Lauterbrunnen limit loads to 60t and 90t (66 and 99 US tons) respectively.

No chances can be taken with the brakes on such grades and five independent systems are provided. First, a normal air brake works on both the rail wheelrims and on a separate braking rack wheel, riding free on one of the axles. There is also a handbrake arranged to come automatically into play when the normal speed is exceeded by 20 per cent. Furthermore, there are two separate screw handbrakes working

Below: *BOB electric locomotive ready to leave Lauterbrunnen Station, Switzerland, with a freight train for Interlaken.*

Right: *BOB rack-and-adhesion electric locomotive. In earlier days the livery was grey and later black was used.*

Nos. 1-13 B₀-B₀

Type: Electric freight locomotive.
Gauge: 4ft 8½in (1,435mm).
Propulsion: Direct-current at 1,500V fed via overhead catenary to four 275hp (205kW) nose-suspended traction motors.
Weight: 166,660lb (76t).
Max. axleload: 41,665lb (19t).
Overall length: 59ft 0in (17,989mm).
Tractive effort: 28,800lb (128kN).
Max. speed: 40mph (64km/h).

The principal reason for building the Stockton & Darlington Railway, the first steam public railway in the world, was to haul coal from coalfields near Bishop Auckland to tide-water at Stockton. The route chosen just happened to run via Darlington. This first steam railway was a prime example of what was to become the classic use for them—bulk movement of minerals. Today it is the only use which enables new railways to be justified upon purely financial considerations.

For many years fortune smiled on the S&D and traffic rose to a point where a by-pass (known as the Simpasture line) had to be built to avoid the congestion of Darlington, and other parts of the line had to be increased from two to four tracks. The route was also a very early candidate for electrification, not because of any of its physical characteristics nor because of the need to increase capacity or avoid pollution, but entirely on the basis of reducing running costs.

Electrification of the 18-mile (29km) route from Shildon Yard (the collecting point for coal from the various collieries concerned) to Newport Yard, the distribution point for the numerous coal-consuming customers and shipping staithes in the Stockton-Middlesbrough area, began in 1914 and was completed in 1917. Because of the complexities of the lines, 50 miles (80km) of track were involved. Technical innovation was not a feature; instead, simplicity and economy were the keynotes of the equipment. For example, the locomotives had no train braking equipment. Fortunately, the public power supply system in a major industrial area was by then already adequate to take on the heavy and highly variable demands involved, so one major complication—construction of a purpose-built generating station—was avoided. Incidentally, the power company contracted for the supply of the actual traction current, building and owning the two substations.

Some features were found to be too simple; for example, hand-worked knife switches on these locomotives had to be replaced by power-worked equipment—a combination of hundreds of amps with over a thousand volts was too much for operation by hand. Also, the distance of 200ft (61m)

on the rail wheels and the braking rack-wheel respectively. Finally, provision is made for electric braking, dissipating the energy generated in the process by a bank of blower-cooled resistances.

Since World War II, most BOB passenger trains have been worked by trailer-hauling railcars, but a number of these neat locomotives are retained for freight haulage, service trains and summer peaks, and accordingly join the select ranks of 70-year old locomotives still in use.

Right: *BOB No. 22 at Wilderswil with a freight in August, 1982. Note the standard-gauge wagon on metre-gauge transporter.*

between structures supporting the overhead wire on straight lengths of track was found to be too great when the wind blew, and intermediate stay poles had to be added. Otherwise success was achieved.

As intended, 1,400t (1,640 US tons) trains of unbraked loaded coal hopper wagons—without even brake vans—could be hauled and, more importantly, held to a reasonable speed on gradients of 1-in-100 (1 per cent).

Left: *North Eastern Railway No. 9 Bo-Bo electric locomotive as built for the Shildon to Middlesbrough line to the design of Vincent Raven by the railway's own shops at Darlington in 1914.*

Primitive bearings on the wagons made the former more difficult but gave modest assistance with the latter!

Commercial success was, however, short-lived. In the 1930s, coal production in the West Auckland field fell to a low level. Moreover, the overhead conductor system needed a good deal of renewal; the wood poles in particular had reached the end of their short lives. Accordingly, these locomotives were laid aside, hopefully for re-use on the electrification soon to be started from Manchester to Sheffield. However, the war delayed this project and before it was completed in the 1950s, all except one of the Newport-Shildon locos were scrapped

DD1 2-B+B-2

Type: Electric passenger locomotive.
Gauge: 4ft 8½in (1,435mm).
Propulsion: Direct current at 600V fed via outside third rail (or by overhead conductors and miniature pantographs at places where third rail was impractical) to two 1,065hp (795kW) motors, each driving two main axles by means of a jackshaft and connecting rods.
Weight: 199,000lb (90.2t) adhesive, 319,000lb (145t) total.
Max. axleload: 50,750lb (23t).
Overall length: 64ft 11in (19,787mm).
Tractive effort: 49,400lb (220kN).
Max. speed: 80mph (129km/h).

The Pennsylvania Railroad gained entry to New York City and its new Pennsylvania Station by single-track tunnels, two under the Hudson River and four under the East River, and for the operation of these tunnels electrification was essential. The third-rail system at 650V was chosen, and between 1903 and 1905 three experimental four-axle locomotives were built, two B-Bs at the Pennsy's Altoona shops and a 2-B by Baldwin. The B-Bs had a separate motor for each axle, whilst the 2-B had a single 2,000hp (2,680kW) motor mounted on the main frame midway between the coupled axles. The motors of both types of locomotive drove through quills, an early version of the drive which

was to be used a quarter of a century later on the "GG1" electrics.

Test were made to determine the forces exerted on the rails by the two types of locomotive and by the most recent steam designs, and it was found that the 2-B, with its higher centre of gravity, exerted less than half the force of the B-B, with its low-slung motors. However, the force due to the 2-B was still twice as great as that from the heaviest steam engine. The next two electric locomotives therefore had the 2-B wheel arrangement, but to give the required power each one comprised two units permanently coupled back-to-back, giving the combined wheel arrangement 2-B-B-2. The impor-

tant change in design from the experimental locomotive was in the drive to the axles, which incorporated a jackshaft mounted in bearings in the main frame of the locomotive, with connecting rods from the motor to the jackshaft and from the jackshaft to the driving wheels. The technical problems with the quill drive were left for solution at a later date.

With 72in (1,829mm) driving wheels, each half of the unit resembled the chassis of an express 4-4-0 steam locomotive. This similarity to steam design was apparent in a number of early electric engines, for example in Prussia, but unusually for such designs the Pennsylvania's was highly successful. It was capable of

Class T B₀-B₀+B₀-B₀

Type: Express passenger electric locomotive.
Gauge: 4ft 8½in (1,435mm).
Propulsion: Direct current at 660V collected from under-contact third rail supplying eight 330hp (246kW) gearless traction motors mounted on the bogie frames, with armatures on the axles.
Weight: 230,000lb (104.3t).
Max. axleload: 28,730lb (13.0t).
Overall length: 55ft 2in (16,815mm).
Tractive effort: 69,000lb (307kN).
Max. speed: 75mph (120km/h).

In 1913 the New York Central Railroad completed its Grand Central terminal, and in the same year it also completed an extension of electrification along the Hudson River main line to Harmon, 33 miles (53km) from Grand Central. The heaviest expresses would

80mph (129km/h), and there was no appreciable clanking of the rods. Maintenance costs were very low, and were helped by the design of the body. The whole casing could be removed in one unit to give access to the motors and control equipment. This feature was repeated in all subsequent PRR electric designs. A small pantograph was fitted to allow overhead current collection on complicated trackwork.

The first two rod-drive units appeared in 1909-10, the individual half-units being numbered from 3996 to 3999. They were followed in 1910-11 by a further 31, numbered from 3932 to 3949 and from 3952 to 3995. The Pennsylvania classified its steam locomotives by a letter, denoting the wheel arrangement, followed by a serial number, letter "D" denoted 4-4-0. For electrics the road used the same system, the letter being doubled when appropriate, so that the 2-B+B-2, being a double 4-4-0, was a DD. The main production batch of 31 units was classified "DD1", and the two prototypes "odd DD"

The Pennsylvania Station project required seven years, from 1903 to 1910, for its execution, and electrification then extended from Manhattan Transfer, near Newark, New Jersey, to the carriage yards at Sunnyside, Long Island, a total of 13.4 route miles (21.5km). At Manhattan Transfer the change was made to or from steam for the 8.8 miles (14.2km) between there and Pennsylvania Station. The heaviest gradient on the descent to the tunnels was 1-in-52 (1.93 per cent).

The "DD" locomotives worked all the express passenger services on this section of line until 1924 when newer types began to appear, but they continued to share the work until 1933 when overhead electrification reached Manhattan Transfer from Trenton, and the remaining section into Pennsylvania Station was converted to overhead. Third-rail current collection was retained between Pennsylvania Station and Sunnyside, because the Long Island Rail Road used this system. After 1933 "DDs" continued to work empty trains between Pennsylvania Station and Sunnyside for many years. After the arrival of newer power in 1924, 23 of the "DD1s" were transferred to the Long Island Rail Road, and these remained in service until 1949-51.

The "DDs" were a landmark in electric locomotive design, with exceptionally high power and unusual reliability for their day, but at the same time their design was conservative. Simplicity of design and the flexibility of the "double 4-4-0" chassis contributed greatly to their success.

Below: *Pennsylvania Railroad Class DD1 direct-current 2-B+B-2 electric locomotive.*

now have some 20 miles of fast running with electric haulage, and a new type of locomotive was therefore commissioned, which would be both more powerful than the "S" class 2-Do-2 and also kinder to the track at high speed.

The new class was designated "T", thereby taking the letter vacated by the earlier locomotives when they were rebuilt. The most important change was adoption of an articulated layout in which every axle was motored, but at the same time the whole chassis was more flexible than in the earlier class. There were two sub-frames, each with two four-wheeled trucks pivotted to it. The trucks were connected by arms, and the sub-frames were hinged together at their inner ends and carried the couplers at the outer ends. The body rested on two pivots, one

Left: *A Class T Bo-Bo+Bo-Bo electric locomotive of the New York Central Railroad.*

on each sub-frame, and one pivot had some end play to allow for changes in geometry on curves. The whole assembly was therefore flexible, but with restraining forces on all its elements to discourage the build-up of oscillations. The wheel arrangement was Bo-Bo+Bo-Bo, and it was equivalent to two Bo-Bo locomotives hinged together.

Nominal power of the original motors fitted to Class "S" was 550hp (410kW), but in Class "T" the motor size was reduced to 330hp (246kW). This enabled the weight of the motors to be reduced, with a corresponding reduction in the forces on the track and with an improvement in riding. The new class was therefore allowed 75mph (121km/h), later reduced to 70 (113), compared with 60mph (97km/h) on Class "S". The motors were of the same bi-polar type as before, with almost flat pole faces to allow for the vertical movement of the axle

(and armature) on its springs.

Another change from Class "S" was that the motors had forced ventilation, which involved some complications of ducting to the bogies. As in the earlier units, in addition to pick-up shoes for the third rail, a small pantograph was fitted. This was used on complicated track layouts where there were long gaps in the third rail, and overhead wires were installed locally. There was an oil-fired train heating boiler, with supplies of water and oil. It seemed anomalous on an electrification introduced to eliminate the smoke nuisance that the locomotive should carry a small stack on its roof emitting oil exhaust!

The first locomotive was completed in March 1918; this was Class "T1a". Nine more, classified "T1b", were delivered later in the year. Sub-class "T2a" of 10 units came in 1914, a further 10 designated "T2b" in 1917, and a final batch of 10 in 1926; these were "T3a". Successive batches differed mainly in the size of train-heating boiler and its fuel supplies, but the "T2s" and "T3s" were 20in (508mm) longer than the "T1s". The bodies of successive batches were a little longer, and the end overhang slightly less.

With a continous rating of 2,610hp at 48mph (77km/h), they were powerful locomotives for their day, and they were highly successful. They continued to work single-headed all express trains out of Grand Central until 1955, when some locomotives surplus from a discontinued electrification in Cleveland began to displace them. They could handle trains up to 980 US tons at 60mph (97km/h).

These locomotives established the practicability of the all-adhesion machine for high-speed work, and they showed that it was possible to avoid the heavy and complicated rod drives of many of their contemporaries.

Class EP-2
"Bi-polar" 1-B-D-D-B-1

USA: Chicago, Milwaukee, St Paul & Pacific Railroad, (CM St P&P), 1919

Type: Express passenger electric locomotive.
Gauge: 4ft 8½in (1,435mm)
Propulsion: Direct current at 3,000V fed via overhead catenary to twelve 370hp (275kW) gearless motors mounted directly on the axles.
Weight: 457,000lb (207t) adhesive, 530,000lb (240t) total.
Max. axleload: 38,500lb (17.5t).
Overall length: 76ft 0in (23,165mm).
Tractive effort: 123,500lb (549kN).
Max. speed: 70mph (112km/h).

When the Chicago, Milwaukee, St Paul & Pacific Railroad was opened to Tacoma, Washington State, in 1909 (through passenger service did not begin until 1911) it was the last railway to reach the West Coast from the east. As a newcomer, then, the company had to try harder, and one of the ways in which it did this was to work the mountain crossings by the clean new power of electricity.

Catenary wires mounted on timber poles started to go up five years after the line was opened, and early in 1917 electric working began over the Rocky Mountain and Missoula divisions, between Harlowton and Avery, Montana, a distance of 438 miles (705km). Many miles of 100,000V transmission lines had to be built through virgin territory from hydro-electric power plants to rotary substations along the right-of-way. By 1919 the 230-mile (370km) Coast Division from Othello to Tacoma, Washington State, had been electrified also.

Electrification measured by the hundreds of miles was something quite new in the world, and the

North American railroad top brass watched with baited breath for the results. Technically, they were totally satisfactory: much heavier loads could be worked than with steam, energy costs were lower, faster running times—and hence better productivity—could be achieved. The system was reliable and one could have been forgiven for thinking that other railroads would quickly follow. Alas, the enormous costs involved proved too frightening at a time when railroads were beginning to feel the effects of competition from road transport. So, with one notable exception, in the USA main line electrification schemes were

confined to shortish lengths of line.

The Milwaukee Railroad itself went bankrupt in 1925, and this caused a further ebb of confidence, although it was claimed that the onset of bankruptcy was *delayed* rather than *caused* by the $24 million spent on electrification.

The original passenger locomotives (Class "EP1"), delivered from 1915 onwards by The American Locomotive Co and General Electric, were the same as those for freight, except that they had higher gearing and oil-fired train-heating boilers. They were formed as twin units, permanently coupled, of the 2-Bo-Bo+Bo-Bo-2 wheel ar-

Above: *A "Bi-polar" in service under the 3,000 volt catenary wires of the Chicago, Milwaukee St Paul & Pacific Railroad.*

rangement and produced 3,440hp (2,570kW) for a weight of 288 tons. Their plain "box-car" style belied their ability to pull and go in an unprecedented manner. Thirty freight and 12 passenger locos were supplied.

When the wires were going up over the Cascade mountains in 1918, something more exotic was proposed; the result was these legendary "Bi-polars", created by General Electric. The name arose from using two-pole motors. The

reason for this lay in a desire to simplify the mechanics of an electric locomotive. The ultimate in simplicity is to put the armatures of the motors actually on the driving axles, thereby doing away altogether with gearing, but it is then necessary to cater for vertical movement. Hence there can only be two poles, one on either side in a position where the critical air gap between poles and armature is not affected by vertical movement. The price of doing it this way is that the power of each motor is limited, partly because it runs at the low speed of the wheels and partly because two-pole motors are less powerful than those with a more usual number of poles anyway.

The result was that, for a power output virtually the same as the "EP1s", the "EP2s" had half as many more driving wheels. The body was articulated in three parts, connected together by the four-axle trucks. All this made for a lot of locomotive, but the effect of size on the public was nothing compared with the impact of very impressive styling. The electrical equipment was contained in round-topped bonnets at each end of the locomotive and this simple change was what gave these engines that little extra the others hadn't got.

The designers were sensible enough to put the train-heating boiler, fuel and water tanks—all items that do not mix well with electricity—in the separate centre section. All things considered, the Cascade Division in 1918 found itself in possession of a reliable class of five locomotives that could

Below: *The Chicago, Milwaukee St Paul & Pacific Railroad's Class EP-2 "Bi-polar", one of the most impressive locomotives of any form of traction ever to have been built.*

haul 900t (1,000 US tons) trains up the long 1-in-45 (2.2 per cent) grades at 25mph (40km/h), as well as hold them back coming down. Some rather fine publicity stunts were arranged showing a "Bi-polar" having a tug-of-war with two big steam engines (a 2-6-6-2 and a 2-8-0) on top of a huge trestle bridge. The electric had no difficulty in pulling backwards the two steam engines set to pull full steam ahead.

Ten more passenger engines (Class "EP3") were delivered in 1921 by rival builders Baldwin and Westinghouse, and these were more orthodox. Even so, 20 per cent more power was packed into a locomotive with only half the number of driving wheels, the wheel arrangement being 2-C-1 + 1-C-2. Their appearance was fairly box-like, although not quite as severe as that of the "EP1s".

So the "Bi-polars" were outclassed as well as outnumbered

by nearly five-to-one soon after they were built, yet these legendary locomotives demonstrated very clearly the value of cosmetics, because they are the ones remembered and regarded as epitomising this longest amongst North American electrification schemes. The great engines gave excellent service, though, and soldiered on through the years. In the late 1950s they were moving the road's crack "Olympian Hiawatha" luxury express over the 438 miles (705km) of the Rocky Mountain Division in 10hr 40min, compared with 15 hours scheduled when the electrification was new

Some modern electric locomotives of even greater power, built for the USSR but undeliverable on account of the so-called "Cold War", became available at this time. These "Little Joes" as they were known, were further nails in the coffins of the now ageing "Bi-

polars". In spite of a rebuild in 1953 which included the addition of multiple-unit capability, all five were taken out of service between 1958 and 1960. One (No. E2) is preserved at the National Museum of Transport in St Louis, Missouri, but the others went for scrap.

In 1973, all electric operations on the Milwaukee came to end, a favourable price for scrap copper being one of the factors. The escalation in the price of oil which followed might have saved the day, although the existence of the whole railroad was soon to be in jeopardy, there being just too many lines in the area. It was no surprise, then, when in 1980 all transcontinental operations over the one-time electrified tracks ceased, and most have now been abandoned.

Below: *"Bi-polar" No. E-2 as preserved at the National Museum of Transport, St Louis, Missouri.*

Nos. 1-20 B₀-B₀

Great Britain:
Metropolitan Railway (Met), 1920

Type: Electric passenger locomotive.

Gauge: 4ft 8½in (1,435mm).

Propulsion: Direct current at 600V fed via third and fourth rails to four 300hp (224kW) nose-suspended motors geared to the driving axles.

Weight: 137,760lb (62.5t).

Max. axleload: 34,440lb (15.4t).

Overall length: 39ft 0in (11,887mm).

Max. speed: 65mph (104km/h).

When a railway which has hitherto been confined to short rapid-transit operations within a great metropolis suddenly starts to run out into the country, it is apt to behave as if it owned a transcontinental. The Metropolitan Railway's extension for 50 miles (80km) from Baker Street Station to Aylesbury and beyond was (among more mundane things) part of a grandiose plan for running trains from such places as Manchester, Sheffield, Nottingham and Leicester to Paris, Berlin and Rome. The Channel tunnel was to be the link between Britain and the rest of Europe, while that between the north and the south of London was the Metropolitan Railway.

Alas, it never happened that the "Orient Express" called at Baker Street to pick up secret agents, but the Met did its best to compensate with such delights as

Pullman parlour cars on its longer-distance suburban trains, taking commuters from what became known as Metroland to earn their daily bread in the city. At the head of them were these handsome, named and beautifully painted electric locomotives.

Electrification had come to the surface lines of London's underground railways around the turn of the century. In 1904, and again in 1906, a batch of 10 electric locomotives was built to work the trains on country extensions as far as the the limit of electrification, which was Harrow-on-the-Hill for a time and later Rickmansworth. These early machines were reconstructed in 1920 by Metropolitan-Vickers to an extent that amounted to replacement, the result being these outwardly magnificent but basically very conventional electric locomotives.

The usual problems caused by the inevitable gaps in the conductor system were solved by providing collecting shoes and a power line, not only for the Metropolitan trains used on the main line but also on the Great Western services which ran through via Paddington, and were electrically worked from there to Liverpool Street. Vacuum as well as air brake equipment was provided, so that stock which was normally steam-hauled could be handled also.

In 1960 electrification was extended from Rickmansworth to

Amersham, and London Transport (into which the Met had been absorbed in 1933) ceased running trains between Amersham and Aylesbury. After this, little work could be found for these engines, and the majority were withdrawn; however, No. 5 *John Hampden* is preserved in the London Transport Museum at Covent Garden and No. 12 *Sarah Siddons* in working order at London Transport's Neasden depot.

Above: *One of the Metropolitan Railway 1920 electric locomotives enters Baker Street station.*

Right: *No. 12* Sarah Siddons, *preserved at Neasden Depot, at Wembley Park, on a special to Watford in September 1982.*

Below: *No. 8, appropriately named* Sherlock Holmes, *who supposedly lodged in Baker Street just opposite the Metropolitan station.*

41

Class Ge 6/6 "Crocodile"

Switzerland:
Rhaetian Railway (RhB), 1921

Type: Electric mountain locomotive.
Gauge: 3ft 3⅜in (1,000mm).
Propulsion: Single-phase current at 11,000V 16⅔Hz fed via overhead catenary and step-down transformer to two 313hp (420kW) motors, each connected to three driving axles by jackshafts and coupling rods.
Weight: 145,460lb (66t).
Max. axleload: 24,240lb (11t).
Overall length: 43ft 7½in (13,300mm).
Tractive effort: 39,600lb (176kN).
Max. speed: 34mph (55km/h).

One of the most famous as well as one of the most spectacular railway systems in the world is the metre-gauge line which serves the Swiss resorts of Davos and St Moritz. Connections with the main stand-ard-gauge railway are made at Landquart and Chur, at around 500ft (150m) altitude, whilst the two main objectives of the line are reached via summits at 5,700ft (1,737m) and 5,980ft (1,823m) respectively. The line from Land-quart to Davos was laid out in 1896 with a ruling gradient of 1-in-22½ (4.5 per cent) while the Chur to St Moritz route, completed in 1902, was built to 1-in-29 (3.4 per cent) maximum including four spiral tunnels and the 3.6-mile (5.9km) Albula tunnel connecting the Rhine and Danube water-sheds.

Even though curvature as sharp as 328ft (100m) radius is the rule rather than the exception, it was not possible to avoid some of the most expensive and spectacular railway engineering in the world. In steam days, operation was

Right: *Rhaetian Railway Class Ge 6/6. Note the big snow-plough as carried in winter and spring until about 1960, when small permanently-fixed ones were fitted at both ends.*

fairly traumatic and the thoughts of Rhaetian Railway engineers turned to this new-fangled power called electricity, which could be generated by the ample water-power available in the district.

Mountain railway electrification in Switzerland had until then tended to follow tramway practice in using low-voltage direct current, but the Rhaetian problem was more that of a main line railway.

When in 1910 construction began of a branch down the Engadine Valley to the Austrian border at Schuls-Tarasp, oppor-tunity was taken to build the line as an electrified railway. The engineers used what was to be-come the Swiss standard main-line system of 16⅔Hz alternating current, but at the nominal lower voltage of 11,000 instead of 15,000. One reason for this was

Above: *Rhaetian Railway Class Ge 6/6 No. 410 leaving Davos-Dorf Station with a Landquart to Davos-Platz train.*

the tight clearances for the over-head wires in RhB's numerous tunnels. Some box-like tractors of the 1-B-1 wheel arrangement were built for local traffic on the lower Engadine line, but also in 1913-14 came eight experimental (and rather longer) 1-D-1 boxes intended as possible main-line power for the RhB. They incorporated various solutions to the problem of obtaining adequate starting torque from a single-phase alter-nating current motor.

A desperate shortage of fuel during the 1914-18 war (the Swiss had no coal of their own) turned this desire to electrify into an iron resolve. After the war was over,

experience with the pre-war electric engines suggested that something completely different would be preferable; and that led to the magnificent locomotives described here.

No.401, the first of 10 C-C electric locomotives, was delivered in June 1921 and this event marked the beginning of an un-interrupted rule of 26 years as the prime power on this spectacular and exacting railway. Two more were built in 1925 and a further batch of three came in 1929. As with most Swiss locomotives, the mechanical parts were supplied by the Swiss Locomotive Works; the electrical equipment was shared by Brown Boveri and Oerlikon.

A timing of 4 hours from Chur to St Moritz (89km) in steam days was improved to 2hr 45min with electrification. In addition, it was possible in due course to provide more comfortable rolling stock (reflected in an increase in weight per seat provided) and such amenities as restaurant cars, for, what was still a fairly long journey. Furthermore, a large increase in traffic could be handled without difficulty, considering that the trailing load for one locomotive had increased from 90t to 200t of the RhB's light bogie coaches averaging 20t each.

The design incorporated two jackshaft and rod-drive six-coupled units, each with a large single-phase motor, set some distance apart. These units were connected (in the exact manner of a Beyer Garratt steam locomo-tive) by a body section which carried the main transformer—always very heavy in the case of a low-frequency supply—as well as

all the switchgear and auxiliaries, the two sets of controls and, on the roof, the two pantograph current collectors. The driver looks out from the windows of this central section over the bonnets of the articulated motor units. A similar layout was used for some standard-gauge locomotives (known as the "Crocodiles") built at the same time for the newly-electrified Gotthard line of Swiss Federal Railways.

Interesting accessories included flange-lubricating gear to assist in negotiating the almost continuous curvature, and there was a vacuum exhauster to provide power for RhB's vacuum brakes. For winter use there were transformer tappings to provide a supply of train-heating current and a massive snowplough for attachment at one end. In later years two smaller ploughs were permanently fixed, which saved turning the engines.

Regenerative braking was a possibility, but a problem arose while RhB's low-frequency power supplies remained self-contained. All the trains on the line *could* be running downhill, and without any load on the system (or special provision for such conditions) braking effect would not be forthcoming with dire results. Accordingly, a system of electric braking was adopted which is similar to that provided on many modern diesel-electric locomotives; the power generated by braking is dissipated in a bank of resistances.

A pleasing feature is the brown livery with elegant brass insignia which has been retained despite the fact that after World War II RhB began applying a rather drab dark green colour with chromium-plated *sans serif* lettering and numbering to its new electric tractors.

After these more conventional Bo-Bo locomotives came along in 1947, the "baby-crocs" (as the "Ge 6/6s" were sometimes known) began to be displaced from the prime assignments but continued to give good service on lesser trains. Even though 20 Bo-Bo and seven Bo-Bo-Bo machines are now available, all the baby-crocs except No.401 (which lost an argument with some avalanche debris at Cavadurli near Klosters in 1973) are still in service at the time of writing.

News that further locomotives are at last on order to replace these superb vintage examples of the locomotive-builder's art saddens those for whom they have for so long been part of the landscape of a favourite holiday area. The RhB management has, however, kept two steam locomotives to satisfy the demands of old train lovers, so perhaps they will apply themselves to the less onerous problem of keeping a baby-crocodile or two in running order with the same end in view.

Above: *Rhaetian Railway Class Ge 6/6 No. 405 comes off the 1-in-22½ (4.5%) ascent at Laret Station above Klosters in the heart of the famous Parsenn skiing area.*

Be 4/6 1-B-B-1

Switzerland:
Swiss Federal Railways (SBB), 1919

Type: Electric mountain passenger locomotive.
Gauge: 4ft 8½in (1,435mm).
Propulsion: Single-phase current at 15,000V 16⅔Hz fed via overhead catenary to two pairs of 510hp (380kW) motors, each pair driving four wheels by jackshaft and coupling rods.
Weight: 169,710lb (77t) adhesive, 234,730lb (106.5t) total.
Max. axleload: 42,427lb (19.25t).
Overall length: 54ft 1½in (16,500mm).
Tractive effort: 44,080lb (196kN).
Max. speed: 47mph (75km/h).

The Gotthard Railway, one of the world's greatest mountain railways and which must take the lion's share of the blame for giving Switzerland's rail routes the nickname "Turntable of Europe", was opened in 1883. The mountain section was double track including the 9¼ mile (14.8km) St Gotthard tunnel, as well as 19 miles (30km) of lesser bores. The ruling grade of 1-in-38½ (2.6 per cent) applied to both the northern and the southern ascents. Even so, heavy traffic was worked satisfactorily by a fleet of well-built compound 2-10-0 and 4-6-0 steam locomotives.

World War I, during which Switzerland was neutral, posed serious problems because coal supplies—mostly originating from Germany—became minimal. Wood-burning was no substitute and even while the war was on plans were afoot to work the railways with Switzerland's only indigenous form of power, that is, electricity produced by water power, the 'white coal' of the Alps.

Proven technology was available, resulting from five years experience with the Lötschberg Railway and now that the will—and the money—was there, there were no obstacles to rapid and confident progress. On May 29, 1921 the main Gotthard line from Erstfeld

Above: *Swiss Federal Railways' Class Be 4/6 electric locomotive shown in the original brown livery, as built for the inauguration of electric working over the Gotthard line.*

No. 13 2-C₀-2

Great Britain:
North Eastern Railway (NER), 1922

Type: Express passenger electric locomotive.
Gauge: 4ft 8½in (1,435mm).
Propulsion: Direct current at 1,500V fed via overhead catenary or under-contact third rail to three pairs of 300hp (224kW) motors, each pair driving a main axle by gearing and spring drive.
Weight: 114,240lb (52t) adhesive, 228,480lb (104t) total.
Max. axleload: 38,080lb (17.25t).
Overall length: 53ft 6in (16,307mm).
Tractive effort: 28,000lb (124kN).
Max. speed: 90mph (144km/h).

When at the end of World War I the railways of the world once more began to look to the future, one of the most far-sighted people involved was Sir Vincent Raven of the North Eastern Railway.

Raven was Chief Mechanical Engineer, and an enthusiast for electric traction. Moreover, the NER's principal activity was the one it had inherited from its earliest constituent, the Stockton & Darlington Railway—the carriage of minerals in bulk. Railways that do this tend, even today, to be rich and so able to afford costly but remunerative investment such as electrification. The NER was no exception.

One of the company's principal mineral lines, that from Shildon to Newport, had been electrified in 1917 with extremely satisfactory results, and Raven's mind turned towards electric traction for the NER's trunk passenger line from York to Newcastle, part of the East Coast route from London to Edinburgh. A great deal of work was done on this project, including construction of a prototype 2-Co-2 electric locomotive capable of as high a speed—90mph (144km/h)—as was then run on railways anywhere.

No. 13 was built at the company's own Darlington Works in 1921-22; Metropolitan-Vickers supplied the electrical equipment. With six motors it was possible to have three running positions of the controls: all motors in series for starting, two sets of three in parallel and three sets of two in parallel. The 6ft 8in (2,032mm) diameter driving wheels had an unusual spoke arrangement to accommodate the fittings of and

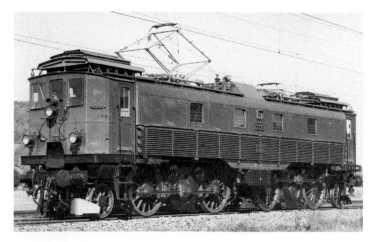

Above: *Swiss Federal Railways' rod-drive electric locomotive No. 12320. Note the buffers and drawgear attached to the bogies rather than to the body of the locomotive.*

passenger traffic, three prototypes were delivered in 1919 for evaluation. A 1-B-B-1 (No. 12301) and a 1-C-1 (No. 12201) came with electrical equipment by Oerlikon, plus a different and rather simpler 1-B-B-1 (No. 12302) from Brown Boveri. After a brief period of trial the last-named was judged the best and a batch of 39 was ordered, the mechanical parts coming as always from the Swiss Locomotive Works of Winterthur. Numbers ran from 12303 to 12341.

The specification for the "BE 4/6s" called for the haulage of a 300t train at a minimum speed of 31mph (50km/h) up the 1-in-38½ (2.6 per cent) gradient and this was easily met. The articulated design, with small guiding wheels on each bogie, was well suited to the continuous sharp curvature of the line, whilst rheostatic braking equipment (fitted originally only

near Lucerne to Bellinzona near the Italian frontier was turned over fully to electric traction, the first electrically-hauled train having crossed the mountains the previous year. As regards locomotives for

to the last 30) helped with holding trains back when coming downhill. The locomotives were used in pairs on the heaviest trains.

In a long period of satisfactory service, these locomotives were the mainstay of passenger and fast freight operations on one of the most exacting railway routes in the world. Latterly the "Be 4/6s" have been outclassed, as will be seen, by single-unit locomotives with the same number of wheels but five times the power output, but a handful still perform less arduous duties in a useful way. Incidentally, another vital part of the Gotthard propulsion system, the original water turbines (of the Pelton wheel pattern) and generators in the purpose-built power stations at Amsteg and Piotta, still provide some of the current for the mighty train movements over the present day Gotthard line.

---

forces from the spring drive geared to the frame-mounted motors.

Two pantograph current collectors were fitted on the roof in what had by now become the conventional manner, but this was not the final intention. For sections of track in open country, Raven had decided to use a side-mounted third rail because of its cheapness. To protect staff from the high voltage used, and also to prevent problems arising through accumulation of ice, this was to be of the cased under-contact pattern. Trials were made at Strensall, between York and Scarborough. A length of conductor rail was laid, and 4-4-4 tank locomotives used on the line were fitted with the sliding contact equipment.

Above: *No. 13 is seen in the Stockton & Darlington Railway centenary cavalcade, July 1925.*

Normal overhead was to be used in stations where points and crossings would have made the

ground-level conductor rail system too complex.

Alas, all this work came to naught, not for technical reasons, but for political ones. In 1923 government action led to amalgamation of the railways of Britain into four main groups. The idea was that the weaker lines could be supported by the stronger ones. So the North Eastern's financial strength went towards supporting its mainly agricultural and weaker partners in the newly-formed London & North Eastern Railway, rather than to improve its own property. So the York-Newcastle electrification was shelved and this great (and rather beautiful) locomotive never fulfilled itself. It was scrapped in 1950.

Left: *Sir Vincent Raven's experimental express electric locomotive built for the North Eastern Railway at their Darlington shops in 1921.*

EASTERN

No.1 B₀-B₀

Type: Diesel-electric switching locomotive.
Gauge: 4ft 8½in (1,435mm).
Propulsion: Ingersoll-Rand 300hp (224kW) 6-cylinder four-stroke diesel engine and GEC generator supplying current to four nose-suspended traction motors geared to the axles.
Weight: 120,000lb (54.4t).
Max. axleload: 30,000lb (13.6t).
Length: 32ft 6in (9,906mm).

These locomotives can be claimed as the "first commercially-successful diesel-electric locomotives in the world". They were the result of co-operation between three well-known specialist manufacturers; Ingersoll-Rand of Phillips, New Jersey, produced the diesel engine, General Electric of Erie, Pennsylvania, the electric equipment and the American Locomotive Company (Alco) of Schenec-

tady, New York, the locomotive body and running gear. Both the principles of design and the configuration are the same as those used for the majority of today's locomotives. The difference is that for the same size and weight GE today could offer 1,000hp (746kW) instead of 300hp (224kW).

A demonstrator had been built earlier in 1924 and this led to a

batch of five locomotives being built later that year for stock; 26 units in all were produced during the years 1924 to 1928. Customers included the Baltimore & Ohio (1), Central of New Jersey (1), Lehigh Valley (1), Erie (2), Chicago & North Western (3), Reading (2), and Delaware, Lackawanna & Western (2). The remainder went to industrial buyers. There were also a few twin-engined models

Nos. 101-103 1-C-C-1

Type. Electric rack-and-adhesion locomotive.
Gauge: 3ft 3⅜in (1,000mm).
Propulsion: Direct current at 3,000V fed via overhead catenary to four 320hp (239kW) traction motors driving the main wheels by gearing and jackshafts for adhesion, plus two 540hp (403kW) motors driving the pinions for rack working.
Weight: 158,700lb (72t) adhesive, 188,450lb (85.5t) total.
Max. axleload: 26,450lb (12t).

Overall length: 52ft 9in (16,070mm).
Tractive effort: 11,000lb (49kN) adhesion, 22,000lb (98kN) rack.
Max. speed: 25mph (40km/h) adhesion, 12.5mph (20km/h) rack.

Railways connecting the Atlantic with the Pacific have always caught people's imagination, often overshadowing sound financial thinking. Of them all, the original

Transandine Railway, built between 1887 and 1908 to connect Argentina with Chile, was both the most spectacular and a case in point. The British company that originally obtained the concession from the two countries did not, however, let enthusiasm for the project carry it away. The deal included a guarantee of a fair but modest profit, but long ago the line was nationalised.

The Transandine Railway provided a metre-gauge line, 159

miles (254km) long, from Mendoza in Argentina to Los Andes in Chile. The summit of La Cumbre, 10,450ft (3,186m) altitude, is also the frontier; on both sides the final stages of the climb—at 1-in-12½ (8 per cent) on the Chilean side —are equipped for rack-and-pinion working using a unique triple rack, an elaboration of the Abt system. There are more tunnels on the Chilean side than on the Argentine, and difficulties encountered in working led to elec-

supplied, generally similar but longer and of twice the power.

Whilst the claim of commercial success was true in the sense that the makers did not lose money, it was not so for the buyers. All these customers had operations for which steam traction could not be used for some extraneous reason such as fire-risk or legislation, and so a more costly form of power was necessary. Amongst them was that famous ordinance whereby steam locomotives were excluded from New York City. Useful experience was gained which eased the general introduction of diesel traction a quarter century later. It says enough, perhaps, of the technical success of these locomotives that, unlike so many firsts, they stood the test of time. Indeed, some were still giving service 35 years later although, like the legendary Irishman's hammer, they had no doubt acquired a few new heads and a few new handles in the meantime. Two units survive, one in the Baltimore & Ohio Railroad Museum at Baltimore, Maryland, and the very first, Central of New Jersey No. 1000, at the National Museum of Transport in St Louis, Missouri.

Alco no longer builds locomotives in the USA, although it does so in Canada. General Electric still produces diesel locomotives, including engines and the mechanical parts, and sells world-wide as well as in the USA.

Below: *The first commercially successful diesel-electric locomotive, used for switching from 1924 until scrapped in the 1950s.*

trification. When completed in 1927 this covered only the highest and most difficult half of the line, that is, the 22½ miles (36km) from Portillo to the summit; in 1942 electrification of the remaining 25 miles (40km) was completed.

The Swiss Locomotive Co. of Winterthur supplied the three original locomotives; Brown Boveri electrical equipment was used. They were designed to haul 150t (165 US tons) up the rack at 9½mph (15km/h).

Several years of closure followed flood damage on the Argentine side in 1937, but relations between Argentina and Chile were never good and, in consequence, traffic and trade between them was not heavy. It says enough that the three original locomotives sufficed to meet all demands on this transcontinental artery for over 35 years.

Right: *Rack locomotive of the Chilean Transandine Railway.*

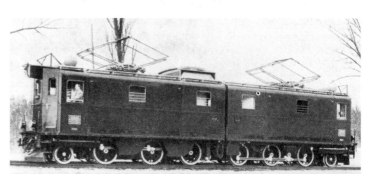

Ganz 2-B-B-2

Type: Electric express passenger locomotive.
Gauge: 4ft 8½in (1,435mm).
Propulsion: Direct current at 1,500V from overhead wires fed to four 1,200hp (895kW) traction motors mounted on the locomotive frame, with each pair of motors connected to pairs of driving axles by a triangular system of connecting rods.
Weight: 158,690lb (72.0t) adhesive, 290,330lb (131.7t) total.
Max. axleload: 39,670lb (18.0t).
Overall length: 52ft 7½in (16,040mm).
Tractive effort: 39,670lb (176kN).
Max. speed: 75mph (120km/h).

The Paris-Orléans Railway electrified its Paris suburban services from 1899 onwards on the 600V dc third-rail system, and by 1920 it had 20 Bo-Bo locomotives at work on these services. During World War I French railways suffered acutely from shortage of coal, and after the war the government sent a party of engineers to the United States to study recent main-line electrification schemes there, and to report on the possibility of main-line electrification in France. The engineers recommended electrification on the overhead system at 1,500V, and in 1919 a programme of electrification was prepared covering 5,300 miles (8,500km) on the PO, PLM and Midi railways. It was intended that power should be generated mainly by hydro-electric stations in the Massif Central and in the Pyrenees.

In 1923 the PO embarked on its first 1,500V conversion under the programme, the Toulouse main line over the 127 miles (204km) between Paris and Vierzon. For this scheme three types of experimental express locomotive were ordered, representing a wide sample of the technology of the day. Each type had some notable features, but the most remarkable of the three were two locomotives ordered from Ganz of Budapest, and delivered in 1926. They were numbered E401-2.

At this time the Managing Director of Ganz was Kálmán Kandó (1869-1931), a brilliant engineer, who had a great influence on development of three-phase electrification, and later the use of alternating current at industrial frequency. He was less known for his work with dc, but the locomotives which he designed for the PO were as distinctive as any of his three-phase machines. Unfortunately this incursion into dc did not enhance Kandó's reputation.

The wheel arrangement was 2-B-B-2, there being two sets of four-coupled wheels in a rigid frame. Each set of wheels was driven by two motors mounted on the main frame, with a complicated set of rods to connect the motors to the wheels. The system included coupling rods connecting cranks on the armature shafts of each pair of motors, and a triangular arrangement of rods to connect the motor shafts to one of the driving wheels of the pair. These arrangements were necessary to allow for movement of the driving wheels on their springs relative to the main frame. The layout of the rods used on No. E401 was of Kandó's own design, and was used on his three-phase

Class WCG1* C-C

Type: Electric locomotive for heavy freight haulage.
Gauge: 5ft 6in (1,676mm).
Propulsion: Direct current at 1,500V supplied via overhead catenary to four 650hp (485kW) motors, geared in pairs to two jackshafts, each of which is connected to three driving axles by connecting rods.
Weight: 275,500lb (125t).
Max. axleload: 46,285lb (21t).
Overall length: 66ft 1in (20,142mm).
Max speed: 50mph (80km/h).

* Indian Railways' classification

The so-called "Crocodile" configuration for an electric locomotive was repeated several times — on standard gauge in Austria or Switzerland and on the narrow gauge in Switzerland also. It is not so generally known that there were also British-built broad-gauge examples, and that they are still running in the Bombay area in India.

In 1929 the Great Indian Peninsula Railway completed electrification of 181 miles (291km) of line connecting the Bombay area with Poona. The ascent of the Western Ghats involved a ruling gradient of 1-in-37 (2.7 per cent), the same as that of the Gotthard main line in Switzerland. Those

Right: *Indian Railways' Class WCG1 C-C electric locomotive on shunting duty in Bombay.*

48

and 50Hz locomotives. It was the most complicated rod drive used anywhere. The arrangement on No. E402 was simpler.

The electrical equipment was advanced for its day, not least in that the total continuous rating of the four motors was 4,800hp. The motors had forced ventilation and the control system made use of series/series-parallel/parallel combinations, and an unusually large degree (for the day) of field weakening. The appearance of the locomotive was striking, with a central cab flanked by two hoods, which were extraordinarily like the hoods of some American diesels of 30 years later. With the tapered ends and smooth sides of the casing above the 69in (1,750mm) driving wheels with their flailing rods, there was no doubt that these were express engines.

Unfortunately, although the loco-motives produced the intended power, they were unreliable in service, to the extent that they were incurring between one and two faults per 100 kilometres. As soon as other express locomotives were available, they were transferred to freight work, where their high power could be put to good effect. It was found that coupling pairs of driving wheels gave better adhesion than the locomotives with individual axle drives. This was significant in the light of the later evolution of the monomotor bogie in France.

In passenger service No. E401 was recorded as averaging 60.6mph (97.5km/h) with 636t between Les Aubrais and Paris, and in freight service maintained between 19mph (30km/h) and 30mph (50km/h) with up to 770t (847 US tons) on a 1-in-100 (1 per cent) gradient. However, this standard was only to be expected, as the specification called for the locomotives to haul 800t at 59mph (95km/h). Despite their indifferent performance, the locomotives were remembered by railwaymen as *Les Belles Hongroises*.

Below: *The unusual lines of Paris-Orléans 2-B-B-2 electric locomotive No. 401 built by Ganz of Hungary. Note the third-rail shoes on the bogies for use in the tunnels in Paris.*

responsible evidently took the view that a proven design was preferable and hence commissioned these distinguished machines, which as regards the mechanical side followed the crocodile locomotives of the Gotthard. An order was placed with the Swiss Locomotive Works of Winterthur for a prototype batch of 10.

The electrical equipment on the other hand, being for direct current, was quite different from that for low-frequency alternating current by which all the Alpine crocodiles worked. Accordingly, Metropolitan-Vickers of Manchester did the electrical work, not only on the 10 Swiss-built engines but also on 31 supplied by the Vulcan Foundry. An advanced feature for the time was the provision of regenerative braking. Six running positions of the controller were provided; the six motors could be grouped in series, in series-parallel or in parallel, and each grouping could be operated with two positions of field strength.

Long and useful lives have followed. Although no longer used on main line work, some of the Indian crocodiles are still in use on shunting work. One is displayed at the Indian Rail Transport Museum in New Delhi.

Right: *An Indian "Crocodile" in ex-works condition at Poona in February 1981.*

Class D 1-C-1

Type: Electric mixed-traffic locomotive.
Gauge: 4ft 8½in (1,435mm).
Propulsion: Single-phase current at 15,000V 16⅔Hz fed via overhead catenary and step-down transformer to two 1,250hp (930kW) motors driving the wheels via gearing, jackshaft and connecting rods.
Weight: 112,400lb (51t) adhesive, 165,300lb (75t) total.
Max. axleload: 37,468lb (17t).
Overall length: 42ft 6in (13,000mm).
Tractive effort: 34,600lb (154kN).
Max. speed: 62mph (100km/h).

Sweden is another of those countries poor in coal supplies but rich in water power, in which engineers early on were able to set about electrifying the railway system. Technical restraint was a characteristic of the way it was done, well demonstrated by the fact that this simple locomotive design worked virtually all the traffic. Construction continued over the years from 1925 to 1952, progressive batches being stretched so that the newest (sub-class "Da") show a 30 per cent improvement in tractive effort over the originals, sub-class "Du". Some of the earliest examples had wooden bodies, sub-class "Dg".

Some of the locomotives in the early batches were supplied with (or altered to) a lower gear ratio for freight working, trading maximum speed for increased tractive

Below: *An early woodenbodied version of Swedish State Railways' standard Class D 1-C-1 general-purpose rod-drive electric locomotive.*

Above and left: *Twenty-five years' development of the Swedish standard 1-C-1 electric locomotive is shown in these two pictures. On the left is a preserved example of the earliest version with a wood-panelled body, while above is shown one of the last batch of units to be constructed, a Class Da built in 1950.*

effort; these became respectively 47mph (75km/h) and 46,400lb (206kN). In all 417 Class "D" 1-C-1 locomotives were built, most being still in service.

It might be considered an objection to this 1-C-1 wheel arrangement that the jackshaft, and hence the positioning of the motors, must be unsymmetrical. However, the need to accommodate a single heavy low-frequency transformer corrected the out-of-balance weight distribution which would otherwise have resulted.

The rod-drive seems to have satisfied the Swedes for many years; few people know more about tricky bearings than they, and moreover rod-drive gives a very simple and total form of control over the slipping of individual wheel pairs, otherwise only achieved with some electrical complication. It was notable that SJ was still taking delivery of powerful rod-drive electric locomotives in 1970.

Overall, the electrification system followed that of Germany and Switzerland, although there was one important difference. Instead of having an independent low-frequency generating and distribution system, supplies of electricity were taken from the national grid at normal frequency and converted to low frequency by rotary-convertor substations. These could be set to take a leading current and improve the power factor of electricity supply in Sweden as a whole—in effect, the resulting watt-less kilovolt-amperes are sold back by the railway to the current supplier, a new chapter in the art of profitable disposal of industrial waste.

GPO A1-1A

Great Britain:
His Majesty's Post Office (GPO), 1927

Type: Driverless electric mail carriage.
Gauge: 2ft 0in (610mm).
Propulsion: Direct current at 440V or 150V is fed via a centre conductor rail to two 22hp (16.5kW) traction motors each geared to one driving axle.
Weight: 6,610lb (3t)*.
Max. axleload: 2,204lb (1t).
Overall length: 28ft 0in (8,535mm).
Max. speed: 30mph (48km/h).

*loaded with mail.

For a period during the 1960s, this writer was one of a group of technically-minded people who were asked to take a long look at freight movement on British Railways, then in steep decline. The thought was that modern technology might have something to offer. One of the ideas put forward was to convert major parts of the railway for running unmanned self-propelled automatic freight railcars. Although a bold and fairly costly idea, the economics were superb. Alas, politics are the art of the possible and selling a "zero option" to the trainmen's unions was not considered feasible, although there would have been ample savings to pay off all the staff handsomely. Further development of such a novel scheme was accordingly the subject of a interdict from on high—even though it was pointed out that for 40 years freight of a kind had moved between important BR stations in London in just such a way.

What might have been the foundation of a really effectively competitive British Railways' freight system runs from Paddington Station in London via the Post Office's Mount Pleasant headquarters to Liverpool Street Station and the Eastern District post office on Whitechapel Road. The distance is 3½ miles (5.5km), the gauge is 2ft (610mm) and the whole railway (except at the seven stations) is laid as a double track in a 9ft (2.75m) diameter cast-iron tube tunnel.

Work began in 1914 and when a year or two later the Zeppelins appeared over London, the deep-level tunnels came in useful as a safe store for various national treasures. Progress afterwards was slow and it was not until 1927 that traffic began to flow. Mail was carried in trains formed of either one or two self-propelled railcars. The technology of 50 years ago found no difficulty in producing a safe system, based on electro-magnetic relays, of automating the movement of these cars. The system is run under the overall control of a "signalman", if that is the correct term on a railway which, not having any train crews, has no need for signals. Really substantial savings are achieved over the cost of moving mail by road at the snail's pace which is all that is possible for motor vehicles in London. This significant advantage keeps the Post Office Railway viable, as witness the recent renewal of the rolling stock.

Below: *One of the original driverless electric mail carriages of The Post Office underground railway in London.*

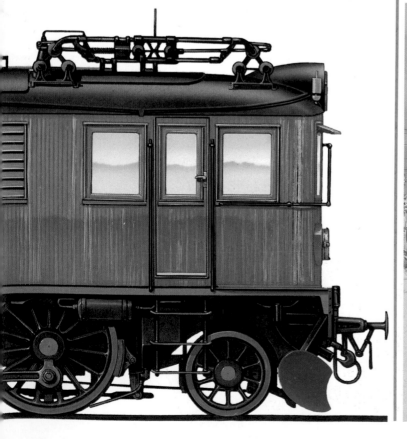

Type: Diesel-steam locomotive for local train duties.
Gauge: 4ft 8½in (1,435mm).
Propulsion: Eight double-acting cylinders in two horizontal banks, with diesel action on the side of the pistons and steam on the other; crankshaft connected to driving wheels by gearing and jackshafts, wheels connected by coupling rods; steam supplied by boiler heated either by diesel exhaust gases or by an oil burner.
Weight: 132,160lb (60t) adhesive, 194,880lb (88.4t) total.
Max. axleload: 44,050lb (20t).
Overall length: 39ft (11,890mm).
Tractive effort: 28,000lb (125kN).
Max. speed: 43mph (69km/h).

A diesel engine converts about 35 per cent of the heat energy of the fuel into useful work, but the remaining 65 per cent is thrown away, mainly in heat in the cylinder cooling water and heat in the exhaust gases. Various methods have been employed to recover some of this waste heat, and the Still engine was an example which enjoyed some success for a time in stationary and marine practice. Heat from the cylinder walls and exhaust gases was picked up by water circulating from and to a boiler, and steam collected in the boiler. The pistons were double-acting, with diesel on the side of the pistons and steam on the other. An oil burner was provided in the boiler so that the engine could operate on steam alone; this enabled the engine to start from rest and accelerate to a speed at which the diesel end of the cylinders would fire. The Still principle raised the efficiency of the engine to about 40 per cent which was well ahead of any other contemporary heat engine.

The ability to start from rest on steam alone made the Still engine attractive for locomotive use, as it afforded a means of achieving the high efficiency of the diesel engine without the steam engineers being carried into the mysterious realms of electric and hydraulic transmissions. Patents were taken out by members of the staff of Kitson's of Leeds for applying the Still principle to a locomotive, and a Kitson-Still engine in accordance with these patents was built at the firm's expense in 1924.

This locomotive was of the 1-C-1 or 2-6-2T layout, and it weighed 87 tons. It had eight cylinders arranged in horizontal banks of four on opposite sides of a crankshaft, which was parallel to the axles, and connected to the wheels through gears, a layshaft and coupling rods. The machinery was thus perfectly balanced. The outer ends of the cylinders were diesel and the inner ends steam. The cylinder casting was above the driving wheels,· and above that was the boiler, with a cylindrical firebox for the oil burner. The exhaust gases were led through tubes in the boiler, and the boiler water circulated through the cylinder cooling jackets.

The oil burner raised steam for starting, and at about 5mph fuel was turned on to the diesel ends of the cylinders. In about two revolutions the diesel cylinders reached full power, and steam was then shut off until the next stop, unless required to supplement the diesel output at maximum powers. Between stops the boiler was kept hot by the exhaust gases and cylinder jackets. The locomotive was designed for a maximum speed of 43mph (69km/h) corresponding to 45rpm but as tests proceeded the speed was increased to 55mph (88km/h).

Tests were run intermittently on the LNER for a number of years, and when certain problems had been solved, the locomotive enjoyed considerable success. It made trial trips over various routes of the former North Eastern Railway in Yorkshire. The heaviest load was 400 tons, which the locomotive restarted from a signal stop on a 1-in-33 (3 per cent) gradient. It was reckoned that the weight of fuel consumed was about one-fifth of that of a coal-burning steam locomotive, but what this represented in cost savings depended upon the relative prices of coal and oil. The makers had a particular eye on countries which had oil but no coal.

The maximum horsepower of 700 (522kW) developed at the drawbar was not very high for a locomotive of 87t weight. For commercial use this would need to be improved upon, and a stage had been reached at which further heavy expenditure was required to convert a successful experiment into a production unit. Unfortunately conditions were not favourable. Kitson's finances declined in the industrial depression, and eventually it went into liquidation. In the meantime no orders had come for Kitson-Still locomotives.

By the time British railways were ready for a serious attack on the diesel locomotive, inhibitions about electric and hydraulic transmissions had been overcome, and the Kitson-Still was forgotten.

Right: The Kitson-Still steam-diesel locomotive as running in later trials during the 1930s.

Below: The Kitson-Still locomotive built by Kitson's of Leeds in 1924, using the Still principle of combining diesel and steam propulsion. It is shown as prepared for early trials in the works.

Class Ae 4/7 2-D₀-1 Switzerland:
Swiss Federal Railways (SBB), 1927

Type: Electric express passenger locomotive.
Gauge: 4ft 8½in (1,435mm).
Propulsion: Single-phase current at 15,000V 16⅔Hz fed via overhead catenary and step-down transformer to four 769hp (574kW) motors each driving one pair of main wheels through gears and Büchli flexible drives.
Weight: 169,710lb (77t) adhesive, 260,070lb (118t) total.
Max. axleload: 42,430lb (19.25t).
Overall length: 55ft (16,760mm).
Tractive effort: 44,100lb (196kN).
Max. speed: 62mph (100km/h).

These superb locomotives, now well into their second half-century, for many years handled the top

Class E432 1-D-1 Italy:
Italian State Railways (FS), 1928

Type: Electric express passenger locomotive.
Gauge: 4ft 8½in (1,435mm).
Propulsion: Three-phase alternating current at 3,600V 16⅔Hz fed to two 1,475hp (1,100kW) synchronous traction motors with provision for speed control by pole-changing, driving the four pairs of main wheels direct by means of connecting and coupling rods.
Weight: 156,484lb (71t) adhesive, 207,176lb (94t) total.
Max. axleload: 39,672lb (18t).
Overall length: 45ft 8in (13,910mm).
Tractive effort: 30,856lb (137kN).
Max. speed: 62.5mph (100km/h).

1928 was a critical year for three-phase main-line electrification. Since 1910, when the Class "550" locomotives described earlier began working the Giovi incline, Italian electrification had moved on apace and virtually all of it was three-phase. Most lines of any significance in the Genoa-Turin area were by now electrified and tentacles had stretched south along the Mediterranean coast to reach Pisa and Leghorn. In addition, there were some isolated miles up near the Austrian border and also between Florence and Bologna. The total amounted to some 940 miles (1,500km).

The moment of truth came in 1928 when a proposal to electrify with three-phase between Naples

and Foggia was modified to make this line a testbed for direct current electrification. The new system worked so well and was so economical that the three-phase system became instantly obsolete, although the three-phasers fought back bravely but unsuccessfully with another experimental installation (104 miles—166km, from Rome to Sulmona) at high voltage and industrial frequency.

A further result was that these "E432s," of which 40 were built by Breda of Milan, were the last class of main-line three-phase locomotives of any importance built in the world. Compared with the original "E550s," the newer engines had their express passenger status recognised by provision of

pony trucks fore and aft and four 64in (1,630mm) driving wheels in place of five of 42in (1,070mm) diameter. Electrical progress now allowed for provision of a larger number of fixed speeds (23, 31, 47 and 63mph—37.5, 50, 75 and 100km/h), by making varying special connections inside and between the two traction motors. "Pole-changing" is the technical term. Some of the class had twin pantograph current collectors instead of the cantilever type more generally fitted—and which were a hall-mark of the three-phase. In fact, the cantilever arrangement allowed the collector bows to be far enough apart to permit operation across inevitable gaps in the double overhead conductor sys-

assignments (including many of the legendary European international trains such as the "Simplon-Orient" expresses) of Swiss Federal Railways. The design was based on that of the extremely successful "Ae 3/6" class of 1921 (3/6 means 3 driving axles out of 6), which were of the 2-Co-1 wheel arrangement; 114 of these were built between 1921 and 1926 and they were way ahead of their time.

When more power was needed

Left: *Swiss Federal Railways' Class Ae 4/7 locomotive hauling a short freight train past Wadenswil on the shore of Lake Zurich early in 1976.*

it was just a case of splicing in, as it were, another driving wheel, motor and body section. Originally SBB had misgivings over such a long rigid wheelbase, and the fourth pair of driving wheels was, as regards side movement, connected to the small single guiding wheel in the form of a Zara truck. This arrangement was common on Italian steam locomotives and provided some flexibility to otherwise rather rigid wheel arrangements. Later, the worries were found to be unjustified, and a conventional pony truck was substituted. The reason for having a four-wheel bogie at one end and only a two-wheel truck at the other lies in the need to accommodate a heavy low-frequency transformer.

The transmission system was of Swiss origin, known as Büchli after its inventor. The motors drove large gear wheels mounted approximately concentric with and outside the main driving wheels on the side of the locomotive. A lever arrangement transmitted torque to the driving wheels, at the same time allowing for vertical movement of the axles relative to the frames, necessary to cope with small irregularities in the track.

Only a few out of the 127 built (30—Nos. 10973-11002) have regenerative braking and 30 more (Nos. 10931-51 and 11009-17) are equipped for running in multiple. Virtually the whole of the series (Nos. 10901-11027) remain in service.

Left: *The handsome but old-fashioned lines of Swiss Federal Railways' Class Ae 4/7. Excellent performances can still be obtained from these powerful machines in spite of their age.*

tem, but the roofs of the "E432" class were long enough to carry two pantographs sufficient distance apart.

During World War II, many railways in Italy were forcibly de-electrified. Re-electrification was usually by dc, but the lines in north-west Italy escaped relatively unscathed and survived as three-phase. The "E432" class also survived intact with them into the 1970s, but conversion to dc and hence extinction of all the three-phase motive power came well before the end of the decade. So ended a heroic chapter in the history of the railway locomotive.

Right: *The FS Class E432 three-phase locomotive.*

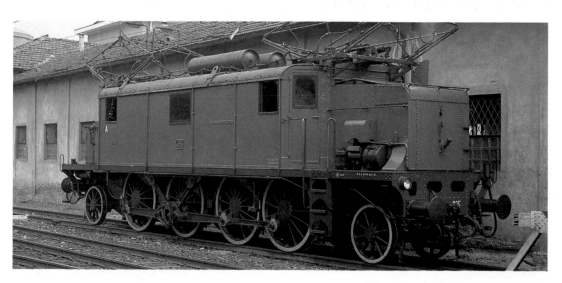

No. 9000 2-D₀-1

Type: Main line diesel-electric locomotive.
Gauge: 4ft 8½in (1,435mm).
Propulsion: Beardmore 1,330hp (992kW) four-stroke V12 diesel engine and generator, originally supercharged, supplying direct current to four nose-suspended traction motors geared to the axles.
Weight: 255,644lb (116t) adhesive, 374,080lb (170t) total.
Max. axleload: 63,920lb (29t).

Overall length: 47ft 0½in (14,338mm).
Tractive effort: 50,000lb (222kN).
Max. speed: 75mph (120km/h).

The shape of things to come! These two locomotives—which usually worked coupled back-to-back as a pair—were the first main-line diesel units in North America. They were a joint product of the Canadian Locomo-

tive Co and Westinghouse Electric. From all accounts they worked quite well when they were actually working—keeping time easily with 700 US tons on the "International Limited" between Montreal and Toronto, for example, on a schedule which involved an average speed of 44mph (70km/h) including 13 stops, some lengthy. Running costs were absurdly low, and yet the locomotives were not successful.

The problem lay in the diffi-

culties of maintenance. CN's own maintenance department was almost entirely steam-orientated and so the basic infrastructure was not there. Secondly, the locomotives themselves had all the small faults typical of any unproven piece of equipment. Thirdly, none of the manufacturers involved nor CN had a stock of spare parts worthy of the name—almost all the parts needed had to be specially made to order, and many hand-fitted thereafter, a process

HGe 4/4 B₀-B₀

Type: Electric rack-and-adhesion locomotive.
Gauge: 3ft 3⅜in (1,000mm).
Propulsion: Low-frequency alternating current at 11,000V 16⅔Hz fed via overhead catenary and step-down transformer to four 160hp* (120kW) ac traction motors, each geared both directly to a driving axle and (at a subtly different gear ratio) to a rack pinion mounted freely on the same axle.
Weight: 103,590lb (47t).
Max. axleload: 26,450lb (12t).
Overall length: 46ft 3in (14,100mm).
Tractive effort: 30,856lb (137kN).
Max. speed: 28mph (45km/h) adhesion, 12½mph (20km/h) on rack.

*Later increased to 230hp (172kW).

When Edward Whymper's party climbed the Matterhorn so disastrously in 1865, the tiny and fiercely independent high-altitude village of Zermatt came out onto the world stage. Accordingly, a rack-and-adhesion railway 22¼ mile (35½km) long to connect the village to Visp in the Rhone valley was proposed and finally completed in 1891. The ruling gradient on the adhesion sections was 1-in-40 (2.5 per cent) and on the rack sections 1-in-8 (12.5 per cent); curves were as sharp as 3 chains (60m) radius and for many summers little 0-4-2T steam locomotives hauled the tourists up to

Zermatt. At other times of the year the Zermatters valued their privacy and visitors had to walk or ride on horseback, no motor cars being permitted.

However, in 1928 a scheme to electrify the line and open it all the year round was put into effect. The 11,000V 16⅔Hz system was adopted in order to match that of the far-off Rhaetian Railway in eastern Switzerland, with which both physical and electrical connection might one day be established—in fact, these things happened in 1930 and 1941, respectively.

Five commendably simple Bo-Bo electric locomotives were supplied by the Swiss Locomotive Works of Winterthur and the Oerlikon

Above: *The mountaineering HGe 4/4 of the Visp-Zermatt Railway (now Brigue-Visp-Zermatt) of 1929.*

company of Zurich. There were no separate motors to drive the rack pinions which were mounted on the adhesion-wheel axles. The pinions were driven by the same appropriate traction motor as the adhesion wheels but at a slightly different and faster rotational speed—the gearing for the rail wheels is 6.2 to 1 and for the rack pinion wheels 5.6 to 1. This compensated for the fact that the rack pinions must clear the rails and so have a smaller effective diameter. Obviously, the rack teeth and the wheel-rim surface must move at

the same speed if satisfactory traction is to be established.

Other features were also similar to those of the Rhaetian Railway. Central buffers with screw couplings on each side were standardised and the vacuum brake was used, supplemented by rheostatic braking for use on the main descents, with hand brakes in reserve for an emergency. There was a "deadman" device to permit operation by a single driver. If this was released involuntarily both the rack brakes and the main brakes were applied and the current switched off.

Electric operation was very successful, running times being reduced from 2hr 5min to 1hr 35min, and much heavier trains hauled. The prohibition of motor traffic which is still enforced by the Zermatters—and which makes a visit to the resort such a delight —means that today's problem is that of moving the traffic offering rather than surviving. This local railway is one of the very few in the world which is run at a profit.

All five of the original electric locomotives are still in service, supplemented by another built in 1939, as well as a number of twin articulated railcar trains, in order to handle a passenger traffic flow now counted in millions.

Right: *Train ready to leave Zermatt behind locomotive of Class HGe 4/4. "H" denotes a rack loco, "G" narrow gauge, "e" means electric, 4/4 means 4 driven axles out of 4 axles total.*

which was both slow and expensive. No progress in dieselisation could be made until a package appeared which included a solution to these problems. This was shortly to happen, as will be seen.

On the other hand, both the overall technology, and the concept were good, one or two quite basic shortcomings being easily resolved. For example, in 1931 the engine manufacturer had to replace both crankcases with stronger ones nearly a ton

heavier. This perhaps underlined the fact that an engine like the Beardmore, which was excellent in a submarine under the watchful eye of highly-qualified "tiffies" (Engine-room Artificer, 1st class, RN), was less satisfactory under railway conditions. Even so, the specific weight of the Beardmore engine at 24.5lb per hp (15kg/kW) had come a long way from the Ingersoll-Rand engines fitted to switchers a few years earlier, which turned the scales at double

that figure. This must be considered against the background of present day North American diesel locomotives, which have engines of specific weights only half that of the Beardmore.

After trials with the locomotive as a twin unit, the two "ends" were operated separately, being then renumbered 9000 and 9001. No. 9000 was scrapped in 1939, but during the war No. 9001 found a use in the west as a coastal defence train. Its bodywork

was altered to give the appearance of a boxcar, as well as a modicum of armoured protection for the crew. After the war, No. 9001 worked for a short time in the east but was withdrawn in 1947. Even so, 20 years later, virtually all Canadian trains were to be hauled by locomotives of totally similar concept.

Below: *Pioneer diesel-electric main line locomotive built in 1929 for Canadian National Rly.*

Diesel Railcar

Ireland:
County Donegal Joint Railways (CDJR), 1931

Type: Trailer-hauling railbus.
Gauge: 3ft 0in (904mm).
Propulsion: Gardner Type L2 74hp (55kW) 6-cylinder diesel engine driving the rear bogie through a mechanical gearbox with four forward speeds and one reverse, a propellor shaft, gearing and— when required— chains coupling the two rear axles.
Weight: 6,720lb (3t) adhesive, 15,680lb (7.1t) total.
Max. axleload: 6,720lb (3t).
Overall length: 28ft 0in (8,534mm).
Max. speed: 40mph (64km/h).

These delightfully economical little vehicles must represent the contribution made by the diesel engine all over the world towards maintaining the sort of little railways that had to think twice before investing in just one rail-spike.

The 3ft gauge County Donegal Railways served a wild and sparsely-populated part of the north-west of Ireland. The system was entirely steam-operated until 1907, when it purchased a four-wheeled petrol-engined vehicle with an open body for use as an inspection car. In 1920 the vehicle needed heavy repairs, and to increase its usefulness it was fitted with an enclosed body seating 10 passengers. In this form it was used occasionally for carrying passengers and mail, but in 1926 the railcar was put into regular service to replace a lightly-loaded steam train.

The experience gained at this time convinced Henry Forbes, the manager of the railway, of the potential of railcars for countering serious competition from motor buses which was already affecting other Irish narrow-gauge lines. From then until his death in 1943, Forbes worked enthusiastically for the extension of railcar services.

Railcars cost less to operate than steam trains, they could be operated by one man, and their acceleration was so good that they could make wayside stops in country areas without seriously affecting their schedules.

By 1930 four more railcars had been acquired, two secondhand from standard-gauge lines and two purpose-built. They were all petrol-engined, but in 1931 railcar No. 7 went into service driven by a 74hp diesel engine. The body was mounted at one end on a bogie which had one axle driven, and at the front, ahead of a projecting bonnet, was a radial axle. The car seated 32 passengers and weighed 7 tons, compared with 5.55 tons for a similar petrol-engined vehicle built in the previous year. No. 7 was the first diesel-engined railcar to enter regular passenger service in the British Isles. A second vehicle of the same type was built in 1931. Usually they worked singly, but at times they worked back-to-back with one or more goods wagons between. Gear changing was then sychronised by hand signals between the drivers.

These two vehicles gave good service for 18 years, and they were followed by 12 further diesel cars, the last of which were mounted on two bogies, and seated 43 passengers. The power unit was at the front, with four wheels connected by coupling rods, and the coach body was hinged to the power unit. These cars prolonged the life of the County Donegal by many years, and one of them ran nearly one million miles. Eventually, however, the line succumbed to road competition, and it closed at the end of 1959. Several of the railcars have been preserved, including Nos. 15 and 16 on the Isle of Man Railway, but unfortunately not No. 7.

Above: *County Donegal petrol railcar No. 10 built in 1932. Note the coupled leading driving wheels and bus-type body.*

Right: *Buses on wheels made the CDJR for many years the only railway in Ireland to be run without a substantial deficit.*

Above: *No. 19, one of the last two CDJR diesel railcars, as built by Walker Bros. of Wigan, England, with Gardner engine.*

Below: *County Donegal Railways' standard diesel railcar. Nos. 12 to 14 were to this style; later units had a full-width cab.*

V40 1-D-1

Hungary:
Royal Hungarian State Railways (MKA), 1933

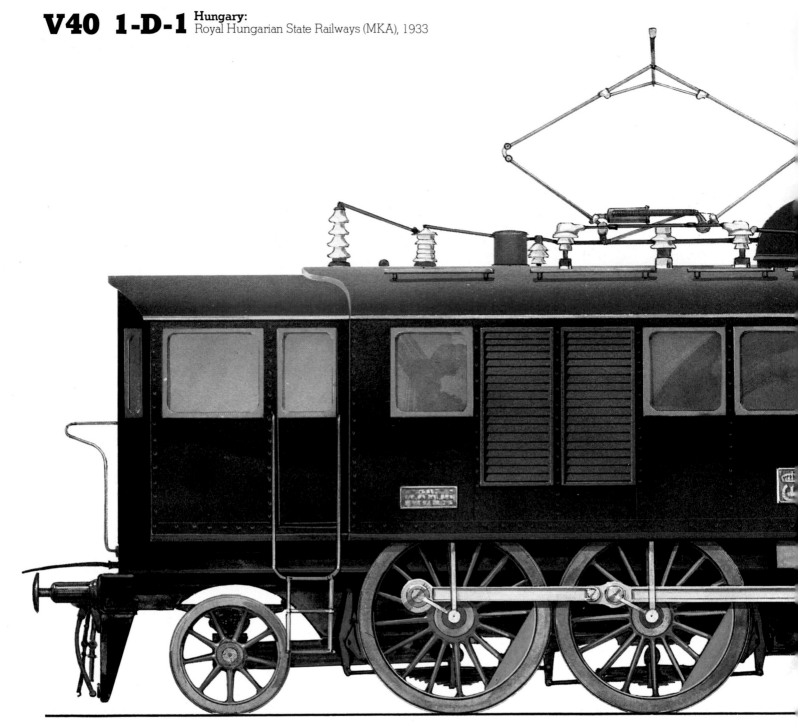

Type: Electric locomotive for express passenger trains.
Gauge: 4ft 8½in (1,435mm).
Propulsion: Single-phase current at 16,000V 50Hz fed via overhead catenary and rotary phase-converter to a single 2,500hp (1,865kW) polyphase motor coupled directly to the driving wheels by connecting rods.
Weight: 154,224lb (70t) adhesive, 215,375lb (97.75t) total.
Max. axleload: 38,556lb (17.5t).
Overall length: 45ft 0in (13,715mm).
Tractive effort: 38,570lb (171kN).
Max. speed: 62.5mph (100km/h).

When electric railways were new, so was electricity supply in general. Hence there was little reason for what was best for the former to be affected by the latter. Later, when electricity supply

became generally available, a few far-sighted engineers began to think that it would be best for railways to take their current direct from the mains and supply it to the trains in this form, just like any other customer. One of these prophetic gentlemen was a Hungarian, Dr Kálmán Kandó, who recommended as early as 1917 that this should be the basis of future electrification schemes. In this respect he was some 50 years ahead of the rest of the world, and it is only recently that the essential rightness of the idea has been demonstrated by the fact that virtually all new electrification follows the example he set. Moreover, extensions to older electrification schemes are also commonly carried out using industrial-frequency current, despite the problems of operating a dual system.

Under Kandó's influence a 9 mile (14.5km) trial line was liad out in 1922 north of Budapest and a 1,600hp (1,280kW) trial

locomotive of 0-E-0 configuration was built by Ganz & Co. The success achieved led to a loan being raised in Britain and in 1928 work commenced on converting the 118 mile (189km) line connecting Hegyeshalom on the Austrian frontier with Budapest. Twenty-eight locomotives were built jointly by Ganz and by the British company Metropolitan-Vickers. There were to be four 0-F-0s for freight traffic and, as described here, 24 1-D-1s for passenger traffic. Two prototypes of each were delivered in 1932.

Kandó avoided the problems of making traction motors to run on high-frequency single-phase current by converting it to current with an alterable number of phases on the locomotives. So in respect of the very sophisticated internal workings of the locomotives he departed significantly from what is now the world norm. Even so, they correspond in certain principles to what may well become that norm tomorrow. All eight

main wheels were coupled directly by massive rodding to a huge polyphase motor of 10ft 6in (3,080mm) diameter, supplied with current at constant frequency but at variable phase by a rotary phase-convertor. As in straight three-phase electrification schemes, but for different reasons, there can only by a certain number of fixed speeds corresponding to the number of phases. In this case the fixed speeds were 15½, 31, 46, and 62mph (25, 50, 75 and 100km/h). Regenerative braking was a built-in feature of the arrangement needing no additional equipment, but the system was a complicated one. For example, the motor had 16 slip-rings to provide electrical access to its innards.

Once some mechanical problems with the running gear had been eliminated, operation was very satisfactory and the locomotives remained in use for many years. The main advantage—that of minimising the cost of the fixed

60

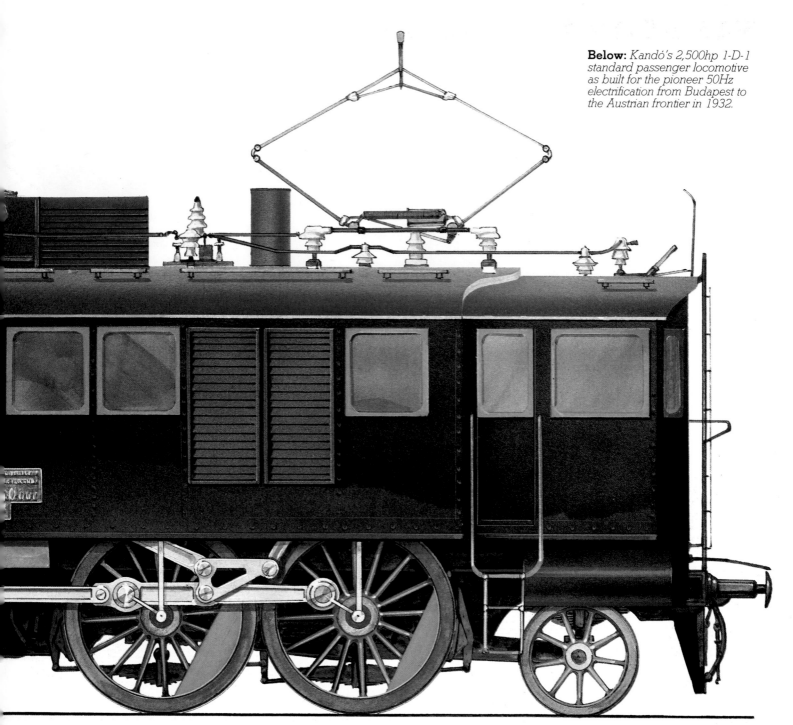

Below: *Kandó's 2,500hp 1-D-1 standard passenger locomotive as built for the pioneer 50Hz electrification from Budapest to the Austrian frontier in 1932.*

installations — was achieved when one considers that the whole line was supplied by four simple substations. Compare this with the 18 more complex substations needed for 97 miles (155km) of dc electrification on the contemporary Croydon to Brighton electrification.

There is one further advantage of the Kandó system which to some extent compensates for its complications. The power factor of a Kandó locomotive was close to unity or even slightly leading. This is an advantage as it counters the poor power factor (that is, with current flow lagging behind the alternating voltage) which is characteristic of a normal industrial loading. Because there were so few power supplies in the area, Hungarian State Railways had to

Left: *Royal Hungarian Railways' 1-D-1 50Hz single-phase class V40 locomotive. Twenty-four of these complex machines were supplied from 1932.*

build their own generating station and supply network, so any savings produced by improving the power factor in this way would accrue to the railway.

So, through the far-sighted genius of one man (who, alas, died in 1931, and so missed seeing his ideas come to fruition) the world's first main-line electrification using single-phase alternating current at industrial frequency came into being, in a country then better known for its agriculture than for heavyweight engineering. Some of the principles may now be changed, but the most obvious has been adopted world-wide in all its detail. This consists of the mast supports for the overhead conductors, with the catenary wire supported by one diagonal and one horizontal rod, another horizontal rod steadying the contact wire. So memorials exist to Kandó and his genius in their tens of thousands, to supplement the one "V40" preserved in the Budapest Transport Museum.

5-BEL Five-car Train
Great Britain:
Southern Railway (SR), 1933

Type: Electric multiple-unit Pullman express train.
Gauge: 4ft 8½in (1,435mm).
Propulsion: Direct current at 650V fed via top-contact outside-mounted third rail to two motor coaches each with four 225hp (168kW) nose-suspended motors geared to the axles.
Weight: 277,700lb (126t) adhesive, 557,760lb (253t) total.
Max. axleload: 35,280lb (16t).
Overall length: 347ft 6in (105,920mm).
Max. speed: 75mph (120km/h).

Although many notable British-built examples existed abroad, it was not until January 1, 1933 that electrically-propelled express passenger trains began running in Britain itself. The Southern Railway and its predecessors had been for many years progessively electrifying the suburban network south of London with excellent results, both financial and technical, and

Below: *A "Brighton Belle" 900hp third class brake-parlour motor coach, of which one was marshalled at each end of a five-car Pullman set.*

a point had now been reached when it was the turn of the main lines. There had recently been a substantial reduction in the costs involved, since it had become practicable to replace manned substations which had rotating machinery by unattended ones which converted ac to dc using static mercury-arc rectifiers.

Above: *The "Brighton Belle" could be formed of two five-car sets, as seen here. Note the "4" headcode which indicates a non-stop express train between Victoria and Brighton.*

If the invisible aspects of the electrification to Brighton, Hove and Worthing represented a bold

step forward in technology, the most visible aspect—the trains—had the solid reliability of hardware tested over many years in the fires of day-to-day operation on one of the world's busiest railways. Even so, what the passenger saw was both fine and new.

Very special in the steam service

AEC Single-unit Railcar
Great Britain:
Great Western Railway (GWR), 1933

Type: Diesel-mechanical railcar.
Gauge: 4ft 8½in (1,435mm).
Propulsion: AEC 6-cylinder four-stroke 121hp diesel engine driving the four wheels of one bogie via a mechanical gearbox, a propellor shaft and a drive enclosed in the axleboxes at one end of the driving axles.
Weight: 24,685lb (11.2t) adhesive, 53,780lb (24.4t) total.
Max. axleload: 12,340lb (5.6t).
Overall length: 63ft 1in (19,228mm).
Max. speed: 60mph (96km/h).

If the "Brighton Belle" pointed the way ahead for main-line express

passenger trains in Britain, then this modest railcar did the same for the branch-line passenger. Numerous other companies produced lightweight diesel trains, but none stayed the course, and it is from this little vehicle that British Railways' large fleet of diesel-mechanical multiple-unit trains are directly descended.

The Associated Equipment Co (AEC) of Southall, Middlesex, were the main builders of London's buses and it was to them that the GWR went in 1932 for something a bit heftier than a railbus, but based on bus practice. The diesel engine was slung below

between London and Brighton was the all-Pullman "Southern Belle" train and in the new scheme of things this became the "Brighton Belle." One innovation for the Southern (but not for Pullman) was that the three five-car Pullman trains built for this service were of all-steel construction. Each set provided 80 first-class seats and 152 third-class seats. The six first-class Pullman cars (two in each set) were named, not after the customary grand ladies such as *Zenobia* or *Lady Dalziel*, but after the girls next door—*Hazel, Doris, Audrey, Vera, Gwen* and *Mona*.

Apart from World War II, for some 40 years the "Belle" sets provided luxury service several times a day in the even hour over the 52 miles (84km) from London's Victoria Station to Brighton. Eventually they had to be replaced by the more mundane trains running today, but such is the affection in which these trains are held that several survive in museums and as restaurant dining rooms.

Right: *The tail of the Brighton Belle at speed near Wandsworth Common, London. The two five-car sets could muster a respectable 3,600hp between them.*

the underframe and drove the wheels via a longitudinal shaft. An interesting feature was that passengers had a view along the tracks as from an observation car.

Later the same year, three express railcars were delivered, generally similar in appearance, but with two engines and geared for a maximum speed of 75mph (120km/h). There was also a small buffet. During the next few years,

Far left: *GWR diesel railcar No. 1, as built in 1933.*

Left: *A trailer-hauling GWR railcar of the 1940 series.*

other cars followed including No.17, which was for parcels traffic, while No.18 had standard railway drawgear and the ability to haul trailers. Experience gained led to an order for 20, all twin-engined. These later cars all had multiple-unit capability, using vacuum-operated servos. They were distinguished by rather more angular bodywork and were delivered in 1940.

Once the war was over and the upheaval of nationalisation surmounted, the experience was used in the design of several thousand generally similar vehicles supplied to BR from 1953.

Pioneer Zephyr Three-car train USA: Chicago, Burlington & Quincy Railroad (CB&Q), 1934

Type: High-speed articulated streamlined diesel-electric train.
Gauge: 4ft 8½in (1,435mm).
Propulsion: Electro-Motive Type 201E 600hp (448kW) in-line two-stroke diesel engine and generator feeding two nose-suspended traction motors on the leading bogie.
Weight: 90,360lb (41t) adhesive, 175,000lb (79.5t) total.
Max. axleload: 45,180lb (20.5t).
Overall length: 196ft 0in (59,741mm).
Max. speed: 110mph (177km/h).

On May 25, 1934 the fastest train between Denver and Chicago (1,015 miles—1,624km) was the "Autocrat", timed to do the run in 27hr 45min including 40 stops, an average speed of 37mph (59km/h). On May 26 a brand new stainless steel articulated streamlined self-propelled train reeled off the miles between the two cities in just over 13 hours at an average speed of 78mph (125km/h). As the little train triumphantly ran into its display position at the Century of Progress Exhibition in Chicago, US railroading had changed for ever.

Preparation for this triumph had begun in 1930 when mighty General Motors purchased both the Electro-Motive Company and their engine suppliers, the Winton Engine Co. GM concentrated their efforts on making a diesel engine suitable for rail transport. 'Softly, softly catchee monkey' was their policy and it was with considerable reluctance that after four years work they agreed to let an experimental engine out of their hands for this *Pioneer Zephyr*. The floodlight of publicity that illuminated its triumph could so easily have lit up a disaster

—indeed, electrical faults occurring during the trip but bravely corrected by the staff whilst the equipment was still live, indicated that it was a very close-run thing indeed.

In some ways, of course, it was a nonsense. Naturally, the manufacturers pressed the view that

Below: *The observation car at the rear end of the Chicago, Burlington & Quincy Railroad's* Pioneer Zephyr *high-speed diesel-electric trainset, now on display at the Chicago Museum of Science & Industry.*

M-10001 Six-car trainset USA: Union Pacific Railroad (UP), 1934

Type: Diesel-electric high-speed passenger train.
Gauge: 4ft 8½in (1,435mm).
Propulsion: Electro-Motive 1,200hp (895kW) V-16 two-stroke diesel engine and generator supplying current to four 250hp (187kW) nose-suspended traction motors geared to the axles of the two leading bogies.
Weight: 143,260lb (65t) adhesive, 413,280lb (187.5t) total.
Max. axleload: 35,815lb (16.25t).
Overall length: 376ft 0in (114,605mm).
Max. speed: 120mph (192km/h).*

* Not operated in regular service above 90mph (144km/h).

In February 1934 the famed Union Pacific Railroad only failed by a technicality to be the first in America with a diesel-electric high-

speed train. A suitable diesel engine was not quite ready and UP's stunning train had to have a spark-plug engine using distillate fuel. This was the yellow and grey No. M-10000, consisting of three articulated streamlined light-alloy cars weighing including power plant 85t (93½ US tons), in total hardly more than a single standard US passenger car as then existing. The train was built by Pullman Standard and seated 116 passengers in air-conditioned comfort; the leading power car included a 33ft (10m) mail compartment. After a coast-to-coast demonstration tour the train went into service as the "City of Salina" on one of UP's few short-distance daytime inter-city runs, that between Kansas City and Salina.

The success of the principles involved led to the first diesel-

Right: *The original Union Pacific M-10000 three-car self-propelled train in Pullman Works, Chicago, 1934.*

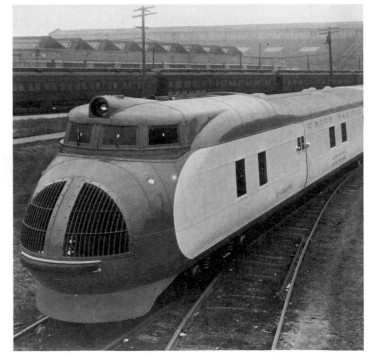

the whole performance was due to diesel traction when it was really due to a different approach to long-distance passenger movement. Various railroads (notably the Chicago, Milwaukee, St Paul & Pacific and Southern Pacific) were quick to demonstrate that equal improvements were possible with steam, at much lower first cost. Of course, once they had been paid for, running costs of the new trains were much lower than with steam, but overall there was little in it. Incidentally, over one-third of the space available was devoted to the carriage of mail and parcels.

Extra comforts such as air-conditioning, radio reception, reclining seats, grill-buffet and observation lounge were very nice, but significantly little has ever been said about the riding of the *Pioneer Zephyr*. One must unkindly suspect, though, that compared with the heavyweight stock the new train replaced, a little was left to be desired. Even so, many other *Zephyr* trains—but never quite as lightly built as the original—were to go into service on the Burlington. It is true that the self-propelled concept was soon dropped in favour of separate locomotives, but the name is still commemorated today with Amtrak's "San Francisco Zephyr" running daily between Chicago and Oakland (San Francisco). The original little 72-seat train. —later enlarged to four cars—ran over 3 million miles in traffic and is today enshrined in Chicago's Museum of Science & Industry.

Right: *The leading end of the original* Pioneer Zephyr *train. Note the special headlight with powerful scanning beam, needed as extra warning in the absence of columns of steam and smoke.*

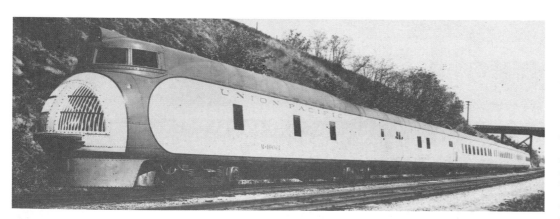

Above: *Six-car diesel-electric train No. M-10001 as supplied to the Union Pacific Railroad in November 1934.*

powered sleeping car train, the articulated six-car M-10001. This train was turned out also by Pullman in November 1934 and this time had a true diesel engine by Electro-Motive in the power car. At first a 900hp V-12 was installed, but later this was replaced by the V-16 engine mentioned above. Behind the power car was a baggage-mail car, then three Pullman sleepers and finally

a day coach with buffet. There was accommodation for 124 passengers.

On October 22, 1934, UP set its new train to capture the existing transcontinental record. The then existing coast-to-coast record was a run of 71½ hours by the Atchison, Topeka & Santa Fe route—described vividly by Rudyard Kipling in *Captains Courageous*—achieved by a special train put on in 1906 for railroad tycoon E. H. Harriman. In 1934, 508 miles (817km) from Cheyenne, Wyoming to Omaha, Nebraska were run off at an average speed of 84mph (135km/h) but no fireworks were

attempted east of Chicago. To avoid breaking New York City's famous no-smoke law, a vintage 1904 New York Central electric loco (described earlier) had to haul the train the final few miles. In spite of such handicaps and some quite lengthy stops for refuelling and servicing, No. M-10001 lowered the record to a so far unbeaten 57 hours for the 3,260 miles (5,216km) from Oakland Pier opposite San Francisco to Grand Central Terminal, New York.

The impact on the public was tremendous. In the following year the same train went into service as the "City of Portland" running the 2,270 miles (3,652km) between Chicago and Portland, Oregon, cutting 18 hours from the previous best schedule of 58 hours. More importantly, in succeeding years, the demand for travel by these trains was such that at first 11-car and then 17-car streamliners had to be put into service on such trains as the "City of Los Angeles" and "City of San Francisco".

Class E428 2-B₀-B₀-2

Italy:
Italian State Railways (FS), 1934

Type: Electric express passenger locomotive.
Gauge: 4ft 8½in (1,435mm).
Propulsion: Direct current at 3,000V fed via overhead catenary to eight 470hp (350kW) frame-mounted motors geared in pairs to the driving axles through flexible drives.
Weight: 163,103lb (74t) adhesive, 297,533lb (135t) total.
Max. axleload: 36,368lb (16.5t).
Overall length: 62ft 4in (19,000mm).
Tractive effort: 48,500lb (215kN)*.
Max. speed: 93mph (150km/h)*.

*Depending on gear ratio; maximum speed.

As electrification proceeded in Italy, the limitations of the three-phase system induced increasing dissatisfaction amongst those responsible. There were the limited

number of fixed speeds, and the complications involved in having to provide twin-insulated conductors above each track. An alternative system used high-voltage direct current, pioneered over long distances by the Chicago, Milwaukee, St Paul & Pacific Railroad of the USA, and experimented with locally on a modest scale over the 63-mile (101km) line between Benevento and Foggia in southern Italy during the late 1920s.

In 1928 the decision was taken that future electrification schemes should be direct current, and by

Left and below: Italian State Railways' E428 electric locomotive. The pictures show the locomotive finished in a light reddish brown colour. More usual was a khaki shade known as Isabella *after the colour of the garments of Queen Isabella who unwisely vowed she would eschew clean ones until her army had taken a certain city.*

"Lyntog" Three-car train

Denmark:
Danish State Railways (DSB), 1935

Type: Articulated diesel-electric express passenger train.
Gauge: 4ft 8½in (1,435mm).
Propulsion: Four Frichs 275hp (205kW) engines and generators, two mounted on each of two end bogies, feeding current to eight nose-suspended traction motors, each geared to one axle.
Weight: 286,520lb (130t).
Max. axleload: 36,366lb (16.5t).
Overall length: 209ft 0in (63,703mm).
Max. speed: 90mph (144km/h).

In the mid-1930s one of the most staid of railway administrations went mad and put on an extraordinary and quite brilliant programme of accelerations in which these diesel-electric trains played a major part. Before the changes were made a traveller from Britain arriving at Esjberg, Denmark, on the excellent ships of the Danish *Det Forende Dampskib Skelskab*, faced a 7½hr 214 mile (342km) journey and a second night in a railway carriage before he reached the capital, including two more sea crossings on train ferries. No less than 2hr 48min was sliced

from the timing of this particular run by the new "Englaenderen" express, corresponding amounts taken out of the schedules connecting other towns and cities in Jutland with Copenhagen.

Accounting for 56 minutes of this acceleration was the huge new bridge across that arm of the sea known as the Little Belt, opened by King Christian (a great railway enthusiast) on May 14, 1935. Both the old and the new trains still faced a 1hr 40min crossing of the Great Belt, leaving these well-named (*Lyntog* means 'Lightning Train') diesel expresses

responsible for cutting 1hr 50min off a journey of which the rail portion was previously only 4hr 40min. Average rail speeds were almost doubled. The trains were fully articulated, with the power plant mounted on the end bogies. This consisted of four paired and relatively small diesel engine and generator sets, thereby ensuring that a fault which shut down an engine would be unlikely to mean a failure out on the road. At the same time the power plants were arranged so that they could easily be run out from under the train for attention or replacement. High

1934 electric working had begun between Rome and Milan—including the brand new 11½-mile (18.5km) Appennine tunnel, opened on April 12, 1934. There was therefore a requirement for heavy-duty express passenger electric locomotives and these formidable machines were the result.

It is only very recently that it has become possible with static devices to convert high-voltage to low—and since traction motors able to cope with voltages as high as 3,000V are not really practical, it was necessary to connect pairs of 1,500V motors in series. Hence, the eight motors for the four pairs of driving wheels which, although it is not obvious from a cursory glance, are mounted in two separate bogies.

The 241 excellent "E428s" are nearly all still in service, although occupied on less glamorous duties than in their heady early days when it was they rather than Mussolini that made the top Italian trains run to time.

Above: *Italian E428 2-Bo-Bo-2 electric locomotive, later version. The earliest ones did not have the streamlined ends.*

acceleration was ensured by having all the axles motored, again with relatively small motors of 104hp (78kW) each. Seating for 36 first-class and 104 third-class passengers was provided. In addition there was a small dining section seating 12, complete with kitchen/pantry.

The success of these trains led shortly to further orders being placed, this time for four-car sets. The most significant thing was that few changes were made, except those necessary to cater for the extra vehicle in the set. The services initiated by these trains

have stood the test of time and those run by their successors could still be found in the timetables until 1982. For some reason recently (the grass always grows greener on the other side of the fence, perhaps!) the Danes, in opposition to the world trend, returned in 1982 to using separate locomotives and new trainsets fitted for push-and-pull working on many main line services.

Left: *Danish State Railways' "Lyntog" diesel-electric train leaving the train ferry after the crossing of the Great Belt.*

Bugatti Single Railcar
France: State Railway (Etat), 1934

Type: Petrol-mechanical express railcar.
Gauge: 4ft 8½in (1,435mm).
Propulsion: Four 200hp (150kW) Bugatti "Royale" petrol engines driving through hydraulic coupling and cardan shafts the middle two axles of each eight-wheel bogie.
Weight: 35,265lb (16t) adhesive, 70,530lb (32t) total.
Max. axleload: 8,820lb (4t).
Overall length: 73ft 2in (22,300mm).
Max. speed: 99mph (159km/h).

The inter-war years saw perfection of the lightweight internal-combustion-engined railcar, particularly in countries where the cost and availability of coal made a change from steam traction attractive. France was such a country and the dozen or more manufacturers of railcars there included such well-known automobile names as Renault and Michelin.

By the early-1930s, technology had reached a stage at which railcars could not only replace steam on secondary routes, but could improve on the best steam schedules on main lines. This period brought a spectacular new entry into the railcar world. Ettore Bugatti was a famed designer of racing cars; Italian by birth, but now a naturalised Frenchman, he built his cars at Molsheim in Alsace Lorraine. He applied his ingenious brain to the problems of rail traction, starting from the proposition that with a suitably-designed railcar it should be possible to double the speeds then being reached on railways.

Bugatti's first railcar was supplied to the Etat system in 1933, and it bristled with novelties. The shape and proportions of the body suggested speed, for it was only 8ft 10in (2,692mm) high for a length of 73ft 2in (22,300mm), and its ends were brought to horizontal wedges, the shape being determined by wind tunnel tests. The driver was placed in a "conning tower" amidships, with an excellent view of the line ahead (but not immediately ahead!). Four of Bugatti's "Royale" engines of 200hp (150kW), burning a benzol-alcohol fuel, were placed across the body at the centre, the drive being taken to the bogies by cardan shafts along one side. The bogies each had eight wheels mounted in a flexible suspension system which allowed the wheels not only to accommodate vertical irregularities in the track, but also to move laterally to suit the radius of curves. Only the middle axles of each bogie were driven. There

SVT 877 "Flying Hamburger" Two-car Trainset

Germany:
German State Railway (DRG), 1932

Type: High-speed two-car articulated diesel train.
Gauge: 4ft 8½in (1,435mm).
Propulsion: One 410hp (305kW) diesel engine and generator mounted on each outer bogie supplying a dc traction motor on the nearer axle of the middle bogie.
Weight*: 72,290lb (32.8t) adhesive, 206,740lb (93.8t) total.
Max. axleload: 36,150lb (16.4t).
Overall length: 137ft 6in (41,906mm).
Max. speed: 100mph (160km/h).

*The weights apply to the final post-war condition of the train; when built it weighed 171,900lb (78t).

At 08.02 on May 15, 1933 a new era in railway speed began, for at that time the *Fliegender Hamburger* (Flying Hamburger) left Lehrter Station in Berlin on its first 77.4mph (124.5km/h) passenger-carrying journey to Hamburg. That it was the fastest schedule in the world was notable, but that it should have been introduced in Germany was quite remarkable. For, despite the brilliant example set by the Zossen-Marienfelde trials in 1903, Germany had lagged behind other countries in passenger train speeds, and in 1933 the speed limit was only just being raised above 62mph (100km/h).

Diesel railcars were first introduced in Germany in 1915, and during the 1920s their use was extended greatly on local services, but the aim here was a reduction of costs compared with steam operation. The novelty in the *Flying Hamburger* was that diesel propulsion was being used to raise train speeds above the level which was practicable with steam.

The official classification of the new railcar was "SVT877" (*Schnellverkehr* = express service, *Verbrennungs* = internal combustion, *Triebwagen* = railcar), and it was a two-car articulated unit with a 410hp engine mounted on each end bogie. Each engine drove a generator which fed a traction motor on the nearer axle of the articulation bogie. Thus the weight was distributed as evenly as possible. The shape of the vehicles was determined by wind tunnel tests at the Zeppelein Works at Friedrichshafen. The unit was permitted to run at 100mph (160km/h) in traffic, but reached 109mph (175km/h) on test.

There was accommodation for

98 second-class passengers in the two coaches, and there were also four seats at the small buffet. The livery was a striking combination of mauve and cream. The weight of the unit was stated to be 78t when it appeared, but in the post-war DB diagram book it was given as 93.8t.

Above: Flying Hamburger *on display at the German National Railway Museum in Nuremburg.*

The schedule allowed 138 minutes for 178.1 miles (286.5km) on the westbound run, and 140 minutes in the opposite direction. Although much of the journey

was a hydraulic coupling between the engines and the cardan shafts. There was no gearbox, as the characteristics of the engines enabled them to start the car from rest with no more help than the hydraulic coupling.

The total engine power of 800hp (600kW) for a vehicle weighing 32t loaded was exceptional, and enabled the car to accelerate and run at unprecedented rates. There were 48 seats in two saloons. The seat and back-rest were identical, and by a simple movement the back could be slid into the seat position, the seat then becoming the back for facing the opposite direction.

Initial tests demonstrated that the car ran smoothly at speeds up to 107mph (172km/h), but when it entered service between Paris and Trouville-Deauville it was subjected to the normal French speed limit of 75mph (120km/h). Later, as a result of favourable experience, maximum speed was raised to 87mph (140km/h).

Shortly after entering service, the first car carried the French President to Cherbourg at an average speed of 73.3mph (118km/h); following the trip this type of car became known as a *Présidential*. Further cars were delivered to the Etat, and in 1934 the PLM took delivery of a double

unit, comprising a power car and trailer permanently coupled. Other versions included a lower-powered lightweight unit and an extra-long car. A total of 76 cars were built up to 1938, of which the État had the largest fleet with 41 sets. One of the 1935 État cars made a demonstration run on the Est from Strasbourg to Paris covering the 311.9 miles (501.8km) at the remarkable average of 88.7mph (142.7km/h).

The cars were little used during World War II, but they made a notable contribution to the revival of express services after the war. SNCF then introduced standard designs of diesel railcar, and the

last of the Bugattis was withdrawn in 1958. Fortunately one of them was retained as a service vehicle, and it was eventually restored to its original condition, and placed in the French National Railway Museum at Mulhouse in 1982.

Bugatti cars are remembered as leaders of French railway speed in their early days, and they well merited the name under which the PLM advertised its services operated by them—"Thoroughbreds of the Rail".

Below: *A Bugatti single railcar of the State Railway of France. Note the central conning tower which was the driving position.*

Above: *The combined* Flying Municher *and* Flying Stuttgarter *high-speed diesel electric trains in the Frankenwald near Mt. Lauénstein.*

was on easy gradients and free from speed restrictions, there was one slack to 37mph (60km/h) near the middle of the run, the first 7 miles (11km) out of Berlin were limited to 50mph (80km/h), and at the Hamburg end 17 miles (27km) were limited to 68mph (110km/h).

Although there were a few problems with the train, it averaged 71 per cent availability over the first six months of operation, and this had reached 90 per cent in two years. Timekeeping was good, and the average load was just over half the capacity.

Success of the *Flying Hamburger* led to an order for 13 more two-car units placed in 1934 to operate similar services from Berlin to Cologne, Frankfurt and Munich, and a second service to Hamburg, as well as one from

Cologne to Hamburg. When the new cars went into service in 1935, the schedules included a booking from Berlin to Hanover at 82.3mph (132.4km/h), which, with a Berlin to Frankfurt run, were the first runs in the world scheduled at more than 80mph (128.7km/h) start-to-stop.

The high-speed services became increasingly popular, and the next step was a three-car version with two 600hp (448kW) engines, and with the traction motors on the end bogies. One of

these sets reached 127mph (205km/h) on test. With these sets the Reichsbahn built up a network of fast services which, for seven years from 1933 to 1940, held the world record for the fastest start-to-stop runs, apart from a short period when the Santa Fe "Super Chief" in the United States was faster.

Fast running in Germany ended early in the war, and the railcars were put into store. After the war they came back into service, but in Federal Germany the main routes were much less suited to high speed than the routes which had radiated from Berlin, and the cars were not able to achieve their pre-war averages. They were withdrawn from service in the late-1950s, by which time some of them had been converted to hydraulic transmission. One power bogie and part of a car body from the first set are preserved in the German National Railway Museum in Nuremberg.

Despite the faith which the old Reichsbahn had in these railcars, large orders for steamlined steam engines had been placed in 1939, and substitution of steam trains for the railcars had to be made from time to time when passengers exceeded the capacity of the cars. It is thus not clear how the pattern of services would have developed had there been no war.

Class E18 1-D₀-1

Type: Express passenger electric locomotive.
Gauge: 4ft 8½in (1,435mm).
Propulsion: Alternating current at 15,000V 16⅔Hz supplied through a transformer to four traction motors mounted on the frame, and connected to the axles through flexible drive.
Weight: 172,130lb (78.1t) adhesive, 239,130lb (108.5t) total.
Max. axleload: 43,200lb (19.6t).
Overall length: 55ft 6in (16,920mm).
Tractive effort: 46,300lb (206kN).
Max. speed: 93mph (150km/h).

From 1926 a succession of express passenger locomotives with individual axle drive was built for the growing electrified network of Deutsche Reichsbahn in Bavaria and Saxony. Amongst these was the 3,750hp (2,800kW) Class "E17" 1-Do-1 of 1927, which set the pattern for the layout of several later types of the same wheel arrangement. In 1933, three types of 1-Co-1 locomotive were introduced for the more easily-graded routes, of which the "E04", with a one-hour output of 2,940hp (2,190kW), was notable for its controller with fine gradations and for other electrical refinements. The 1-Do-1 locomotives were limited to 74mph (120km/h) but some of the 1-Co-1s were geared for 83mph (130km/h).

By this time the great revolution in German passenger train speeds was under way, with diesel railcars running at 100mph (160km/h) and steam locomotives at 93mph (150km/h). The next series of electric locomotives, the "E18" 1-Do-1 of 1935, therefore took a major step forward in that its maximum speed was 93mph (150km/h). The specification required the locomotive to be capable of reaching 87mph (140km/h) with a 700t train. To achieve this the continuous power output was increased to 3,800hp (2,840kW) at 76mph (122km/h), compared with 3,080hp (2,300kW) at 60mph (97km/h) in the "E17".

Experience with existing 1-Do-1 locomotives had shown that their riding was steady, despite a firm belief amongst many locomotive engineers that a locomotive with a symmetrical wheelbase was potentially unsteady at speed. The layout of the "E18" therefore followed closely that of the "E17". The electrical equipment was based on that of the "E04" 1-Co-1, with one traction motor per axle and Kleinow flexible drive. Previous German electric locomotives had been angular in shape, but the "E18" had an air-smoothed casing with rounded ends. This fell short of the streamlined shapes of the high-speed railcars and steam engines, but showed clearly that this was a new generation of fast locomotives.

To assist the driver at the higher speeds now contemplated, there was more power operation of controls. Above 44mph (70km/h)

greatly increased brake power was available than in the earlier classes. As in the previous types with end carrying axles, those axles were connected to the adjoining driving axles by Krauss-Helmholtz trucks, which made the locomotive flexible but guided it into curves. When the "E18s" were tested at high speed, troubles were encountered with oscillations in the KH trucks. Air cylinders were therefore fitted which could lock the truck so that the driving axle in it had no lateral freedom and the carrying axle had a small amount of individual play. This control came into effect automatically at the trailing end whenever the controller was reversed in direction, and it cured the trouble.

The "E18s" proved to be very successful and plans were approved for construction of 92. By the time work was suspended at the beginning of World War II, 53 had been completed, and after the war they were the mainstay of express passenger workings in West Germany until the new generation of electric locomotives appeared in the 1950s. Two of the locomotives were in Austria at the end of the war, and Austrian Federal Railways retained them. Eight more were built by the Austrians, and for many years they were the fastest express locomotives in that country.

The "E18s" were followed by further locomotives of the same basic dimensions, but designed for normal operation at 112mph (180km/h) and for test running at

up to 140mph (225km/h). The continuous power rating was raised to 4,900hp at 112mph (180km/h). Four of these locomotives, Nos. E19.01-4, were built in 1939-40, and until the coming of the "E03" Co-Co locomotives in 1965 they were the most powerful West German express passenger locomotives. They were never exploited to the full, and in the post-war years they worked alongside the "E18s," both classes being limited to 75mph (120km/h) by that time.

Simultaneously with the development of the "E19" series of electric locomotives, the German railway authorities embarked on an extensive assessment of the use of 50Hz industrial frequency current. A line in the Black Forest area, known as the Hollental railway, was converted on this system. It involved gradients as steep as 1-in-20 (5 per cent) and was a severe test. Had the war not intervened, this combination of high-speed locomotive design with cheaper supply systems might have put Germany decades ahead of the rest of the world.

Right: *German Federal Railway's Class E18 1-D-1 electric locomotive No. 118 049-6 passes Aschaffenburg with a relief express from Fulda to Dortmund.*

Below: *The E18 was a classic 1930s electric loco, with independently driven driving wheels in a rigid frame, guided by pony trucks.*

262 BD1 2-C$_o$-2+2-C$_o$-2

France: Paris, Lyons & Mediterranean Railway (PLM), 1937

Type: Twin-unit express passenger diesel-electric locomotive.
Gauge: 4ft 8½in (1,435mm).
Propulsion: In each unit, two 1,025hp (765kW) MAN 6-cylinder four-stroke diesel engines in a common frame, each driving a generator supplying three traction motors mounted on the main frame, with flexible drive to the axles.
Weight: 238,000lb (108t) adhesive, 493,700lb (224t) total.
Max. axleload: 39,670lb (18.0t).
Tractive effort: 70,500lb (314kN).
Max. speed: 81mph (130km/h).

In the mid-1930s the PLM Railway experimented with diesel traction on its Algerian offshoot, and then, in 1935, ordered two large diesel-electric locomotives for its main line from Paris to the Riviera. The specification laid down precise conditions: to haul 450t from Paris to Menton on a schedule which would require maximum speeds of 81mph (130km/h) and a minimum of 53mph (85km/h) on the steepest gradients; to haul 600t trains from Paris to Nice on prevailing schedules; maximum axleload 18t; to cover a mileage of 171,000 (275,000km) in each of the first two years after introduction into service.

To achieve this performance required an engine power of 4,000hp, and this was provided in two ways; first by four MAN 6-cylinder in-line engines, and secondly by two Sulzer 12-cylinder 12LDA 31 double-crankshaft engines. The power available at the rail required a total of six driving axles, and in addition eight carrying axles would be needed to support the total weight. To satisfy these requirements each locomotive was a double 2-Co-2, the two halves being semi-permanently coupled at the centre with a connecting gangway. The bogies had inside frames, like those of a steam locomotive. Each pair of

MAN engines had a common casing, with two independent parallel crankshafts, each with its own generator, one at each end of the casing. The twin crankshafts of each Sulzer engine were geared together, and drove a single generator.

The MAN engines developed 1,025hp (765kW) each, giving a total of 4,100hp (3,060kW), of which 300hp (224kW) was absorbed by auxiliaries, leaving 3,800hp (2,835kW) for traction. The Sulzer engines developed 1,900hp (1,420kW) each, with 3,550hp (2,650kW) available for traction. There was a single traction motor for each axle mounted on

Class 11* C

Great Britain: London, Midland & Scottish Railway (LMS), 1936

Type: Six-coupled diesel-electric shunter (switcher)
Gauge: 4ft 8½in (1,435mm).
Propulsion: One English Electric Type 6K 350hp (260kW) four-stroke 6-cylinder in-line engine and generator supplying two 175hp (130kW) nose-suspended traction motors geared to the outer axles, the axles being connected by cranks and coupling rods.
Weight: 116,260lb (52.7t).
Max. axleload: 38,750lb (17.6t).
Overall length: 28ft 6¾in (8,705mm).
Tractive effort: 30,000lb (133kN).
Max. speed: 30mph (48km/h).

*BR class designation

The first locomotive in the world to be driven by an oil engine was built in England in 1894, and from then onwards numerous firms experimented with internal-combustion locomotives. Some of these were general engineering firms, and some were amongst the smaller steam locomotive builders. By the 1920s several had standard designs of small shunting locomotives, and the first main line or road locomotives were produced by Armstrong-Whitworth of Newcastle-upon-Tyne, an old-established armaments manufacturer which had entered the locomotive field after World War I.

The main line railways still showed little interest, apart from granting facilities for trials of various machines. They bought a few small shunters for use where sparks were dangerous, but in general the steam engine reigned supreme; coal, labour and steam shunting engines were all cheap, and the relatively expensive diesel seemed to have little to commend it. However, in 1932 Armstrong-Whitworth built a demonstration 0-6-0 or C shunter with a single-traction motor mounted on the frame, connected to the driving wheels through gearing, a layshaft and connecting rods. The engine was of Armstrong-Sulzer design,

Above: *British Railways class 08 diesel shunting locomotive based on the LMS 1936 design.*

with an output of 250hp (187kW). This locomotive was tested by the LNER and GWR in busy marshalling yards, and it created a great impression by its economy and reliability.

In 1933 there came a breakthrough. The LMS, the largest British railway, recognised that diesels might effect some economies, especially in yards where shunting went on round the clock. The company therefore ordered nine locomotives of six different types from five manufacturers. It

was an indication of the extent of diesel locomotive activity amongst British builders that all these locomotives were virtually standard models. All had mechanical transmission except for the Armstrong-Whitworth contribution, which was very similar to the earlier demonstrator.

Concurrently, another six-coupled diesel-electric shunter was built by Hawthorn Leslie of Newcastle, incorporating an English Electric engine and equipment. The 300hp (234kW) 6-cylinder in-line engine drove a generator which supplied two traction motors geared to the outer axles; the three axles were connected by coupling rods. The LMS tested this locomotive and bought it.

With the experience gained from these locomotives, the LMS ordered two batches of 350hp (260kW) machines, one batch from Hawthorn Leslie with geared drive and the other from Armstrong-Whitworth with jackshaft drive. The success of these locomotives encouraged the railway to build more. At this point Armstrong-Whitworth gave up locomotive construction, and the LMS therefore produced its own design, in which an English Electric engine and electrical equipment was mounted on a chassis with jackshaft drive from one motor. Thirty of these units were built by Derby Works between 1939 and 1942. In the latter year

the frame, and connected to the axles by a Kleinow quill drive, a well-tried arrangement used in many electric locomotives.

The locomotives were completely enclosed down to rail level in a streamlined casing. In later years the bottom of the casing was cut away slightly.

The MAN-engined machine, No. 262BD1, appeared at the end of 1937, and hauled the first diesel-worked train in France on December 29 of that year. It was at that time the most powerful diesel locomotive outside the United States. No. 262AD1 was completed in April 1938, and for a short time took over from No.

262BD1 the distinction of being the most powerful diesel locomotive, but in July of that year the German firm Henschel completed a double locomotive for Hungary with two 2,200hp (1,640kW) versions of the Sulzer engine fitted to No. 262BD1.

Although they met with various troubles, the two locomotives were soon at work on express trains between Paris and Lyons. By the time they were put into storage in September 1939 they had achieved good mileages, albeit short of the figure laid down in the specification. In January 1945 they returned to service, and helped to relieve the acute post-war locomo-

tive shortage in France. At first they worked between Paris and Lyons, but later they moved to Nice, where they performed some notable work on expresses of up to 750t. They were finally withdrawn from service in 1955, 262AD1 having covered a grand overall total of 985,000 miles, (1,585,000km).

These locomotives were remarkable for their time, and they marked an important step in the development of the main line diesel in Europe. Their significance was obscured by two things—their immobilisation for four years and the post-war electrification of main lines of the SNCF, including the

Paris, Lyons & Mediterranean line for which they had been built. As a result of the progress of electrification, no more large diesel locomotives were needed on SNCF until the mid-1960s, by which time the influence of 20 years of post-war development of the electric locomotive masked the significant contribution made to diesel design by these pioneer machines.

Below: *The Paris, Lyons & Mediterranean Railway diesel-electric locomotive No. 262BD1, built in 1937. Two 1,900hp Sulzer engines were provided, one in each half-unit.*

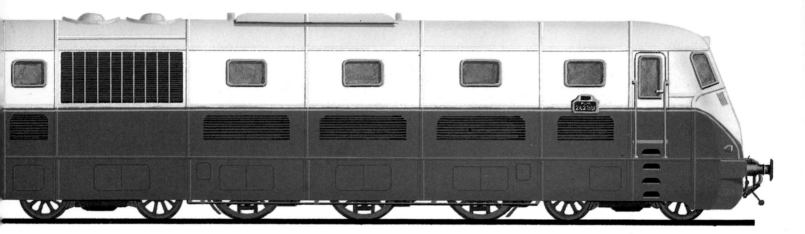

the LMS directors authorised 100 more, but as the long wheelbase which was inherent in the jackshaft drive had proved to be a disadvantage on the sharp curves of some sidings, there was a reversion to the Hawthorn Leslie layout with two geared motors. Twenty of these locomotives were built for the War Department, and then between 1949 and 1952 the order for 100 was executed. In the meantime the other three grouped railways had all built small numbers of very similar locomotives, so that for the first time there was virtually a British standard shunting locomotive.

With this background it was natural that British Railways should adopt a very similar design, and soon after nationalisation, long before it showed any interest in main line diesels, BR embarked on a plan to eliminate steam shunting, for which purpose a total of 1,193 of the 350hp shunters were built, all identical except for a few with different engines for trial purposes.

In a country where railways traditionally designed their own locomotives, the adoption of the Hawthorn Leslie/English Electric design was notable, and it eventually led to construction of the most numerous locomotive class in Britain.

Right: *Netherlands Railways shunting locomotive also based on the pre-war LMS design.*

GG1 2-Co-Co-2

Type: Heavy-duty express passenger electric locomotive.
Gauge: 4ft 8½in (1,435mm).
Propulsion: Medium-frequency alternating current at 15,000V 25Hz fed via overhead catenary and step-down transformer to twelve 410hp (305kW) traction motors, each pair driving a main axle through gearing and quill-type flexible drive.
Weight: 303,000lb (137t) adhesive, 477,000lb (216t) total.
Max. axleload: 50,500lb (22.9t).
Overall length: 79ft 6in (24,230mm).
Tractive effort: 70,700lb (314kN).
Max. speed: 100mph (160km/h).

The Pennsylvania Railroad devised a keystone herald to underline the position it justifiably felt it held in the economy of the USA. The keystone, displayed both front and rear of these superb locomotives, might equally well stand for the position they held in Pennsy's remarkable passenger operations. Since 1928, PRR had been pursuing a long-considered plan to work its principal lines electrically. The statistics were huge; $175 million in scarce depression money were needed to electrify 800 route-miles (1,287km) and 2,800 track-miles (4,505km) on which 830 passenger and 60 freight trains operated daily.

The medium-frequency single-phase ac system with overhead catenary was adopted. The reason lay in the fact that the dc third-rail system used in New York City was not suitable for long-distance operations and, moreover, since 1913 Pennsy had been gaining experience working its Philadelphia suburban services under

Below: *Pennsylvania Railroad Class GG1 electric locomotive in tuscan-red livery. These noble machines could also be seen in black or dark green.*

the wires on 25Hz ac. Only a corporation of colossal stature could have kept such a costly scheme going through the depression years, but by 1934 impending completion of electrification from New York to Washington meant a need for some really powerful express passenger motive power. There were two contenders for the prototype, the first being a 2-Do-2 which was based on the 2-Co-2 "P5a" class already in use. For comparison, a rather plain articulated locomotive of boxcar appearance and 2-Co-Co-2 configuration was borrowed from the neighbouring New York, New Haven & Hartford.

The latter proved superior, but first a further prototype locomotive was built. The main difference was a steamlined casing, which for production members of the class was stylishly improved by the famous industrial designer Raymond Loewy. Between 1935 and 1943, 139 of these "GG1s" were built; only very recently have they been superseded on prime express work.

Some of the "GG1s" were constructed in-house by the railroad's Altoona shops, others by Baldwin or by General Electric. Electrical equipment was supplied

Above: *After the demise of the Pennsylvania Railroad and its successor Penn Central, Amtrak took over the GG1s. Here is No. 902 at Paradise, Pennsylvania.*

Below: *A Pennsylvania Railroad GG1 passes through Glenolden, Pennsylvania, with the Chesapeake & Ohio Railroad's "George Washington" express.*

by both GE and Westinghouse. The philosophy behind the design was the same as that of the railroad—solid, dependable and above all, well tried. For example, the arrangement of twin single-phase motors, the form of drive, and many other systems were essentially the same as had been in use for 20 years on the New Haven. An interesting feature was the continuous cab-signalling system whereby coded track circuits conveyed information regarding the state of the road ahead, which was displayed on a miniature signal inside the "GG1" cabs. It was a remarkable tour-de-force for those days, especially considering that the rails also carried the return traction current.

At this time fortune was smiling on the Pennsy, because low traffic levels during the depression years meant that the physical upheaval of electrification was almost painless, while its completion (there was an extension to Harrisburg, Pennsylvania, in 1939) coincided with the start of the greatest passenger traffic boom ever known, that of World War II. The peak was reached on Christmas Eve 1944 when over 175,000 long-distance passengers used the Pennsylvania Station in New York. It was true that anything that had wheels was used to carry them, but coaches old and new could be marshalled in immense trains which the "GG1s" had no problem at all in moving to schedule over a route which led to most US cities from Florida to Illinois.

In numerical terms, a "GG1" rated at 4,930hp (3,680kW) on a continuous basis, could safely deliver 8,500hp (6,340kW) for a short period. This was ideal for quick recovery from stops and checks. In this respect one "GG1" was the totally reliable equivalent of three or four diesel units 30 or 40 years its junior. It is perhaps telling tales out of school, though, to mention an occasion when

brakes failed on a "GG1" and it came through the ticket barrier on to the concourse of Washington Union Station. This was built for people not "GG1s", and the locomotive promptly descended into the basement!

Of the fate of the Pennsylvania Railroad in the post-war years, perhaps the less said the better. It is enough to state that the "GG1" fleet passed piecemeal to the later owners of the railroad, or parts of it—Penn Central, Conrail, Amtrak, and the New Jersey Department of Transportation. At this time it would have been laughable had it not also been tragic how various highly-advertised successors to what were now regarded as relics of a bad past failed to match up to these contemptible museum pieces. But finally, and very recently, the coming of Amtrak's "AEM7" class has put an end to the use of "GG1s" on main-line passenger trains.

Conrail also recently de-electrified the parts of the ex-Pennsylvania lines it inherited on the bankruptcy of Penn Central and so it too had no use for even a handful of "GG1s". Only the New Jersey

DoT has—at the time of writing—a humble and, alas, emphemeral operation of suburban trains upon which a few of these noble machines perform. Two as least will survive, though, in museums at Altoona and Strasburg, but no longer will it be possible to see one of these mighty people-movers effortlessly in action at 90mph (144km/h) plus, treating a 20-coach passenger train like a sack of feathers.

Above: *The 10,000hp of two rather shabby GG1s was ample power for a Pennsylvania Railroad freight train in the latter days of that great institution.*

Below: *GG1 No. 4835 restored to Pennsylvania Railroad black livery, ahead of two further GG1s in Amtrak colours, pantographs raised in salute. The fourth loco is a modern E60P unit. A further GG1 is visible on the left.*

4-COR Four-car trainset
Great Britain:
Southern Railway (SR), 1937

Type: Electric express
passenger multiple-unit set.
Gauge: 4ft 8½in (1,435mm).
Propulsion: Direct current at
660V fed via side-mounted top-
contact third rail to four 275hp
(205kW) nose-suspended
traction motors geared to the
wheels of the outer bogies of
each set.
Weight: 130,816lb (59.4t)
adhesive, 349,890lb (159t) total.
Max. axleload: 32,704lb
(14.8t).
Overall length: 264ft 5in
(80,620mm).
Max. speed: 75mph
(120km/h).

For many years the Southern
Railway claimed to have the most
extensive suburban electrification
in the world. Its final flowering
was the extension in 1937 and
1938 to Portsmouth by two main
routes plus a good deal of in-
filling. Completion of this ambitious
scheme involved electrification of
407 miles (650km) of track. On
summer Saturdays more than 120
express trains and 70 stopping
trains were to run between

Right: *A Waterloo to Portsmouth
express formed of 4-COR and
4-RES units at speed near
Clapham Junction, London.*

"Electroliner": Four-car trainset

USA:
Chicago, North Shore & Milwaukee Railroad (North Shore), 1941

Type: High-speed articulated
electric interurban train.
Gauge: 4ft 8½in (1,435mm).
Propulsion: Direct current at
550V (600/650V post-World
War II) fed via trolley wire and
poles (or 600V on third rail on
the Loop) to eight 125hp
(200kW) Westinghouse nose-
suspended traction motors
geared to the driving axles of all
except the third of the five
Commonwealth cast steel
bogies.
Weight: 171,030lb (77.6t)
adhesive, 210,500lb (95t) total.

Max. axleload: 21,380lb (9.7t).
Overall length: 155ft 4in
(47,345mm).
Max. speed: 85mph
(136km/h)*.

*after World War II

At a time when high-speed electric
multiple-unit trains seem set to
provide the inter-city transport of
the future, it is worth considering
that the United States has already
developed and discarded a huge

network, 18,000 miles (29,000km)
in extent, of fast interurban electric
trains. Some were faster than
others but virtually all have now
vanished. Some of the longest

lasting, as well as the fastest and
best, ran on the Chicago, North
Shore & Milwaukee Railroad. On
this line, travellers started their
journeys at selected stops on the

Below: *The legendary Chicago,
North Shore & Milwaukee
Railroad Electroliner trains
consisted of five articulated cars
of which the outer two pairs are
depicted here. They were financed
by employees' pay cuts, staving
off closure until 1963.*

London and Portsmouth, and the whole south coast was now served by electric traction from Portsmouth as far as Hastings. The service was on average doubled in frequency, as well as becoming cleaner, and was faster and more reliable. It was railway modernisation of a quality that to us, nearly 50 years later, is totally out of reach.

To work the new services, 193 multiple-unit sets were built, of which 87 were four-car corridor units for the fast services. These could be marshalled to make up eight and twelve car trains, vestibuled throughout; hence the classification "4-COR". Nineteen of the units ("4-RES") included a restaurant car and 13 ("4-BUF") a buffet car.

All the electrical equipment of the two driving motor cars was carried below the underframe, leaving the body free for traffic purposes. The control equipment was electro-pneumatic, but the multiple-unit equipment allowed for older sets with electro-magnetic control to be operated in multiple with the new trains. The driving cabs could be closed off by a hinged vestibule door to provide a through way for passengers when units were coupled together. Air brakes were provided as

standard on SR electric stock.

The Portsmouth sets—sometimes affectionately known as "Nelsons"—gave over 30 years of excellent service. Nominal maximum speed was easily exceeded, 90mph (144km/h) often being observed, although at this speed the riding was a trifle lively. More important than speed though was reliability. Constant use of these trains during the period which included World War II and before

British Railways had seriously tried its hand at modernisation, gave this writer a totally false impression of the shape of things to come elsewhere. Enough to say then of these trains that at high speeds they might ride like steam-rollers with square wheels, but they never failed to deliver the promises implicit in the timetables. Now they have all gone, except for one motor coach set aside for display in the National Railway

Above: *This 12-car express electric train bears the headcode "80", indicating that it is on a non-stop run from Waterloo, London, to Portsmouth Harbour.*

Museum at York, and a demotored but otherwise complete four-car set which is used behind air-braked steam power on the Nene Valley tourist railway near Peterborough.

---

famous central loop of Chicago's elevated railway—which meant that trains had to be flexible enough to turn street corners on 90ft (27.5m) radius curves. This was achieved by making the cars articulated as well as rather short. Only a few minutes later they

would have to be rolling along at 85mph (135km/h) on the North Shore's excellent main line tracks. In Milwaukee, the trains made their final approach to the city centre terminal on street-car tracks, with all that that involves in control at crawling speeds. It was as if a Bristol to London High Speed Train came on from Paddington Station up Oxford Street and then happily made the right turn into Regent Street!

The famous trains that did all this so spectacularly had some

unusual features, not least the fact that the line's employees had agreed to finance improvements to the line, including the "Electroliners" by taking a wage cut! This was because the trains were a last-ditch attempt to hold off abandonment.

St Louis Car built the trains, using electrical equipment from Westinghouse. They seated 146 and boasted a tavern-lounge car. The two "Electroliner" trainsets were scheduled to make the 88-mile (141km) journey from Chi-

cago to Milwaukee and return five times daily from February 9, 1941 until the flexibility of the motor car finally won out. The North Shore's last full day of operation was January 20, 1963.

The "Electroliners" were sold to the Red Arrow lines of the Southeastern Pennsylvania Transportation Authority in Philadelphia. In 1964 they went into service as "Liberty Liners" *Valley Forge* and *Independence Hall,* complete with a vivid maroon, white and grey colour scheme.

EMD E Series A1A-A1A

United States:
Electro-Motive Division, General Motors Corporation (EMD), 1937

Type: Express passenger diesel-electric locomotive; "A" units with driving cab, "B" units without.

Gauge: 4ft 8½in (1,435mm).

Propulsion : Two EMD 567A 1,000hp (746kW) 12-cylinder pressure-charged two-stroke Vee engines and generators, each supplying current to two nose-suspended traction motors geared to the end axles of a bogie.

Weight: "A" unit 212,310lb (96.3t) adhesive, 315,000lb (142.9t) total. "B" units 205,570lb (93.3t) adhesive, 305,000lb (138.4t) total.

Max. axleload: "A" 53,080lb (24.1t), "B" 51,390lb (23.3t).

Overall length*: "A" 71ft 1¼in (21,670mm), "B" 70ft 0in (21,340mm).

Tractive effort: 53,080lb (236kN).

Max. speed: 85mph (137km/h), 92mph (148km/h), 98mph (157km/h), or 117mph (188km/h) according to gear ratio fitted.

*Dimensions refer to the E7 variant of 1945

In 1930 the General Motors Corporation made two purchases which were to have dramatic effects on the American locomotive scene. The first was the Winton Engine Co, a firm specialising in lightweight diesel engines. The second was Winton's chief customer, the Electro-Motive Corporation, an organisation established in 1922 to design and market petrol-electric railcars, which had sold some 500 units in 10 years. With the engine-building facility and the expertise acquired in

Below: *A 2,000hp E9 cab unit supplied to the Chicago, Rock Island & Pacific Railroad and specially painted in the livery of the line's "Rocket" express trains.*

these purchases, EMD was a major partner in the sensational pioneer streamlined trains introduced in 1934, and in the following year the firm produced its first locomotives. There were four Bo-Bo units with rectangular "boxcar" bodies, each powered by two 900hp (670kW) Winton 12-cylinder Vee engines. Pending the completion of its own plant, EMD had to employ other builders to assemble them.

In 1936 EMD moved into its own purpose-built works at La Grange, Illinois, and work commenced on the next locomotives. These were the first of the "E" series, known also as the "Streamline" series. Like the four earlier locomotives, they had two 900hp Winton engines, but the chassis and body were completely new. The body had its main load-

bearing strength in two bridge-type girders which formed the sides. The bogies had three axles to give greater stability at high speeds, but as only four motors were needed, the centre axle of each bogie was an idler, giving the wheel arrangement A1A-A1A. The units were produced in two versions, "A" units with a driver's cab and "B" units without. The Baltimore & Ohio was the first purchaser, taking six of each type to use as 3,600hp (2,690kW) pairs. Santa Fe bought eight As and three Bs, and the "City" streamliner roads bought two A-B-B sets for the "City of Los Angeles" and the "City of San Francisco". These latter at 5,400hp were the world's most powerful diesel locomotives when they appeared in 1937. The B&O units were classed "EA" and "EB", the

Above: *A passenger train of the Gulf, Mobile & Ohio RR hauled by EMD E9 cab unit (leading) and E3 booster unit.*

Santa Fe were "E1A" and "E1B", and the City units "E2A" and "E2B".

All these locomotives were an immediate success, not only by their performance but also by their reliability. The reliability was a striking tribute to the quality of the design, for there had been no demonstrator subsequent to the "boxcar" Bo-Bos. In multiple-unit working it was possible for some maintenance to be done on the road on the easier stretches, on which one engine could be shut down. With servicing assisted in this way, remarkable feats of endurance could be achieved. One of the B&O A-B sets gained

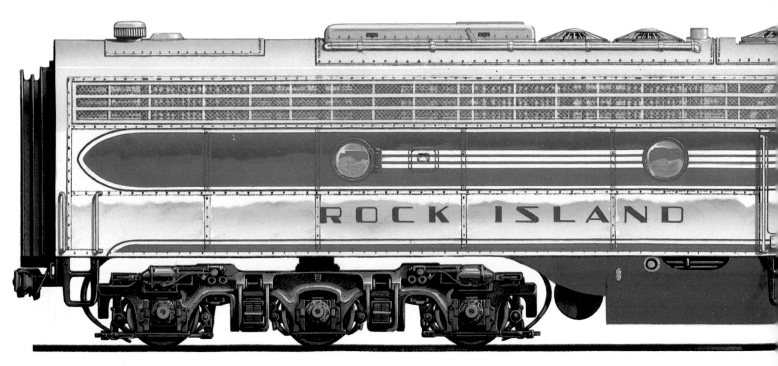

ROCK ISLAND

national publicity when it completed 365 continuous days of service between Washington and Chicago, covering 282,000 miles (454,000km) at an average scheduled speed of 56mph (90km/h).

Progress at La Grange was rapid. At 900hp the Winton engine was reaching its limit, and an EMD engine was therefore developed. Designated 567 (the capacity of a cylinder in cubic inches), it was available in three sizes with 8, 12, and 16 cylinders, giving 600, 1,000 and 1,350hp (448, 746 and 1,007kW). Simultaneously La Grange began to manufacture its own generators, motors and other electrical equipment.

The first all-EMD locomotives were an order from Seaboard Air Line for 14A and five B units, which appeared from October 1938 onwards. They had two 1,000hp engines and were operated as 6,000hp three-unit "lash-ups" (in the US jargon). These were the "E4s". "E3" and "E5" followed, the former comprising 18 units for the Sante Fe and the latter 16 for the Burlington.

So far each railroad's order had incorporated some individual variations—hence the different designations—but EMD aimed to gain the maximum benefits from production-line assembly of locomotives, to which end individual variations were to be discouraged. The next series, the "E6", which appeared in the same month in 1939 as the first freight demonstrator, was therefore a standard off-the-shelf unit, with the minimum of options. This was the start of real diesel mass production and 118 units had been built by the time the War Production Board terminated building of passenger locomotives in February 1942.

Construction of passenger locomotives was resumed in February 1945 with the first of the "E7" series. These locomotives bene-fited from the experience gained from both the "E" and the "F" series freight units. Improvements included a new and larger cooling system for the engine. Externally there was a noticeable difference in that the front of the body was sloped at 80° to the horizontal, as in the "F" series, instead of 70°, as in previous "E" series bodies. Apart from this change, there were few differences in external appearance throughout the range of "E" series, and most of them concerned windows and portholes.

With locomotive fleets rundown by wartime traffic, the railroads were even more eager to acquire passenger diesels, and Electro-Motive Division (as it had now become) settled down to a steady production of "E7s", averaging 10 per month for four years. During this time 428 A units and 82 B units were built, so that the "E7" outnumbered the passenger diesels of all other US makers put together. In general it was roads

Below: *Early E-series "A" or "cab" unit of the Atchison, Topeka & Santa Fe Railway, 1936.*

which had fast passenger services on easy gradients which bought "E7s"; for mountain work the all-adhesion "F" series was favourite.

Amongst "E7" buyers were the Pennsylvania and the New York Central. With 60 and 50 units respectively they had the largest numbers of any owner. On the NYC the most through comparison ever made between steam and diesel was conducted during October 1946. Two twin "E7" locomotives were tested against six of the new "Niagara" 4-8-4 steam engines working between Harmon, New York, and Chicago, 928 miles (1,493km). The "E7s" averaged 28,954 miles in the month and the 4-8-4s 27,221. Average operating costs per mile were $1.11 for the "E7" and $1.22 for the 4-8-4. However, a succession of coal strikes and then some trouble with the alloy steel boilers of the "Niagaras" ensured that the NYC did not allow its lingering love of steam to interpret the results in favour of the 4-8-4s, but the tests were still encouraging to steam enthusiasts in showing how small was the improvement when the best of

steam locomotives, intensively used and adequately serviced, were replaced by diesels. But on most roads the margin was much wider, and there was a handsome saving from diesels, quite sufficient to offset the greater capital cost.

In 1953 the 1,125hp (840kW) 567B engine was available, and this was incorporated in the next series, the "E8". By this time most of the principal passenger services were dieselised, so the impact of the "E8" was less spectacular than that of the "E7". By the time the final version appeared, the "E9" with 1,200hp (900kW) 567C engines, the need for passenger diesels had almost been met, and only 144 units were sold between 1954 and 1963, compared with 457 "E8s".

In the 1960s the American passenger train declined rapidly in the face of air and coach competition, and many of the later "Es" had short lives, being traded in against the purchase of new general-purpose locomotives.

The "E" series instituted the general conversion of the American passenger train to diesel operation, and they eventually saw many of the most famous trains out. In their heyday the US had an undisputed world lead in passenger train speeds. Geared for up to 117mph (188km/h), (although few roads operated them above 100mph (160km/h), the "Es" were the fastest diesel locomotives in the world, and yet their construction was rugged and straightforward. In particular they had nose-suspended traction motors, which the heavy North American rails with their close-spaced sleepers seemed able to accept without distress.

In 1980 Amtrak operated the last run of "E" locomotives in multiple and the ranks were very thin by this time. Fortunately the body of the first B&O unit is preserved.

EMD "F" Series B₀-B₀

Type: All-purpose diesel-electric locomotive, "A" units with cab, "B" units without.
Gauge: 4ft 8½in (1,435mm).
Propulsion : One EMD 5,67B 1,500hp (1,120kW) 16-cylinder pressure-charged two-stroke Vee engine and generator supplying current to four nose-suspended traction motors geared to the axles.
Weight: 230,000lb (104.4t) (minimum without train heating steam generator).
Max. axleload: 57,500lb (26.1t).
Overall length*: "A" 50ft 8in (15,443mm), "B" 50ft 0in (15,240mm).
Tractive effort: 57,500lb (256kN).
Max. speed: Between 50mph (80km/h) and 120mph (164km/h) according to which of eight possible gear ratios fitted.

*Dimensions refer to the "F3" variant of 1946

The railway locomotive leads a rugged existence, and only the fittest survive. Evolution has thus tended to move in moderate steps, and few successful developments have been sufficiently dramatic to merit the term "revolutionary". One such step was the pioneer four-unit freight diesel, No. 103, produced by the Electro-Motive Division of General Motors in 1939. When that unit embarked on a 83,764-mile (134,780km) demonstration tour on 20 major American railroads, few people, other than EMD's Chief Engineer Richard M. Dilworth, even imagined that it would be possible for the country's railroads to be paying their last respects to steam only 20 years later.

By 1939 EMD had some six years' experience of powering high-speed passenger trains by diesel locomotives tailored to suit the customer's requirements. Their

Below: *A pair of F3s supplied to the Baltimore & Ohio. The left-hand unit is a "cab" or "A" unit, while the right-hand unit has no driving car and is designated "B" or "Booster".*

ability to outrun the best steam locomotives had gained them acceptance in many parts of the country, but this was a specialised activity, and even the most diesel-minded motive power officer did not regard the diesel as an alternative to the ten, twelve or sixteen coupled steam locomotive for the heavy grind of freight haulage.

Dilworth had faith in the diesel, and his company shared his faith to the tune of a four-unit demonstrator weighing 912,000lb (414t) and 193ft (58,830mm) in length. Most of the passenger diesels built so far incorporated the light-weight Winton 201 engine, which EMD had acquired, but in 1938 EMD produced its own 567 series of two-stroke Vee engines (numbered from the cubic capacity of the cylinder in cubic inches). The 16-cylinder version was rated at 1,350hp (1,010kW), and this fitted conveniently into a four-axle Bo-Bo layout, with the whole weight thus available for adhesion.

Two such units were permanently coupled, an "A" unit with cab and a "B" or booster unit without; two of these pairs were coupled back-to-back by normal couplings. Multiple-unit control enabled one engineer to control all four units, but they could easily

be separated into pairs, or, with a little more work, into 1 + 3. Dilworth reckoned that a 2,700hp pair was the equal of a typical steam 2-8-2 or 2-10-2, and that the full 5,400hp (4,030kW) set could equal any of the largest articulated steam engines. As the combined starting tractive effort of his four units was almost double that of the largest steam engine, his claim had some substance. The demonstrators were geared for a maximum of 75mph (120km/h) but could be re-geared for 102mph (164km/h), producing a true mixed-traffic locomotive.

The units were built on the "carbody" principle, that is, the bodyshell was stressed and formed part of the load-bearing structure of the locomotive. The smooth streamlined casing was in sharp contrast to the Christmas-tree appearance of most large American steam engines, festooned as they were with gadgets. But this was one of the revolutionary ideas demonstrated by No. 103. Bright liveries on the passenger stream-liners had attracted great publicity; now there was the possibility of giving the freight locomotive a similar image.

Despite the scepticism of steam locomotive engineers, 20 railroads

Above: *A single "F" cab unit belonging to the Denver & Rio Grande Western Railroad at the head of a short and now defunct three-car train on the D&RGW's Moffatt Tunnel route.*

spread over 35 states responded to EMD's invitation to give No. 103 a trial, and everywhere it went it improved on the best steam performance by a handsome margin. From sea level to 10,240ft (3,120m), from 40°F below zero (−40°C) to 115°F (46°C), the story was the same. Typical figures were an average speed of 26mph (42km/h) over 98 miles (158km) of 1-in-250 grade with 5,400t, compared with 10mph (16km/h) by a modern 4-6-6-4, or an increase of load from 3,800t with a 2-8-4 to 5,100t. The booster units were equipped with steam generators for train heating, and this enabled No. 103 to show its paces on passenger trains. The impression it made on motive power men was profound.

Not least amongst the startling qualities of No. 103 was its reliability. Throughout the 11-month tour no failure occurred, and even when allowance is made for the close attention given by accompanying EMD staff, this was a remarkable achievement.

Production locomotives, designated "FT", followed closely on the heels of the demonstrator, and orders were soon received from all parts of the country. EMD's La Grange Works was tooled-up for quantity production, and over a period of six years 1,096 "FT" units were built, Santa Fe being the biggest customer with 320 units. The War Production Board was sufficiently impressed by the contribution which these locomotives could make to the war effort to allow production to continue with only a short break, despite the use of scarce alloys.

By the end of the war the freight diesel was fully accepted on many railroads, and total dieselisation was already in the minds of some motive power chiefs. The first post-war development was production of the 567B engine rated at 1,500hp (1,120kW) to replace the 1,350hp 567A model. After 104 interim units designated "F2", there came a four-unit demonstrator of the "F3" model, with a larger generator to suit the 1,500hp engine, and a number of other improvements based on six years' experience with the "FTs". Amongst these were automatically-operated cooling fans; the fans fitted to the "FTs" were mechanically-driven through clutches, and had manually-worked shutters. The fireman had a frantic rush to de-clutch the fans and close the shutters when the engine was shut down, particularly in severe cold when the radiators would freeze very quickly.

EMD proclaimed the "F3" as "the widest range locomotive in history", and the railroads seemed to agree, for new sales records were set with a total of 1,807 units sold in little more than two years up to 1949. Railroads took advantage of the scope which the smooth curved shape offered for imaginative colour schemes, and an EMD pamphlet showed 40 different liveries in which these locomotives had been supplied.

Simplicity of maintenance, and improvements in the engine to reduce fuel consumption, were two of EMD's claims for the "F3", and these same claims were re-

peated for the next model, the "F7", launched in 1949. The main change from the "F3" was in the traction motors and other electrical equipment. With the same engine power, the new motors enabled 25 per cent more load to be hauled up heavy grades. The model was offered with the usual options, including eight different gear ratios.

The "F7" proved to be a best-seller; 49 US roads bought 3,681 "F7s" and 301 "FP7s", the version with train-heating boiler, whilst Canada and Mexico took 238 and 84 respectively. They handled every type of traffic from the fastest passenger trains to the heaviest freight. Measured by sales, the "F7" was the most successful carbody diesel ever. "F7" production ended in 1953, to be replaced by the "F9". The main change was the 567C engine of 1,750hp (1,305kW). By this time the US market for carbody diesels was drying up, as "hood" units gained popularity, and only 175 "F9s" were built over a

Right: *F cab and booster units of the Canadian Pacific Railway on a passenger train at London, Ontario, in January 1963.*

period of three years.

By the 1960s steam had been replaced totally, and diesel manufacturers were now selling diesels to replace diesels. Trading-in of old models became popular, and trucks in particular could be re-used. Many "Fs" were replaced in this way as the more powerful hood units became more popular, and the decline of passenger traffic helped the process. Nevertheless many units of the "F" series were still to be found at work in 1982, and the Canadian locomotives, in particular, could

Above; *A Gulf, Mobile & Ohio Railroad train leaves Chicago behind a single F unit.*

still be seen on important passenger trains.

The "F" series, more than any other model, showed that improvements in performance and economies in operation could be achieved in all types of traffic by dieselisation, despite the high initial cost compared with steam, and despite uncertainties about the life which could be expected from a diesel locomotive.

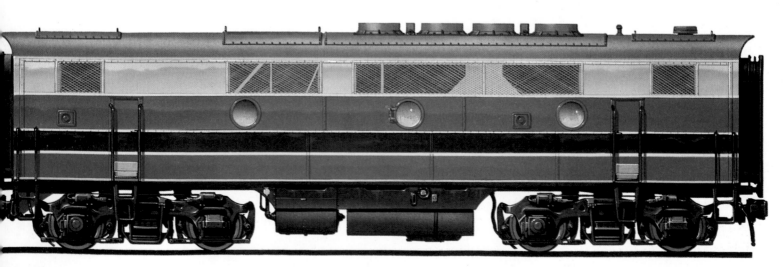

Class 1020 C₀-C₀

Type: Electric locomotive for heavy freight traffic.
Gauge: 4ft 8½in (1,435mm).
Propulsion: Alternating current at 15,000V 16⅔Hz fed by overhead catenary and step-down transformer to six 725hp (540kW) nose-suspended traction motors driving to the axles via resilient gearing.
Weight: 264,480lb (120t).
Max. axleload: 44,080lb (20t).
Overall length: 61ft 0in (18,600mm).
Tractive effort: 65,300lb (290kN).
Max. speed: 56mph (90km/h).

These handsome locomotives, with lines which are a pleasant change from the plain box structures normal amongst today's locomotives, were built in large numbers during and after World War II both in Austria and in Germany, while the former country was occupied by the latter. They were a development of the earlier Ger-man Class "E93" (now Class "193"). Of 202 constructed, 47 are in service in Austria, two were destroyed in the war and of the remainder some still run in West Germany and a few in East Germany, where they are now designated classes "194" and "254" respectively.

The layout is not strictly that of a normal bogie locomotive, for the

Right: Austrian Federal Railways No. 1020.41 in original colours at St. Auton on June 2, 1967.

CC1 C₀-C₀

Type: Electric mixed-traffic locomotive.
Gauge: 4ft 8½in (1,435mm).
Propulsion: Direct current at 660V fed via third-rail or alternatively by an overhead wire to a motor-generator set with flywheel which supplies current to six nose-suspended traction motors each geared to an axle.
Weight: 222,990lb (101.2t).
Max. axleload: 37,296lb (16.9t).
Overall length: 56ft 9in (17,297mm).
Tractive effort: 45,000lb (200kN).
Max. speed: 75mph (120km/h).

From 1932 onwards the Southern Railway extended its third-rail suburban network to main lines, operating passenger services by electric multiple-units. Freight traffic on the SR was in a minority, and the Operating Department was content for freight services, many of which ran at night, to be worked by steam engines which were employed on the remaining non-electrified lines. However, Alfred Raworth, the Chief Electrical Engineer, was anxious to build an electric freight locomotive, and in 1937 he obtained authority to build three. The mechanical parts of all the company's locomotives were the responsiblity of the Chief Mechanical Engineer, and when O. V. S. Bulleid joined the company as CME in 1938, he became involved in the project.

Bulleid argued that the high cost of an electric locomotive could only be justified if it worked passenger trains by day and freight trains by night, and that it had a capacity to work the heaviest passenger and freight trains which the company could envisage. The specification of the engines was thus fixed at the haulage of passenger trains of 475 tons (523 US tons) at 75mph (120km/h) and freight trains of 1,000 tons (1,100 US tons) at 40mph (64km/h). As at this time most British freight trains had no continuous brakes, the engines must be able to stop these trains of 1,000 tons by the engine brakes, aided modestly by the guard's brake van. To achieve this level of braking required an adhesive weight of 100 tons, for which six axles would be needed, giving the wheel arrangement Co-Co.

Above: *British Railways' electric locomotive No. 20001 (ex-Southern Railway CC1) brings HM The Queen from Victoria to Tattenham Corner Station for the races on Derby day.*

couplings and buffers are mounted on the two chassis units, while the cab and main equipment compartment is suspended between them in the manner of a Beyer Garratt steam locomotive, the heavy low-frequency transformer being housed therein. The class is equipped with rheostatic braking and this, combined with the high tractive

Left: *Twenty-four driving wheels! OBB Class 1020 (leading) and Class 1110 Co-Co locomotives.*

effort and short rigid wheelbase, makes them very suitable for general service over the heavy grades and sharp curves of Austria's mountain routes. The very orthodox nature of their design and construction has led to this very impressive longevity for, although no longer pressed into service on prime express train work, most of the Austrian examples anyway are still occupied on the heavy freights for which they were designed.

In West Germany, a start was at one time made on re-equipping the Class "194s" so as to enhance their power output, but only a few examples were treated. Apparently the richer nation preferred the extravagant and dubiously economic alternative of scrapping and building again from new.

Left: *Austrian Federal Railways Class 1020 electric locomotive, originally German State Railway Class E94.*

The performance required of the locomotives was not exceptional, but there was a further requirement which was more difficult. Gaps in the third rail could leave even a three-car set momentarily without power. It was therefore essential that the electric locomotives should be able to start a 1,000 ton (1,100 US tons) train and travel a short distance with it, if the engine should happen to stop on a gap in the third rail. It was equally important that when the locomotive passed over a gap in the third rail while pulling hard, there should not be a sudden loss of tractive effort which could cause dangerous jerking of loose-coupled freight wagons. This was a novel problem and a novel solution was devised jointly by Raworth's staff and English Electric. It involved supplying the traction motors through a motor-generator set, one for each bogie, in which a dc generator fed from the third rail drove a 600V generator. The generator was connected in series with the third-rail supply, so that a total of 1,200V was

connected across the traction motors. The three conventional traction motors of each bogie were connected in series, so that each took 400V. On each motor-generator shaft was a flywheel weighing 1 ton.

When the engine lost the third-rail supply, the motor-generator continued to turn under the influence of the flywheel. The motor, deprived of its external supply, acted as a generator, and the generator proper continued as before. As the two were connected in series, the traction motors continued to receive a supply at 1,200V until the flywheel slowed down.

Control of the traction motor supply was effected by varying the field strength of the generator, and as the resistances concerned was small, it was possible for each of the 26 positions of the controller to be maintained indefinitely without heating problems (by contrast the contemporary LNER Bo-Bo 1,500V locomotives had only 10 running notches). However, the cost of these advan-

tages was that two heavy electrical machines were running whenever the engine was in use.

The mechanical construction of the locomotive was novel in that there were no pivots to the bogies. The underside of the body carried pads which rested on guides on the top of the bogies. The guides had lips shaped to a circle 9ft (2,743mm) in diameter, and these lips limited the relative movement of the body and bogie to rotation. The absence of pivots left a clear space for the traction motor of the middle bogie axle. All flexibility in the suspension was in the springs of the axle-boxes. This arrangement appeared to violate the rules for the springing of bogie locomotives, but it proved sufficiently acceptable to be used later on 396 diesel-electric locomotives for the SR and BR.

The first locomotive No. CC1, was completed in 1941 and proved that it fulfilled the specification. After testing, it entered freight service, and in February 1942 it spent two weeks hauling

an express from London to Portsmouth in substitution for an emu. This was notable as the first time in Britain that a main-line express had been hauled by an electric locomotive.

After the war the locomotives, now two in number, found a niche in working the London to Newhaven boat trains, which had locomotive-hauled coaches on an electrified line otherwise worked by emus. In 1948 they were joined by a third locomotive, and from then until 1969 they divided their work between the boat trains, special passenger trains and freight services. Their BR numbers were 20001-3. By 1969, due to the heavy fall in freight traffic, the SR had a surplus of motive power, so the "flywheel" engines were withdrawn, and their duties taken over by more flexible electro-diesels.

In the meantime BR had built 24 Bo-Bo locomotives with a much simplified version of the flywheel control for the Southern Region, but these also succumbed to electro-diesels after a short life.

Class Ae 4/4 B₀-B

Switzerland:
Berne-Lötschberg-Simplon Railway (BLS), 1944

Type: Electric mixed-traffic mountain locomotive.
Gauge: 4ft 8½in (1,435mm).
Propulsion: Single-phase low-frequency alternating current at 15,000V $16\tfrac{2}{3}$Hz fed via overhead catenary to four 1,000hp (746kW) traction motors driving the axles through a flexible system of discs, shafts and gears.
Weight: 176,320lb (80t).
Max. axleload: 44,080lb (20t).
Overall length: 51ft 2in (15,600mm).
Tractive effort: 52,900lb (236kN).
Max. speed: 78mph (125km/h).

A great leap forward in the art of locomotive building came in 1944 when this small but progressive Swiss railway put into service a deceptively ordinary-looking double-bogie locomotive. The amazing thing was that 4,000hp was offered, when more typically a locomotive of similar size and configuration would offer only half as much.

The early BLS rod-drive locomotives of Class "Be 5/7", built in 1913, have already been discussed. At 2,500hp (1,865kW) they were the most powerful in Europe and for a time handled adequately the heavy traffic on this exacting main line. In 1926 four new 1-Co-Co-1 locomotives (Class "Be 6/8")

Below: *Berne-Lötschberg-Simplon electric locomotive of Class Ae 4/4, which introduced the concept of 1,000hp per axle.*

raised the power available to 4,500hp (3,360kW) but these engines, although effective, had a heavy, complex and consequently expensive basic layout.

The idea that even the most important and powerful locomotives should have their wheels arranged in two bogies, just like other vehicles on a railway, was then quite a new one, but many problems had first to be solved. Not least was that of weight in order to keep the axleload down to 20t. A more complex main transformer with a core star-shaped in plan led to a fundamental reduction in the weight of this item (always critical when low frequency current was involved) from 16t to 9½t. Light alloys were also used extensively in the all-welded body.

Reduction of weight brings in problems of providing adequate

Above: *Simple-looking, but complex in reality, the Ae 4/4 Bo-Bo electric locomotive was introduced in 1944.*

adhesion, and this was tackled by a combination of mechanical and electrical measures. The voltage was regulated on the high-tension side of the transformer and provided for a much larger number of steps (28) than usual so that slipping of the wheels is less likely to be initiated by a move from one control notch to the next. At the same time the bogies are arranged so that the connection with the body is as near to the ground as possible, so as to minimise transfer of weight from the front wheels of each bogie to the rear when pulling. Mechanical linkages also minimise transfer of weight from the front bogie to the rear and, should slipping occur, an anti-

wheelspin brake comes into play. The ancient remedy of sanding gear is also provided. Coming downhill, there is automatic regulation of brake force according to speed to prevent skidding of the wheels when moving slowly, as well as electrical rheostatic (dynamic) braking. Full regenerative braking was rejected because of the extra weight and maintenance involved; by anyone else's standards, the "Ae 4/4s" were already too complex.

Perhaps it says enough to remark that nowadays the majority of high-powered electric (and for that matter diesel-electric) locomotives follow the layout of these path-finding machines. The original four (Nos. 251 to 254) had become eight by 1955; three double units classified "Ae 8/8", which were two "Ae 4/4s" permanently coupled (Nos. 271 to 273), came next, following which in the late-1960s Nos. 253 to 256 were rebuilt to make two further double units (Nos. 274 and 275). The remaining "Ae 4/4s" were equipped for working in multiple, or as push-pull units controlled from a remote driving cab. This was no reflection of any inadequacy on the part of these excellent locomotives, but rather was due to an upsurge in traffic on the Lötschberg route.

A single "Ae 4/4" was rostered to haul 400t (440 US tons) up the 1-in-37 (2.7 per cent) gradients, but this was by no means the end of the matter. A further series, which could handle 630t (693 US tons) on the same climb, was

ordered from 1964 onwards, later reclassified "Re 4/4" on account of a high maximum speed. The main difference was abandonment of the single-phase low-frequency ac traction motors so typical of Swiss practice, and their replacement by dc motors fed via solid-state rectifiers. This arrangement is well known for its built-in anti-slipping control but other measures, including water ballast which can be pumped from one end of the locomotive to the other, have enabled the maximum traction effort to be increased by 33 per cent and power output by 65 per cent as between the old and the new designs. There are now a total of 35 examples of the later class.

Incidentally, the Swiss use their own locomotive classification system, where the figures show the number of driving axles/total number of axles. The capital letter indicates the permissible speed range or usage, while the small letter 'e' indicates an electric locomotive.

Left: *A Berne-Lötschberg-Simplon express for Berne awaits departure from Brig, at the southern end of the Lötschberg railway.*

Below: *A development of the Class Ae 4/4 was this Re 4/4, depicted with a heavy train at Kandersteg in September 1980.*

PA Series A1A-A1A

United States: American Locomotive Company (Alco), 1946

Type: Diesel-electric express passenger locomotive; "A" units with cab, "B" units without.
Gauge: 4ft 8½in (1,435mm).
Propulsion: One Alco 244 2,000hp (1,490kW) 16-cylinder turbocharged four-stroke Vee engine and gearbox, supplying four nose-suspended traction motors geared to the end axles of the bogies.
Weight: 204,000lb (92.6t) adhesive, 306,000lb (138.8t) total.
Max. axleload: 51,000lb (23.1t).
Overall length: "A" unit 65ft 8in (20,015mm), "B" unit 63ft 6in (19,350mm).
Tractive effort: 51,000lb (227kN).
Max. speed: 80mph (129km/h), 90mph (145km/h), 100mph (160km/h), or 117mph (188km/h) according to gear ratio fitted.

The American Locomotive Company was mainly a builder of steam locomotives until the end of World War II, but it had already achieved considerable success with diesel shunters (switchers), and in 1940 had produced a 2,000hp (1,490kW) twin-engine passenger locomotive, of which 78 were built before construction ceased during the war. In the following year Alco produced a 1,500hp (1,120kW) road-switcher, but the railroads were not yet accustomed to the idea of a locomotive which could combine two functions. All these locomotives had engines made by specialist firms, but in 1944 Alco produced its own engine, designated the 244, the last two digits indicating the year in which it first ran. It was a turbocharged Vee engine made in two versions, one with 12-cylinders producing 1,500hp (1,200kW) and the other 16 cylinders giving 2,000hp (1,490kW).

With these two engines Alco launched three models in 1945, a 1,500hp "Bo-Bo combination switching locomotive" (in the terminology of the day), a 1,500hp road freight locomotive, and a 2,000hp A1A-A1A passenger locomotive. The first of these was a hood unit, and the others were "cab" or "carbody" units. All three had GE electrical equipment and were marketed as Alco-GE brand. Great emphasis was laid on the fact that 98 per cent of the electrical parts and 96 per cent of the mechanical parts were interchangeable between the three types.

The freight locomotives, the "FA" cab units and the "FB" booster units—note that "cab" is used to denote a locomotive with a driver's (engineer's) cab as well as any locomotive with a totally enclosed body—appeared at the end of 1945, and the passenger locomotives, the "PA" and "PB" series, in September 1946. With high cab windows and a projecting bonnet, both types bore a resemblance to existing EMD and Baldwin designs, but the front and the roof were flatter. The bonnet of the "PA" was quite distinctive. The first units were for the Sante Fe and were finished in a remarkable livery of red, orange and silver, which earned them the nickname of "warbonnets". The three-axle trucks were unusually long, and these combined with the long bonnets to give an appearance of great length, although in fact the locomotives were 5ft (1,525mm) shorter than the corresponding EMD "E" type.

Over the next three years a total of 170 A units and 40 B units were sold, designated "PA1" and "PB1". There was then a pause in production until the "PA2" and "PB2" series appeared in 1950 with the engine uprated to 2,250hp (1,680kW). Finally there came the third version, "PA3" and "PB3", also with the 2,250hp engine, but with a number of detail changes. The last of these was built in 1953, and although a 2,400hp (1,790kW) version was offered, none was built. The day of the carbody was over, and passenger trains were in decline. There was also an export model, which looked very similar but was usually a Co-Co. Some of these were built by Alco licencees in the country concerned.

Above: *American Locomotive Co's PA-series diesel-electric locomotive. A PA cab unit is followed by a PB booster.*

Below: *Atchison, Topeka & Sante Fe A1A-A1A PA-series diesel-electric locomotive No. 51 supplied by the American Locomotive Co. in 1946.*

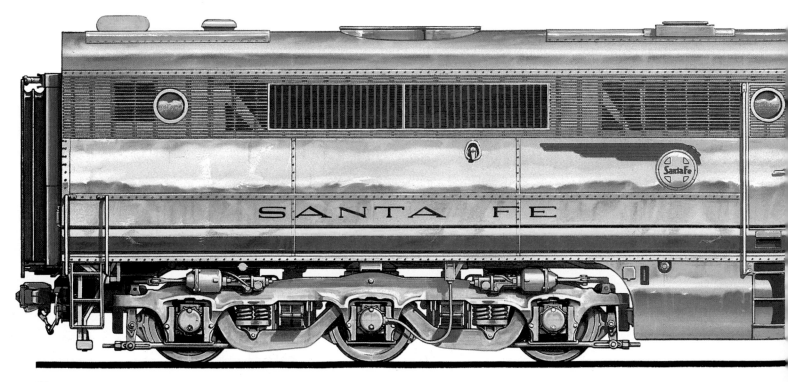

The 244 engine had a number of troubles, particularly the 2,000hp version when used intensively on long-distance passenger trains. The "PA" locomotives had several protective devices to prevent damage to the electrical equipment, and at times these were over-protective, giving false warnings. Compared with their EMD competitors, the Alco "PAs" had the simplicity of one engine, whereas the EMD passenger units had two, but the "PAs" never equalled the reliability of the EMD locomotives. Although 16 roads bought them, and used them on the best passenger trains, they were usually outnumbered by EMD units. As passenger traffic declined, the "PAs" were either withdrawn from service or transferred to freight work, often with altered gear ratios. The large GE traction motors could take a heavy overload, and were well suited to freight work. A few "PAs" were re-engined with EMD 1,750hp (1,305kW) engines, but none received the later Alco 251 engine.

The last four "PAs" ended their days in Mexico, having been leased by the Delaware & Hudson

Above: *A 6,000hp three-unit diesel-electric locomotive formed of Alco PA, PB and PA units in Cajon Pass, California.*

to the National Railways (NdeM) in 1978. The "FA" freight series, by contrast, of which a total of 1,072 were built, were still active in the 1980s in the United States, Canada and Mexico.

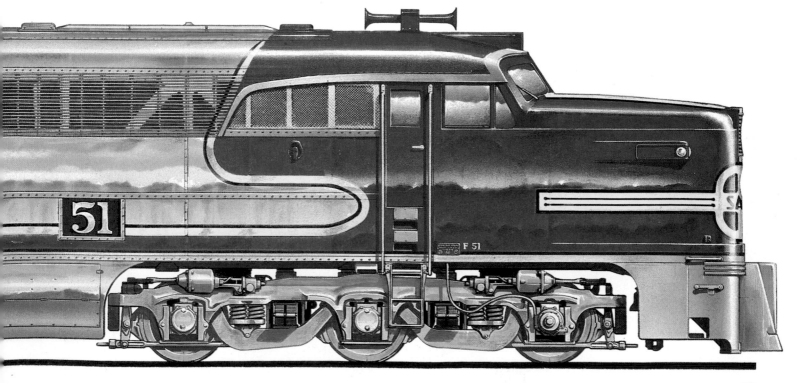

No. 10000 Co-Co

Great Britain:
London Midland & Scottish Railway (LMS), 1947

Type: Mixed traffic diesel-electric locomotive.

Gauge: 4ft 8½in (1,435mm).

Propulsion: English Electric 1,600hp (1,200kW) Type 16SVT V-16 turbocharged diesel engine and generator supplying current to six nose-suspended tractiom motors geared to the axles.

Weight: 285,936lb (129.4t).

Max. axleload: 47,824lb (21.7t).

Overall length: 61ft 2in (18,644mm).

Tractive effort: 41,400lb (184kN).

Max. speed: 90mph (144km/h).

The LMS was the first British railway to put diesel locomotives into regular service. It first experimented with diesel shunters in 1932, and by World War II it had adopted 350hp six-coupled machines as standard for its large marshalling yards. However, the 1930s were the high noon of steam in Britain, and there was no interest in main-line diesels. In 1942 there was a change on the LMS; Sir William Stanier was succeeded as Chief Mechanical Engineer by C. E. Fairburn, who had joined the LMS in 1934 as Chief Electrical Engineer after years of experience of electric and diesel traction with English Electric. Under wartime conditions, Fairburn could do no more than arouse interest in the extension of diesel traction, but after his early death his successor, H. G. Ivatt, had the opportunity to develop this interest when English Electric produced a 1,600hp engine, by far the largest diesel

Below: *London Midland & Scottish Railway No. 10000 as completed at Derby Works shortly before the LMS Company became nationalised.*

Above: *Ex-LMS Co-Co diesel-electric locomotive No. 10000 at work on the Southern Region with an up express at Basingstoke in May 1953.*

engine for rail traction thus far produced in Britain.

Ivatt was interested in innovation, and he was already planning various experiments with steam traction. Among these was construction of two Pacific locomotives which would differ from their predecessors in various details, the changes being directed at reducing maintenance and increasing the annual mileage. He therefore planned to build two diesel-electric locomotives which could be compared with the Pacifics. As the Pacifics could develop up to 2,500hp at the drawbar, twin diesel locomotives of 1,600hp would be needed to make a fair comparison.

There followed a remarkable period of intense activity at Derby Works, in which the first of the locomotives was built in six months. The reason for the hurry was that the LMS was to disappear into the new British Railways at the end of 1947, and Ivatt was determined that the first diesel should legitimately carry the initials "LMS", he having no enthusiasm for nationalisation. The second locomotive followed eight months later when Derby had made up the arrears of other work!

Several layouts were considered, but when English Electric decreed that six traction motors would be needed, the wheel arrangement Co-Co was adopted. The limited height of the British

loading gauge presented problems which do not arise in other countries, and a novel arrangement was devised to support the pivot of the bogie without it fouling the traction motor of the middle axle. The weight of the body was distributed from a pivot at the centre of an H-shaped frame to four nests of springs at the corner of the H.

It was felt that former steam drivers would be disturbed by the sight of sleepers passing close under them, so the cabs were placed away from the ends, with the view of track partly blocked by a "nose". The resultant styling showed a marked similarity to contemporary EMD styling.

For pioneer locomotives, designed by a steam-orientated staff, Nos. 10000-1 were remarkably successful. But as BR policy was to retain steam traction until electrification, there was little interest in the main-line diesels for some years, and the close comparison with the Pacifics which Ivatt envisaged was never made. Furthermore, the sheer length of the twin unit was a disadvantage on a railway on which some of the longest trains already strained the capacity of platforms at terminal stations. Nevertheless, they demonstrated that 3,200hp of diesel could improve significantly on the work of a single Pacific, and that, barring failures, the diesels could amass tremendous mileages. Sadly, maintained in dirty steam locomotive depots and requiring special attention at a time of acute labour shortage on the railways, the diesels spent a lot of time out of action.

In 1953 they were borrowed by the Southern Region, which had high hopes of alleviating some of its maintenance problems with the unconventional Bulleid Pacifics by the use of its own three diesel locomotives plus the LMS pair. In due course enthusiasm on this region also declined in the face of maintenance problems with the diesels, and all five engines then went to the London Midland Region for the remainder of their lives. Again their fortunes fluctuated. At times they worked the "Royal Scot" and sleeping car trains as a pair, and services from London to Birmingham and Manchester working singly, but they were dogged by heating boiler troubles, and eventually they were confined to freight trains during the train heating season.

In 1955 there was a change of policy on BR, and preparations began for a major conversion to diesel traction. Although the pioneer locomotives continued to yield valuable information for future development, their frequent visits to Derby Works became an increasing nuisance as new diesels were built in quantity, and after long periods out of use they were withdrawn from stock in 1963 and 1966 respectively. Sadly the historical significance of No. 10000 was ignored, and nothing survived of the first main-line diesel to be built or owned by a British railway.

Above: *Just out of the box! No. 10000 at Derby, December 1947.*

Below: *3,200hp for the "Royal Scot"! Nos. 10000 and 10001 in double harness make easy work of a 13-car train on the famous ascent to Shap Summit.*

M-1 2-1 C₀-1-C₀ B₀

Type: Steam turbo-electric express passenger locomotive.
Gauge: 4ft 8½in (1,435mm).
Propulsion: Coal-fired fire-tube boiler supplying steam at 310psi (21.8kg/cm²) to a 6,000hp (4,475kW) turbine coupled to two generators, providing current for eight axle-hung motors.
Weight: 508,032lb (230.5t) adhesive, 1,233,970lb (560t) total*.
Max. axleload: 63,475lb (28.8t).
Tractive effort: 98,000lb (436kN).

Overall length: 154ft 1in (46,965mm).
Max. speed: 100mph (160km/h).
*Including tender

Almost since its earliest constituent, the James River Company, got its charter and had George Washington himself as President, the Chessie (as the Chesapeake & Ohio RR has long been affectionately known) has had coal for its life-blood. Small wonder then that it resisted a change to diesel oil as a fuel.

Most electric current is genera-

ted by steam-driven turbines and in 1945 there seemed no good reason why locomotives should not with advantage be powered that way. Accordingly, in that year Chessie ordered from Westinghouse Electric and the Baldwin Locomotive Works, three of what were to become the heaviest and largest steam locomotives ever built.

The intention was to use the turbines on a proposed high-speed streamliner to run between Washington and Cincinnati. Mountainous terrain en route gave advantages to a locomotive with a

high proportion of its axles powered and this could be arranged to order on any locomotive with electric transmission. Incidentally, the driven axles on the "M-1s" were not the obvious ones; three axles out of the four on each of the central rigid trucks, plus both axles of the rear guiding truck, were the ones motored. The locomotive-type boiler with a grate area of 112sq ft (10.4m²) was placed so that the firebox was at the leading end, the opposite of normal practice, while right at the front of the engine was a bunker holding some 27t of coal. The

W1 B₀-D₀-D₀-B₀

Type: Mixed-traffic electric locomotive for mountain grades.
Gauge: 4ft 8½in (1,435mm).
Propulsion: Alternating current at 11,500V 25Hz, fed via overhead catenary to two motor-generator sets supplying direct current to twelve 275hp (205kW) nose-suspended traction motors geared to the axles.
Weight: 527,000lb (239t).
Max. axleload: 43,917lb (20t).
Overall length: 101ft 0in (30,785mm).
Tractive effort: 180,000lb (900kN).
Max. speed: 65mph (104km/h).

The fourth great transcontinental railroad to reach the West Coast of the USA was the Great Northern Railway, built by famed railroad tycoon James J. Hill. The "Big G" crossed the Cascade mountains beneath the Stevens Pass, named after GN's Chief Engineer. After seven years of trouble with a temporary alignment involving 4 per cent grades, the first 2.6 mile (4.2km) Cascade tunnel opened in 1900. In 1909, working through the tunnel was electrified on the three-phase system, the only example in North America. In 1927, three-phase was abandoned and single-phase electrification installed; this time the approach ramps were included, as well as a new Cascade tunnel, at 7.8 miles (12.5km) the longest railway tunnel in America, eliminating the most exposed part

Right: *Great Northern Railway Class W1 Bo-Do-Do-Bo electric locomotive. This machine had no fewer than 24 driving wheels.*

tender at the rear was for water only, no condenser being provided.

The "M-1s" were expensive to run and maintain, offering no serious competition to conventional steam, let alone diesel traction. All three were scrapped in the early 1950s after only a few years' service.

Right and below: *Class M-1 steam-turbine-electric locomotive built for the Chesapeake & Ohio Railroad Company in 1947. Three of these immense machines were built.*

of the route. The scheme covered 73 miles (117km) from Wenatchee to Skykomish, Washington State.

In its principles, this electrification was far ahead of its time, for the single-phase current was converted to dc for use in the traction motors of the locomotives. Of course, solid-state devices for this purpose were still in the future and rotary convertor sets, consisting of synchronous motors coupled to dc generators, had to be used. The technology had been placed in two locomotives constructed in of all places the Ford Motor Works, but equipped electrically by Westinghouse for use on a railroad (the Detroit, Toledo & Ironton) that Henry Ford owned. The GN electrification had four "Y1" 1-C-C-1s and twelve "Z1" 1-D-1s; the latter again heralded the future of US railroading by virtue of their multiple-unit capability. Put another way, they were building blocks from

which locomotives of any desired power could be assembled.

The final fling of this little system was purchase of the very large "W1" class, of which two examples were constructed by General Electric in 1947. Modest power, combined with the huge tractive effort possible with all axles motored, was appropriate to a locomotive confined to the mountains. They could be run in multiple both with each other and with the "Y1s" and "Z1s". As with all the GN electric fleet, regenerative braking of trains on the down grades could provide a proportion of the current needed for other trains climbing. The electrification was totally successful but even so, in 1956, after new ventilating equipment had been installed in the second Cascade tunnel, diesels took over. One "W1" was rebuilt as a gas-turbine locomotive for the Union Pacific Railroad, but all the others were scrapped.

Above: *Only two examples of these huge Class W1 electric locomotives were built in 1947. In spite of their vast size, the power output of 3,300hp was only very modest.*

Below: *A Class W1 electric locomotive draws a Great Northern Railway freight train out of the eastern portal of the Cascade tunnel in Washington State, north-western USA.*

No. 18000 A1A-A1A
Great Britain:
British Railways (BR), 1950

Type: Express passenger gas-turbine locomotive.
Gauge: 4ft 8½in (1,435mm).
Propulsion: Brown Boveri 2,500hp (1,865kW) gas turbine and generator feeding four 528hp (394kW) traction motors geared with flexible drive to the two outer axles of each bogie.
Weight: 174,000lb (79t) adhesive, 260,000lb (118t) total.
Max. axleload: 43,000lb (19.5t).
Overall length: 63ft 0in (19,202mm).
Tractive effort: 31,500lb (140kN).
Max. speed: 90mph (144km/h).

The aircraft gas turbine made a spectacular entry into the engineering world in the latter days of World War II, and after the war there were high hopes that this mechanically simple machine, with a very high power-to-weight ratio, could replace the more complex diesel engine in various applications. In fact, unostentatiously, development work on industrial gas turbines had been in progress for many years, and a gas-turbine electric locomotive was completed in Switzerland in 1940 by Brown Boveri and the Swiss Locomotive

Works (SLM). By the end of the war it had several years of successful running to its credit.

In Britain, after the war, the railways began to make fundamental studies of their future motive power policy, especially in the light of the rapid growth of diesel traction in the United States. The Great Western Railway, maintaining its tradition of being different from other railways, decided that the gas turbine offered the prospect of eventually supplanting the diesel engine, and that it would be worth moving directly to what

Above: *Swiss-built gas-turbine-electric locomotive Brown Boveri No. 18000 in service with an express.*

might be the ultimate motive power. The company therefore ordered a gas turbine electric locomotive from Metropolitan-Vickers, a firm with long experience of electric traction, but one which had also entered the field of aircraft gas turbines quite early. Metro-Vick was to design and build the locomotive, which was to burn diesel oil, and the cost

would be shared by the makers and customer.

The GWR technical staff then visited Switzerland to study the work done by Brown Boveri, and they were so impressed that the railway ordered a second gas turbine locomotive from Switzerland. It was to be closely based on the Swiss prototype, adapted to the British loading gauge, and designed to burn heavy Bunker C oil, except at starting when diesel oil would be used. Although ordered in 1946, the locomotive did not reach Britain until February 1950, by which time the former GWR had been the Western Region of British Railways for two years, and BR had adopted the policy of continuing to build steam locomotives until money was available for electrification.

The gas turbine was a 2,500hp unit driving a generator which supplied current to four traction motors. Each bogie had a carrying axle between the motored axles, giving the wheel arrangement A1A-A1A. A heat exchanger transferred part of the heat of the exhaust to the air moving between the compressor and the combustion chamber. Detail work was to Swiss standards, but the locomotive was equipped with a

---

RDC Single Railcar
USA:
The Budd Company (Budd), 1949

Type: Self-propelled diesel-mechanical railcar.
Gauge: 4ft 8½in (1,435mm).
Propulsion: Two General Motors Type 6-110, six-cylinder 275hp (205kW) diesel engines mounted beneath the floor, each driving the inside axle of one bogie, via longitudinal cardan shafts and gearing.
Weight: 63,564lb (29t) adhesive, 126,728lb (57.5t) total.
Max. axleload: 31,782lb (14.5t).
Overall length: 85ft 0in (25,910mm).
Max. speed: 85mph (136km/h).

After World War II, the Budd Company made a bid to extend their passenger car-building business using stainless steel construction which had started with the "Pioneer Zephyr" streamline train in 1934 as previously described. By 1948 Budd ranked second in the USA after Pullman and their plan now was to produce not long-distance streamliners but equipment for lesser services—'plug runs', in US vernacular.

To some extent this market had been explored in the 1920s with the gas-electric "doodlebugs" (qv), but something with a more up-to-date aura and still lower costs was needed. Budd's Vice-President for Engineering, Maj-Gen G.M. Barnes, had heard of a new V-6 diesel engine developed by General Motors for tank propulsion. Furthermore, he had had experience of torque-convertor transmission while in the army.

Combined with the weight-saving possibilities of Budd's normal stainless steel construction, a pair of these engines married to two such transmissions would give an excellent self-propelled passenger railcar with an ample power-to-weight ratio of some 8hp/ton. This would provide rapid acceleration from stops and give better than 40mph (64km/h) on a 1-in-50 (2 per cent) grade as well as a maximum speed as high as would be acceptable to the generality of railroad companies. Disc brakes with anti-slide control would also provide superior stopping power. Moreover, the proposal was to produce the car first, then demonstrate it to the railroads, rather than try to sell a mere idea.

Accordingly, in 1949 a demonstrator RDC (Rail Diesel Car) was built and it performed with impressive reliability. In fact, the Budd RDCs sold so well that by 1956

more than 300 were running. The largest fleet was that of Boston & Maine with 64, while RDCs provided a local train service over more than 924 miles (1,478km) from Salt Lake City to Oakland (San Francisco). The longest RDC service was that of the Trans-Australian Railway from Port Pirie to Kalgoorlie, 1,008 miles (1,613km). Varying amounts of passenger accommodation could be provided in proportion to mail/parcels space according to customers' requirements, while trains could be made up of any number of RDCs without reducing speed or acceleration, or needing extra crew.

Generally speaking, the Budd cars managed to save their own first cost in less than a year by reducing costs and improving revenue. However, many of these results were obtained against a background of compulsion to

Above: *A train of Canadian Pacific RDC railcars leaves Montreal in summer 1958.*

provide local passenger services. When this compulsion disappeared, as it had generally in the USA by the 1970s, then not even an RDC could be operated cheaply enough to run the service at a profit. Even so, a large number are still in service more than 33 years after the prototype took to the rails, notably in Canada. No doubt the ever-lasting stainless bodywork and the ease with which replacement engines can be fitted have contributed to this great span, but the main reason for such un-American longevity is the brilliance of execution of the original concept.

Right: *Chicago & North Western Railway RDC railcars at Chicago, summer 1952.*

train heating boiler and vacuum train brakes to meet British requirements. There was a 150hp diesel engine to supply the auxiliaries when the turbine was shut down, and this could move the locomotive at walking pace in depots. The maximum speed was 90mph (145km/h) and the unit was numbered 18000.

After three months of trial running No. 18000 went into service between London Paddington and Plymouth. Various troubles were encountered and overcome, but it was found that the traction motors were better suited to fast running than to the heavy gradi-

Below: *Brown Boveri 2,500hp gas-turbine-electric locomotive as ordered by the Great Western Railway but supplied to BR.*

ents of Devon, and the locomotive was therefore transferred to the Paddington to Bristol route. The combustion chamber proved to be the most troublesome part, as it distorted and cracked. Dynamometer car trials established the performance of the locomotive, and they revealed the fundamental weakness of the gas turbine in this application. The efficiency of the turbine fell off seriously at part-load, and a British locomotive of that period spent only a small proportion of its time working at full load. The overall consumption of oil by weight was therefore little better than the average consumption of coal by a "King" class 4-6-0, although at its best the turbine locomotive was more than twice as efficient as a "King".

The Metro-Vick locomotive, No.

18100, was delivered in December 1951. It had the Co-Co layout, and its gas turbine followed aircraft practice. There was no heat exchanger, which lowered the efficiency, but this was partly compensated by higher gas temperature which increased blade maintenance problems. The turbine output was 3,500hp and the starting tractive effort 60,000lb, which was the highest of any British passenger locomotive of the day, and enabled it to start 600t (672 US tons) on the steepest West Country gradient, compared with 290t (325 US tons) for No. 18000. In due course No. 18100 went into service on the West England route, where its high tractive effort could be utilised. However, as there was only one locomotive of each type, inevitably there was no possibility of recasting timetables to exploit them to the full.

As experience was gained on the Western Region with gas turbine locomotives, other regions of BR were gaining experience with diesel-electrics, and it was clear that both types required further development. However, the diesels had much better fuel consumption than the turbines, and were closer to the stage

when series-production could begin. When the GWR ordered the locomotives, the British government was sponsoring development work on a coal-burning gas turbine, but a few years later this was abandoned. So valuable imported oil would have had to be used in any production gas turbines—which was another factor weighing against turbine development.

When in 1955 BR finally embarked on a programme to eliminate steam traction, national enthusiasm for gas turbine had waned. The need for production prototypes was urgent, the capacity of the British rail traction industry was limited, and it was inevitable that diesels should prevail. No. 18000 remained in intermittent service for 10 years, and was nominally booked to work the 09.15 from Paddington to Bristol and the 16.15 back. It was withdrawn from service in December 1960, and after being stored for some years it was returned to the makers, who used it for test purposes. No. 18100 had a shorter career, and in 1958 it was converted to an ac electric locomotive for test work and crew training in preparation for the West Coast electrification.

EMD GP Series B₀-B₀

United States:
Electro-Motive Division, General Motors Corporation (EMD), 1949

Type: Diesel-electric road switcher locomotive.

Gauge: 4ft 8½in (1,435mm).

Propulsion : One EMD 567D2 2,000hp (1,490kW) 16-cylinder turbocharged two-stroke Vee engine and generator, supplying current to four nose-suspended traction motors geared to the axles.

Weight: 244,000lb (108.9t) to 260,000lb (116.0t) according to fittings.

Max. axleload: 61,000lb (27.2t) to 65,000lb (29.0t) according to fittings.

Overall length*: 56ft 0in (17,120mm)*.

Tractive effort: 61,000lb (271kN) to 65,000lb (289kN) according to weight.

Max. speed: 65mph (105km/h), 71mph (114km/h), 77mph (124km/h), 83mph (134km/h) or 89mph (143km/h) according to gear ratio fitted.

*Dimensions refer to the GP20 variant of 1959

For the post-war boom in diesel sales EMD offered a range of models based on three main series. First the "E" series of A1A+A1A express passenger locomotives, secondly the "F" series of Bo-Bo locomotives for freight work, but with optional gear ratios covering passenger work to all but the highest speeds, and thirdly a number of switchers (shunters) and transfer locomotives for work within and between marshalling yards. There was an important difference between the switchers and the other models. In the switchers the structural strength was in the underframe, on which

Right: The GP 38-2 standard road-switcher 2,000hp diesel electric locomotive as supplied by General Motors (Canada) for the Canadian Pacific rail system.

rested the engine, generator and other equipment. The casing or "hood" was purely protective and had no structural strength. The "E" and "F" series, on the other hand, had load-bearing bodies, or "carbodies", which provided an "engine-room" in which maintenance work could be carried out whilst the train was in motion, and which were more satisfactory aesthetically than a hood.

With these models EMD captured about 70 per cent of the North American market. Its ability to do so stemmed from a combination of quality of performance and reliability in the locomotive, low maintenance costs, which were helped by the large number of parts which were common to the different types, and competitive prices made possible by assembly line methods of manufacture. Full benefit of assembly line methods could only be achieved by limiting the number of variants offered to

Above: *General Motors GP9 1,750hp road-switcher unit belonging to the Chesapeake & Ohio Railroad Company.*

customers, and this, in turn, helped EMD's competitors to pick on omissions from, or weaknesses in, the EMD range by which to hold on to a share of the market. At first EMD's main theme in its diesel sales talk was the benefit accruing from replacing steam by diesel traction, but as its competitors achieved modest success in finding gaps in the EMD range, more and more was that firm concerned with proclaiming the superiority of its products over those of its competitors.

To achieve this superiority some changes were made in the range, of which the most important originated in customer enquiries received before the war for a locomotive which was primarily a switcher, but which could also

haul branch line trains, local freights and even local passenger trains. To meet this need a small number of locomotives were built with switcher bodies, elongated to house a steam generator, and mounted on trucks (bogies) of the "F" series; these were "road switchers". Construction was resumed after the war, still on a small scale, and with the design adapted to meet individual customer's requirements.

By 1948 EMD's competitors, particularly Alco, were achieving success with a general purpose hood unit for branch line work. For this application, ability to gain access to the working parts was more important than protection for technicians to work on the equipment on the road, and the hoods also gave the enginemen a much wider field of view. In 1948, therefore, EMD offered a branch line diesel, designated "BL", incorporating the 1,500hp (1,120kW) 567B engine, and other equipment including traction motors from the "F" series. These were accommodated in a small semi-streamlined casing, whose main advantage compared with a carbody was the improved view from the cab. There was, however, a serious snag—the "BL" was too expensive.

EMD then designed a true hood unit for general purpose duties, designated "GP". Richard Dilworth, EMD's Chief Engineer, said that his aim was to produce a locomotive that was so ugly that railroads would be glad to send it to the remotest corners of the system (where a market for diesels to replace steam still existed!), and to make it so simple that the

price would be materially below standard freight locomotives.

Although the "GP" was offered as a radically new design, many parts were common to the contemporary "F7" series. The power plant was the classic 567 engine, which like all EMD engines was a two-stroke Vee design; this was simpler than a four-stroke but slightly less efficient. Much development work was devoted over the years to improving the efficiency of the EMD engines to meet the competiton of four-stroke engines. The trucks were of the Blomberg type, a fairly simple design with swing-link bolsters, which were introduced in the "FT" series in 1939 and are still, with changes in the springing system, standard in EMD Bo-Bo models in the 1980s. EMD's success with this long-running design is in contrast to the radical changes which have been made in truck design in other countries over that period.

The cab afforded a good view in both directions, the hood gave easy access to the equipment, and, despite the designer's intentions, EMD's stylists produced a pleasing outline. Electrical equipment was simplified from the "F" series, but nevertheless it gave the driver tighter control over the tractive effort at starting, and a more comprehensive overall control to suit the wide range of speeds envisaged.

First production series of the new design was the "GP7", launched in 1949. It was an immediate success, and 2,610 units were supplied between 1949 and 1953 to US roads, plus 112 to Canada and two to Mexico — and this at a time when the "F7" was still selling in record numbers.

In 1954 the next development of the 567 engine, the C series of 1,750hp (1,305kW), was introduced into the range, giving the "GP9". This differed in detail from the "GP7", mainly to bring still further reductions in maintenance. By this time the hood unit was widely accepted, and sales of the "GP" at 4,157 established another record. The "GP" was now America's (and therefore the world's) best selling diesel locomotive.

Below: *A pair of GP-series EMD diesel units, typical freight power for Conrail's huge 17,700-mile (28,485-km) network.*

So far the EMD engines had been pressure-charged by a Roots blower driven mechanically from the engine, but with its competitors offering engines of higher power, EMD now produced a turbocharged version of the 567 engine, 567D2, giving 2,000hp (1,490kW). For customers for whom the extra power did not justify the expense of the turbo-blower, the 567D1 at 1,800hp (1,340kW) was availble. Both these models had a higher compression than their predecessors, which, combined with improvements in the fuel injectors, gave a fuel saving of 5 per cent. These engines were incorporated in the "GP20" and "GP18" series, respectively.

By this time US railroads were fully dieselised, and this, combined with a decline in industrial activity, reduced the demand for diesels. EMD therefore launched its Locomotive Replacement Plan. The company claimed that three "GP20s" could do the work of four "F3s", so it offered terms under which a road traded in four "F3s" against the purchase of three "GP20s", parts being reused where possible. It was claimed that the cost of the transaction could be recovered in three to four years, and the railroad then had three almost new units in place of four older ones with much higher maintenance costs. Despite this, only 260 "GP20s" and 390 "GP18s" were sold over 13 years.

The final phase of "GP" development with the 567 engine came in 1961 with the 567D3 of 2,250hp (1,680kW) in the "GP30." The designation "30" was a sales gimmick, based on there being 30 improvements in the new model; it was claimed that maintenance was reduced by 60 per cent compared with earlier types. The "GP30" was in turn succeeded by the "GP35" of 2,500hp (1,870kW). With trade reviving, and many more early diesels in need of replacement, these models achieved sales of 2,281. At this stage the 567 engine was replaced by the 645 with which the "GP" series remains in full production in the 1980s.

The "GP" series with the 567 engine totalled 10,647 units, or about one-quarter of the total of North American diesels, and it established the hood unit as the norm for all future construction.

Class 9100 2-D₀-2

France:
French National Railways (SNCF), 1950

Type: Express passenger electric locomotive.

Gauge: 4ft 8½in (1,435mm).

Propulsion: Direct current at 1,500V from overhead catenary supplied to four 1,330hp (990kW) traction motors connected to the axles through flexible drives.

Weight: 180,730lb (82t) adhesive, 317,380lb (144t) total.

Max. axleload: 45,180lb (20.5t).

Overall length: 59ft 3¾in (18,040mm).

Tractive effort: 50,800lb (226kN).

Max. speed: 87mph (140km/h).

For 25 years the 2-Do-2 locomotive was the most advanced express electric type in France. For the electrification from Paris to Vierzon in 1925-26 the PO Railway built a number of types of express locomotives. All these were in various ways troublesome, particularly in the amount of maintenance required, except for two 2-Do-2 units built in 1925. These were destined to have a major influence on French locomotive practice for 25 years. Nos. E501-2 were designed by Swiss builders Brown Boveri and SLM, and they incorporated a number of features based on contemporary Swiss ac practice.

At this time, many electric locomotives were still driven by clumsy and complex rod drives, and an important feature of Nos. E501-2 was the Büchli drive, a system of links incorporated in the large gear wheel of the traction motor reduction gear between the motor and driving wheels. These allowed for movement of the driving wheels on their springs when they were driven from a motor

mounted rigidly on the frame of the locomotive. There was a notable difference between the PO and Swiss machines, in that the former had the Büchli drive at each end of each driving axle, whereas on the Swiss machines it was applied at one end only. French engineers considered this difference to be a major contribution to the small amount of wear which their Büchli drive

incurred between overhauls.

After a lengthy test period, 48 further 2-Do-2 locomotives were built between 1933 and 1943; they were numbered E503-50 and became SNCF Nos. 5503-50. The maximum power was 3,520hp (2,625kW). Twenty-three very similar machines were built in 1938 for the Etat Railway electrification from Paris to Le Mans.

For the post-war electrification

Above: *French National Railways' Class 9100 2-Do-2 electric locomotive No. 2D2.9119 enters Dijon Station with a rapide from Paris to Marseilles in 1967.*

of the former PLM main line from Paris to Lyons, a new class of 2-Do-2, the "9101", was built, based on the last of the PO locomotives, but with a number of improvements. The control system was extensively modified by introduction of additional stages of field weakening, made possible by improvements in the compensating windings of the motors. There were considerably more notches on the controller, so that the discontinuity in tractive effort, or "jerk", when a resistance step was cut out was reduced to about one fifth of that with the "5500" class. The extra field weakening improved the whole range of performance at higher speeds. The maximum speed was 87mph (140km/h), an advance of 10km/h on the earlier 2-Do-2s.

The specification for the class required it to haul 900t on the level at 87mph (140km/h), and 1,000t on 1-in-200 (0.5 per cent) at 62mph (100km/h). This requirement had been increased during the design period, following the spectacular tests of the Chapelon 4-8-4 steam locomotive. Although electrification was the logical step for a country with no oil and little coal, and SNCF was fully committed to it, nevertheless the electrical engineers were concerned that their latest product

should not be outdone by the older type of motive power. The power output was 4,400hp (3,280kW) continuous and 4,880hp (3,640kW) for one hour. Despite the increase in power, the "9101" class weighed only 3.5t more than the "5500" series.

An initial order for 35 of the new locomotives was placed, and it was expected that a total of 100 would be needed eventually. However, the design was already dated when the class was delivered in 1950. All-adhesion locomotives for express work were well established in Switzerland, and the cumbersome Büchli drive had been rendered unnecessary by improvements in motor design which allowed motors to be fitted on a bogie. When further units were ordered they were of the Co-Co layout.

Nevertheless Class "9101" took a major part in the working of the *Ligne Impériale*, and in Summer 1951 they were working the four fastest schedules in France. The class achieved remarkable standards of reliability, and built up mileage as quickly as their more modern contemporaries. By January 1982 several of the class had exceeded 4.5 million miles (7.25 million km). Withdrawal of this hard-working class of locomotive began in May 1982.

Below: *This French National Railways Class 9100 2-Do-2 electric locomotive built in 1950 was the last of a long line with this elegant layout.*

Above: *A Class 9100 2-Do-2 electric locomotive. Note the double current-collecting contact bows provided to cope with the heavy current flows involved.*

Nos. 10201-3 1-C₀-C₀-1 Great Britain:
British Railways, Southern Region (BR), 1951

Type: Diesel-electric mixed-traffic locomotive.
Gauge: 4ft 8½in (1,435mm).
Propulsion: English Electric 1,750hp (1,305kW) Type 16SVT V-16 four-stroke diesel and generator supplying current to six nose-suspended traction motors geared to the axles.
Weight: 246,950lb (112t). adhesive, 302,400lb (137t) total.
Max. axleload: 41,440lb (19t).
Overall length: 63ft 9in (19,430mm).
Tractive effort: 31,200lb (139kN).
Max. speed: 90 mph (144km/h).

The post-war development plan of the Southern Railway had included introduction of diesel traction on certain routes on which electrification was not justified, and main-line locomotives of 2,500hp were mentioned. Responsibility for diesel locomotives, other than the electrical equipment, rested with the Chief Mechanical Engineer, O. V. S. Bulleid, a strong advocate of steam, who was at this time building large

numbers of unconventional Pacific locomotives, and planning even more unconventional steam types. Bulleid was not convinced of the need for diesels, but he believed that the best way to meet competition was to beat it, and he therefore embarked on the design of a large diesel-electric locomotive. As the largest diesel engine then available in Britain was of only 1,600hp, which fell far short of the 2,500hp envisaged, Bulleid had no fear of his Pacifics being outshone.

Three prototype locomotives were approved, and design work began in earnest in 1946. Limitations of axleload on the SR made eight axles inevitable, so Bulleid took the bogie of his electric locomotive as the basis, and added a pair of carrying wheels at one end, this giving the wheel arrangement 1-Co-Co-1. This carrying axle was constrained by two horizontal links to move laterally as if turning about a pivot. Most of the weight was applied to the bogie through central segmental pads, but two additional sliding bearers were

provided nearer to the outer ends of the bogies. As in the electric locomotives, the only flexibility in the bogie was in the leaf springs over each axle and their rubber pads. A difference from the electric locomotives was that the couplings and buffers were attached to the bogies instead of the body.

The engine was English Electric's 16-cylinder design, which had already been ordered by the LMS and Egyptian State Railways,

Above: *Ex-Southern Railway diesel-electric locomotive No. 10201 at speed on BR's London Midland Region near Kenton, Middlesex, in June 1960.*

and English Electric also supplied the electrical equipment. The body was shaped to the profile of SR postwar passenger stock, and there were numerous access doors, so that, if necessary, the engines and equipment could be withdrawn

Fell 2-D-2 Great Britain:
British Railways (BR), 1951

Type: Diesel-mechanical mixed-traffic locomotive.
Gauge: 4ft 8½in (1,435mm).
Propulsion: Four 500hp (370kW) two-stroke Davey Paxman 12-cylinder diesel engines driving a set of four coupled axles through a patented system of hydraulic clutches and constantly-meshing differential gears.
Weight: 170,240lb (77t). adhesive, 268,800lb (122t) total.
Max. axleload: 42,560lb (19.4t).
Overall length: 50ft 0in (15,240mm).
Max. speed: 78mph (125km/h).

At the end of World War II electric transmission was well established in North America as the norm for diesel locomotives, but in Europe there were still engineers who hoped to perfect a hydro-mechanical system. Their aim was higher efficiency and lower weight. Most of this effort was concentrated in West Germany, but one Englishman was active in the field. Lt Col L. F. R. Fell was trained as a steam locomotive engineer, and after an army career joined an aero-engine firm. In his spare time he took out nearly twenty patents for matters concerning diesel engines and mechanical transmissions for locomotives.

Fell favoured a multi-engined locomotive, partly to insure against engine failure and partly for easier maintenance of the smaller engines. In a normal diesel engine horsepower increases with speed, but Fell believed that engine power should remain almost constant over the working speed range of the engine, so that tractive

effort would fall as speed increased, as it does in a steam locomotive. His idea, therefore, was to boost the engine with an independent supercharger, so controlled that as engine speed rose the boost fell, keeping power almost constant.

The Fell gearbox not only geared together the engines (four in number in the experimental locomotive to be described) but it also gave a high gear ratio at low speeds for starting, decreasing as speed increased. It made use of differential gears, but whereas in a motor vehicle power is fed in to the planet carrier and is taken out through the sun wheels, in the Fell gearbox an engine was connected to each sun wheel, and the combined power was taken out through the planet carrier. If, with the engine running at steady speed, one rear wheel of a car is brought to rest, the other wheel accelerates to twice its previous speed. The gear ratio between the planet carrier and the sun wheel of the rotating wheel is thereby doubled compared with the condition when both wheels are turning at the same speed. In the Fell system, if one engine of a pair started whilst the other remained at rest, the gear ratio to the planet carrier was doubled compared with the condition when both engines were running.

In a four-engined locomotive, the output from each pair of engines was combined in a third differential and then fed to the wheels. With only one engine running, the gear ratio was four times its value when all four were working. The change in gear ratio took place progressively and smoothly as successive engines

were started and connected to their driving shafts.

The LMS had early experience of diesel-electric shunters, and in 1946 it undertook construction of two experimental 1,600hp diesel-electric passenger locomotives. In the following year Fell persuaded H. G. Ivatt, the LMS Chief Mechanical Engineer, to build an engine incorporating his ideas for comparison with the diesel-electrics. The directors of the LMS approved the project shortly before their railway was merged into BR. The locomotive had coupling rods connecting all driving axles; the middle pair of axles were in fact connected by the gearing, and for some time the engine ran with the middle section

of the coupling rods removed.

Four 510hp Paxman engines housed under the end "bonnets" provided traction power, and two 150hp engines supplied the superchargers and other auxiliaries. One engine sufficed up to 7mph, two from 7 to 19, three 19 to 27 and four engines from 27 to the maximum speed of 75mph (120km/h). In practice, all four engines were in use for most of the running time. A fluid coupling enabled each engine to idle whilst its output shaft was locked against rotation.

Below: *British Railways' "Fell" 2-D-2 experimental diesel locomotive with mechanical transmission, built in 1951.*

sideways in a workshop which did not have facilities for lifting them through the roof of the locomotive. On a railway on which electric motormen were accustomed to driving positions at the end of vehicles, no projecting "nose" was deemed necessary and the cabs were at the ends.

Work proceeded slowly; the SR was merged into the newly-nationalised British Railways, in which there was little interest in main-line diesels, and in any event post-war austerity made extensive dieselisation of the SR a very distant prospect. Eventually in 1951 the first locomotive, No. 10201, was completed at Ashford Works. By this time the diesel engine had been uprated to an output of 1,750hp for one hour. The locomotive had been optimistically geared for a maximum speed of 110mph (177km/h), but this was soon changed to a more practicable 90mph (144km/h), with a corresponding increase in tractive effort at lower speeds. The locomotive soon established that it was able to work the trains normally hauled by the Bulleid

Pacifics, although it fell short of their maximum achievements. But it could work two return trips a day over the 171.8 miles (276km) between London and Exeter, which was more than the steam engines could do at that time. When the second engine No. 10202 appeared, their duties were extended to services between London and Bournemouth.

By this time the railways were in the fifth year of nationalisation, and although BR's policy was to retain steam as the main motive power until electrification was possible, there was a strong feeling in some quarters that main-line diesel locomotives should be given a thorough trial. The completion of the third SR locomotive was therefore delayed pending consideration of improvements which could be made to a design which was already some six years old.

When No. 10203 was at last completed in 1954, the main differences were that the engine had been further uprated to 2,000hp, and that the control system was much improved. In Nos. 10201-2

the driver's controller had eight positions only, and some difficulty was experienced in adjusting the power to control the train speed precisely. In No. 10203 the controller was infinitely variable, an arrangement which became standard for subsequent BR diesel locomotives.

Whereas Nos. 10201-2 could barely equal a Pacific in good form, No. 10203 could better it, and for a time enthusiasm for the diesels ran high on the SR, to the extent that the region borrowed the two LMS locomotives, Nos. 10000-1. Steam locomotive maintenance was at the time at a low ebb on the SR, and the diesels covered workings which could have needed up to 10 steam engines. However, steam maintenace gradually improved, and at the same time the difficulties of servicing diesel locomotives in the crude surroundings of steam locomotive depots became severe, so reliability declined. The SR lost enthusiasm for the new power, and the five locomotives were transferred to the LMR.

Here their fortunes also varied.

They took over some of the heaviest duties on the routes from Euston Station, London. Usually the smaller locomotives worked in pairs on long-distance trains, but No. 10203 could not work in multiple, and it proved able to handle trains of up to 500t (560 US tons) on the modest schedules of the period with average speeds of about 55mph (88km/h). They also had periods of working on the former Midland Railway route from London St Pancras.

At their best these locomotives achieved annual mileages unheard of in Britain, but their reliability still varied, and when Derby Works become involved in major dieselisation under the 1955 BR modernisation programme, the pioneer locomotives spent increasingly long periods awaiting repair. The SR locomotives were withdrawn from service in 1963.

Despite their fluctuating fortunes, these locomotives had provided invaluable experience to BR designers, and No. 10203 was the prototype for the first generation of large BR diesel locomotives.

The locomotive was completed at BR's Derby Works in 1951, and was subjected to a long series of trials on the Midland Division of the London Midland Region. Eventually it went into service, mainly between Derby and Manchester, hauling passenger trains of up to 12 coaches.

In its early years, BR took little interest in main-line diesels, but in 1956, when the modernisation programme was being initiated, dynamometer car trials were conducted with the Fell locomotive to assess its potential. The test report

Left: *The Fell diesel locomotive was withdrawn in 1957 after the main gearbox had sustained some accidental damage.*

was generally favourable, but only to the extent that with the Fell system "a locomotive could be developed to give a close approach to the required (drawbar) characteristics." In fact the locomotive gave a higher tractive effort than a 2,000hp diesel-electric at speeds between 40 and 60mph (64 and 97km/h), but fell far below at low speed. The maximum tractive effort actually recorded was 29,000lb (129kN) compared with figures of 50,000lb (222kN) which had been obtained with a diesel-electric. The Fell transmission had a higher efficiency than an electric transmission, but this was offset by the much greater power required to drive the auxiliaries in the Fell.

Class Ew B₀-B₀-B₀

Class Ew B_o-B_o-B_o

New Zealand:
New Zealand Railways (NZR), 1952

Type: Mixed-traffic electric locomotive.
Gauge: 3ft 6in (1,067mm).
Propulsion: Direct current at 1,500V fed via overhead catenary to six 300hp (480kW) nose-suspended traction motors each geared to one axle.
Weight: 167,505lb (76t).
Max. axleload: 27,770lb (12.6t).
Overall length: 62ft 0in (18,900mm).
Tractive effort: 42,000lb (187kN).
Max. speed: 60mph (95km/h).

Mountainous and oil-less New Zealand is one of those countries where electrification would seem to be a natural choice, but in which little has taken place. In 1932, a start was made with electrification at one end of the 428 mile (685km) North Island trunk route from Wellington towards Auckland. Fifty years later, only the 26 miles (42km) as far as Paekakariki had been achieved.

To handle traffic on this short section, English Electric and Robert Stephenson & Hawthorn in 1952 supplied electrical equipment and mechanical parts respectively for seven articulated locomotives of unusual configuration. In contrast, though, their electrical equipment was very conventional and the power output modest in relation to the weight of the locomotive.

The "Ews" are one of those classes best described by what they didn't have rather than what they did. The traction motors were of the elementary axle-hung pattern so there was no flexible drive. There was no electric brake and also, since New Zealand surprisingly follows US rather than British traditions over rolling stock, there was no vacuum exhauster to work the train brakes, as these were fed by air-compressor sets which the system needed anyway. The Bo-Bo-Bo arrangement was excellent for NZR's sharply curved alignments, while arrangement of the six motors could be permutated

to give several natural running connections. An absence of external fittings and frills made for a neat and tidy appearance, exceptionally easy on the eye. On the debit side, though, one must compare the "Ews" with some contemporary locomotives of similar wheel arrangement, weight and gauge, built for the Swiss Rhaetian Railway, that could develop 50 per cent more power.

In 1967, diesel locomotives began taking long distance trains through over the electrified lines into Wellington. The "Ews" were then transferred to suburban trains

Above: *A short Ew-hauled passenger train about to pass beneath a diesel-hauled freight.*

Right: *New Zealand Government Railways Class Ew electric loco leaving Wellington station.*

which were confined to the electrified district. And, although electrification of the main part of the Wellington to Auckland trunk is now in progress, the use of very high-voltage ac makes it unlikely that a wider sphere of action will arise for these neat and useful machines.

Class 277* C_o-C_o

Spain:
Spanish National Railways (RENFE), 1952

Type: Electric mixed-traffic locomotive.
Gauge: 5ft 6in (1,668mm).
Propulsion: Direct current at 3,000V fed via overhead catenary and rheostatic control system to six 600hp (447kW) nose-suspended traction motors geared to the axles.
Weight: 264,480lb (120t).
Max. axleload: 44,080lb (20t).
Overall length: 67ft 9½in (20,657mm).
Tractive effort: 69,000lb (307kN).
Max. speed: 68mph (110km/h).

*Originally designated Class 7701.

This class of rather solid-looking electric tractors was one of the very few export successes of the British locomotive industry in Europe. They were intended to serve the electrification of two mountain lines in north-western Spain. The main line from Madrid to the port of Gijon on the Atlantic coast crosses the Cantabrican mountains by a tunnel 1.9 miles (3.1km) long beneath the Pajarks pass at an altitude of 4,170ft (1,271m). The northern ascent to this pass from Ujo (817ft—249m)

Right: *Spanish National Railways' Class 277 Co-Co electric locomotive No. 277-004-8 at Oviedo in September 1975.*

in 39 miles (62km) is exceptionally severe, an additional hindrance in steam days being the existence of 71 tunnels. The ruling grade is 1-in-48 (2.1 per cent). This short section was electrified as early as 1924.

When recovery began after the Civil War, priority was given to extending this electrification back to Leon and on to Gijon, a distance of 108 miles (172km). Furthermore, another mountain line was also electrified, leading from Leon as far as Ponferrada in the direction of Corunna. Hence this order placed with English Electric, the Vulcan Foundry producing mechanical parts for some of the series. Similar locomotives had been supplied to the Santos-Jundiai Railway in Brazil in 1950 and by a fortunate chance the Spanish Purchasing Mission visited the works while the Brazilian locomotives were being erected, so they were used as the basis of the design, many parts being in common.

In accordance with normal dc practice, the running steps in the control system were provided by the usual combination of motor groupings and field weakening, and the locomotives were assisted in their mountain-crossing role by being equipped with both multiple-unit control and regenerative braking. Vacuum brakes were then standard in Spain, so an exhauster system was provided.

A further sale of locomotives built to this basic design — with a few detail differences — was made in 1954 to the Central Railway of India. These in their turn became the basis of the first main line non-steam locomotive class built at Indian Railways' Chitteranjan Works in 1961.

Since then the dc electrification in this area of north-west Spain has been extended to 387 miles (605km) and Class "277" (originally Class 7701) eventually reached 75

Above: *Spanish National Railways Class 277 electric locomotive at La Robla.*

in number, the last being delivered in 1959. The whole class was still in service at the time of writing.

ETR 300 "Settebello" Seven-car train

Italy:
Italian State Railways (FS), 1953

Type: De-luxe articulated electric express passenger train.
Gauge: 4ft 8½in (1,435mm).
Propulsion: Direct current at 3,000V fed via overhead catenary to twelve 250hp (187kW) traction motors driving the axles of six of the 10 bogies by gearing and hollow-axle flexible drives.
Weight: 449,620lb (204t) adhesive, 716,300lb (325t) total.
Max. axleload: 37,468lb (17t).
Overall length: 542ft 0in (165,202mm).
Max. speed: 98mph (158km/h).

The day was July 20, 1939 and World War II was barely a month away, when Italian State Railways took a record for long-distance travel by rail which was to stand for over 25 years. The instrument used was a three-car high-speed electric trainset (Class "ETR200") nominally rated at 1,475hp (1,100kW), and the route was from Florence to Milan via the then new 11½-mile (18.4km) Appennine tunnel. The 196 miles (314km) were run off in 1hr 55min, an average speed of 102mph (163km/h). To increase the power available, the line volt-age of 3,000 was temporarily increased to over 4,000V and normal speed restrictions were relaxed. The maximum speed recorded was a thrilling 126mph (203km/h)—for those in the know perhaps a little too thrilling, like the rest of the run.

When World War II was over and the worst of the physical destruction in Italy repaired, the expertise that had produced this world-beating train was used to build a new and even better one, this time super-de-luxe as well as fast. And remember that this was a period when austerity ruled the roost elsewhere, particularly on railways.

The "ETR300", *Settebello* or 'Lucky Seven', is a seven-car set seating a mere 160 first-class passengers in considerable comfort. In addition to this, there are spacious observation lounges front and rear, (the driver having been banished to an eyrie upstairs) which seat 11 each. Both driving-observation cars are articulated to another passenger car and these two pairs originally constituted the whole of the revenue-earning accommodation. Style, comfort and decor were luxurious to a

degree which has seldom been approached elsewhere.

There is a separate dining car with 56 seats, and two cars articulated to the dining car in the centre of the train provide kitchen, staff, mail and luggage accommodation plus a small shop. Later, room was found for 30 extra seats, by encroaching on this rather over-ample allowance of space for service use.

Six out of the 10 bogies are motored, each with a pair of 1,500V motors permanently connected in series. Seventeen running notches on the controller are produced by using the motor-pairs in series, series-parallel and parallel, plus field-weakening stages. A hollow-axle flexible drive arrangement is used as the final element in the driving system. Brake force is arranged to lessen automatically as speed reduces.

At a later stage, rheostatic electric braking was added to the system. At the same time new motors with a rated output 28 per cent higher than the originals were substituted. Cab signalling was also fitted and the maximum speed raised theoretically to 125mph (200km/h). In practical terms, though, 100mph (160km/h) was the best permitted out on the line.

It must not be forgotten that there is more to running high-speeds than the trains themselves. That the track has to be improved is obvious, but there are other things as well. The signalling system must provide enough braking distance between the point at which a driver is warned and the place at which he has to stop. Furthermore, if cab signalling is a requirement, then there is a costly ground installation to -be

provided. Another problem is line capacity. On a busy route (and Rome to Milan is a very busy route indeed), a few trains that run faster than the rest have a quite disproportionate effect on the number of trains that can be run each day.

So, for all these reasons, the new trains were not originally able to better the best pre-war timing of 6 hours for the 392 miles (627km) between Rome and Milan. However, construction of a new *direttissima* railway between Rome and Florence, aligned to permit speeds as high as 156mph (250km/h), has been in progress for some time. The first and southernmost section of 76 miles (122km), over half of which is in tunnel or on bridges and viaducts, was opened in 1977. Although speeds on the new line are still limited to 112mph (180km/h), it was possible then for the *Settebello* schedule between Rome and Milan to be cut to 5hr 35min inclusive of stops at Bologna and Florence. Since then the timings have been eased again and 6 hours or just over is once more the best offered.

There remains just one odd point. In the past the best trains in Britain and France were locomotive-hauled, whereas in Italy they were self-propelled. Now, however, when the best British trains as well as the French are self-propelled, the Italians are going back to locomotives. The Class "E444" Bo-Bos, named "Tortoises" (!), hauling trains of new coaches of a luxury comparable with those of "ETR300", have the same speed potential; that is, a design speed of 125mph (200km/h), but as yet no railway suitably equipped on which to use it.

Left: *The Leading end of an* ETR 300 Settebello *train. The wide windows are for the passengers' view, not the driver's.*

Below: *A* Settebello *express train at speed crosses a handsome viaduct on the Rome to Milan trunk route.*

Above: *The driver's eyrie is clearly visible above roof level of the leading end in this view of a* Settebello *train.*

Below: *De luxe accommodation for 160 passengers was provided in the seven cars of an Italian ETR 300 trainset.*

Gas Turbine B₀-B₀-B₀-B₀

United States:
Union Pacific Railroad (UP), 1951

Type: Gas-turbine electric freight locomotive.
Gauge: 4ft 8½in (1,435mm).
Propulsion: One 4,500hp (3,360kW) oil-burning gas turbine driving a generator and supplying direct current to eight nose-hung traction motors.
Weight: 551,720lb (250.3t).
Max. axleload: 68,970lb (31.3t).
Overall length: 83ft 6½in (25,464mm).
Tractive effort: 135,000lb (600kN).
Max. speed: 65mph (105km/h).

Union Pacific is a big railroad; its last three designs of steam engine were all, in some way, the largest or most powerful of their type, and there was a dramatic contrast when the road began to buy off-the-shelf diesels of 1,750hp instead of 6,000hp steam engines. But UP is also a road of contrasts. One main line crosses deserts where coal and water are scarce, but oil is available; this was an obvious line for dieselisation. In other districts, however, the company owns coal mines, and there the economic case for dieselisation was less clear. In particular, any alternative to the diesel which might burn coal was of interest.

In the post-war surge of interest

Above: *Union Pacific Railroad three-unit 8,500hp gas-turbine locomotive. The lead unit has the turbine, the others house auxiliary equipment and fuel.*

Trainmaster H-24-66 C₀C₀

United States:
Fairbanks Morse & Co (FM), 1953

Type: General-purpose diesel-electric locomotive.
Gauge: 4ft 8½in (1,435mm).
Propulsion: One Fairbanks Morse 38D-12 2,400hp (1,790kW) 12-cylinder turbocharged opposed-piston diesel engine and generator supplying six nose-suspended traction motors geared to the axles.
Weight: 375,000lb (170.1t).
Max. axleload: 62,500lb (28.4t).
Overall length: 66ft 0in (20,120mm).
Tractive effort: 112,500lb (500kN).
Max. speed: 65mph (105km/h), 70mph (113km/h), or 80mph (129km/h) according to gear ratio fitted.

Fairbanks Morse of Beloit, Wisconsin, was an engineering firm which had for a long time supplied general equipment to railroads, such as water stand pipes. In the 1930s the firm developed a specialism, an opposed-piston diesel engine, with two pistons in each cylinder, and two crankshafts connected by gearing. This engine was fitted to a number of railcars, but further railway applications were delayed by the US Navy, which took the total production for four years to power submarines. After the war, FM introduced a range of switcher and transfer locomotives, and then in 1950 it produced the "Consolidation" line of carbody or cab units, with a choice of engines rated at 1,600hp (1,190kW), 2,000hp (1,490kW) or 2,400hp (1,790kW), supplying four traction motors. Twenty-two units with the 2,400hp engine were sold in 1952-53, but the market was changing rapidly, and carbody designs were giving way to the more versatile hood-type road switcher.

Fairbanks Morse acted quickly, and in 1953 produced a 2,400hp hood unit designated "H-24-66" (Hood, 2,400hp, 6 motors, 6 axles). It was mounted on two three-motor three-axle bogies of new design. Compared with its competitors everything about it was big—the dynamic brake power, the train heating boiler (if fitted), the fuel supplies, the tractive effort. Although EMD offered a twin-engined 2,400hp carbody unit, the FM engine was the largest then on the market. With some justification, the firm chose the pretentious name "Trainmaster", and showed the first unit at a Railroad Manufacturers' Supply Association Fair at Atlantic City, where it stole the show. This publicity, combined with the impression made by the four demonstrator units, soon brought orders.

The peak year for Trainmaster production followed all too quickly in 1954, when 32 units were built, but orders then slowed down. Railroads encountered problems with the opposed-piston engine and with the electrical systems. One of the characteristics of EMD service had always been the prompt and thorough attention which was given to faults in the field, but customers found that the smaller FM company could not give such good service. During 1954-55 the firm was still dealing with engine problems, including pistons and bearings, but then came a blow to the future of all FM products.

The Morse family had large holdings in the company, and family feuding cast doubts upon the whole stability of the firm, which led to a takeover by another company. By the time conditions were stable, the diesel market was in the doldrums, and competitors had been busy catching up. One result of this trouble was that Illinois Central decided against

in the gas turbine, General Electric was well placed, with years of successful steam turbine work behind it. As far back as 1904 it had begun work on gas turbines. In 1946, development of a gas turbine for locomotive work was begun, and an experimental locomotive appeared in 1948. The attractions of the gas turbine for locomotives were the high power-to-weight ratio, simple mechanical parts and the ability to use low grade fuel. This turbine burned a heavy oil commonly termed "Bunker C", but already work was in progress on the use of pulverised coal in a turbine.

The gas turbine drove a generator, which supplied direct current to eight traction motors of normal design mounted on four bogies, giving the wheel arrangement Bo-Bo-Bo-Bo. The main frame of the body formed the fuel tank, and a boiler was provided to heat the oil in the tank, as it was too viscous to flow when cold.

With a horsepower of 4,500, it was the most powerful internal-combustion locomotive in the world, and it soon attracted the attention of UP, to which it was loaned for trials.

Success of these trials brought a quick response. UP was led by a new President, A. E. Stoddard, a convinced "big engine" man to whom the 4,500hp unit appealed, and 10 were ordered. These where delivered in 1952-53; numbered from 51 to 60, they closely followed the design of No. 50, but had a cab at one end only. They went quickly into freight work between Ogden, Utah, and Green River, Wyoming, where their rated tonnage was 4,890. So successful were they that when only six of them had been delivered, a further 15 were ordered.

Thirteen months after the delivery of the 25th gas turbine, UP was sufficiently enthusiastic to take a second plunge, this time with an order for 15 locomotives

(later increased to 30) with an 8,500hp turbine. The new design differed from the previous one in its layout, there being two Co-Co units, one carrying the turbine and generator and the other the control and auxiliary equipment. In addition a converted steam-engine tender was attached as a fuel tank. They took over from the earlier turbines the distinction of being the most powerful internal combustion locomotives in the world—by a considerable margin.

The gas turbine was, by its working cycle, inherently less efficient than a diesel, and the key to its ability to better the diesel in running costs was the use of cheaper fuel. However, this heavy oil brought penalties of corrosion and fouling of the blades, as well as difficulties in handling the viscous fluid. An attempt was made to use liquefied propane gas, but this was expensive and even more difficult to handle than heavy oil. Similarly, blade erosion was the

main reason for the attempt to burn coal in a gas turbine being unsuccessful.

Despite the excellent work which the 55 "Big Blows" performed, time was against them. Changes in the petro-chemical industry made Bunker C oil more valuable, whilst developments in diesel locomotives made them more efficient and powerful, and thus more competitive with gas turbines. By the time the turbines needed heavy repairs, UP already had the world's most powerful diesel locomotives in service, and further expenditure on the turbines could not be justified. They were gradually replaced by diesels, and the last of them finished work in December 1969.

Below: *The Union Pacific Bo-Bo-Bo-Bo 4,500hp gas-turbine electric locomotive. An ex-steam locomotive tender adapted as a fuel tank was normally attached when in service.*

placing an order for 50 to 60 units which it had contemplated, an order which could have changed the whole outlook for the model. In the event a total of 105 were sold to eight US railroads, and a further 22 were built in Canada.

Major users were the Norfolk & Western, which acquired 33 Trainmasters as a result of mergers,

and Southern Pacific, which used them extensively on commuter trains. Most of the locomotives ended their days on switching duties, where their high adhesive weight was still appreciated after they had been displaced from main line work by more powerful locomotives from other makers.

A 1,600hp version of the Train-

master, sometimes known as the "Baby Trainmaster" also failed to achieve satisfactory production, with a total of 58 sales. The opposed-piston engine had failed to make the grade in railway work. The fate of the Trainmaster was sealed when, by three years after its introduction, it had failed to achieve a level of sales which

Above: *Two Fairbanks-Morse prototype "Trainmaster" Co-Co diesel-electric units coupled together to form a locomotive of 4,800hp, a high figure for diesels of thirty-odd years ago.*

made its production economically viable, but for a time it enjoyed well-earned acclaim.

Class CC7100 C₀-C₀

France: French National Railways (SNCF), 1952

Type: Electric express passenger locomotive.
Gauge: 4ft 8½in (1,435mm).
Propulsion: Direct current at 1,500V from overhead catenary fed to six bogie-mounted traction motors geared to the axles through Alsthom spring drive.
Weight: 235,830lb (107t).
Max. axleload: 39,230lb (17.8t).
Overall length: 62ft 1in (18,922mm).
Tractive effort: 50,700lb (225kN).
Max. speed: 100mph (160km/h).

French locomotive design has always been distinctive; much of the distinctiveness has been purely French in origin, but from time to time a foreign influence has been seen. Thus in the development of express passenger locomotives for the main line electrification of the Paris-Orléans Railway (PO), adoption to the Swiss Büchli drive led to a notable series of 2-D-2 locomotives, which bore an external likeness to contemporary Swiss designs. The last 2-Do-2 type, the "9100", was introduced by SNCF as the principal passenger locomotive for the electrification of the former PLM main line to Lyons. However, before those locomotives had been built in the quantity originally intended, another Swiss influence changed the course of French locomotive design.

Until this time, end bogies or pony trucks had been thought essential for fast passenger work, not only to support part of the weight of the locomotive but also to guide it into curves. All-adhesion Bo-Bo locomotives, which constituted the majority of French electrics, were considered suitable only for medium-speed work.

Two notable Swiss designs changed the status of the all-adhesion locomotive. In 1946 Swiss Federal Railways introduced the 56t "Re4/4I" Bo-Bo, designed for speeds up to 78mph (125km/h). This class soon attracted attention by its ability to haul trains of 400t at its maximum permitted speed, while, two year earlier the Lötschberg railway had introduced its 80t Bo-Bo, classified "Ae4/4". The success of these classes established the respectability of the double-bogie locomotive for express work, and SNCF commissioned two Bo-Bo machines from Swiss makers, based on the Lötschberg design, together with two Bo-Bo and two Co-Co machines from French builders.

The Co-Co was produced by Alsthom to a specification based on the requirements of the PLM electrification. This called for speeds up to 100mph (160km/h) on the level with 600t, 87mph (140km/h) on the level with 850t, and the ability to start a 600t train on a 1-in-125 (0.8 per cent) gradient and haul it at 75mph (120km/h) on that gradient.

The locomotive has a motor for each axle mounted in the bogie

frame, with Alsthom spring drive. The novelty in the bogie was in the pivoting and in the axle guides. The pivots are of Alsthom design, and comprise two vertical links situated mid-way between the pairs of axles on the centre line of the bogie, with their ends resting in conical rubber seatings. Lateral movement of each link is controlled by two horizontal springs. The springs have two effects; when the body of the locomotive swings outward on curves, they provide a restoring force resisting centrifugal action, and when the bogie rotates, the links swing in opposite directions, and exert forces tending to restore the bogie to the straight line. Thus, if the bogie rotates on straight track due to irregularities in the permanent way, the action of the springs tends to damp this motion and discourage the flanges from striking the rails.

Each axlebox is restrained by two horizontal links, which allow vertical movement but not fore-

Above: *French National Railways' Class CC7100 No. CC7135 stands under 1,500V catenary in this wintry railway scene.*

and-aft movement, and they eliminate the wearing surfaces of traditional steam-type axleboxes. End movement of the axles is controlled by stiff springs fitted between the ends of the axles and the axlebox cover plates. These springs reduce the shocks transmitted to the bogie frame when the flanges strike the rails. Extensive use was made of rubber in the pivots of the suspension system, which was unusual at that date.

The electrical equipment was notable for the large number of running notches, made possible by the large amount of field weakening. The clean external lines were enhanced by the two-tone blue livery, set off by light metal beading of the window frames and of the horizontal flashing.

The two locomotives, Nos. CC7001-2, were delivered in 1949 and were subjected to intensive testing on the Paris-Bordeaux main line, which was then the longest electrified line in France. Early in these tests, No. 7001 hauled a train of 170t from Paris to Bordeaux at an average speed of 81.4mph (131km/h), reaching a maximum of 105.6mph (170km/h), which was a world record performance for an electric locomotive and a token of more stirring events to come.

After three years of testing, orders were placed for a further 35 locomotives, differing in detail from Nos. 7001-2. They were delivered in 1952, and are numbered from 7101 to 7135. A further order for 23 brought the class of a total of 60. Compared with Nos. 7001-2 the production units had an increase in maximum power from 4,000hp (2,980kW) to 4,740hp (3,540kW), and the weight increased from 96t to 107t. Compared with the "9100" class

2-Do-2, the adhesive weight had increased from 88t to 107t, but the axleload had fallen from 22t to 17.8t, so that the locomotive was much kinder to the track. Six of the locomotives were fitted with collecting shoes for working on the former PLM line from Culoz to Modane (the Mont Cenis route), which was at that time equipped with third rail current collection.

Electrification from Paris to Lyons was completed in 1952, and the "7100" class then shared with the "9100" 2-Do-2s the heaviest and fastest runs. By the summer of 1954 there were three runs between Paris and Dijon or Paris and Lyons booked at 77.1mph (124km/h) start-to-stop with permissible loads of 650t. Another run from Paris to Dijon was booked at 76.1mph (122.4km/h) with 730t. These were the outstanding speed exploits in Europe at the time—on a railway which 10 years before was devastated by war.

In February 1954 the first very high-speed tests were made with No. CC7121 in standard condition, on a level stretch between Dijon and Beaune. The purpose of the tests was to investigate the effect of high speed on various parameters, including the forces exerted on the rails and the behaviour of the pantograph. With a train of 111t a speed of 151mph (243km/h) was reached, which was a world record for any type of traction, beating the figure of 143mph (230km/h) attained in 1931 in Germany by a curious propellor-driven railcar.

Testing then moved to the former PO railway, where a long stretch of almost straight line was available south of Bordeaux. First the problem of picking up a very heavy current was investigated with two "7100" class locomotives double-heading. With the line

voltage boosted by 25 per cent, these two reached 121mph (195km/h) with 714t and 125mph (201km/h) with 617t.

The next target was a speed of 300km/h (185mph), for which purpose No. CC7107 was fitted with gears of higher ratio than normal. The train comprised three coaches weighing 100t, with a streamlined tail attached to the rear vehicle. The target of 300km/h was reached in 21km (13 miles) from the start, and was maintained for 12km (7½ miles), but, very remarkably, speed rose to 330.8km/h (205.6mph) for 2km (1¼ miles), which required an

output of 12,000hp (8,950kW). Equally remarkably, the performance was repeated exactly on the following day by an 81t Bo-Bo, No. BB9004, one of the French-built experimental locomotives mentioned earlier. The two locomotives thus became joint world record holders, and as subsequent developments in very high-speed trains have been with railcar-type units, it is likely that this record for locomotives will stand.

The achievement of No. BB9004 was significant; a locomotive costing little more than half a "7100" had achieved the same performance, such was the pace

of locomotive development at this time. French activity was then concentrated on four-axle machines, and no more six-axle electric locomotives were built until 1964, by which time design had changed greatly with introduction of the monomotor bogie.

Although the Co-Co locomotives were soon overshadowed by their smaller successors, they took a full share in express work on the former PLM for many years, and in 1982 No. CC7001 became the first French locomotive to cover 8 million km (4.97 million miles), at an overall average of 658km (409 miles) per day.

Above: *French National Railways' Class CC7100 Co-Co 1,500V dc electric locomotive at Paris (Gare de Lyon) in February 1979.*

Below: *French National Railways' Class CC7100 electric locomotive. One of this class, No. CC7107, held the world speed record for many years after 1954.*

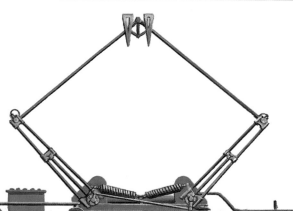

Class EM2 C₀-C₀

Great Britain:
British Railways (BR), 1954

Type: Electric express-passenger locomotive.
Gauge: 4ft 8½in (1,435mm).
Propulsion: Direct current at 1,500V supplied via overhead catenary to six 490hp (366kW) nose-suspended traction motors, one geared to each axle.
Weight: 217,280lb (97t).
Max. axleload: 36,288lb (16.2t).
Overall length: 59ft 4½in (18,000mm).
Tractive effort: 44,600lb (198kN).
Max. speed: 84mph (134km/h).

Seven of these solid reliable machines (inappropriately named after rather flighty Greek godesses) were built in 1958 by British Railways at Gorton Works in order to work the sparse passenger services over the then newly-electrified 70-mile (112km) line across the Pennine Hills from Manchester to Sheffield. Who would then have guessed that the time would come when top luxury international expresses on the continent of Europe would begin their journeys behind one of them?

Before World War II the London

& North Eastern Railway put in hand with govenment assistance an ambitious scheme to electrify the busy coal-hauling route from

Above: *Ex-British Railways EM2 class electric locomotive at Hook of Holland, with "Lorelei Express" to Basel, May 1971.*

South Yorkshire via the Woodhead tunnel to Manchester. There were major problems with steam haulage over the line but work on the project had to cease with the outbreak of war. Afterwards, a decision to resume was delayed first by nationalisation and later by a state organisation being more cautious (after all, it was someone else's money) and finding it necessary to bore a new 3-mile (4.8km) double-track tunnel for the electric trains. Accordingly, electric traction was not introduced until 1954. The LNER had been intending to re-employ on this project the North Eastern Bo-Bo locomotives already described, but BR discarded them in favour of increasing the fleet of new freight locomotives of dissimilar appearance but similar configuration.

Extravagances over matters like these were accompanied by penny-pinching on more basic things such as reballasting the permanent way, and inevitably the result was an unhappy object lesson in the effects of the heavy unsprung weight of nose-suspended motors on weak track. This did not matter as regards

Class 4E 1-C₀-C₀-1

South Africa:
South African Railways (SAR), 1954

Type: Electric mixed-traffic locomotive.
Gauge: 3ft 6in (1,067mm).
Propulsion: Direct current at 3,000V fed via overhead catenary and rheostatic control to six 505hp (377kW) nose-suspended traction motors, each geared with resilient gearwheels to one driving axle.
Weight: 288,960lb (131.1t) adhesive, 347,200lb (157.5t) total.
Max. axleload: 48,160lb (21.85t).
Overall length: 71ft 8in (21,844mm).
Tractive effort: 72,000lb (320kN).
Max. speed: 60mph (97km/h).

It almost says enough about the foresight, continuity and restraint of those who made the decisions about South African Railways' extensive electrification, that after 25 years they had only reached their fourth locomotive class. Even so, these Class "4Es" represented a brief excursion away from plain double-bogie designs by adding to a double six-wheel bogie locomotive guiding pony wheels at the outer ends. Otherwise the same solid, reliable, well-tried technology took great trains effortlessly up the long and severe climb on to the high African central plateau and across the wild Karoo as brings suburban daily-breaders up to London from

Sevenoaks or Surbiton.

North British of Glasgow and General Electric of Manchester supplied 40 of these locomotives to South African Railways in 1954 to work traffic on a 149-mile (238km) extension of electrification to Touws River. The new locos represented a 12½ per cent increase in power output over the previous best on the system. A 1,000t (1,100 US tons) freight train could be started and hauled up a 1-in-66 (1.5 per cent) grade at 25mph (40km/h) by these locomotives.

An implicit part of the scheme was a realignment of the notorious climb up the Hex River Pass, so as to improve the gradient from

1-in-40 (2.5 per cent) to this 1-in-66, and the capacity of the locomotives had been designed accordingly. However, construction of the new line was delayed and electric trains had to use the old one, hence double-heading was necessary. Fortunately multiple-unit capability was available and so the second locomotive did not need a second crew. At the end of the steepest portion, the second locomotive could be dispensed with and it was the economical

Below: *South African Railways' Class 4E 1-Co-Co-1 electric locomotive built by North British of Glasgow and General Electric of Manchester in 1954.*

slow-moving mineral trains, but passenger trains hauled by the fine new electric locomotive had to face a semi-permanent speed restriction of 60mph (96km/h) or so over the whole line. And this on a railway region whose steam trains regularly exceeded 100mph (160km/h)!

In 1968, through passenger traffic between Manchester and Sheffield was transferred to another route and so, after what would have been a fair life for a diesel but was barely a moment in time for an electric, the "EM2s" became redundant, other possible routes having been electrified on different systems. Happily a buyer appeared who found the locomotives to his liking and after a few details had been attended to (fitting of electric train heating, air brakes and different vigilance equipment as well as a major overhaul) the "EM2s" have become Netherlands Railways (NS) Class "1500".

The intention was that these locomotives should be an economical stop-gap to cover a temporary power shortage in The Netherlands. It does not, however, seem to have turned

out like that; the "EM2s" robust simplicity has found much favour and a further lease of life is now expected. For example, the use of resilient gearwheels to connect the axle-mounted motors to the wheels has ameliorated much of the bad effect on the track of this simple convenient arrangement, whilst still retaining its simplicity. Further simplification has been possible, too, since the original

Metropolitan-Vickers electrical equipment provided for regenerative braking, appropriate for the mountain grades of the "EM2s" native heath. For use in the flatlands of Holland the relevant apparatus could be dispensed with, as also could the vacuum-brake exhauster and the electrically-fired steam-heat boiler.

As a postscript, 1981 saw complete closure of the 1,500V dc

Above: *British Railways' Class EM2 Co-Co electric locomotive supplied for working between Manchester and Sheffield.*

route from Manchester to Sheffield, apart from a suburban service to Hadfield and Glossop at the Manchester end. As a result, the freight version of the "EM2"—"EM1", later Class "76"—went to the scrap heap.

practice to shunt it into an unmanned siding there. The next suitable train proceeding downhill would then collect a locomotive and use it to assist braking, using the regenerative electric system with which the "4Es" were equipped. Naturally, straight air brakes were provided for the locomotive and vacuum brake equipment for the train. The latter brake is automatically applied should there be an electrical failure during regeneration.

Right: *Class 4E locomotive No. 219. Although railways in South Africa are narrow-gauge, the locomotives are as big and as heavy as any in Europe.*

Class 12000 B₀-B₀

Type: Mixed-traffic electric locomotive.
Gauge: 4ft 8½in (1,435mm).
Propulsion: Alternating current at 25,000V 50Hz passed through transformer and mercury arc rectifier to bogie-mounted traction motors with flexible drive to axles; axles of each bogie geared together.
Weight: 188,660lb (85.6t).
Max. axleload: 47,170lb (21.4t).
Overall length: 49ft 10⅜in (1,5200mm).
Tractive effort: 54,000lb (240kN).
Max. speed: 75mph (120km/h).

At the end of World War II the standard system for main-line electrification in France was 1,500V dc, but French engineers, like those of a number of other countries, were interested in the possibility of using alternating current at the standard industrial frequency of 50Hz. This offered a number of advantages: 50Hz current could be taken from the public supply at any convenient point and only a small transformer would be needed to reduce the voltage to that required for the overhead wires. As alternating current could be reduced on the locomotives by transformer, the supply could be taken from the overhead at high voltage; the higher the voltage, the smaller the current, and the lighter the overhead wires and their supports. With high voltage, the supply points could be spaced more widely, because voltage drops in the line would be proportionally smaller than with a lower-voltage system.

The second most comprehensive test so far made with electric traction at 50Hz was on the Höllenthal line in West Germany, which happened to be in the French zone of occupation after the war. French engineers thus had an opportunity to study closely this line and the results of ten years' operation of it. They formed a favourable opinion of the system, particularly as a means of electrifying lines with lower traffic densities than had previously been considered economic for electrification. SNCF therefore chose for an experimental ac system the line from Aix-les-Bains to La Roche-sur-Foron in Savoy. This was mainly single track without complicated track layouts, but it had gradients sufficiently severe to test the equipment thoroughly. French and Swiss manufacturers supplied a number of locomotives and motor coaches for this conversion, some to work on ac only and some on both ac and dc.

Above: *A new era of railway traction was ushered in by these Class 12000 electric locomotives.*

Success of the Savoy scheme led to a bold step forward—conversion of 188 miles (303km) of the Thionville to Valenciennes route in northern France to electric working at 25,000V 50Hz. Although a secondary route, it carried three express trains and up to 100 freight trains in each direction daily, and it had gradients up to 1-in-90 (1.1 per cent).

The ac traction system in West

Below: *French National Railways' Class 12000 locomotive built for early industrial-frequency electrification. Later examples had open frameworks to support the pantographs (as shown in photograph above) instead of the plate brackets shown here.*

Germany and Switzerland used current specially generated at 16⅔Hz. A normal type of electric motor as used on dc will operate on ac, but each time the current reverses there are induced effects which tend to upset the working of the commutator. These effects are proportional to the square of the frequency. At 16⅔Hz they can be coped with, but 50Hz is a different proposition, and up to and including the Höllenthal line experiment satisfactory traction motors for this frequency had not been produced, but the target was still worth striving for.

Two main alternatives were available in a 50Hz system: to persevere with 50Hz motors or to convert the supply to some other form on the locomotive for supply to the traction motors. In fact SNCF decided to test four arrangements, conversion to dc by static convertor, direct use of the 50Hz supply, conversion to dc by rotary convertor, and conversion to three-phase by rotary machines.

For this purpose four types of locomotive were designed, two B-Bs for the first two systems and two Co-Cos for the second two. Of these systems the simplest was the second, for as with the 16⅔Hz locomotives in other countries, it involved only a transformer to step down the voltage to a value suitable for the motors, and a tap changer on the transformer to vary the voltage. For the ac to dc conversion by static convertor the Ignitron was selected. This was a form of steel-tank mercury-pool rectifier developed by Westinghouse in the United States. The two types of Co-Co locomotive had heavier equipment involving one or more rotating machines. The four classes were designated "12000", "13000", "14000", and "14100" respectively.

Layout of the locomotives was unusual in that they had centre cabs, an arrangement normally found only on shunting locomotives. The main reason for this was that SNCF had found that 50 per cent of failures of equipment in electric locomotives on the road were in the control equipment. With cabs at both ends of the locomotive, remote control of equipment was unavoidable, but with a central cab, in which the driver could use the same controls for both directions of travel, some of the equipment could be controlled directly. Further advantages were the good all-round view and more protection for the driver in collisions. A conspicuous feature of the locomotives was the platform mounted on the cab roof, and protruding beyond it, to support the pantographs.

Bogies of the B-B locomotives were derived from those of the experimental high-speed B-B machines, Nos. 9003-4, with the axles geared together, but as the new locomotives were intended for lower speeds than Nos. 9003-4, the bogie was shortened and the suspension simplified. For the Thionville line it was sufficient for one of the four classes to be capable of express passenger work, so the "12000s" were geared for 75mph (120km/h), the "13000s" for 65mph (104km/h) and the two C-C types for 37mph (60km/h).

The first of the "12000" class, No. 12001, was delivered in July 1954 and was put to work immediately on passenger and freight trains ranging from 500t to 1,300t. Control of voltage to the motors was by a tap changer on the high-tension side of the transformer as is common in ac practice. On test No. 12006 achieved some remarkable results. It started a train of 2,424t on a gradient of 1-in-100 (1 per cent), with a maximum tractive effort of 38t, or 47 per cent of the adhesive weight. At 8.5km/h the tractive effort was still 33.7t. These were outstanding figures, and the ability of the locomotive to sustain this high tractive effort, just on the point of slipping, but without actually "losing its feet", was considered to be a notable achievement of the Ignitron control in conjunction with the gearing together of the axles on each bogie. The other classes performed well, but not so well as the "12000s", and furthermore the "12000s" proved to be the most reliable.

The other classes were not extended beyond the initial orders, but a total of 148 of Class "12000" were eventually built. The success of the Thionville-Valenciennes scheme led to a major policy decision—that future electrification, except for certain extensions of existing dc routes, would be as ac at 25,000V 50Hz. The first scheme to be affected by this decision was the main line of the former Nord Railway, and this scheme met the Thionville route at its northern extremity. The last of the "12000" class were ordered as part of the Nord scheme.

Before construction of the class was complete, there was a major development in electrical equipment with introduction of the silicon diode rectifier. This was a simpler, more compact and more robust piece of equipment than the ignitron, and well suited to the rough life of equipment on a locomotive. The last 15 of the "12000s" were built with silicon rectifiers, and others have been converted over the years. As the most successful and the most numerous of the four types for the Thionville electrification, these locomotives still dominate traffic on that route.

Experience with these four classes settled finally the type of traction equipment to be used on a future ac lines. Once again, the direct 50Hz motors proved unsatisfactory, whilst the simplicity of the silicon rectifier ruled out decisively any system with rotating machinery.

FL9 B₀-A1A

Type: Electro-diesel passenger locomotive.
Gauge: 4ft 8½in (1,435mm).
Propulsion: General Motors 1,750hp (1,350kW) Type 567C V-16 two-stroke diesel engine and generator—or alternatively outside third-rail—feeding current to four nose-suspended traction motors geared to both axles of the leading truck and the outer axles of the trailing one.

Weight: 231,937lb (105.2t) adhesive, 286,614lb (130t) total.
Max. axleload: 57,984lb (26.3t).
Overall length: 59ft 0in. (17,983mm).
Tractive effort: 58,000lb (258kN).
Max. speed: 70mph (112km/h).

These unusual and interesting machines, like a number of others, were the result of that famous ordinance of the City of New York prohibiting the use therein of locomotives which emitted fumes. It occurred like this: the New Haven railroad was in the 1950s considering abandonment of its path-finding single-phase electrification, which dates from as early as 1905, and changing over to diesel traction. The only problem was how to run into New York.

New Haven trains used both the Grand Central terminal (of the New York Central RR) and the Pennsylvania Station. Both routes were equipped with conductor rails (of different patterns) supplying low-voltage direct current. This corresponded closely to the current produced in the generator of a diesel-electric locomotive and it

Mv A1A-A1A

Type: Diesel-electric mixed-traffic locomotive.
Gauge: 4ft 8½in (1,435mm).
Propulsion: General Motors Electro-Motive Division Type 567C 1,700hp (1,268kW) 16-cylinder two-stroke diesel engine and generator supplying current to four nose-suspended traction motors, one geared to each of the outer axles of the two bogies.
Weight: 154,280lb (70t) adhesive, 227,675lb (103.3t) total.
Max. axleload: 38,570lb (17.5t).
Overall length: 62ft 0in (18,900mm).
Tractive effort: 39,700lb (176kN).
Max. speed: 83mph (133km/h).

Danish State Railways were not strangers to diesel-electric motive power—their excellent *Lyntog* or "Lightning" trains had been running since the 1930s. By 1954 the time had come to put a tentative toe in the water and order a small batch of five large modern diesels for main line locomotive-hauled passenger and freight trains. With

commendable good sense they settled on more or less standard locomotives of US design produced by General Motors Electro-Motive Division, then almost the only really experienced diesel locomotive builders in the world. They were actually supplied by the Swedish locomotive-building firm of Nydqvist & Holm, better known as Nohab, who had a licence to produce EMD products in Europe. By taking bits out of EMD's comprehensive Meccano set, Nohab were able quickly to put together a suitable package for DSB. The locomotives, classified "Mv" were basically "F" cab units, but with the car body modified so that there was a driving cab at both ends. To reduce the axleload to the lower values appropriate to Europe, six-wheel trucks each with a central unmotored axle were provided. They were the same as those used on EMD's "E" units, but for differences in the springing. Indeed apart from buf-

Right: *General Motors A1A-A1A diesel-electric locomotive built by the Swedish firm of Nydqvist & Holm under licence for Danish State Railways.*

was suggested that a standard General Motors "FP9" passenger cab unit could be modified easily to work as an electric locomotive when required. The ac electrification could then be dismantled, yet trains could continue to run without breaking the law. In fact axleload restrictions led to one quite substantial change—substitution of a three-axle trailing truck for the standard two-axle one; hence a unique wheel arrangement. The end product was designated "FL9" and 60 were supplied between 1956 and 1960. The most obvious evidence of their unique arrangements were the two-position retractable collecting shoes mounted on the trucks, to cater for New York Central's under-contact conductor rail and Long Island RR's top-contact one. Otherwise the presence of additional low-voltage control gear inside the body was the principal technical difference between an "FP9" and an "FL9".

In the event the New Haven changed its mind over dispensing with the electrification, but the "FL9s" still found employment, surviving long enough to be taken over by Amtrak in the 1970s. While they existed, the "FL9s" represented a spark of originality in a country whose locomotives were and are much of a muchness (apart from their livery) from Oregon to Florida or Arizona to Maine.

Below: *New York, New Haven & Hartford Class FL9 Bo-A1A electro-diesel locomotive. These locomotives could run on current drawn from two types of third rail in New York City.*

fers, screw couplings and a Danish Royal Crown on each end, everything was totally trans-Atlantic.

It was Nohab's secret how much they did themselves and how much came over ready-assembled from EMD, but DSB made it clear they liked what they got by ordering a production batch of 54, more or less identical but with uprated engines developing 1,950hp (1,455kW). This was Class "My". Not only that, but other locomotives subsequently ordered followed the same recipe. Next came 45 of the 1,425hp (1,063kW) "MX" class and then, more recently, 46 of 3,300 to 3,900hp (2,462 to 2,910kW) "MZ" class of 1967-79. Locomotives very similar to the "Mv/My" classes went to Norway, Belgium and Hungary, and many other countries and railway administrations were to follow this excellent principle of buying locomotives off-the-shelf from the most experienced people in the business.

Left: *The Norwegian State Railways also had locomotives similar to the Danish Mv and My classes. Here is No. 3.641 at Andalsnes in August 1981.*

V200 B-B

West Germany:
German Federal Railway (DB), 1953

Type: Diesel-hydraulic express passenger locomotive.
Gauge: 4ft 8½in (1,435mm).
Propulsion: Two 1,100hp (820kW) diesel engines each driving the axles of one bogie through Voith hydraulic transmission.
Weight: 162,000lb (73.5t).
Max. axleload: 40,500lb (18.4t).
Overall length: 60ft 7in (18,470mm).
Tractive effort: 52,680lb (234kN).
Max. speed: 87mph (140km/h).

A major discouragement to the development of large diesel locomotives in the 1930s was their great weight in relation to power. By comparison with later diesel-electric locomotives, it can be seen that there were three main contributions to this weight. First the low speed of the engines; secondly heavy electrical equipment; and thirdly body construction based on steam locomotive practice with all the strength in the underframe. Apart from North America, where permissible axle-loads were up to 50 per cent greater than elsewhere, a large diesel locomotive of the 1930s inevitably had several carrying axles because the total weight was well above what was needed for adhesion.

German engineers tackled the first of these factors by developing higher-speed engines, and the second by developing hydraulic transmissions, which were inherently lighter and simpler to control than the electrical type. By 1939 many hydraulic transmissions had been made for shunting locomotives and a 1,400hp (1,040kW) 1-C-1 locomotive had been built in 1937. Further experience was gained from large numbers of locomotives in the power range 130 to 360hp which were built for the German forces.

After World War II construction of diesel-hydraulic locomotives

Right: *German Federal Railway Class V200 diesel-hydraulic loco near Lingen in 1976.*

was resumed, and the new Deutsche Bundesbahn began to develop larger units to replace steam traction on routes not scheduled for electrification. A decisive step forward was taken in 1952 with construction of a batch of 10 B-B locomotives of 800 to 1,100hp (600 to 820kW) in which three types of engine were fitted at various times. The transmission was made by Voith, who supplied about 70 per cent of all German hydraulic transmissions, and the weight was kept down to 57t by use of lightweight inside-framed bogies, by careful body design,

and by extensive use of welding. The class was originaly known as "V80", later becoming "280", and with a maximum speed of 62mph (100km/h) it was intended for freight and secondary passenger work.

The "V80" design was prepared by Krauss Maffei in conjunction with DB. Although no more locomotives of this class were built, the same firm now produced a design for an express passenger B-B locomotive incorporating two 1,100hp engines, and capable of 87mph (140km/h). Each engine drove the axles of

one bogie through a Voith transmission. The main structural members were two steel tubes, and the casing was of a distinctive streamlined form, the upper part tapered to suit the loading gauge. Five prototypes were built in 1953, with three different makes of 1,100hp engine, giving total weights of 70.5 to 73.5t. For the period, this gave a quite remarkable power-to-weight ratio. The class was designated "V200", later becoming Nos. 220.001-5.

After three years of testing, a production batch of 50 locomotives was ordered and delivery

ChS2 Cₒ-Cₒ

USSR:
Soviet Railways (SZD), 1958

Type: Electric express passenger locomotive.
Gauge: 5ft 0in (1,524mm).
Propulsion: Direct current at 3,000V fed via overhead catenary and rheostatic control system to six 828hp (618kW) traction motors driving the axles through Skoda pattern flexible drives and gearing.
Weight: 271,080lb (123t).
Max. axleload: 45,185lb (20.5t).
Overall length: 62ft 1in (18,920mm).
Tractive effort: 70,500lb (314kN).
Max. speed: 100mph (160km/h).

For many years after World War II, the pace of electrification in the USSR was such that locomotive building plants were fully occupied constructing electric locomotives for freight traffic. To obtain motive power for working electric passenger trains the Soviet Union had to look to imports, and fortunately a source was conveniently to hand in one of its satellite countries. This was the world-famous Skoda Works in Pilsen, Czechoslovakia, whose products could compete with any of those of the great industrial nations.

Two prototypes were built in 1958 for trial purposes. Evaluation was satisfactory and production

began in 1962. It did not end until 1972, after a quite amazing 944 units had been built of this very plain and straightforward design. Later examples had rheostatic (dynamic) braking as an additional feature and locomotives so fitted are designated "ChS2T" instead of "ChS".

Unusual features were few, but of interest is the glass-fibre body-work, more or less to European rather than Russian profile. As a result the pantographs have to be mounted on stilts high above the roof to compensate for the fact that the USSR loading gauge is some 2ft (600mm) higher than the European one. Top speed is

100mph (160km/h), but on few lines outside the Moscow to Leningrad trunk is such fast running relevant to day-by-day operation.

Having said that "ChS2T" production ended in 1972, it did in fact continue but with a version so different as to constitute another class, but rather confusingly not so designated. These later examples have a tall steel body, taking advantage of the full height of the SZD loading gauge. Consequently the appearance is completely different, while the electrical equipment offers 30 per cent more installed horsepower.

To add further confusion, similar-looking Skoda locomotives

began in 1956. Three makes of engine could be fitted, but the majority were of Maybach manufacture. The "V200s" proved to be very successful machines, and little trouble was experienced with the transmission equipment for five to six years. In 1960 loadings of trains were increased, and track improvements enabled the locomotives to run greater mileages at their maximum speed. A crop of transmission failures now occurred, which were traced to inadequate lubrication of part of the Voith transmission. This defect was remedied and in 1962 the class averaged 145,000 miles (233,000km) per locomotive on duties which were 30 per cent more onerous than the performance specified for the design. They were capable of hauling 700t on the level at 62mph (100km/h) and a 305t train at a sustained 50mph (80km/h) on a 1-in-100 gradient.

A further batch of 50 locomotives was now built with larger engines of 1,350hp. A number of improvements were made to the design, including the bogies, and

the weight was between 78 and 79.5t. These units went into service in 1962. By the early 1980s further electrification had made some of the "V200" series redundant, and several were sold. The remaining units were concentrated in northern Germany.

Although German locomotives were designed with an eye to the export market, few of the twin-engined machines were exported. Their largest application outside West Germany was on the Western Region of British Railways, but those locomotives were built in Britain.

Right: *A Class V200 diesel hydraulic locomotive No. 220 023-6 leaves Aalen with a German Federal Railway Nuremburg to Stuttgart express in Autumn 1969.*

Below: *For use on lines which are not electrified, the German Federal Railway developed powerful diesel-hydraulic locomotives instead of the diesel-electric designs favoured in other countries.*

(classes "ChS4" and "ChS4T") have been built for 25,000V 50Hz lines in the Soviet Union. Quite distinctive in appearance, but belonging to the same family, is a still experimental small batch of double Bo-Bo+ Bo-Bo locomotives for the dc lines, with a power output of 10,720hp (8,400kW). These Class "ChS200" machines are geared for 125mph (200km/h) running, ready for the day when such speeds can be offered to SZD's patient customers.

Right: *Czech-built Class ChS2 electric locomotive on trials in the USSR at Kalinin on the October Railway, 1959.*

Class 30* A1A-A1A
Great Britain:
British Railways (BR), 1957

Type: Mixed-traffic diesel-electric locomotive.
Gauge: 4ft 8½in (1,435mm).
Propulsion: Mirrlees 1,250hp (933kW) JVST12T 12-cylinder Vee diesel engine and generator supplying direct current to four nose-suspended traction motors geared to the outer axles of the bogies.
Weight: 163,100lb (74t) adhesive, 232,520lb (105.5t) total.
Max. axleload: 40,775lb (18.5t).
Overall length: 56ft 9in (17,297mm).
Tractive effort: 42,800lb (190kN).
Max. speed: 80mph (128km/h).

*As classified in 1968; later, these locos were re-engined and became Class 31.

These low-key machines were some of the very earliest to be supplied under British Railways' so-called pilot scheme for dieselisation, under which a multitude of builders were asked to supply locomotives of various powers and weights. Orders for this programme were placed in late-1955. Brush Engineering of Loughborough based the design on a batch of 25 locomotives supplied to Ceylon in 1953, and in October 1955 No. D5500, the first of an order of 20, was handed over to British Railways.

Originally a Mirrlees 1,250hp (933kW) engine was fitted, but later examples had the more powerful 1,470hp (1,097kW) English Electric 12VV 12-cylinder Vee engine, which later became standard for the whole batch, leading eventually to reclassification as Class "31". One unusual feature of an otherwise very conventional machine was addition of an idle axle between each pair of driving axles to reduce axleload. Steam heating boilers were fitted as well as the usual vacuum train brake equipment. The bogies are one-piece steel castings and they and the underframes were supplied by Beyer Peacock of Manchester.

Although they possessed a quite extraordinarily low power-to-weight ratio of only 11.8hp (8.8kW) per tonne of locomotive weight, the recipe of solid, simple, conventional engineering was in one way successful, for over the years this class proved itself one of the most reliable in the whole of BR's diesel fleet. This in spite of the fact that one disgraced itself by failing when hauling HM The Queen on the first occasion that the Royal Train was entrusted to diesel traction. However, steam came quickly to the rescue and the incident was soon forgotton.

More important was that the class was good enough to be built up to a total of 362 over the years, and that even today well over 200 are still giving good service as Class "31", although withdrawal is proceeding slowly. Even so, it has been thought worthwhile to make improvements to 24 of them (sub-class "31.4") which have been modernised by provision of dual air and vacuum brakes, and electric train-heating equipment.

Right: *British Railways' Class 31 A1A-A1A diesel-electric locomotive at York, September 1982.*

Below: *British Railways' No. D5603 at Oakleigh Park on the Welwyn to King's Cross train.*

Kodama 8-car Trainset
Japan:
Japanese National Railways (JNR), 1958

Type: Express passenger electric train.
Gauge: 3ft 6in (1,067mm).
Propulsion: Direct current at 1,500V supplied via overhead catenary to two power cars and then fed to sixteen 135hp (100kW) traction motors, geared to the axles of the two power cars and to those of two adjacent cars.
Weight: 322,560lb (146t) adhesive, 609,280lb (276t) total.
Max. axleload: 21,280lb (9.6t).
Overall length: 546ft 0in (166,420mm).
Max. speed: 75mph (120km/h).

Electrification of the Tokaido line, the most important in Japan and connecting the capital with the city of Osaka, was an opportunity for the railway to take a considerable step forward. It is generally assumed that high speeds cannot be run on narrow-gauge tracks. Of course, the two things are not necessarily interdependent—it is more that heavy well-maintained track is not common on narrow-gauge railways. So far the best achievement had been by steam before 1939 in the island of Java where 70mph (120km/h) was run, but these spectacular Japanese trains—known as *Kodama* or "Echo"—are something else again. The 344 miles (553km) from Tokyo to Osaka were timed in 6hr 50min, an average speed of 50mph (80km/h), certainly a record for any narrow-gauge line.

The two outer cars of each eight-car unit, which look as if they do the work, are in fact mere driving trailers. The main power

Right: *Japanese National Railways' eight-car "Kodama" high-speed electric train.*

cars are the second and seventh; traction motors are provided on the bogies of the power cars and the adjacent cars (the third and sixth). In each of the latter a small buffet is provided. The two centre cars are plain trailers providing 104 second-class seats. The rest of the train provides seating for 321 third-class passengers. Features provided for the benefit of travellers include air coolers fitted on the roof for use in hot weather, drinking water, telephone booths, earphones for receiving radio programmes and even speedometers in the buffet cars. Impressed as the first travellers must have been by 120km/h plus, little did they know that in a few years they would regard such speeds by a train on this route

Right: *The streamlined nose and conning-tower of a Japanese "Kodama" (Echo) trainset.*

as practically standing still.

These *Kodama* trains (now Class "481") became the prototypes for a dynasty of high-speed electric self-propelled trains that relatively soon were to provide the majority of express services in Japan on the state-owned narrow-gauge lines. Twelve-car units came soon, as well as sets which could also run on lines electrified with alternating current at standard industrial frequency. Things were further complicated by the fact that different areas of Japan have different standards in this respect —necessitating tri-current power equipment for dc and 50Hz and 60Hz ac. Even so, the challenge was met in providing for this requirement without encroaching on all-important revenue space. In addition to the electric sets, some diesel-hydraulic trains of similar appearance have been built for use on non-electrified lines.

Class 40 1-C₀-C₀-1

Great Britain:
British Railways (BR), 1958

Type: Mixed-traffic diesel-electric locomotive.
Gauge: 4ft 8½in (1,435mm).
Propulsion: English Electric 2,000hp (1,480kW) Type SVT V-16 four-stroke turbocharged diesel engine and generator supplying current to six 240hp (180kW) nose-suspended traction motors geared to the main axles.
Weight: 238,032lb (100t) adhesive, 293,132lb (134t) total.
Max. axleload: 29,672lb (18t).
Overall length: 69ft 6in (21,037mm).
Tractive effort: 52,000lb (231kN).
Max. speed: 90mph (145km/h).

After the formation of British Railways in 1948, the controlling body, the Railway Executive, decided that its motive power policy would be based on the use of home-produced fuel. As Britain had little indigenous oil at that time, this implied that steam traction would be retained until electrification was possible. There was an exception in that the use of diesel shunters would be extended, as experience on the LMS had shown marked economies despite the use of imported fuel. The five main-line diesel-electric locomotives which BR acquired from the LMS and SR therefore commanded little interest, although they were used as fully as circumstances permitted, and gave valuable information to BR engineers. The fifth of these locomotives, No. 10203, which was the third of the SR machines, incorporated some important changes from the preceding four, notably in having a 2,000hp engine. This pointed the way ahead, but no immediate steps were taken to incorporate the lessons learned from No. 10203 in an up-to-date design.

By 1955 it was clear that the deteriorating quality of coal, and the difficulty of getting labour for the more disagreeable tasks of steam locomotive maintenance, made a change of policy urgently necessary. The government therefore agreed to a massive modernisation programme, in which several of the busiest main lines from London would be electrified on the overhead system, the SR third-rail system would be extended, and the whole of the remainder of BR would be turned over to diesel traction. Plans were made for a fleet of diesel locomotives which were to be divided into four main groups, numbered in ascending order of power. The highest was Type 4, which embraced locomotives in the power range 2,000 to 2,300hp; a fifth group was added later to include the 3,300hp "Deltic" locomotives.

Right: An Aberdeen to Edinburgh express, hauled by No. 40151, leaving Montrose. Note the "arrow" warning board indicating a temporary restriction of speed to 40mph (64km/h).

At this time Britain had one industrial group, English Electric, which could build complete diesel-electric locomotives, including engines and electrical equipment. It had supplied either complete shunting locomotives, or the engines and electrical equipment for them, to each of the four groups before nationalisation, and also the engines and equipment for the five existing main-line diesels. At first English Electric had built diesel locomotives in its works at Preston, but after World War II it made an agreement to sub-contract the assembly of locomotives to a locomotive manufacturer of great historical importance. This company was an amalgamation of Robert Stephenson, Hawthorn Leslie and the Vulcan Foundry, with a continuous record of steam locomotive construction from 1825. In 1955 this company was absorbed into English Electric.

Apart from English Electric, there were firms which could supply diesel engines, supply electrical equipment, or assemble locomotives, but not all three. A scheme was considered for importing some EMD diesels from the USA, to be followed by the granting of licences for several British companies to build to EMD designs, but this was rejected on political grounds. BR then embarked on a pilot scheme of 171 locomotives of 13 different types. Manufacture of these units was spread over a number of companies, to exploit to the full the expertise and capacity of the industry and of BR's workshops.

Not surprisingly, English Electric received the largest share; 40 locomotives were ordered, including 10 of Type 4. Although English Electric was to execute the detailed design, the broad layout was specified by BR. In view of the urgency of the pilot scheme there was no time for more design work than was absolutely necessary. The Co-Co arrangement of

Above: *British Railways' Class 40 1-Co-Co-1 diesel-electric locomotive No. 40183 at Scarborough in August 1982.*

the LMS locomotives was ruled out for general use on BR by its high axleload, and the only tried layout with eight axles was that of the SR locomotives. This design was therefore adopted, including the plate frames of the bogies, the axleboxes closely derived from steam practice, and the segmental pads for transmitting body weight to the bogies. By contemporary diesel and electric standards this was a crude arrangement, but it

had been successful so far on the SR units, and it enabled the axle-load to be kept down to 18t.

The general equipment of the locomotives was very similar to the third SR locomotive, No. 10203, but, as on the LMS main-line diesels, it was thought advisable to position the cabs slightly away from the ends to give the enginemen some protection. Doors were provided in the ends to allow a gangway to connect two locomotives working in multiple, but these were little used and were later removed. All locomotive-hauled passenger trains on BR were at this time steam heated, and the new locomotives not only had a boiler and a large water tank, but also scoops for replenishing the tanks from the water-troughs provided for steam engines.

The 10 locomotives were delivered between March and September 1958, and were divided between the East Coast main line from King's Cross to the north and the former Great Eastern line from London Liverpool Street; they were numbered D200 to D209, and until the introduction of a new classification system in 1971 were generally known as "EE Type 4". Their reception was mixed; they suffered from a number of teething troubles, one of which was indicative of a problem which was to plague BR until steam heating was eliminated — the train-heating boiler. Although unable to equal an LNER or BR Pacific at its very best at high speed, the diesels' high starting tractive effort and high adhesive weight gave them an advantage over steam engines at lower speeds.

More importantly, whatever they could do, they could continue to do for long periods day-in, day-out, and it was this ability which gave them a lead over indifferently-maintained and poorly-fuelled steam engines. They soon undertook daily workings which

were well beyond the capacity of contemporary British steam, although, as was often demonstrated during the teething troubles of the diesels, steam engines could approach their performance remarkably closely when given special attention.

Before the first 10 locomotives had been delivered, political pressure was applied to BR to accelerate the elimination of steam, and despite the intention to test the pilot-scheme locomotives thoroughly before placing further orders, five more orders had been placed for "EE Type 4" locomotives by 1960, bringing the total to 200 units.

The most important fields of

activity of the class were the East Coast and West Coast main lines. On the former they largely replaced the LNER Pacifics until they in turn were displaced by the "Deltic" locomotives and the 2,750hp Brush Type 4s. On the West Coast route they dominated passenger traffic until completion of electrification from Euston to Liverpool and Manchester in 1967, by which time the larger English Electric 2,700hp locomotives were taking over West Coast traffic north of Crewe. The "EE Type 4" machines were then transferred to less demanding duties, largely freight traffic in the north of England. Although various troubles with the class had now been

cured, they continued to suffer from cracks in the frames and other troubles associated with the primitive frame and axlebox construction. The locomotives suffered and the track suffered, but overall they became dependable and popular machines. Under the 1971 classification scheme they became Class "40."

In the late-1970s BR's requirement for diesel locomotives declined, and a number of the earlier classes were scheduled for elimination. General withdrawal of Class "40" began in 1980, but was prolonged, and they continued on passenger workings to North Wales each summer when train-heating was not required.

The class was originally painted in standard BR green, which was actually Great Western locomotive green. From 1967 this gradually gave way to BR rail blue, but such was public interest in the class in its latter days that BR repainted one of them in its old livery for working special trains.

The 2,000hp engine fitted to Class "40" was one of a long series of English Electric engines with 10in × 12in (254mm × 305mm) cylinders. The first locomotive application was a six-cylinder version for shunters made in 1934. Subsequently a total of 1,233 engines of this type were supplied to BR and its predecessors between 1934 and 1962. In the late-1930s the development of an engine of Vee-form was undertaken with a two-cylinder test unit, and the first outcome of this work was the 16-cylinder engine fitted to the LMS and SR main-line diesels and to Class "40."

For the BR modernisation programme eight-cylinder and 12-cylinder versions were built. The former was used in a Bo-Bo locomotive of 1,000hp of which 228 were built, and the latter in 309 1,750hp Co-Co locomotives of Class "37." It was Class "37" which was the most direct successor to the pioneer LMS locomotives Nos. 10000-1, but the latter, with a weight of 127½t, were limited in the routes over which they could work, whereas Class "37" weighed between 101t and 105t (according to fittings) and could work very widely over BR. Altogether English Electric had supplied 2,082 diesel engines to BR by 1975, and development of the same family of engines continued under the auspices of GEC.

Class "40" was neither the most powerful nor the most numerous of early BR main-line diesels, but it was the first successful production main-line diesel on the system, and the contribution it made towards acceptance of diesels on a largely steam-operated railway was of great historical importance. The class will be remembered also for the high-pitched whistle of its supercharger, which made it one of the easiest of BR diesels to identify by sound alone.

Above: *A train of empty hopper wagons leaves York for Morpeth, Northumberland, behind Class 40 No. 40152 in October 1979.*

Below: *Class 40 1-Co-Co-1 No. D312 with a London to Carlisle express, climbing the 1 in 75 (1.33%) past Shap Wells in September 1964.*

Class 44 "Peak" 1-Co-Co-1
Great Britain:
British Railways (BR), 1959

Type: Diesel-electric express passenger locomotive.
Gauge: 4ft 8½in (1,435mm).
Propulsion: 2,300hp (1,715kW) Sulzer Type 12LDA28 twin-bank turbocharged diesel engine and generator supplying current to six nose-suspended traction motors geared to the axles with resilient gearwheels.
Weight: 255,360lb (116t) adhesive, 309,120lb (140t) total.
Max. axleload: 42,560lb (19.5t).
Overall length: 67ft 11in (20,701mm).
Tractive effort: 70,000lb (311kN).
Max. speed: 90mph (144km/h).

The famous "Peaks" when new were the highest-powered diesel-electric locomotives supplied to BR. They were the first of a huge and unprecedented order for 147 express passenger locomotives (later increased to 193) with Sulzer twin-bank engines (with two parallel crankshafts in the same crankcase). Most of the latter were made under licence by Vickers

Armstrong of Barrow-in-Furness, England. After the first 10, engines rated 200hp (150kW) higher were provided.

Above: *No. 46004 takes a Newcastle to Liverpool express across the King Edward Bridge over the Tyne in April 1977.*

Running gear was similar to that of the Class "40" locomotives already described. This, together with the bodywork, was built at BR's Derby and Crewe works where the locomotives were erected. Electrical equipment for the first 137 engines came from Crompton Parkinson (CP) and for the remainder from Brush Engineering.

Originally the class was numbered D1 to D193, in the prime position in BR's diesel list. Later, the 10 original 2,300hp Sulzer/CP locomotives became Class "44", the 2,500hp Sulzer/CP batch Class "45" and the 2,500hp Sulzer/Brush batch Class "46". All were provided with such usual equipment as an automatic train-heating steam boiler, a vacuum exhauster for train brakes, straight air brakes for the locomotives, multiple-unit control gear and a toilet. Later, the locomotives were fitted for working air-braked trains and (in some cases) heating electrically-heated carriages. The first 10 were named after mountain peaks in Britain; a few others received names of regiments and other military formations.

TEP-60 Co-Co
USSR:
Soviet Railways (SZD), 1960

Type: Diesel-electric express passenger locomotive.
Gauge: 5ft 0in (1,524mm).
Propulsion: Type D45A 3,000hp (2,240kW) turbocharged 16-cylinder two-stroke diesel engine and generator supplying current to six spring-borne 416hp (310kW) traction motors geared to the axles via flexible drives of the Alsthom floating-ring type.
Weight: 284,316lb (129t).
Max. axleload: 47,390lb (21.5t).
Overall length: 63ft 2in (19,250mm).
Tractive effort: 55,750lb (248kN).
Max. speed: 100mph (160km/h).

These powerful single-unit machines form one of the Soviet Union's principal diesel-electric passenger locomotive classes, although at the time of writing they are due to be displaced from the very top assignments by the 4,000hp "TEP-70" class. Production of the "TEP-60" continued for a least 15 years, though the total number built has not been revealed. For many years it has been the only type of Soviet diesel locomotive passed for running at speeds above 140km/h (87mph), although neither the need nor the opportunity for such fast running really exists as yet on the SZD network.

Russian experience with diesel locomotives was minimal (and, as

far as it went, totally unsatisfactory) before World War II. Therefore in 1945 the mechanical engineers began with a clean sheet and the early diesels were based very sensibly on US practice. By 1960, however, sufficient confidence had been attained so that original ideas could be incorporated.

A serious weakness in early adaptations of freight locomotives to passenger work was the bad tracking of the bogies. Having regard to SZD aspirations towards faster passenger trains, some electric locomotives had been ordered from Alsthom of France, maker of the bogies for world railway speed record-breaker, French National Railways' Co-Co No. 7107.

Alsthom features were used in the bogies for the "TEP-60" in particular the flexible drive which enabled the traction motors to be spring-borne, and the prototype was able to reach 118mph (189km/h) on test. This was claimed at the time to be a world record for a diesel locomotive and certainly vindicated the restrained wisdom of those responsible for the design. Other features of note in these locomotives included electric braking and the ability to cope with temperatures both hot and cold considerably more extreme than are found in conjunction on other railways.

Right: *Typical Russian diesel locomotives in double harness.*

Although there was 15 per cent more power available than on the Class "40s", the "Peaks" also had very little margin in hand when working to the best steam schedules. But even though one may criticise the design as being unenterprising, with little to offer over and above steam traction, it must be said that this slow-solid approach has paid off in longevity. At the time of writing after more than 20 years, 130 of the original 193 are still in service, while many of their more enterprising successors have taken their brilliant performances with them to the scrapyard.

Right: *A Newcastle to King's Cross relief express passes Brandon, County Durham on Easter Monday, 1978, hauled by Class 46 1-Co-Co-1 No. 46042. Apart from peak periods this class is now mainly confined to freight work.*

Below: *One of the original "Peak" class 1-Co-Co-1 diesel-electric locomotives, now Class 44, depicted in original colours, style and numbering.*

Class 060DA Cₒ-Cₒ

Romania: Romanian State Railways (CFR), 1960

Type: Mixed-traffic diesel-electric locomotive.
Gauge: 4ft 8½in (1,435mm).
Propulsion: Sulzer Type 12LDA28 2,300hp (1,690kW) turbocharged twin-bank 12-cylinder diesel engine and generator supplying direct current to six traction motors driving the axles via resilient gearwheels.
Weight: 257,870lb (117t).
Max. axleload: 42,980lb (19.5t).

Overall length: 55ft 9in (17,000mm).
Tractive effort: 64,125lb (285kN).
Max. speed: 62mph (100km/h).

The bulk of the diesel-electric locomotive fleet used by Romanian State Railways is based on six prototypes constructed in Switzerland during 1959. Mechanical parts were built by the Swiss Locomotive Works, the electrical

equipment by Brown Boveri, and the diesel engines supplied by Sulzer. There are of the "twin bank" configuration with two parallel rows of cylinders, each driving a separate crankshaft.

The elegant bodywork is typical of Swiss locomotives and is of welded construction. No train heating equipment is included; separate heating vans are used when required.

A 550t freight train can be started by one of these locomotives

on the ruling grade (1-in-40 — 2.5 per cent) of the Brasnov to Bucharest main line and accelerated up to 9mph (14km/h). For heavier loads, the locomotives can be run in multiple. There is no rheostatic or regenerative braking, but the usual straight and automatic air brakes are provided. Automatic detection and correction of wheelslip is a help on these severe grades.

Production of these locomotives has continued in Romania and they are also offered for export.

Class 124 "Trans-Pennine"

Great Britain: British Railways (BR), 1960

Type: Diesel-mechanical express passenger train.
Gauge: 4ft 8½in (1,435mm).
Propulsion: Two 230hp (172kW) Leyland-Albion Type EN602 six-cylinder horizontal diesel engines mounted beneath each of four motor coaches. Each motor drives one bogie through a fluid coupling four-speed Wilson epicyclic gearbox, cardan shafts and gearing.
Weight: 361,455lb (164t) adhesive, 500,310lb (227t) total.
Max. axleload: 23,140lb (10.5t).
Overall length: 395ft 10in (120,650mm).
Max. speed: 75mph (120km/h).

In 1955 British Railways announced a modernisation plan, a central feature of which was replacement of steam traction by diesel and electric. The first aspect of this plan to make an impact on the

public was on trains for rural lines and local services. The necessary experience was to hand in a series of diesel-mechanical railcars built for the Great Western Railway between 1933 and 1941, and in a very short time a fleet of self-propelled diesel multiple-unit (DMU) trains eventually totalling 3,740 cars had taken over most local and short-distance trains on non-electrified lines. Although few of these routes actually became viable as a result of the change over, in general expenses fell sharply and revenue rose.

After a few years the same attention was given to shorter-distance express passenger services and outstanding amongst these schemes was the Trans-Pennine services between Liverpool, Manchester, Leeds and Hull. The remarkable trains built in 1960 for this service were the ultimate development of the basic DMU layout, using small multiple

underfloor-mounted diesel engines driving the wheels through remotely-controlled mechanical gearboxes.

For the "Trans-Pennine" sets, formed of six cars, 230hp (172kW) engines were used rather than the 150hp (112kW) more typical of the average DMU. Each set

Above: *A British Railways' Class 124 "Trans-Pennine" diesel-mechanical train set near Selby, Yorkshire, in Autumn 1976.*

had eight engines mounted in twos under the two end cars and two intermediate cars. There was a buffet/grill, and first-class pass-

Left, right and below:
Romanian State Railways' Class 060DA diesel-electric Co-Co locomotive No. 06204333. These multi-purpose machines of Swiss origin have been produced over a long period, and are used extensively on passenger and freight train workings all over the network. The bright livery is an innovation—a drab green typical of European railway systems was the rule in Romania for many years.

engers at each end had an observation car ride, looking through wrap-around end windows. Seating was provided for 60 first and 232 second class passengers in main-line comfort. The control system allowed these trains to run in multiple with other DMUs in the area.

The central section of the line is steeply-graded and the relatively high power-to-weight ratio of 8hp (6kW) per tonne could be used to advantage. A steam timing of 3hr 30min for the 128 miles (204km) from Hull to Liverpool was brought down to 2hr 51min. Of this improvement, no less than 5½ minutes was attributable to faster running on the 7.1 mile (11.4km) climb from Huddersfield to Standedge tunnel, mostly at 1-in-96 (1.04 per cent).

Existence of eight independent propulsion systems gave reliability, although one or two were usually "out" on any particular journey which meant a small loss of time. Even so, for some years many people who had previously

used their cars to cross the Pennines by indifferent narrow roads "let the train take the strain"—in the words of a BR slogan of more recent days.

Construction of the M62 motorway, however, following the same route, came at a time when these trains were beginning to show their age, and restored the status quo. Loss of patronage led to economy measures such as withdrawal of the buffet cars, extra stops, removal of power equipment from intermediate cars and speed restrictions on track overdue for renewal; it all added up to a 20 minute increase in journey time. This in its turn has led to further loss of patronage and a reorientation of the service, which now consists of locomotive-hauled trains running from North Wales or Liverpool to Leeds and Scarborough and DMUs running from Leeds to Hull.

Right: *A re-formed four-car "Trans-Pennine" set at Hessle near Hull in October 1980.*

TEE Four-car train

Type: High-speed diesel-electric luxury train.

Gauge: 4ft 8½in (1,435mm).

Propulsion: Two Werkspoor 1,000hp (746kW) Type RUHB1616 16-cylinder diesel engines and generators supplying current to four traction motors geared with flexible drive to the outer axles of the power car bogies.

Weight: 176,320lb (80t) adhesive, 506,920lb (230t) total.

Max. axleload: 44,080lb (20t).

Overall length: 318ft 0in (96,926mm).

Max. speed: 87mph (139km/h).

One of the most distinguished men of the rail was a Dutch engineer called F.Q. den Hollander. It was he who in a few short years after World War II transformed mountains of twisted wreckage into the modern Netherlands Railways—an efficient (though small) railway which was and is a model system and which the rest of the world has for so long rightly tried to emulate. Later, den Hollander left his mark on the European scene as the driving force behind creation of a network of high-speed international luxury express routes known still as Trans-Europe-Express or TEE.

It was a firm principle of the operation that frontier delays should be minimal and accordingly it was arranged that all customs and immigration formalities should be conducted aboard while the train was in motion. Furthermore, locomotive changing was eliminated and carriage-shuffling made impossible by making the trains self-propelled and self-contained. Frontier halts measured in hours for regular trains became momentary for the TEEs, a notable example being the 3 minutes allowed in Basle. The objective was to provide an attractive service for business travellers, with the fastest

possible timings compatible with smooth riding, air-conditioning and superior cuisine. First class fares plus a supplement were charged. France, West Germany, The Netherlands, Belgium, Italy and Switzerland were the principal partners in the enterprise—as well as, and in spite of a change of gauge, Spain. Admittedly the gauge-changing operation at the Spanish frontier was not absolutely momentary. Each of the partici-

Below: *A Dutch-Swiss TEE near Mörschwil, Switzerland, on the Zurich-Munich "Bavaria" express, October 1972.*

Above: *The power car of the Dutch-Swiss type of diesel-electric high-speed luxury Trans Europe Express set.*

Right: *TEE Dutch-Swiss unit ready to leave Paris Est on the evening "L'Arbaléte" service to Basle in June 1966.*

pants provided trains for different services and the sets described here were jointly owned, provided and developed by Dutch and Swiss enterprise. They include 114 seats, kitchen, and driving positions at both ends, as well as accommodation for customs and immigration staff.

The power car is essentially a powerful locomotive equipped for remote control. In addition to the pair of 1,000hp (746kW) diesel engines for traction, a further 350hp generator set is provided to supply power for train heating, cooking, air-conditioning and lighting. In those days it was not possible to muster all this equipment with a total weight sufficiently low to keep within the permissible axleload, using a pair of two-axle bogies. Hence the two idler axles in the centre of each bogie.

The principal service provided by the Dutch-Swiss TEEs was the "Edelweiss" express once daily each way from Amsterdam via Brussels and Luxembourg to Basle

and Zurich. The 656 miles (1,050km) were covered in 9hr 33min including 13 stops at a remarkable average speed of 69mph (110km/h). In 1957, electrification over the whole route was not quite complete; even when it was, four electric supply systems were involved (1,500V dc in The Netherlands, 3,000V dc in Belgium, 25,000V 50Hz in France and 15,000V 16⅔Hz in Switzerland), so diesel traction was the only possible choice. The trains also shared in operating TEE services between Paris, Brussels and Amsterdam.

Developments of economic quadri-current power equipment in due time led to substitution of electric trains but it was not the end of the line for the diesels. A buyer in faraway Canada took three sets which moved from one of the most highly developed areas of the world to one of the least—the Ontario Northland Railway's "Northlander" makes daily 243-mile (388km) runs between

Toronto and Timmins, equipped with these ex-TEE trains, serving places so remote that roads have only recently been built.

Below: *Basle to Paris Trans-Europe Express-train passes Culmont-Chalindrey, France, with Dutch-Swiss set, June 1966.*

Class Dm3 1-D+D+D-1

Sweden: Swedish State Railway (SJ), 1960

Type: Electric locomotive for heavy mineral traffic.

Gauge: 4ft 8½in (1,435mm).

Propulsion: Single-phase low-frequency current at 15,000V 16⅔Hz fed via overhead catenary and step-down transformer to six 1,609hp (1,200kW) motors, driving the wheels by gearing, jackshaft and connecting rods.

Weight: 528,960lb (240t) adhesive, 595,080lb (270t) total.

Max. axleload: 44,080lb (20t).

Overall length: 115ft 8in (35,250mm).

Tractive effort: 210,000lb (932kN).

Max. speed: 47mph (75km/h).

To exploit the vast deposits of iron ore found in the interior of northern Sweden, a railway was needed. It was comparatively easy work to build from the Baltic port of Lulea to the mining area around Kiruna, but the Baltic at this latitude, near to the Arctic circle, freezes over in the winter. Accordingly, the railway was continued further north still as well as westwards, crossing not only the Ofoten mountains but the Arctic circle itself, and what is now the Norwegian frontier, to reach the sheltered port of Narvik, kept free of ice year-round by the friendly Gulf Stream. The iron ore railway from Lulea to Narvik, which began in 1883, extends for a total of 295 miles (473km).

Steam operation was fairly traumatic, especially in winter, because of the heavy loads, the very low temperatures, the mountain gradients, not to speak of continuous darkness. Apart from the mosquitos, in summer things were more pleasant—for example, the lineside tourist hotel at Abisko (with no access except by train!) boasts a north-facing sun verandah to catch the midnight sun!

It is not surprising then that the Lappland iron ore railway was the first important line in Scandinavia to be electrified. Electric working began in 1915 and conversion was completed throughout in 1923. The low-frequency single-phase system was adopted, by then well-proven in Switzerland and elsewhere.

The quality of the iron ore from Kiruna, together with the ease with which it can be won—plus, it must be said, the long-standing neutrality of Sweden, which means that customers are never refused on political grounds—always kept demand high and, in the long term, ever-rising. The problem for the railways, then, has in most years been concerned with the ability to handle the traffic offering.

Below: *A Swedish State Railways Class Dm3 electric locomotive hauls an iron ore train through the forests of Swedish Lappland.*

So far, doubling the line has been avoided by increasing the weight of the trains, and today they are the heaviest in Europe.

It is typical of the Swedish way of railroading that the motive power there today is a modest adaptation of the early standard and essentially simple Class "D" locomotive, already described. The result is this Class "Dm" locomotive of 9,650hp (7,200kW), designed to haul the now legendary ore trains. Loads of up to 5,200t (5,720 US tons) are taken up 1-in-100 (1 per cent) gradients, as well as started in polar temperatures—thereby explaining the need for a tractive effort exceeding 200,000lb (900kN).

One might be puzzled why Swedish State Railways designate this mighty hauler as a sub-class (the "m" in Dm stands for *malm* or iron) of their modest and ubiquitous Class "D" 1-C-1 standard electric locomotive. The reason was that the original Class "Dm" could be said to be two "Ds" with an additional coupled axle substituted for one pony truck on each unit, which also had a cab at only one end. Two units coupled permanently back-to-back originally formed a Class "Dm" locomotive and these were introduced in the late 1940s. Eventually there were 19 twin locomotives plus four owned by Norwegian State Railways (the NSB class is "el 12"). Both the brown Swedish engines and the green Norwegian ones operate indiscriminately over the whole line.

In 1960 still more power was required and three cab-less units (also without pantographs) were built and put in the middle of three existing pairs. By 1970 all the Swedish "Dm" pairs had been converted to triples in this way.

Each individual unit bears a separate number although units are not separated in normal operation. The huge tractive effort available has caused problems with

Below: *A 9,600hp three-unit Class Dm3 iron ore locomotive of the Swedish State Railways. The use of rod-drive in a locomotive constructed after 1960 is an unusual feature.*

the traditional screw couplings and a start has been made on fitting Russian-pattern automatic knuckle couplers.

As a rod-drive locomotive the "Dm3" was the last of its line. Since 1970 a need for additional power has been met, and history made to repeat itself, by modifying

the current standard Swedish high-power Class "Rc4" express passenger locomotive. The alterations include lower gearing, very sophisticated wheel slip control and addition of 10t (12 US tons) of ballast, all in aid of improving tractive effort, while cabs are insulated against arctic temperatures.

Above and below: *Swedish State Railways' Class Dm3 heavy freight locomotive. These mighty haulers are used for the iron ore traffic from Kiruna in northern Sweden to the ice-free port of Narvik situated well north of the Arctic Circle in northern Norway.*

U25B B₀-B₀

United States:
General Electric Company (GE), 1960

Type: Diesel-electric road switcher locomotive.
Gauge: 4ft 8½in (1,435mm).
Propulsion: One GE FDL16 2,500hp (1,870kW) four-stroke 16-cylinder Vee engine and generator supplying four nose-suspended traction motors geared to the axles.
Weight: 260,000lb (118.0t).
Max. axleload: 65,000lb (29.5t).
Overall length: 60ft 2in (18,340mm).
Tractive effort: 81,000lb (360kN) with 65mph gear ratio.
Max. speed: 65mph (105km/h), 75mph (121km/h), 80mph (129km/h) or 92mph (148km/h) according to gear ratio fitted.

If, in the 1920s, one had said to an American locomotive engineer: "The diesel-electric locomotive seems to have great potential; which locomotive manufacturer is capable of exploiting it?" he would almost certainly have said "General Electric", for that company was then building on 30 years' experience of electric traction of all sorts by turning out diesel switchers (shunters) incorporating various makes of engine. However, the prophet would have been wrong, for it was the massive resources of General Motors Corporation thrown into its Electro-Motive Division which sparked off, and largely fuelled, the steam-to-diesel revolution in the United States.

GE was thus destined to take a minor part in the overall process, but within the 25 per cent or so of the market which did not fall to EMD, it has always had a major share. When the American Locomotive Company (Alco) embarked seriously on production of road

diesels, it made an agreement with GE to use only GE electrical equipment in its products, in return for which GE agreed not to compete with Alco. From 1940 to 1953 both companies benefited from this agreement; Alco profited from the expertise of the biggest firm in the electric traction business, and GE acquired an easy market for products which it was well qualified and equipped to supply. A second manufacturer, Fairbanks Morse, likewise offered GE equipment in its models.

By the early-1950s, total dieselisation of the US railroads was certain, and although Alco was well established in the market, its sales ran a poor second to EMD and were not improving. GE then took the plunge; it quietly terminated its agreement with Alco and embarked on development of its own range of large diesels. Although most of its previous diesels had been small switchers, it had in fact built a 2,000hp (1,490kW) Sulzer-engined unit in 1936, which

for 10 years was North America's most powerful single-engined diesel locomotive, and in the post-war years the company had built up an export market in road locomotives.

The essential requirement for GE to enter the home road-diesel market was a large engine. At this time its switchers were fitted with Cooper-Bessemer 6-cylinder in-line and 8-cylinder Vee engines, so the company acquired the rights to develop this engine. Two versions were made, the 8-cylinder developing 1,200hp (895kW) and the 12-cylinder developing 1,800hp (1,340kW).

First outward sign of GE's new venture was a four-unit locomotive, with "cab" or totally-enclosed bodies, two units fitted with the V8 engine and two with the V12. These units were tested on the Erie Railroad from 1954 to 1959, and based on their successful performance the company launched a new series of export models in 1956, designated the

Above: *General Electric U36C 3,600hp (2,690kW) Co-Co diesel-electric locomotive supplied to the Union Pacific Railroad.*

"Universal" series. With the experience gained from V8 and V12 engines, GE now embarked on a major step forward, a 16-cylinder version developing 2,400hp (1,790kW). Two of these engines were installed in Bo-Bo hood units, and were tested on the Erie, covering 100,000 miles (160,000km) in 11 months. Although masquerading under the designation "XP24", denoting 2,400hp export test units, these were in fact destined to be the demonstrators of a new model for the home market.

In 1960, seven years after the ending of its partnership with Alco, GE announced its new model, the 2,500hp (1,870kW) "Universal" Bo-Bo, denoted "U25B". Its most obvious sales point was that it had the highest horsepower of any locomotive on

the US market, by 100hp (75kW), but to have any chance of breaking into the EMD/Alco markets, it had to have many attractions which were less obvious, but equally important to customers.

In preparing the design, GE had asked the motive power chiefs of 33 railroads what they liked and disliked in the diesels which they already operated. The costs of operating these units were also analysed, and it was found that repairs accounted for 28.7 per cent of total diesel operating costs. The designers' aim was therefore to improve performance, but at the same time to simplify equipment to make it more reliable and maintenance-free. A major cause of complaint was the air system, both for supplying the engine and for cooling. The incoming air was filtered, and in most contemporary designs the filters needed cleaning at about 2,500 miles (4,000km). Alco designed a self-cleaning mechanical filter. Another complaint was that air for ventilating the equipment compartments commonly passed through the engine compartment, becoming heated and polluted in doing so. On the "U25B" the air from the fan to the equipment compartment passed through ducting in the main frame, well away from the engine. Another simplification was elimination of electrically-controlled shutters to the radiator ventilating system.

In contrast to these changes much of the electrical equipment was well tried, including the traction motors, and roads which operated Alco locomotives would already have many of the parts in stock. However, there was an electrical innovation—use of modular electronic equipment.

Launching of the new model

Above: *GE U25C Co-Co units belonging to the Lake Superior & Ishpeming RR and leased by the Detroit, Toledo & Ironton.*

coincided with unfavourable economic conditions on the railroads, and more than a year passed before any orders came in. The first came from Union Pacific, which was always on the lookout for higher-powered locomotives, and other roads which had a specific need for higher power followed. Over a period of six years a total of 478 "U25Bs" were sold, not a great number by EMD standards, but sufficient for GE to displace Alco from second place in the US diesel sales league.

It was already established practice for a US road switcher to be offered both as a four-axle and as a six-axle unit, the latter appealing to railroads which needed more adhesive weight or a slightly lower axleload. The "U25C" therefore appeared in 1963, and added a further 113 units to GE sales. With the spread of the "U" designation, someone referred to "U-boats' and the nickname caught on.

The effect on other manufac-

turers of GE competition was to spur them to modify their own models. Competition was keen, particularly horsepower competition. GE's 16-cylinder engine and its generator were rated modestly, so that uprating would be possible without major alterations (and more spare parts to stock!), and so in 1966 came the 2,800hp (2,090kW) engine, in the "U28B" and "U28C" models.

UP bought 16 "U25Bs", but then ordered a special model to suit the addiction of its motive power chief, D. S. Neuhart, to very powerful locomotives. Already his road was operating 8,500hp (6,340kW) GE gas turbine locomotives, and the builder

Below: *A four-axle "U-boat" road-switcher of the Louisville & Nashville Railroad.*

now produced a 5,000hp (3,730kW) twin-engined version of the "U25B" mounted on four bogies and weighing 247t; these were the "U50Bs". Later came a simplified Co-Co version of the same power. Neither of these types was entirely successful, and with the coming of standard models of 3,000hp (2,240kW) UP was content to fall into line with other railroads and buy off-the-shelf.

The next landmark in diesel development in the US was the 3,000hp engine, produced by EMD, Alco and GE in 1965-66. The GE models, "U30B" and "U30C", appeared late in 1966, and were followed less than a year later by 3,300hp (2,460kW) versions. In 1969 yet another increase, to 3,600hp (2,690kW), was achieved. The GE decision to use a moderately-rated engine in the first "U-boats" paid good dividends at this time, for whereas GE attained these increases in power by development of the 16-cylinder engine, EMD had to move to 20 cylinders. However, the railroads soon lost their enthusiasm for engines above 3,000hp when they discovered the extra maintenance costs incurred.

In 1976 a further revision of the GE range, known as the "7-series" was accompanied by a change in designation, the 3,000hp Co-Co becoming the "C30-7". With these models GE remains firmly in the US market, and also exports them directly or through overseas associates. There has also been a revival in sales of 3,600hp locomotives.

GE demonstrated that it was possible to compete with EMD. Its models offered some attractive technical alternatives to the EMD products, and by doing so they prevented the larger builder from achieving a monopoly.

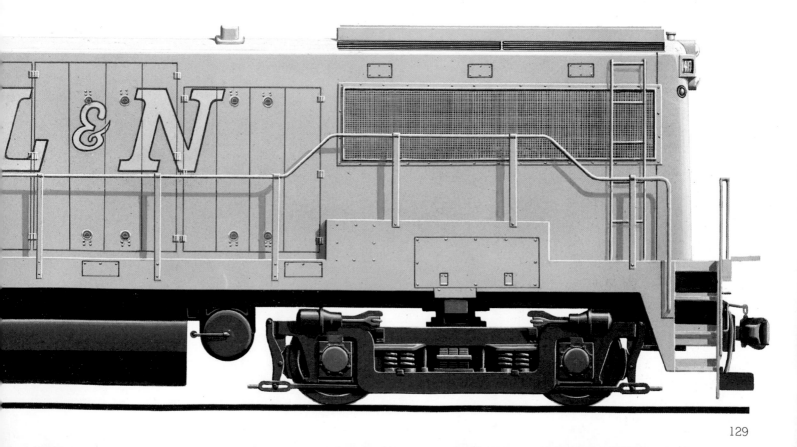

Class 47 Cₒ-Cₒ

Great Britain:
British Railways (BR), 1962

Type: Diesel-electric mixed-traffic locomotive.

Gauge: 4ft 8½in (1,435mm).

Propulsion: Sulzer 2,750hp (2,052kW) 12LDA28C 12-cylinder twin-bank engine and generator supplying direct current to six nose-suspended traction motors geared to the axles.

Weight*: 264,480lb (120t).

Max. axleload*: 44,080lb (20t).

Overall length: 63ft 5in (19,329mm).

Tractive effort: 62,000lb (275kN).

Max. speed: 95mph (152km/h).

*Variations between different sub-groups.

These useful locomotives are the workhorses of BR's diesel fleet and form almost half the total stock of large diesel locomotives of 2,000hp or over. A total of 528 were built between 1962 and 1967 by Brush Engineering and BR's Crewe Works. All have Brush electrical equipment and use the same Sulzer engine—with modest enhancement of power output—as the "Peak" class, but the overall weight was reduced by careful design to the point where the two outer idle axles of the older type could be dispensed with. The engines were built under licence by Vickers-Armstrong of Barrow, England. Originally the "47s" were numbered D1500 to 99 and from D1100 upwards, but renumbering in 1968 to incorporate the class designation brought them into the 47xxx series.

Details vary; the "47.0" group (243 strong) originally had steam

Above: *British Railways' Class 47/0 diesel-electric locomotive No. 47083* Orion *with a freight train at York in September 1981.*

Below: *A relief express hauled by a Class 47 diesel-electric locomotive rounds a curve south of Durham in 1979.*

heating boilers and these run on to include the "471xxx" and "472xx" series. There is a "47.3" sub-class (81 in number) which have no train heating equipment either steam or electric but do include special low-speed control for assisting automatic loading or unloading of merry-go-round coal trains. The 185 "47.4s", which include the "475xx" series, all have electric heating arrangements (and some steam as well). One interesting example of the class, originally No. 47046, has been used as a test bed for a more powerful engine. With a Paxman 3,250hp (2,425kW) 16RK3CT engine fitted in 1975 it became the sole member of sub-class "47.6", later class "47.9" No. 47901. Lastly there is a group fitted for working push-and-pull express trains between Edinburgh and Glasgow; these are renumbered and reclassified "47.4". All the "47s" are equipped with dual brakes for working both air and vacuum-braked trains, automatic wheelslip detectors and correctors as well as an anti-slip brake. The bogies are made from one-piece steel castings.

It must be said that the electric train heating system absorbs power from the engine and affects the amount of power available to haul the train by a noticable amount—several hundred horsepower in fact. In this case the diminution nicely absorbs the amount of power gained by several years of diesel engine development! When considering these locomotives as express passenger power,

then, this loss must normally be taken into account. Of course, it is of lesser importance now that most of the prime diesel express passenger assignments in Britain have been taken over by HST125 sets. However, the "47s" equipped for electric train heating have a device whereby, if the full engine power is temporarily needed for traction, the driver can push his controller handle against a spring return which temporarily interrupts the heating supply.

One noticeable thing missing from the Class "47" armoury is multiple-unit capability and this perhaps underlines BR's general philosophy which is (with some exceptions in special cases) to provide a single locomotive of the power needed to haul any given train. It is in complete contrast to the North American principle that diesel units should be building-blocks from which locomotives of any desired power can be assembled.

The experimental Class "47.9", fitted in 1975 with a more powerful engine, spawned in 1976 the BR Class "56". These are a class of Co-Co similar in size, weight and appearance (apart from the style of painting) to the standard "47s" but given 26 per cent more power by installing the same engine as powers No. 47901.

Above: *Before the days of automation, provision was made on locomotives for displaying train reporting numbers. This is no longer needed, hence the group of unevenly set zeros.*

Class 309 "Clacton" Four-car train

Great Britain:
British Railways (BR), Eastern Region, 1962

Type: Electric express-passenger train.
Gauge: 4ft 8½in (1,435mm).
Propulsion: Alternating current at 25,000V 50Hz (and originally at 6,250V 50Hz as well) fed via overhead catenary, step-down transformer and solid-state rectifiers to four 282hp (210kW) nose-suspended traction motors geared to the axles of an intermediate non-driving power car.
Weight: 127,830lb (58t) adhesive, 376,885lb (171t) total.
Max. axleload: 31,960lb (14.5t).
Overall length: 265ft 9in (81,000mm).
Max. speed: 100mph (160km/h), but speed limit of railway 90mph (144km/h).

In the late-1950s, the decision was taken to adopt industrial-frequency as a future standard for British Railways' electrification. A proposed extension of the then new suburban electrification out of London's Liverpool Street Station, using 1,500V direct current, then posed the question whether conversion of these lines to the new standard should be attempted before the extension was begun. To answer this, the branches from Colchester to Clacton-on-Sea and Walton-on-the-Naze were electrified on the new system as a trial. After some traumas, the suburban electrification was converted to ac and in 1961 the gap from its outer limit at Shenfield to Colchester was wired. For the first time then, there was a need for express ac electric sets for the new standard ac system, in order to cover fast London to Clacton trains.

The result was these four-car "Clacton" sets, eight with "griddle" car and seven without, plus eight

matching two-car sets to strengthen the trains at peak hours. Four, eight or ten-car trains could be run, vestibuled throughout. Although costly both in weight and expense, one-piece cast-steel Commonwealth bogies were used in order to give good riding. Very adequately-powered traction equipment was provided, with 3,380hp (2,520kW) for a 460 ton (506 US tons) 10-car train. There was automatic changeover between the two voltages, and silicon rectifiers, then quite new, were used. Both electro-pneumatic and ordinary automatic air brakes were provided.

The best working was the "Essex Coast Express" which ran the 70 miles (113km) from Liverpool Street to Clacton in 80 minutes; the hourly interval trains, which made five intermediate stops and shed a unit at Thorpe-le-Soken for Walton, took 8 minutes longer. Of course, the high-speed capability of these units could not be used to full advantage amongst the dense traffic of the Liverpool Street suburban area.

It was clear that these fine trains were really intended for better things; electrification beyond Colchester to Ipswich, Harwich and Norwich then seemed imminent, although this work was actually authorised only in 1982. Since 1962 there has most surprisingly been no futher requirement for high-voltage ac express electric trains (unless you count the APT!) and accordingly the Clacton trains, now all reformed as four-car sets and minus their griddle cars, remain sole examples of their kind in Britain.

Below: *Class 309 electric multiple-unit set at Clacton Station, Essex, forming the "Centenary Express", September 1982.*

Krauss-Maffei C-C

Type: Diesel-hydraulic freight locomotive.
Gauge: 4ft 8½in (1,435mm).
Propulsion: Two 2,000hp (1,500kW) four-stroke pressure-charged 16-cylinder Maybach MD870 engines driving through two Voith three-stage hydraulic transmissions, each geared to the axles of one bogie.
Weight: 330,600lb (150t).
Max. axleload: 55,100lb (25t).
Overall length: 65ft 11⁵/₁₆in (20,100mm).
Tractive effort: 90,000lb (400kN).
Max. speed: 70mph (113km/h).

During the 1950s the proportion of the world's single-unit diesel locomotives above 2,000hp (1,500kW) which were fitted with hydraulic transmission rose from 4 per cent to 17 per cent due to vigorous development work in West Germany. In 1960, of the world's major diesel users, the United States alone, with more than half the world's 54,000 diesel locomotives, adhered exclusively to electric transmission. Furthermore, diesel-hydraulics were made in West Germany, and the US had imported no locomotives since the earliest days of railways. There was thus a sensation on both sides of the Atlantic when it was announced that two US railroads, the Denver & Rio Grande Western and Southern Pacific, had each ordered three diesel-hydraulic C-C locomotives from Krauss-Maffei of Munich, and furthermore that they would be 4,000hp (2,980kW) units, which was 1,600hp more than any model a US manufacturer could offer.

D&RGW was the first to

approach KM, but to make a viable production run a second order was needed; SP responded. The reasons for this revolutionary step were threefold: diesel-hydraulics gave a much greater horsepower per unit weight than diesel-electrics; German experience showed that with hydraulic transmission adhesion was much improved; and in US experience electrical transmission was the biggest item of repairs in diesels, accounting for up to two-thirds of failures on the road. The improved power-to-weight ratio made it possible to mount two 2,200hp engines in a C-C locomotive.

The engines for the US orders were enlarged versions of the Maybach units used in most German diesel-hydraulics, and were notable for their speed of 1,500rpm, which was almost 50 per cent more than the highest in an American engine. The rating of 2,000hp was the engine output, and after allowing for the losses in the transmission the power was 3,540hp (2,640kW), which was the figure more truly comparable with a US rating (which is power available for traction).

Each engine was connected by a cardan shaft to a Voith gearbox near the outer end of the

frame. From this gearbox an inclined cardan shaft led to a final gearbox on the inner end of the bogie, whence a further cardan shaft led to the axles. The gearbox provided for hydro-dynamic braking, and the controls were pneumatic with provision for multiple-unit working.

The first locomotive completed was D&RGW No. 4001. To test the locomotive in Europe under US mountain railroad conditions, the makers arranged for No. 4001 to work for a week on the famous Semmering line in Austria, with gradients of 1-in-40 (2½ per cent). On the steepest gradient the loco-

Above: *12,000 horse-power provided by three Krauss-Maffei diesel-hydraulic units takes a freight over the Rockies on the Rio Grande Denver to Salt Lake City trans-continental route.*

Left: *The later batch of Krauss-Maffei diesel hydraulic locomotives supplied to Southern Pacific were designed as "hood" rather than "cowl" units.*

Below: *Denver & Rio Grande Krauss-Maffei diesel-hydraulic locomotive No. 4003.*

motive started, and hauled at 16mph (26½km/h), a train of 867t. Only once did the wheels slip, and then only slightly, and the dynamic brake was found to work well.

The six units were duly shipped to the US and put to work in 1961. On the D&RGW the loco-motives worked in duplicate or triplicate on trains of 4,000t to 7,000t on 1-in-50 (2 per cent) gradients. Although their work was satisfactory, the road decided not to continue with the experi-ment, and when the locomotives

had covered 200,000 miles (320,000km) they were sold to the Southern Pacific. The latter, by contrast, was sufficiently im-pressed to order 15 more, which were delivered in 1963. With a total of 21 of the German machines, SP was able to assess their economic and technical per-formance.

The verdict came in 1968; the hydraulic transmission "could provide a reliable means of pro-pulsion with competitive main-tenance costs" but the engines suffered from "complexity of con-

struction and inaccessibility for repairs". Air intake problems arose in tunnels, and the pneumatic controls were troublesome. Some modifications were made, but as the diesel-hydraulics came due for heavy repairs they were with-drawn from service.

This was not quite the end of diesel-hydraulics on the SP, for in 1964 Alco built three C-C versions of its Century series fitted with Voith transmission. These showed promise, but the closure of Alco in 1969 ruled out any possibility of further development.

GT3 2-C
Great Britain:
English Electric Co Ltd, 1960

Type: Direct-drive gas turbine locomotive for mixed traffic.
Gauge: 4ft 8½in (1,435mm).
Propulsion: Double-shaft turbine producing an output of 2,780hp (2,075kW), driving the main wheels direct via gearing and coupling rods.
Weight: 132,720lb (60t) adhesive, 276,416lb (125t) total*.
Max. axleload: 44,800lb (20.5t).
Overall length: 68ft 0in (20,726mm).
Tractive effort: 38,000lb (169kN).
Max. speed: 90mph (144km/h).

*Including tender.

There was great enthusiasm for the gas turbine in post-war Britain, and when the Great Western Railway ordered a gas turbine locomotive from Metropolitan Vickers, it was not surprising that the gas turbine department of English Electric, Metro-Vick's main rival, should embark on the design and manufacture of such a locomotive as a private venture. But there were great differences between the two projects, not least that Metro-Vick delivered its locomotive in five years, whereas EE took as long as fourteen.

The Metro-Vick locomotive conformed to the practice of Brown Boveri of Switzerland and General Electric in the USA, in that the turbine drove a generator from which current was supplied to conventional dc traction motors. EE, on the other hand, took advantage of the capacity of a turbine to transmit a high torque at rest, making direct drive of a locomotive possible, as in some steam

Below: *From a casual glance No. GT3 appeared little different from a steam locomotive, yet it had no boiler, no cylinders and no complex transmission system.*

turbine locomotives. To effect the necessary direct drive to the wheels, the chassis was made in the form of a 4-6-0 or 2-C steam locomotive.

The turbine rested on the frame ahead of the leading coupled wheels and, unlike those of other gas turbine locomotives, it was a two-shaft machine. The high-pressure end of the turbine drove the compressor, while the low-pressure end was on a separate shaft which was connected to a gearbox mounted on the middle coupled axle. Clutches in the gearbox selected forward or reverse gear as required. Use of two power turbines was essential for direct drive, but it also enabled the unit to be designed with a less unfavourable part-load fuel consumption than the other gas turbine locomotive, thus alleviating one of their great weaknesses. There was a heat exchanger above the turbine, transferring heat from the exhaust gases to the air passing from the compressor to the combustion chamber. The driver's cab was in the conventional steam locomotive position, and there was a six-wheeled tender carrying the train heating steam generator and main fuel tank.

Another unique feature of this design was the extensive developing and testing of individual components before and after they were assembled in the locomotive. For this purpose much use was made of British Railways' Locomotive Testing Station at Rugby, the first time that this plant had been used for outside work of that type. Much ingenuity was displayed in the design, particularly in the

Above: *The English Electric Company built this direct-drive gas turbine locomotive in 1960. It was very simple indeed and performed well, and is shown hauling a 12-car train in the northern hills.*

Below: *The 2-C on display at the Institution of Locomotive Engineers Exhibition at Marylebone Goods Yard in 1961.*

transmission, which was the most novel part. The turbine was an existing type of industrial machine.

The reason for adopting the steam locomotive type of chassis was that it enabled the drive to be taken to an axle which was rigid in the frame, except for movement on its springs. This eliminated a major design problem which would have arisen had the drive been transmitted to wheels on a bogie.

The locomotive was completed in 1960, and after tests in sidings adjoining Rugby Testing Station, it eventually emerged for road trials—and such a sight had never been seen on a British railway, for the early trials were made without the casing in position, to that the turbine, heat exchanger and other components were exposed to view.

In 1961 the locomotive, now decently encased and numbered cryptically GT3, was tested on various parts of the London Midland Region of BR. The climax was a series of runs between Crewe and Carlisle, in which loads of up to 15 coaches (about 450t—490 US tons) were hauled up to Shap Summit at speeds as high as had ever been recorded with steam or with 2,000hp diesels. The performance of the unit was deemed satisfactory, although the turbine never quite reached its designed output of 2,700hp. The tractive effort recorded at starting was 36,000lb (16,500kg), and at speeds between 30 and 80mph (48 and 130km/h) the tractive effort was about equal to that of a rebuilt "Merchant Navy" class 4-6-2 steam locomotive working at a maximum rate which a fireman could sustain, and it was well above that of a 2,000hp diesel.

With the tests concluded, the point was reached at which the experience gained, together with, in this case, 14 years of development work on other types of locomotive, could be incorporated

in a production design. There was, however, an essential requirement—money—and this could not be justified unless there was some prospect of orders. BR had withdrawn its two gas turbine locos by this time, and was already testing the experimental second generation diesels in which engines of 2,700 to 2,750hp were installed in a locomotive of less than 120 weight. BR was thus committed to diesels, and was so deeply involved in the problems of dieselisation that it had no interest in alternatives, nor were any export orders forthcoming. Furthermore English Electric's finances were declining, and the time was near when it would join its former rival Metro-Vick in the GEC group. Inevitably, further

Above: *Although occasionally featuring in scenes such as the above, the masterpiece in simplicity that was the GT3 never gained recognition.*

work on the gas turbine locomotive was cancelled, and GT3 was broken up. There was thus no lasting benefit from 14 years' work.

Class 55 Deltic C₀-C₀

Type: High-speed express passenger diesel-electric locomotive.
Gauge: 4ft 8½in (1,435mm).
Propulsion: Two Napier Type 18-25 18-cylinder 1,750hp (1,305kW) "Deltic" two-stroke diesel engines and generators connected in series, feeding current to six nose-suspended traction motors geared to the axles of the two bogies.
Weight: 222,600lb (101t).
Max. axleload: 36,920lb (16.25t).
Overall length: 69ft 6in (21,180mm).
Tractive effort: 50,000lb (222kN).
Max. speed: 100mph (160km/h).

The sad thing about diesel locomotives is that, unlike steam, all the fascinating mechanism is hidden deep within. That is why it is exceptional for what they are like inside to be reflected in what they are called. But on the "Deltics" the mechanism was so very fascinating that its name spilled out into the lay world. In Greek, the capital letter Δ or delta is a triangle which, when inverted, exactly describes the layout of some diesel engines of remarkably high power for their weight and size. They were developed by English Electric's subsidiary Napier soon after World War II for fast motor gun-boats for the Royal Navy. They were to replace engines fuelled by petrol, which presented a serious fire hazard, in action and otherwise.

The advantages of an "opposed piston" engine are well known. Instead of having one piston per cylinder, with a massive cylinder head to take the thrust, there are two pushing against one another. It is not quite two for the price of one, but part way to it. The only problem is that complications arise in making the two opposed thrusts turn a single shaft. In the "Deltic" engine, three banks of double cylinders, each with a pair of opposed pistons and arranged as three sides of a triangle, are connected to a crankshaft at each apex. Each crankshaft is then geared to the central drive shaft of the engine. The result was specific weight of only 6.2lb per

hp, (3.8kg/kW), some 2½ times better than contemporary medium-speed conventional diesel engines normally used for traction. There was also perfect balance both of the forces generated and of the reciprocating parts.

English Electric's Traction Division was a main supplier of locomotives to BR, and EE's chairman Lord Nelson realised that by putting this Napier engine on to an English Electric chassis, he had the means to double the power of a typical diesel-electric locomotive. During 1955, in the teeth of opposition from the Traction Division, and at EE's own expense, a prototype was put in hand. During several years' testing the locomotive did everything that might be expected of a machine that had 3,300hp (2,462kW) available compared with the 2,000hp or so of her competitors. Moreover, it proved unexpectedly reliable.

Under BR's modernisation plan, electrification was envisaged from London to the north of England both from Euston and from King's Cross. In the event, the former scheme was the only one put in hand and the Eastern/North Eastern/Scottish Region authorities accordingly sought a stop-gap alternative which would give electrification timings for minimal expenditure. The result was an order in 1959 for 22 of these superb locomotives, a class destined to become a legend in their own lifetime. When built they were by a considerable margin the most powerful single-unit diesel locomotives in the world.

Two separate "Deltic" engine-

Left: "Deltic" No. 55021 with a King's Cross to Edinburgh express at Ouston Junction, County Durham, in July 1978.

Below: A "Deltic" Co-Co diesel-electric locomotive depicted in the original livery applied to these excellent and powerful units when first built.

D 9002

BRITISH

and-generator sets were installed, normally connected in series, but in the event of failure the failed engine could be switched out and the locomotive could continue to pull its full load using the other one, but at reduced speed.

Auxiliary equipment on the "Deltics" included an automatic oil-fired steam generator for heating trains. The water tanks for this equipment were originally arranged so they could be filled from steam-age water cranes and also—amazingly—at speed from water troughs by means of a scoop! Later, windings were added to the generators to provide for electric heating of the train although this abstracted several hundred horsepower from the output available for traction. Both compressors and vacuum exhauster sets for brake power were provided, as well as cooking facilities and a toilet.

The bogies were standard with the contemporary English Electric 1,750hp Type "3" locomotives (now BR Class "37") and automatic detection and correction of wheelslip was provided for. The controls were also generally similar to other English Electric locomotives, although drivers could not run them exactly the same as other locomotives, because the low angular inertia of a "Deltic" engine precluded heavy-handed throttle movements, which were liable to lead to automatic shutdown. Even so, the possibility of climbing the 1-in-200 (0.5 per cent) gradient to Stoke Summit, north of Peterborough, at a minimum speed of 90mph (144km/h) with a heavy East Coast express was something that earned the total respect of footplatemen. In the old LNER tradition, the "Deltics" were all named—some after race horses that also had won their races and others after English and Scottish regiments. Originally the class was numbered D9000 to D9021; later Nos. D9001 to 21 became Nos. 55001 to 21 and

D9000 became No. D55022.

One of the crucial measures in the scheme to acquire the "Deltics" was that the deal should include maintenance at an inclusive price, with penalties to be incurred if, through faults arising, the locomotives were unable to perform an agreed mileage each year. The task of keeping the "Deltic" fleet in running order was simplified because the engines were maintained on a unit-replacement basis. After a few anticipated problems in the first year or so, the "Deltics" settled down to running about 170,000 miles a year, or about 500 miles a day, with a very low failure rate.

After a few improvements to the route, including major track realignments, the "Deltic"-hauled "Flying Scotsman" ran (for example in 1973) from King's Cross to Newcastle, 271 miles (433km) in 3hr 37min and to Edinburgh, 395 miles (632km), in 5hr 30min, average speeds of 74.9 and 71.8mph (119.8 and 114.5km/h) respectively. Such timings as these

Right: *An East Coast express hauled by a "Deltic" in BR standard blue livery rolls southwards through the hills.*

Above: *"Deltic" No. 55010 King's Own Scottish Borderer under the wires at King's Cross.*

were applied not just to one or two 'flag' trains but to the service as a whole; they represented substantial gains in time—a 1½ hour acceleration compared with 12 years before between London and Edinburgh, for instance. Teesside customers could have as much as 1¾ hours extra time in London for the same time away from home, compared with what was possible in the pre-"Deltic" era. British Rail reaped their reward in the form of a substantial

increase in traffic, and this far more than outweighed the fact that the cost of maintenance of these complex engines was admittedly higher than those of lower specific power output.

Fifteen years and 50 million "Deltic" miles later, electrification seemed as far away as ever, and a further stage of development without it became desirable. In the event, a possible "Super-Deltic" based on two "Deltic" engines of increased power was discarded in favour of the self-propelled High-Speed Trains, with more conventional Paxman engines. It might have been hoped that the existing "Deltics" could be moved on to rejuvenate operations on less important lines, where their low axleload would permit usage. In the end, though, because their engines were expensive to maintain, it was not possible to make a case for keeping them, based on the kind of rather uninspiring arithmetic BR's accountants use in such matters.

So, on January 2, 1982 the last "Deltic"-hauled train ran into King's Cross. Now all that remains are memories of the monumental labours of these fabled machines. Two at least are to be preserved —the prototype in the Science Museum, London, and *King's Own Yorkshire Light Infantry* in the National Railway Museum at York.

Class 52 "Western" C-C

Great Britain:
British Railways, Western Region (BR), 1962

Type: Diesel-hydraulic express passenger locomotive.

Gauge: 4ft 8½in (1,435mm).

Propulsion: Two 1,350hp (1,000kW) Bristol-Siddeley/Maybach 12-cylinder Vee-type MD655 "tunnel" engines each driving the three axles of one bogie via a Voith-North British three-stage hydraulic transmission, cardan shaft, intermediate gearbox, further cardan shafts and final-drive gearboxes.

Weight: 242,440lb (110t).

Max. axleload: 40,775lb (18.5t).

Overall length: 68ft 0in (20,726mm).

Tractive effort: 72,600lb (323kN).

Max. speed: 90mph (144km/h).

The episode of the "Western" class diesel-hydraulics was like a glorious but futile last cavalry charge on the part of some army facing inevitable defeat. Of all the companies absorbed into British Railways on January 1, 1948, the Great Western Railway found nationalisation much the hardest to bear. Its own apparently superior standards evolved over more than a century were largely replaced by those emanating from inferior "foreign" (non-GWR) companies. For some time the regional management at Paddington had largely to content itself with words—the General Manager even issued an instruction to the effect that no locomotive of other than GWR design should be rostered for any train on which he was due to travel!

But after a decade had passed, action became possible. Under BR's Modernisation Programme, a thorough trial of diesel hydraulic locomotives was planned on one of the regions, and the Western Region was suitable for this equipment. This was Paddington's chance to do its own thing with locomotives which followed the hallowed Great Western tradition of being as different as possible from anyone else's.

At that time the choice of hydraulic transmission as an alternative to electric for high-power diesels was less radical than it is now. BR's central management had plumped (quite correctly, seen with hindsight) for electric transmission in most of the proposed diesel locomotives, but hydraulic transmission had some great attractions. Since West Germany was the country in which such motive power had developed furthest, German practice was the basis of what was done. In addition to hydraulic-transmission, the German locomotives had high-speed lightweight diesel engines. They revolved at speeds twice those of diesel engines used in other BR locomotives and weighed less than half as much for the same power.

The first class of importance was the 2,000hp B-B "Warship" of 1958, designed to give similar performance to BR's 1-Co-Co-1 Class "40", but weighing 40 per cent less. Sixty-six "Warships" were built, but equality with the

Above: *Class 52 No. D1005 passes Lostwithiel, Cornwall, with the down "Cornish Riviera Express", in October 1974.*

Below: *Class 52 No. 1028 Western Hussar on humble duty at the head of a five-wagon train of milk tanks.*

FIREBRAND

rest of BR was not enough. What was wanted was a machine that would run BR's other diesels into the ground.

No. D1000 *Western Enterprise* appeared in late-1961, soon to be followed by 73 more "Western" sisters. The names chosen were mostly evocative and many, like the first, provocative to BR's headquarters at 222 Marylebone Road, London. For example, No. D1001 *Western Pathfinder*, D1019 *Western Challenger*, D1059 *Western Empire*. GWR tradition was also followed in the matter of spelling mistakes—No. D1029 *Western Legionnaire* was at first *Western Legionaire*.

Alas, the locomotives did not cover themselves with Western Glory (D1072). For one thing, the opposition did not allow their lead in power output to be held for long. In the following year came the Brush Class "47" CoCo (described here), with a fraction more power than the "Westerns", for only just over the same weight, and by 1967 the Class "50" diesel-electrics hired from English Electric also matched the diesel-hydraulics for power. Moreover, even by 1963, central management had decided that diesel hydraulics had no real advantage over diesel electrics, of which it had a growing surplus. So some time before the high-speed HST125 trains took over most long-distance passenger services from Paddington in the late-1970s, the "Westerns" had been taken out of service. Withdrawal began with No. 1019 in mid-1973 and all had gone by early-1977. No less than six have survived in preservation but, in contrast, the rival diesel-electric classes "47" and "50" remain virtually intact in normal service.

The "Westerns" had their own kind of good looks, the unusualness of their appearance being enhanced by inside bearings to the wheels. The Maybach engines were also unusual (but invisibly

so) in that they were of the tunnel pattern in which the circular crank webs actually form the bearing journals of the crankshafts. Power was transmitted to the wheels via various hydraulic and mechanical transmission boxes connected by numerous cardan shafts. This mechanical complexity was a source of problems with obscure causes but unfortunate results —substitution of hydraulic fluid and mechanical components for electricity as a medium of transmission tended to lower rather than raise as promised reliability and efficiency. Also, there were festoons of electrical circuitry serving the control systems and instrumentation, and these gave the problems to be expected of

Below: *Class 52 diesel-hydraulic locomotive No. D1048 with a Birmingham to Paddington express emerges from the short Harbury tunnel between Leamington and Banbury.*

electrics amongst the oil-mist of a diesel locomotive interior.

The Western Region's mechanical department managed to solve the problems, being especially triumphant when the bad riding which had held down speeds was overcome by altering the bogies (with much simplification) to resemble in principle GWR standard ones dating from Victorian times. Such timings as a 3hr 30min schedule for the 225½ miles (363km) between Paddington and Plymouth then became possible, at last a significant improvement (of 30 minutes) over the best previously achieved with steam.

The reliability problem was eventually solved also by a long and painstaking process of diagnosis, trial and error, and finally by cure of many faults of detail in the design. Alas, by then a decision had already been taken to withdraw the diesel-hydraulic fleet from service prematurely and

Above: *British Railways Western Region Class 52 C-C diesel-hydraulic locomotive No. D1012* Western Firebrand *in the red livery originally adopted. Other liveries, including one known as "desert sand", were applied experimentally.*

replace them by the Class "50" diesel-electric locomotives. It then was a case of heaping insult upon injury because (taking 1971 as an example) the "Westerns" were running 15,000 miles per failure while their diesel-electric replacements, the Class "50s", were only managing to achieve an appalling 9,000.

One benefit did arise; some badly needed self-confidence. This quality, previously lacking, was generated on BR by the fact that a foreign import was shown to be very far from the perfect thing it had been cracked up to be, and its designers to be only human like the rest of us.

Class 16500 B-B

France:
French National Railways (SNCF), 1962

Type: Mixed-traffic electric locomotive.
Gauge: 4ft 8½in (1,435mm).
Propulsion: Alternating current at 25,000V 50Hz fed through a rectifier (ignitron, excitron or silicon) to a traction motor mounted on each bogie; motor connected to axles through two-speed gearing.
Weight: 156,500lb (71t) to 163,100lb (74t) according to fittings.
Max. axleload: 39,100lb (17.8t) to 40,800lb (18.5t) according to fittings.
Overall length: 47ft 3in (14,400mm).
Tractive effort: Low gear 71,410lb (318kN), high gear 42,320lb (188kN).
Max. speed: Low gear 56mph (90km/h), high gear 93mph (150km/h).

The performance of the Class "12000" B-B locomotives on SNCF's Thionville-Valenciennes line established the superiority of the ignitron over other types of rectifier then available, and it also established the advantage of connecting the axles of a bogie by gearing. Wheelslip develops locally, and rarely do both axles of a bogie begin to slip at the same instant. Coupling the axles enables a locomotive to be worked much nearer to the limit of adhesion than with independent axles, and SNCF engineers reckoned that a 60t locomotive with connected axles could maintain as high a tractive effort as an 85t locomotive with independent axles.

The next electrification after the Thionville-Valenciennes line was the Paris to Lille route of the Northern Region. For this scheme two new types of locomotive were introduced, one of which was a high-speed Bo-Bo geared for 100mph (160km/h). The other was a mixed-traffic B-B machine which introduced another novelty, the monomotor bogie with two-speed gearing. The monomotor bogie had already been tested experimentally and used on two dual-voltage locomotives. As its name implies, each bogie has a single motor mounted above the bogie frame and connected to the axles through gearing and spring drives. Between the small pinion on the motor shaft and the large gear wheel of the reduction gear there is an intermediate gear. Two gear wheels of different sizes are mounted on opposite ends of an arm, and by means of a vertical lever the arm can be rocked to bring one or other of these inter-mediate gears into mesh; the gear ratio is thereby changed. The changeover can be effected only when the locomotive is stationary. The high-speed gear is the "passenger" gear, and the low-speed is the "freight" setting.

In a monomotor bogie the axles can be brought closer together than in a bogie with two motors situated between the axles, and the whole bogie is more compact. With the motor almost vertically above the centre, the bogie is less susceptible to developing oscillations at speed.

SNCF announced that these locomotives, designated "16500", would weigh only 60t, but in fact they weigh between 71 and 74t. Even so this is low for a locomotive of nearly 3,500hp, capable of developing a starting tractive effort in low gear of 32.4t (318kN).

ELD4 Four-car set

The Netherlands:
Netherlands Railways (NS), 1964

Type: Fast electric passenger train.
Gauge: 4ft 8½in (1,435mm).
Propulsion: Direct current at 1,500V supplied via catenary with twin contact wires to eight 180hp (134kW) nose-suspended traction motors geared to the axles of the bogies of the two intermediate coaches in the set.
Weight: 200,564lb (91t) adhesive, 370,270lb (168t) total.
Max. axleload: 50,695lb (23t).
Overall length: 331ft 7in (101,240mm).
Max. speed: 88mph (140km/h).

Electrification came early to the Netherlands, for it was as long ago as 1924 that electric traction at 1,500V dc was introduced between Amsterdam, The Hague and Rotterdam. The first stream-lined stock came in 1934, various features of which set the pattern for the future. Streamlined ends to the sets precluded through access for passengers when units were coupled, but coupling and uncoupling were made painless with automatic couplers which also made all the brake-pipe and electrical connections needed. Amongst these early units there were sets of varying lengths, two-three- four- and five-car and, to suit longer runs then becoming possible under the wires, better facilities were provided on the larger units. Matching diesel-electric sets were built too, and there were also matching travelling post office vans.

The trains were designed to suit a pattern of working appropriate to a small country with a density of population 70 per cent greater than even Britain's, but which had no overwhelming single metropolis such as London. They provided an hourly (or more frequent) pattern of service and gave great emphasis to making jour-neys possible between all the principal cities without changing trains. Hence those automatic couplers to enable trains to be divided or combined without fuss.

Although the Dutch emerged from World War II facing almost complete destruction of their railways, they very quickly set about restoring not just the status quo, but something very much better, by extending electrification to all important lines in the country. It was decided to continue the use

Below: *Netherlands Railways' four-car electric train set at Amsterdam Station, 1981.*

When the class was introduced, the ignitron was the current type of rectifier on SNCF, and with this regenerative braking could be fitted.

Outwardly the most noticeable difference from the Thionville locomotives was reversion to a completely enclosed rectangular body, the advantages of the centre cab having been outweighed by the limited space for equipment in the end bonnets. A total of 294 of the "16500" class were built, and they were divided between the Northern Region and the subsequent Paris-Strasbourg electrification of the Eastern Region. The first 155 had bogie suspension

Right: *French National Railways' Class 16500 B-B electric locomotive No. 16506 en route from Paris to Lille.*

similar to that of the "7100" class C-C locomotives, with two Alsthom spring-loaded conical pivots. The remaining bogies had swing links at the corners.

During construction of the class a new type of rectifier known as the excitron came into use, and these were fitted to Nos. 16656 to 16750 (and a few others). Finally came the silicon rectifier which was fitted to the last 44, and has since been fitted to others.

Class "16500" fulfilled the designers' intentions that they should be a universal locomotive capable of undertaking, singly or in pairs, every type of duty except the fastest expresses. For these a 100mph (160km/h) version was developed, the "17000" class, and the "8500" dc class and "25500" dual-voltage class were in turn developed from the "17000".

of multiple-unit self-propelled trains, with a few international and other trains remaining locomotive hauled. This was in order to give employment during the day to motive-power used for freight, which in the Netherlands moves during the night.

New designs of electric and diesel-electric trains put into service during the 1950s followed the lines of their predecessors, except that they were not articulated and only came in two- and four-car form. They also had bulbous extended fronts, provided not for aesthetic reasons but to give protection to the driver. There are also some units with dual-voltage capability, used for working through between Amsterdam and Brussels on to Belgium's 3,000V dc system.

In the 1960s, further stock was required and these Class "501" units, whilst in appearance very like their immediate predecessors, represent a considerable step forward. Two prototypes appeared in 1961 and the production version in 1964. By a remarkable feat of design, the overall weight of a four-car unit is 23 per cent less than before, while the rate of acceleration is approximately doubled.

Automatic doors are provided and this, combined with better performance, enabled schedules to be cut. One other major difference is that the two end vehicles of each set are driving-trailer cars, the intermediate carriages being non-driving motor cars. Since the trains were built, denser traffic, higher speeds and a bad accident in 1962 have made it seem prudent to instal signalling continuously displayed in the driver's cab, actuated by coded track circuits, for use on the busiest sections.

Right: *The front end of a Dutch electric multiple-unit train showing the automatic coupling which facilitates joining and splitting trains.*

C630 "Century" Co-Co

United States:
Alco Products Incorporated (Alco), 1965

Type: Diesel-electric road-switcher locomotive.
Gauge: 4ft 8½in (1,435mm).
Propulsion: One 16-cylinder four-stroke turbocharged 3,000hp (2,240kW) Alco 251E Vee engine and alternator, supplying three-phase current through rectifiers to six nose-suspended traction motors each geared to one axle.
Weight: 312,000lb (141.5t).
Max. axleload: 52,000lb (23.6t), but could be increased to 61,000lb (27.7t) if desired.
Overall length: 69ft 6in (21,180mm).
Tractive effort: 103,000lb (458kN).
Max. speed: 80mph (129km/h) according to gear ratio.

The old-established American Locomotive Company, long known in the trade as Alco, had pioneered one of the most important types of diesel locomotive, the road switcher, when in 1946 it produced a 1,500hp (1,120kW) A1A+A1A hood unit, the first really successful American diesel to be equally at home on switching (shunting) or freight duties. It incorporated the Alco 244 engine, which had performed well in switchers, but which revealed weaknesses under the more arduous conditions of road working.

The 244 was therefore replaced by a new engine, the 251, which officially displaced the 244 from the Alco range in 1956. It was available in 6-cylinder in-line and 12-cylinder Vee formation, to which were added V16 and V18. At first it was installed in existing designs of locomotives, but in 1963 a new range of road switchers was launched, the "Century" series.

Despite the success of its new engine, the position of Alco at this time was increasingly difficult. From 1940 to 1953 the company had an agreement with General Electric that only GE electrical equipment would be used in Alco locomotives, in return for which GE agreed not to compete with Alco in the diesel locomotive market. In 1953 GE withdrew from the agreement, and began to develop its own range of road switchers, which were launched in 1960. This was formidable competition. With the railroads now fully dieselised, the diesel salesman had to convince potential customers that it would pay them to replace their "first generation" diesels by his latest product.

A very strong selling point in any new model must be reduced maintenance costs, and this point was pressed very strongly in

Right: *A Co-Co road-switcher unit of the Alco C630 design, belonging to the British Columbia Railway, Canada.*

Shin-Kansen Sixteen-car train

Japan:
Japanese National Railways (JNR), 1964

Type: High-speed electric passenger train.
Gauge: 4ft 8½in (1,435mm).
Propulsion: Alternating current at 25,000V 50Hz fed via overhead catenary and step-down transformers and rectifiers to sixty-four 248hp (185kW) motors each driving an axle by means of gearing and flexible drive.
Weight: 2,031,200lb (922t).
Max. axleload: 31,738lb (14.4t).
Overall length: 1,318ft 6in (401,880mm).
Max. speed: 130mph (210km/h).

It took more than 60 years for the promise implicit in the Zossen trials of 1903 (already described) to become reality. Public high-speed trains averaging more than 100mph (160km/h) start-to-stop, with normal running speeds 30 per cent above this, appeared first during 1965, when Japanese National Railways put into full service the new *Shin-Kansen* line from Tokyo westwards to Osaka. The line had been opened in 1964, but a preliminary period of operation at more normal speeds had been deemed prudent.

In spite of the impression they gave, the *Shin-Kansen* (the words simply mean "New Line") trains are quite conventional in a basic sense. The high speed is obtained by having plenty of power; a 16-car train has a continuously-rated installed horsepower as high as 15,870 (11,840kW), while high acceleration is achieved by having every axle motored.

No, the interesting thing is to realise how much can be achieved by using existing railroad state-of-the-art if you begin with a clean sheet. Until 1964, Japanese National Railways used 3ft 6in (1,067mm) gauge exclusively, but their new line was to be totally separate even to the extent of being of different gauge. The investment involved in building a new standard-gauge (1,435mm) railway connecting some of Japan's major cities was very great, but the courage of those who promoted it was fully justified, mainly by a three-fold increase of traffic between 1966 and 1973.

The price of high speed was considerable. Not only are there land costs involved in building new lines into and out of the centres of large cities, but since very flat curves of 125 chain (2,500m) radius are required for this degree of fast running, the engineering works in open country are also very heavy. If you cannot turn quickly to avoid natural obstacles, you have to go through them. Of course, with such high power in relation to weight, gradients on the heavy side (1-in-65—1.5 per cent) are no obstacle.

The principal innovation is the self-signalling system of the trains. Acceleration and deceleration is not only automatic but is also

Above: *High-speed "Bullet" trains, capable of 130mph (210km/h) speed, of the Japanese National Railways' Shin-Kansen.*

automatically initiated when required, only the final approach to a stop being directly under the motorman's control. There are no lineside signals and all relevant information about the state of the line is passed on to the driving position by coded impulses passing down the main conductor wires. The trains themselves originate signals which set the route ahead, in places where a choice exists. Seismographs in the main control centres automatically stop all trains if an earthquake is recorded.

Originally there were 480 cars arranged in 40 12-car sets, each

support of the Century range. The makers claimed that a saving in maintenance of up to two-thirds could be expected compared with existing 10 year-old designs.

The new series was designated by three figures, of which the first was the number of axles, all powered; the second and third denoted the engine power, in hundreds of horsepower. The first models launched were "C420", "C424" and "C624", of which the two latter were in the range of power which was most popular at this time. The 16-cylinder turbocharged engine developed 2,600hp (1,940kW), with an output from the generator for traction of 2,400hp (1,790kW); in accordance with US practice it was thus designated a 2,400hp model.

In 1964 a new version of the engine appeared, uprated to 2,750hp (2,050kW) by a combination of increased speed and intercooling. This was the most powerful engine on the US locomotive market. At a time when railroads were increasingly attracted by higher-powered locomotives, this was a strong selling point, but it was only strong enough to sell 135 units in the US.

In 1965 there came another increase in engine speed, raising the power to 3,000hp (2,240kW) for traction. More significantly this

model, the "C630", had an alternator generating three-phase ac, which was then rectified for supply to the traction motors. This was the first alternator sold by a US manufacturer, and it led to the general adoption of alternators by other builders.

Finally in 1968 the engine power was raised to 3,600hp (2,690kW), producing the "C636." These increases in power were all achieved with the same 16-cylinder engine. Other variants in the Century range were the

"C855" for Union Pacific, a massive Bo-Bo-Bo-Bo with two 2,750hp (2,050kW) engines, and the "C430H", a diesel-hydraulic incorporating two 2,150hp (1,600kW) engines and Voith hydraulic transmission. Neither of these was repeated.

Despite this enterprise, Alco was edged steadily out of second place in the US locomotive market by GE. Major improvements at the Schenectady Works could not save the day. Orders declined and in 1969 the works was closed.

Above: *British Columbia Railway C630 No. 712 at Lillooet, Canada. Note snowplough to cope with the extremely heavy snows of Canadian winters.*

Fortunately for the Alco tradition, the firm's Canadian associate, Montreal Locomotive Works, was in better shape, with continued sales in Canada and Mexico. MLW took over all Alco designs and patents, and in 1982 was still marketing its own versions of the Century series.

12-car train being divided electrically into six two-car units, one of which would have a buffet car, with the bullet-shaped ends and driving cabs placed at the outer ends of the train. In 1970, the 12-car trains were strengthened to 16 including two buffet cars, and train frequency increased from 120 to over 200 both ways daily. The fleet of cars had by then become 1,400, arranged in 87 16-car sets.

In 1970, as soon as success was assured, a national plan was prepared to extend the high-speed passenger network from the 320 miles (515km) of the original line twenty-fold. So far, four *Shin-Kansen* lines have been built—extending the network from Tokyo to Okayama and Hakata, and from Omiya (Tokyo) to Niigata and Morioka, a total of 1,188 miles (1,912km) of standard-gauge line.

The scale of work involved in the mountain regions—not to speak of an 11.6 mile (18.6km) inter-island undersea tunnel—can be seen from the amount of civil engineering work needed. Of the

247 miles (398km) between Okayama and Hakata, 55 per cent is in tunnel, 31 per cent on bridges or viaducts, leaving only 14 per cent as a conventional railway built on the ground. This was partly due to the minimum radius of curvature being increased to 200 chains (4,000m), with a view to raising speed from 130mph (210km/h) to 162mph (260km/h), while at the same time reducing the gradient to 1-in-65 (1.5 per cent). Even though this increase in speed has not yet been realised in public service, the fast hourly *Hikari* trains make the 735-mile (1,176km) overall journey from Tokyo to Hakata in 6hr 40min at an *average* speed of 110mph (176.5km/h). To put this in perspective, a *Shin-Kansen* style journey over the comparable distance between New York and Chicago would more than halve the best current rail time of 18½ hours, to 8¼ hours!

Incidentally the trains built for the Hakata extension provide for raising speed sometime in the future by having installed power increased by 48 per cent to 23,600hp (17,600kW), whilst the extra weight of electrical equipment needed to achieve this is compensated for by building the car bodies in light alloy. Work is now in progress replacing the original trains; on a time basis their lives have been short—but not in relation to the miles run.

Above, left: *A Japanese Shin-Kansen train with snow-capped Mount Fuji in the background.*

Below left: *Construction of an entirely new 1.435mm gauge railway was Japan's successful way of cutting journey times.*

WDM2 C₀-C₀

India:
Indian Railways (IR), 1962

Type: Mixed-traffic diesel-electric locomotive.
Gauge: 5ft 6in (1,676mm).
Propulsion: Alco 251D 2,600hp (1,940kW) 16-cylinder Vee diesel engine and generator supplying current to six nose-suspended traction motors geared to the axles.
Weight: 279,910lb (127t).
Max. axleload: 47,385lb (21.5t).
Overall length: 58ft 10in (17,932mm).
Tractive effort: 63,000lb (280kN).
Max. speed: 75mph (120km/h).

In spite of India being a country with little oil and much coal, the railway authorities had decided by 1960 that diesel traction would have advantages. Although with hindsight, it was a decision that might prove to be an expensive

Class 40100 C-C

France:
French National Railways (SNCF), 1964

Type: Express passenger electric locomotive.
Gauge: 4ft 8½in (1,435mm).
Propulsion: Current supply from overhead wires at 1,500V dc, 3,000V dc, 15,000V 16⅔Hz, or 25,000V 50Hz; ac supplies transformed to 1,500V and rectified by silicon rectifiers; current then supplied to two bogie-mounted 2,910hp (2,170kW) traction motors with divided armature windings, allowing series, series/parallel and parallel grouping (parallel not used on 3,000V dc); motor geared to all three axles of the bogie through Alsthom flexible drive.
Weight: 235,830lb (107t).
Max. axleload: 39,300lb (17.8t).
Overall length: 72ft 3¼in (22,030mm).
Tractive effort: 45,000lb (200kN).
Max. speed: 112mph (180km/h).

Through locomotive workings from Paris to Brussels were introduced well back in the days of steam, and were later continued with diesel railcars. Electrification of this route by French and Belgian railways permitted through electric working, but as the French part of the route uses ac at 25,000V 50Hz whilst the Belgians use 3,000V dc, a new type of locomotive was required. At this time, in the early 1960s, a network of *Trans-Europ* expresses had been established, worked by diesel railcars, but SNCF decided to build a small number of locomotives which could work not only into Belgium, but also into other Western European countries, if the TEE trains were ever electrically operated. The requirement was therefore for the locomotives to work on four systems, 1,500V dc (in France and the Netherlands), 3,000V dc (in Belgium and Italy),

15,000V 16⅔Hz (in Austria, West Germany and Switzerland), and 25,000V 50Hz (in France).

Design of the locomotives, the "40100" class, was entrusted to Alsthom, and they were the first of a new generation of electric and diesel classes incorporating mono-motor bogies. So far the principle had been applied only to two-axle bogies, and SNCF had not built any six-axle locomotives since 1952. The specification reflected the prevailing ambitious thinking about TEE trains: to haul 210t at 137mph (220km/h) on the level and at 68mph (110km/h) on the 1-in-37 (2.6 per cent) gradients of the Gotthard and Lötschberg routes; to handle 450t at 100mph (160km/h) on the Paris to Brussels route, and at 68mph (110km/h) on the 1-in-70 (1.4 per cent) gradient between Mons and Quévy in Belgium. These characteristics would enable the

locomotive to haul 800t at 100mph (160km/h) between Paris and Aulnoye, and at 77mph (125km/h) on 1-in-200 (0.5 per cent).

The basis adopted for accommodating the four types of current is that the traction motor windings are designed for 1,500V dc. On the ac supplies, the current is transformed to 1,500V and rectified by silicon rectifiers. On 3,000V the motor windings are connected in pairs in series, whilst on 1,500V dc the motors take the incoming supply directly. Motor control is through starting resistances and there is provision for rheostatic braking.

The weight of this equipment required six axles. To allow for the regrouping of the motors to accept 3,000V, the armature winding of each motor is in two sections. There are four pantographs to suit the characteristics of the four supply systems, and there are

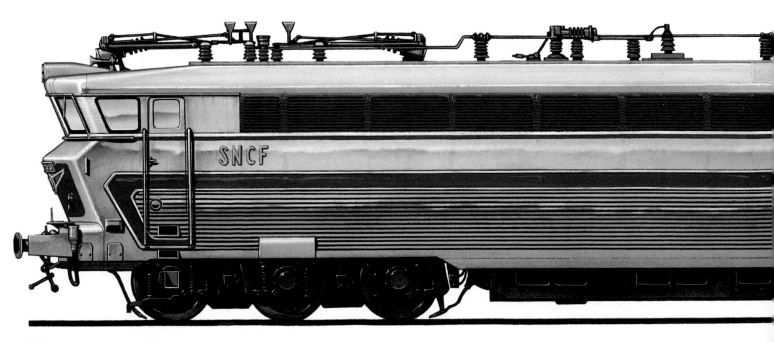

one, they at least went about implementing it in a way that commands admiration. They ignored the temptation succumbed to by so many other "third world" countries, of a big fleet of ready-made diesels, which would have left India for ever in the power of the suppliers. At the same time they recognised that "do-it-yourself" was not possible without assistance from an overseas manufacturer.

In 1961 then, those entrusted with the project looked over the field and decided that the United States firm Alco Products Inc had the best deal to offer. The agreement provided for Alco to supply

Left: *Indian Railways' Class WDM2 standard broad-gauge diesel-electric locomotive No. 17462, built to an Alco design at the railway's own locomotive-building factory at Varanasi.*

technical help as well as complete designs to Indian Railways and, at the start, finished parts for locomotive production at a diesel locomotive works to be established in Varanasi (Benares), India. When completed, the covered shops had an area over 20 acres (8Ha) in extent, while the whole factory complex, inclusive of a self-contained township, extended to 550 acres (220Ha).

The first 40 locomotives came over from America early in 1962 in completed form, followed in 1963 by a batch sent over in knocked-down condition. Ten years later production was of the order of 75 units per year and import-content was down from 100 per cent to 25 per cent. The three types which have been or are being produced are the large broad-gauge "WDM2" class (W = broad gauge, D = diesel, M = mixed traffic) described here,

a smaller broad-gauge Class "WDM1" and a metre-gauge type, smaller still, Class "YDM4". All three have the Alco 251 engine, the difference being in the number of cylinders— 16, 12 and 6 respectively for the three classes.

Alco's designation for the "WDM2" is "DL560" and in many ways it is similar to locomotives in the "Century" series. The six-wheel bogies have had to be modified to allow for the broad gauge, but they are of the familiar unsymmetrical pattern, taking account of the necessarily unsymmetrical arrangement of three nose-suspended traction motors. One change is the installation of a combined compressor-exhauster, provided to cater for vacuum-braked trains. Axleload is also lower than for models produced for the North American market. Although Alco went out of locomotive manufacture in 1969, its

Canadian associate, previously the Montreal Locomotive Works but now known as Bombardier, is still very much in business and continues to give support to the Indian enterprise.

A scheme to update the "WDM2" design has been proposed, using an alternator in place of a dc generator and replacing the 16-cylinder engine by a 12-cylinder one developing the same horsepower. However, the advantages of building locomotives to the same good design over a long period very often outweigh any advantage accruing from some technical improvement. A factor which occasionally affects sensible judgements is the need on the part of the engineers concerned to be seen to be abreast of the latest techniques, but those in charge of locomotive development in India have so far shown a sensible contempt for such motives.

interlocks and "feeler" relays to ensure that the dc supplies are not applied to the transformer and that the correct pantograph is in use. The bogies have provision for changing the gear ratio, but unlike the other French two-speed locomotives, this is not simply a matter of moving a lever; changing of the gearwheels is a workshop job. The first four locomotives are geared for a maximum speed of 100mph (160km/h) and the second batch of six for 112mph (180km/h). None has so far been regeared for 220km/h.

Styling of the locomotives was undertaken by an industrial artist, Paul Arzens, who also styled the "CC6500" and "BB15000" electric locomotives, and the "67000" and "72000" diesel-electrics. This was the first of his designs which incorporate a steeply inclined driver's front window to reduce glare from the sun. The other

classes have a larger cellular box of steel plates in front of the driver's position to act as a shock-absorber in a collision, but the "40100s" have a smaller structure than the other classes, so that the roof has an overhanging effect. The fluted stainless-steel sides are unique to these locomotives.

The first of the class appeared in 1964. They are based at La Chapelle depot, Paris, and work between Paris, Brussels and Amsterdam. In the event, the international TEE network did not develop further, and the "40100s" have never worked in countries other than France, Belgium and the Netherlands, nor, so far, have the high-speed lines designed for 220km/h running yet materialised.

Six very similar locomotives were built for Belgian National Railways (SNCB) using French electrical equipment in bodies built in Belgium. These locomotives work into West Germany.

Above: *French Railways' quadri-current electric locomotive No. 40101 at full speed.*

Below: *No. 40101 has the capability of running on four types of current— 1500 and 3,000V dc, 25,000V 50Hz and 15,000V 16⅔Hz ac. An alternative gear-ratio allows a higher max. speed of 137mph (220km/h) if needed.*

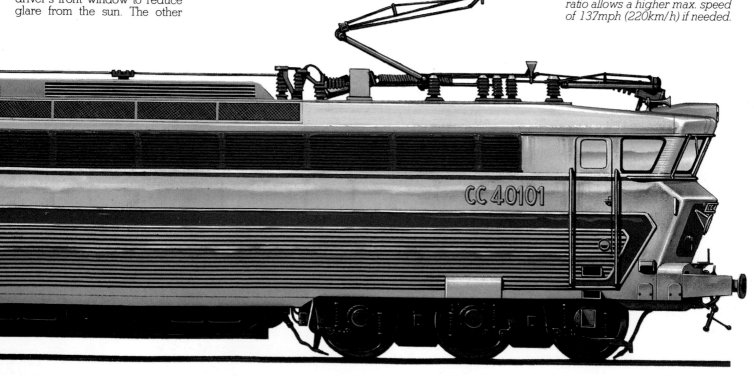

CC 40101

Nos. 111-120 1-E-1

Type: Mineral-hauling gas-fired coal-consuming steam locomotive.
Gauge: 2ft 5½in (750mm).
Propulsion: Gas-producing firebed 26sq ft (2.43m²) in aera generating steam at 228psi (16kg/cm²), which is supplied to a pair of 16½in bore × 17⅜in stroke (420 × 400mm) cylinders, each driving the main wheels directly by connecting and coupling rods.
Weight: 83,700lb (38t). adhesive, 190,529lb (86.5t) locomotive and tender.
Max. axleload: 16,740lb (7.6t).
Overall length: 61ft 7¾in (18,790mm).
Tractive effort: 12,420lb (55.5kN).
Max. speed: 28mph (45km/h).

The many attempts to improve the efficiency of the steam locomotive in the 20th Century fall into two main groups: first, those which involved radical changes in the Stephenson locomotive, such as complex high-pressure boilers or turbine drive; and secondly, those which concentrated on improving the proportions and detailed design of the conventional locomotive. In the second category the work of Andrè Chapelon was outstanding, and his rebuilds developed up to twice the power of the original locomotive, and at the same time used fuel more efficiently.

Above: *A double-shotted train of empty coal hopper wagons prepares to leave the port of Rio Gallegos, Argentina, for the mines at Rio Turbio, hauled by two Porta-Chapelon steam locos.*

QJ "Forward" 1-E-1

Type: Steam freight locomotive.
Gauge: 4ft 8½in (1,435mm).
Propulsion: Coal fire burning on a firegrate 73sq ft (6.8m²) in size generating steam at 213psi (15kg/cm²) in a firetube boiler and supplying it via a main steam pipe mounted above the boiler and a superheater to two 25⅝ x 31½in (650 x 800mm) cylinders which drive the main wheels directly through connecting and coupling rods.
Weight: 221,500lb (100.5t) adhesive, 486,080lb (220.5t) total.*
Max. axleload: 44,300lb (20.1t).
Overall length: 86ft 1½in (26,251mm).
Tractive effort: 63,500lb (282kN).
Max. speed: 50mph (80km/h).

*With small tender holding 15t (16.5 US tons) of coal and 7,700gal (35m³-9,620 US gal) of

water. With large tender the total weight is increased to 546,592lb (248t), the length to 95ft 9in, (29,180mm) and the coal and water capacity to 21.5t (23.7 US tons) and 11,020gal (50m³-13,775 US gals) respectively.

China began seriously to build steam locomotives after the rest of the world had stopped. Production still continues at a rate approaching one per working day and, not only that, has recently been reprieved indefinitely. In fact, this "QJ" class is currently, at 4,000-strong, the largest class of locomotives in the world, of whatever type of propulsion; it also comprises about a fifth of all the steam locomotives left active in the world.

The reasons for China being out of step with the rest of mankind are plain. Ample indigenous supplies of coal, modest oil reserves and plenty of people to serve a

rather labour-intensive form of traction are three of them. More important, perhaps, is the pressing need to keep the capacity of the railways abreast of the rising demands of a rapid industrial growth. This need is best met by continuing with steam locomotives which can be mass-produced in a purpose-built factory for one seventh of the cost, like-for-like, of diesel-electric ones. In Western money, a Chinese steam 2-10-2 costs some £70,000 ($ US105,000), while a diesel of equivalent capacity built in China is priced at £500,000 ($ US800,000). Fuel costs are also now lower with steam than with diesel. A last factor is that the Chinese suffer less pressure to follow the example of neighbouring railway administrations than others. No need to "keep up with the Joneses" if you live by yourself.

The first steps in development of the "QJ" began in 1946 when,

after 12 years of struggle, Mao's communist government took over a war-torn and ramshackle railway system. To improve the motive power situation in the long-term, Russian assistance was given in setting up a works at Datong in northern China, to build large freight locomotives. Delays occured through withdrawal of Russian help and the confusion that resulted, and also because of Mao's "Great Leap Forward", during which embryo locomotive factories were ordered to produce diesel locomotives—Datong's attempt is said to have been called *Sputnik*.

It was 1962 before production of this class (then called *Ho Ping* or "Peace") began at Datong. The design was basically the "Lv" class of 2-10-2 from Russia; some prototypes were built in 1956 at Dalien works in Manchuria. Certain modifications, principally to the boiler, were made in the version for production, which built up

Amongst disciples of Chapelon were several Argentinian engineers, notably Dante Porta. Under the direction of Porta and his colleagues, and with Chapelon's aid, a number of classes were improved beyond recognition, with increases of power of up to 55 per cent despite limitations imposed by the quality of labour compared with France. These rebuilds followed Chapelon's doctrine—increased cross-section of flow throughout the path of the steam, increased steam temperature by redesigning the superheater, and improved blast to increase the steaming rate without restricting the exhaust from the cylinders.

The designs incorporated a number of advances on Chapelon's work, of which the most notable was the gas-producer firebox. In this the firebed is at a comparatively low temperature, and almost all the combustion takes place in the firebox above the fire, air and steam being blown into the firebox under careful control so that almost perfect combustion can be maintained up to the highest rate of steaming. This remedied a major weakness in the normal locomotive boiler —that combustion deteriorates at high rates of steaming, thus reducing the efficiency.

Porta's most spectacular results were achieved on the world's most southerly railway, the Rio Turbio line in Argentina, a 2ft 5½in (750mm) gauge line which carries coal 160 miles (257km) from the Rio Turbio mines to the port of Rio Gallegos on the Atlantic, with grades of 1-in-333 (0·3 per cent) against loaded trains and winds of up to 100mph (160km/h). Light rail limits the axleload to 7½t and the maximum speed is 25 to 28mph (40 to 45km/h).

In 1956, ten 2-10-2 locomotives, based on a design of the Baldwin Locomotive Company, were built for this line in Japan, and Porta later applied his ideas, including the gas-producer firebox, to three of them. As a result, the sustained drawbar horsepower was increased from 700 to 1,200. Despite the poor quality of the coal, which is small for firing in locomotives and has a high ash content, combustion is almost smokeless. The improvements enabled the locomotive to haul 1,700t regularly, and on test as much as 3,000t was hauled on the level, a remarkable achievement for a locomotive weighing 48 tons on a rail gauge little more than half the standard gauge.

In 1964 ten more locomotives were built incorporating Porta's modifications, and one had a circular firebox of his design, arranged to give even more intense combustion by mixing the gases, steam and air in a swirling motion.

Not the least remarkable feature of these engines, is that, for a grate area of 22.5sq ft (2.1m²), a mechanical stoker is provided; many European and North American grates of twice that size were hand fired, but, although it had not been provided for that purpose, the controlled firing which the stoker permitted was of great help to Porta in his modifications to the firebox.

Porta produced a design for a two-cylinder compound 2-8-0 which was aimed at railways in under-developed countries which had coal but no oil, and in which the railways had difficulty in obtaining skilled labour. However, climbing on the diesel band wagon was already a characteristic of the railways in countries which could have benefitted from Porta's work, aided by countries which made cheap loans available to the third world to aid their own diesel locomotive industry. By the time the crisis in oil prices showed the folly of total dependence on oil, dieselisation had proceeded too far in most countries, and no country has built an engine to the Chapelon/Porta design, although, as recorded later, Porta's ideas are being applied in South Africa at the present time.

Below: *No. 108* André Chapelon, *a modern coal-hauling steam locomotive of the Rio Turbio Industrial Railway.*

Left: *A QJ class 1-E-1 steam locomotive of the Chinese People's Republic Railways steams past Jilin outskirts in October 1980.*

board. The standard models (numbered with a few exceptions chronologically from QJ 100 upwards) have eight-wheel tenders, but a few in the QJ60xx series have large 12-wheeled versions for use in dry areas.

Though designed for heavy freight movement, these superb locomotives can often be seen on passenger work on heavily-graded mountain lines. With extensive new railway construction going on, it is possible to travel in China on a 1980s railway behind a 1980s steam locomotive. With 2,980hp (2,223kW) available at the wheel-rim—equivalent to say 3,700hp (2,760kW) developed in the cylinders of a diesel engine —an excellent level of performance is available.

steadily as experience was gained. The 500th "QJ" was built in 1968, the 1,000th in 1970, the 2,000th in 1974 and the 3,000th in 1979, all except the very first at Datong. Datong has also built a number of "JS" or "Construction" class 2-8-2s and a series of mobile diesel-electric generating plants.

The "QJs" are very well-equipped and, apart from having the main steam pipe in trunking above the forward part of the boiler instead of out of sight inside, very much in the North American genre. They have mechanical stokers, exhaust steam injectors, feed water heaters, electric lighting, an air-horn as well as a dragon-scaring steam whistle, and even cooking facilities and a toilet on

Class 103.1 C₀-C₀

Type: Express passenger electric locomotive.
Gauge: 4ft 8½in (1,435mm).
Propulsion: Alternating current at 15,000V 16⅔Hz fed through a transformer to six 1,580hp (1,180kW) traction motors mounted on the bogie frames, connected to the axles through spring drive.
Weight: 251,260lb (114t).
Max. axleload: 41,880lb (19.0t).
Overall length: 63ft 11½in (19,500mm).
Tractive effort: 70,000lb (312kN).
Max. speed: 125mph (200km/h).

Above: *A high-speed inter-city train of the German Federal Railway hauled by a Class 103.1 electric locomotive.*

Below: *German Federal Railway's Class 103.1 Co-Co high-speed electric locomotive, introduced in 1970.*

In 1960 Deutsche Bundesbahn began to plan a network of high-speed inter-city trains with which to meet the competition of internal air services. The fast diesel trains in pre-war Germany had operated mainly on routes radiating from Berlin, on which high speeds could be sustained for long distances. In West Germany, however, the principal routes had more frequent stops and speed restrictions, and the ability to reach high speed quickly was thus as important as the ability to sustain it. The specification which was drawn up in 1961 therefore required that a speed of 125mph (200km/h) should be maintained on a gradient of 1-in-200 (0.5 per cent) with 300t, and that the train should be accelerated to this speed in 150 seconds.

In accordance with German practice a number of companies submitted proposals. These in-

VL80T B₀-B₀+B₀-B₀

Type: Electric locomotive for heavy freight haulage.
Gauge: 5ft 0in (1,524mm).
Propulsion: Alternating current at 25,000V 50Hz fed via overhead catenary, step-down transformer and silicon rectifiers to eight 790hp (590kW) nose-suspended dc traction motors, each geared to one axle.
Weight: 405,535lb (184t).
Max. axleload: 50,695lb (23t).
Overall length: 107ft 9in (32,840mm).
Tractive effort: 99,500lb (433kN).
Max. speed: 68mph (110km/h).

Soviet Railways' "VL80" series of electric locomotives, one of the most numerous in the world, is

the main motive power used for moving heavy freight trains over the USSR's huge 11,600 mile (18,700km) network of industrial-frequency electrification. The letters VL pay tribute to Vladimir Lenin, no less, whose personal enthusiasm for railway electrification has now, many years after his death, had such impressive results.

The eight-axle locomotive has double-bogie units permanently coupled in pairs, and is a favourite for freight work in the USSR. Some 1,500 of Class "VL8" were built for the 3,000V dc lines from 1953 onwards, followed in 1961 by the start of production of the "VL10" class, also for dc lines. For ac lines, the first "VL80s", externally very similar to the "VL10s", began coming into use in 1963

with the class variant "VL80K".

The first "VL80Ks" had mercury-arc rectifiers, but it is difficult to avoid problems when (in lay terms) mercury sloshes around under the influence of vibration and traction shocks. Solid-state silicon rectifiers were soon substituted. The "VL80T" was a modification of the "VL80K" which had rheostatic electric braking, and this has been the main production version of the "VL80" class of which over 2,000 have now been built. After some years of experiment, "VL80" series-production has now changed to a version ("VL80R") with thyristor control and—made painlessly possible by the scope of this system—full regenerative electric braking. This is claimed to reduce current con-

sumption by over 10 per cent.

Experiments are in progress on a "VL80A" version which uses three-phase asynchronous induction motors supplied with variable-frequency current by a solid-state conversion system. Another interesting development, which is obviously very similar to the "VL80A" arrangement theoretically but very different practically, is to use thyristors inside each motor as a substitute for the commutator and brushes. In this way the associated problems of mechanical wear and vulnerability to flashover at the commutators can possibly be avoided. A three-unit version ("VL80S") with 13,100hp (9,780kW) available for hauling 10,000t (11,000 US tons) trains has been produced and

cluded 1-Bo+Bo-1 and A1A+ A1A schemes with four motors of 1,250kW (1,675hp), but it was considered that six motors should be fitted to keep the motor weight down, and despite some doubts about its riding qualities, the Co-Co arrangement was chosen.

Four prototypes were ordered in 1963 from Siemens Schuckert and Henschel; delivered in 1965 they were numbered E03.001-4. They made a spectacular entry into service, for in connection with an international transport exhibition in Munich that year they worked a special train twice daily from Munich to Augsburg at an average of 88mph (142km/h) with sustained 200km/h running.

The locomotives followed the pattern already established in DB standard designs, with an ac motor mounted above each axle and fully-sprung drive. Control was by tap changers on the high-

tension side of the transformer. Automatic speed control was fitted, with increments of 10km/h on the driver's controller. The motors were of light weight for their power, specially designed for high speed. The one-hour rating was 6,420kW (8,600hp) at 200km/h, and the 10-minute rating was no less than 9,000kW (12,000hp). The locomotives were subjected to a lengthy period of testing, from which it was found that, when employed on heavy expresses running at lower speeds, they suffered from high transformer temperatures, and so larger transformers had to be fitted.

For a time, DB favoured the idea of working the inter-city network by multiple-units, but eventually it was decided that, except for any services which might in the future exceed 200km/h, locomotives would be

used, and 145 more of the Co-Co units were ordered. They were delivered from 1970 onwards; under the computerised numbering system then in use they were designated Nos. 103.101-245. They incorporated various improvements to the motors and control equipment which allowed them to work trains of up to 480t at 200km/h. The earlier locomotives had also developed heavy brush and commutator wear when their high-speed motors were subjected to heavy currents at low speeds, and the new machines had an additional tap-changer on the low-tension side of the transformer which made them suitable for working 600t trains at normal speeds.

The body shape of the original locomotives had been determined by wind-tunnel tests, but the resultant curved ends had the effect of making the driver's cab more

cramped than in other classes. The last 30 of the new locomotives were 700mm (27½in) longer in the body, to allow for more roomy cabs. Experience with 200km/h running showed that wear on the track and locomotives was greater than had been expected, and it was suspended from 1967. It was not until 1977 that the intended network of *IC-Züge* came into operation. The Class "103" then came fully into its own, for the admission of second-class passengers to these trains had increased the number of coaches above the original proposals.

No. 103.118 is geared for a maximum speed of 155mph (250km/h), and has been used for much high-speed testing. It also has some electrical differences, and has a short-term rating of 14,000hp (10,400kW), making it the most powerful single-unit locomotive in the world.

prototypes have been built of a "VL84" version with increased power.

Also associated with the "VL80s" are the "VL82" series of dual-current locomotives for 3,000 dc and 25,000V 50Hz ac, dating from 1966. Adding together both systems of electrification the overall picture is quite amazing — more electrically-hauled rail freight traffic than the whole of the rest of the world put together, moved on a 28,000 mile (44,800km) network of electrified lines by a fleet of some 4,000 of these massive dc, ac, and dc/ac machines.

Right: *One half of a Soviet Railways' VL82 series Bo-Bo+Bo-Bo dual current electric locomotive.*

Class 73 B₀-B₀

Type: Electro-diesel mixed-traffic locomotive.
Gauge: 4ft 8½in (1,435mm).
Propulsion: Direct-current at 675V fed via an outside third rail, or alternatively generated on the locomotive by an English Electric 600hp (448kW) Type 4 SRKT diesel engine, to four 395hp (295kW) nose suspended traction motors.
Weight: 168,000lb (76t).
Max. axleload: 42,000lb (19t).
Overall length: 53ft 8in (16,358mm)*.
Tractive effort: 42,000lb (187kN).
Max. speed: 90mph (145km/h).

*Buffers extended

One of the problems of an electrified railway is the need to provide for working over lines which, either permanently or temporarily, have no current supply. With

third-rail systems this need is accentuated by the impossibility of providing conductor rails uninterruptedly; BR's Southern Region had solved the problem by electric locomotives which could store energy in fly-wheels to pass trains over short gaps.

As the SR's electrification became more widespread, the use of normal diesel locomotives to cover workings over shorter and shorter portions of a journey became less and less satisfactory. So a powerful electric locomotive

Left: *The Honeymoon Special of the Prince and Princess of Wales (note special Charles-Diana headcode) enters Romsey station, Hants, hauled by electro-diesel No. 73142.*

Below: *British Railways Southern Region Class 73 electro-diesel locomotive No. 73142, Broadlands.*

Class ET22 C₀-C₀

Type: Electric mixed-traffic locomotive.
Gauge: 4ft 8½in (1,435mm).
Propulsion: Direct current at 3,000V fed via overhead catenary to six 705hp (520kW) traction motors, geared with quill-type flexible drive to the axles.
Weight: 264,480lb (120t).
Max. axleload: 44,080lb (20t).
Overall length: 63ft 1½in (19,240mm).
Tractive effort: 92,568lb (411kN).
Max. speed: 78mph (125km/h).

Poland is a country which, seen from the West, appears as a small (and reluctant) Russian satellite state. Yet its land area and railway

mileage—the latter at 15,078 miles (24,125km)—is 30 per cent greater than Britain's, while the population is 40 per cent less. The startling difference is that Polish State Railways (PKP) move seven times as much freight as BR. In fact, apart from the USSR, Poland has more rail traffic than any European country. Poland is also a coal-rich but oil-poor land so, despite relative poverty, 4,438 miles (7,100km) of electrification has been carried out.

Even so, there are some 2,000 diesel locomotives in Poland including shunters (the exact number is not revealed), but it is a sign of the times that—alone in Europe —more than 1,000 steam locomotives continue to contribute their now substantially lower fuel

costs (not to speak of zero capital cost) to the economy. But there is no doubt that the electrified network, already carrying over one-third of the country's rail traffic, will be increased.

Heavy density of traffic over many lines still to be electrified means that there is little temptation to depart from the 3,000V dc system adopted in the 1930s. All Polish electric locomotives from the beginning have been of the universal double-bogie pattern, all axles powered, of Bo-Bo or Co-Co wheel arrangement.

These Class "ET22" locomotives are the most common type in Poland and were originally designed for freight traffic. Over 500 have been built by Panstwowa Fabvyka Wagonow (Pafawag) of

Wroclaw (mechanical parts) and Kolmex of Warsaw (electrical equipment) since 1971. They follow an anglo-saxon tradition of simplicity introduced to Poland in 1936 with a batch of Bo-Bos from Britain. Hence no frills such as dynamic braking, although some of the units have multiple-unit capability for working heavy trains of coal from Silesia to Gdansk.

Another complication is the use of flexible drive of the quill pattern to ease dynamic loadings and so assist the permanent way to remain permanent. Maximum speed is usefully high and the "ET22s" are equipped for passenger work with electric train heating, a fairly simple matter with medium-voltage dc traction. This is perhaps the reason why some references to

was conceived which carried a modest (but standard) diesel generating plant for movements away from the conductor rail. The result was this versatile group of locomotives (now designated Class "73") of which 42 were built in 1967 following six prototypes of 1962.

Details of interest include provision for multiple-unit operation not only with other electro-diesels, but also with straight electric and diesel-electric trains and locomotives. The weight of the diesel engine and generator, housed at one end of the locomotive, is balanced by a massive buffer beam at the other. Both screw couplings with buffers (for coupling to freight stock) and automatic buck-eye couplers with central buffing plates (for passenger trains) are provided.

The versatility of Class "73" was demonstrated to the world in July 1981, when Charles and

Diana, Prince and Princess of Wales, left London for their honeymoon at Romsey, Hampshire, behind No. 73 142 *Broadlands*: 82 miles (131km) of electrified travel down the main line was followed by 5 miles (8km) on a lesser and non-electrified route.

Above: *BR Class 73 electro-diesel. Yellow ends make the locomotive more conspicuous for men working on the track.*

this class designate it "EU22". "E" means electric and "T" means 'Towarowy' or freight, while "U" seems to signify mixed-traffic. Incidentally, Bo-Bo classes are numbered from 01 to (currently) 08, Co-Cos from 20 to 23, and double Bo-Bos from 40 to 42. "P" stands for "Pospiszny" or passenger, and hence a recent 100mph (160km/h) version of the "ET22" is classified "EP23".

The "ET22s" are very successful machines and have extended the once thriving Polish export trade in steam locomotives to include electric, when an order for 23 for Morocco (Class "E-1000") was delivered in 1973.

Right: *No. ET22-112 takes a freight through Lublin, Poland.*

151

Class 72000 C-C

France: French National Railways (SNCF), 1967

Type: Diesel-electric dual-purpose locomotive.
Gauge: 4ft 8½in (1,435mm).
Propulsion: Société Alsacienne de Constructions Mécaniques 3,550hp (2,650kW) 16-cylinder four-stroke diesel engine and alternator supplying current through silicon rectifiers to two traction motors, one on each bogie; motors connected to the axles through two-speed gearing and spring drive.
Weight: 251,260lb (114t).
Max. axleload: 41,880lb (19t).
Overall length: 66ft 3in (20,190mm).
Tractive effort: Low gear 81,570lb (363kN), high gear 46,300lb (206kN).
Max. speed: Low gear 53mph (85km/h), high 87mph (140km/h).

When SNCF embarked on construction of large main-line diesel locomotives in 1961, it was recognised that a more powerful unit than the 2,650hp Class "68000" would be needed eventually for the heaviest work. So two pairs of twin-engine experimental locomotives were ordered, which could develop up to 4,800hp (3,580kW). However, enthusiasm for the complications of the twin-engine machines was never great, and development of new diesel engines in the range 3,500 to 4,000hp encouraged SNCF in 1964 to invite manufacturers to submit proposals for a powerful single-engine locomotive. Alsthom made a successful submission of a C-C design, based on the AGO16 engine of 3,600hp (2,700kW). "A" denotes the maker, Société Alsacienne de Constructions Mécaniques of Mulhouse, "G" and "O" denote the designers, Grosshaus and Ollier. This engine

was a 16-cylinder version of the 12-cylinder engine already fitted to the "68500" series of A1A+A1A locomotives.

Eighteen of the new design were ordered from Alsthom in 1966, and delivery commenced in the following year; the class was allocated numbers from 72001. SNCF was at this period developing a new family of electric locomotives incorporating monomotor bogies, and the "72000s" incorporated various parts in common with the electric units. The bogies followed closely the design recently introduced in the Class "40100" quadricurrent locomotives, with two gear ratios, the maximum speeds in the two settings being 53mph (85km/h) for freight and 87mph (140km/h) for passenger work. The traction motors are identical electrically with those of the "BB8500," "BB17000" and "BB25500" electric locomotives. SNCF estimated that the monomotor bogie saved 9t in weight compared with conventional bogies with individual axle drive, and it enabled the axleload to be kept within the stipulated 18t.

Main innovation in the electrical system was use of an alternator instead of a dc generator. This delivers three-phase current which is rectified by silicon diodes for supply to the dc traction motors. The electrical equipment includes Alsthom's "Superadhesion" system, in which the excitation of the field of the motors is controlled to give an almost direct relationship between motor voltage and current. By this means the tendency for incipient wheelslip to develop

Right: *French National Railways Class 72000 diesel-electric loco.*

Class 68000 A1A-A1A

France: French National Railways (SNCF), 1963

Type: Express passenger diesel-electric locomotive.
Gauge: 4ft 8½in (1,435mm).
Propulsion: CCM-Sulzer 2,650hp (1,980kW) 12LVA24 12-cylinder four-stroke Vee-engine and generator supplying current to four semi-sprung traction motors geared to the end axles of the bogies through spring drive.
Weight: 176,320lb (80t) or 158,690lb (72t) adhesive, 233,620lb (106t) total.
Max. axleload: 44,080lb (20t) or 39,670lb (18t) adjustable.
Overall length: 58ft 9½in (17,920mm).
Tractive effort: 66,140lb (294kN).
Max. speed: 83mph (130km/h).

During the 1950s, electrification spread rapidly over the busiest main lines in France and many of the most powerful steam engines became available for transfer to non-electrified routes. Until the end of the decade no major steps were taken to introduce large diesel locomotives for the ultimate replacement of these steam engines on routes on which the traffic density was insufficient to justify electrification, and in 1962 only 8 per cent of total tonne-km on SNCF were diesel worked.

By 1960 diesel engines were available which made possible design of locomotives to replace even the largest steam engines, and in 1961 orders were placed for four new types of diesel locomotive, 20 B-Bs of 2,000hp (1,500kW), 18 A1A-A1As of 2,650hp (1,980kW), and two each of two twin-engined machines destined ultimately to have a power of 4,800hp (3,580kW).

It was intended that the 2,650hp Class "68000" should take over the heaviest workings on the routes from Paris to Cherbourg and Basle, pending completion of development of the larger units.

The engine is of Sulzer design, produced by Sulzer's French associate, CCM. It is a 16-cylinder unit of Vee-formation, in contrast to the 2,750hp Sulzer engine then being built in large numbers for British Railways, which had twin crankshafts. It was Sulzer's first Vee engine for traction since 1927.

The engine drives a dc generator, which supplies the semi-sprung nose-hung traction motors. The weight of the engine, generator and train boiler made it necessary to have six axles, but only four traction motors were required, so the middle axle of each bogie is an idler. A novel system was applied whereby wedges can be inserted above the springs of the intermediate axles to vary the distribution of weight. On routes on which a 20t axleload is allowed, the intermediate axles carry 13t, but on routes with an 18t limit, the intermediate axles carry 17t. In the latter arrangement, a servo-operated mechanism enables the load on the driving wheels to be increased to 20t at starting, until a speed of 18½mph (30km/h) is

Above: *A pair of Class 68000 diesel-electric locomotives with an express near Noyelles in 1978.*

Below: *French National Railways No. 68067 enters Angers with a Paris express in June 1967.*

is greatly reduced, and it is claimed that the effective starting tractive effort can be increased by 15 to 20 per cent.

The body resembles closely those of the corresponding electric classes but has a higher roof to accommodate the engine. The treatment of the ends incorporates cab windows steeply inclined backwards to reduce glare, as introduced on the "40100" class, but the appearance was much altered by restyling of the ends due to inclusion of massive cellular boxes in front of the cab to protect the driver in case of collision.

They were immediately put to work on the Paris to Brittany and Paris to Basle routes, where they enabled modest increases to be made in train speeds over the "68000" class, but consistent with SNCF's target of not developing full power for more than 60 per

cent of the run, compared with 67 per cent recorded with the earlier locomotives, and also consistent with supplying electric train heating from the engine power. The class eventually reached a total of 92, and they took over the heaviest work on most non-electrified routes. Ten had modifications made to enable them to run at 100mph (160km/h).

In 1973 No. 72075 was fitted with an SEMT-Pielstick PA 6-280 12-cylinder engine, initially rated at 4,200hp, but increased a year later to 4,800hp (3,580kW), making it the most powerful diesel engine in a locomotive (at least in the Western world). At the end of 1978 the engine was found to be in good condition, and it embarked on a further period of service. This modification increased the weight to 118t. There were no further conversions.

WAM4 Co-Co
India:
Indian Railways (IR), 1971

reached. Maximum speed is 83mph (130km/h).

Control equipment is also novel for a diesel locomotive in that it resembles the "notch-up, notch-down, hold" type of controller, already in use on electric locomotives. The driver's controller has four positions, "stop", "run", "faster", "slower". Moving the controller from "stop" to "run" energises the motor circuits with the engine running at idling speed, and engine speed is increased by holding the controller at "faster" against the pressure of a spring until the desired engine speed is reached. Similarly holding the controller at "slower" reduces the engine speed. Body sides are finished with a distinctive chevron design, destined to characterise all subsequent large French diesel locomotives, and the livery is blue and white.

The first 18 Class "68000" locomotives were ordered in 1961 from Cie des Ateliers & Forges de la Loire of St Chamond, and delivery commenced in 1963. A further 18 were ordered in the following year's programme, and eventually the class totalled 82. The first locomotives were put to work between Paris and Mulhouse and Paris and Cherbourg, but it was soon apparent that they could only just equal the everyday work of the "241P" 4-8-2 steam engines on trains of 800t, and then only at the cost of working at full power for a higher proportion of the time than was considered desirable in the interests of reliability.

A second version of the class was introduced late in 1963, fitted with the AGOV12 engine made by Société Alsacienne de Constructions Mécaniques of Mulhouse. This engine is a smaller version of that used in the "72000" class C-C locomotives. Since the appearance of the "72000", the two series of A1A-A1As have been moved to less-demanding duties.

Type: Electric mixed-traffic locomotive.
Gauge: 5ft 6in (1,676mm).
Propulsion: Alternating current at 25,000V 50Hz fed via overhead catenary, step-down transformer and solid-state rectifiers to six 600hp (448kW) nose-suspended traction motors, each geared directly to one of the six axles.
Weight: 249,050lb (113t).
Max. axleload: 41,876lb (19t).
Overall length: 62ft 3in (18,974mm).
Tractive effort: 74,600lb (332kN).
Max. speed: 75mph (120km/h).

When in the 1950s use of industrial-frequency current combined with rectifier locomotives became the world norm, India like most other countries previously wedded to dc systems made the change.

Since French developments then led the field, the locomotives supplied at first followed that country's practice, whether built in France or in India. Before long it became apparent that some of their more sophisticated features such as spring-borne traction motors did not suit Indian conditions. The result was the first Indian-designed and Indian-built electric locomotive class, which appeared from the railways' own Chittaranjan Loco Works in 1971.

A feature is the use of the same power bogies as on Indian diesel-electric locomotives. So many electric and diesel-electric loco designers pursue separate and divergent courses, those of British Rail being a notorious example. The fleet of these machines has now reached over 300, rheostatic electric braking and multiple-unit capability being provided on all. Silicon-diode rectifiers and tap-

changing on the high tension side of the main transformer are used.

A dual-current series, Class "WCAM1", is also being built, as well as 'WCG2s' for freight traffic on dc lines. Both are similar in appearance to and have many components in common with the "WAM4s". A small group of "WAM4s" have been given a lower gearing for heavy iron-ore trains ("WAM4B"), while a high-speed version is also reported to be under construction.

Class "WAM4" illustrates how sound thinking and a bold approach to self-help have given Indian Railways an enviable foundation on which to build a sound future.

Below: *Indian Railways' Class WAM4 Co-Co 3,600hp electric locomotive built "in-house" at the Chittaranjan Locomotive Works for ac-electrified lines.*

"Virgin" B-B
Spain:
Spanish National Railways (RENFE), 1964

Type: High-speed diesel-hydraulic express passenger locomotive.
Gauge: 5ft 6in (1,668mm).
Propulsion: Two Maybach-Mercedes MD6557 12-cylinder Vee diesel engines of 1,200hp (895kW), each driving a Mekydro K104U hydraulic transmission unit and via cardan shafts and gearing, the main axles.
Weight: 163,100lb (74t).
Max. axleload: 40,775lb (18.5t).
Overall length: 57ft 3in (17,450mm).
Tractive effort: 54,000lb (240kN).
Max. speed: 87mph (140km/h).

Vehicles with less than four wheels are rare in the railway world, except in Spain. There the coaches of the famous "Talgo" trains are not only two-wheeled (the wheelless end being supported by the next car), but so low-slung that the floors are typically only 14in (356mm) above rail level. This compares with 42in (1,067mm) typically for conventional stock. This gives the "Talgos" excellent stability for fast running on heavily-curved routes. The weight per passenger seat is also low, being only about 672lb (305kg) compared with 1,014lb (460kg) of, say, a British Rail MKIII coach.

In 1964, with many "Talgos" running and planned, Spanish National Railways went to Krauss-Maffei of Munich, West Germany, for a batch of five low-slung matching diesel locomotives. These machines, now officially designated Class "352", were the result. The Spanish share with the British a feeling that locomotives need names, but being a devout nation chose for these names of shrines to the Holy Virgin. Further batches have followed down the years, the next five being virtually identical, except that they were constructed under licence in Spain by Babcock y Wilcox of Bilbao.

Eight more of a stretched version (Class "353") came from Krauss-Maffei in 1969, offering 25 per cent more power than the originals. In 1982, Krauss-Maffei delivered a further eight, with power output increased to 4,000hp (2,980kW), designated Class "354". The last of the original batch, No. 3005 *Virgen de la Bien Aparecida* is interesting in that it originally ran for a time on standard-gauge bogies. This was to haul the "Catalan Talgo" Trans-Europe-Express on the French portion of its journeys between Barcelona and Geneva. The train itself has adjustable axles for a quick change between Spanish broad gauge and French standard gauge.

The locomotives have to have special low drawgear for hauling the "Talgo" sets and, in addition, must provide power for lighting, heating, air-conditioning and cooking on the train. This is taken care of by two 250hp (187kW) diesel-generator sets. The basis of the design was the German Class "V-200" diesel-hydraulics (qv) but modifications were needed to obtain the "Talgo" height of 10ft 9in (3,277mm) overall, compared with that of conventional Spanish trains of 14ft 1in (4,293mm).

The "Talgo" principle has recently been extended to encompass a Paris to Madrid sleeping car express, running the 911 miles (1,458km) in a very creditable 12hr 55min, including gauge change for the carriage units. The most interesting innovation on this and other recent "Talgo" trains is inclusion of a passive tilting system to permit higher speeds on curves.

Right: *A low-slung "Virgin" diesel-hydraulic locomotive of Spanish National Railways,* Virgen Sante Maria, *hauling a Talgo express at Pancorbo on the Miranda to Burgos line.*

Metroliner Two-car Trainset
USA:
Pennsylvania Railroad (PRR), 1967

Type: High-speed electric multiple-unit trainset.
Gauge: 4ft 8½in (1,435mm).
Propulsion: Alternating current at 11,000V 25Hz fed via overhead catenary, step down transformer and rectifiers to eight 300hp (224kW) nose-suspended motors, one geared to each pair of wheels.
Weight: 328,400lb (149t).
Max. axleload: 41,880lb (19t).
Overall length: 170ft 0in (51,816mm).
Max speed: 160mph (256km/h)*.

*Design speed; yet to be achieved in normal service.

In the 1960s, the United States passenger train was at a very low ebb. Most railroads were reporting massive deficits on passenger services as well as a steady loss of traffic. Over long distances the jet airliner had a twenty-fold advantage in time, which hardly affected the time disadvantage between city centre and operational terminal, compared with rail. Over short distances, though, the opposite was the case and there seemed a possibility of the train continuing to compete, were it not for out-dated equipment and image.

One such route was the Pennsylvania Railroad's electrified main line between New York, Phila-delphia and Washington, now known as the North East Corridor. It was in order to offer better service on this route that these remarkable trains came into being. Possible prototypes had been acquired from the Budd Company of Philadelphia in 1958 ("MP 85") and in 1963 some cars—the Budd *Silverliners*—were acquired on behalf of Pennsy by the City of Philadelphia.

Later in the decade the railroad received some government assistance towards a $22 million scheme for new high-speed self-propelled trains plus $33 million for some improvements to the permanent way; 160mph (256km/h) operation was envisaged.

Orders were placed in 1966 with Budd for 50 (later increased to 61) stainless steel cars to be called *Metroliners*. They drove on all wheels, could attain considerably more than the specified speed and had a fantastic short-term power-to-weight ratio of 34hp per tonne. They also had dynamic braking down to 30mph (48km/h), automatic acceleration, deceleration and speed control using new sophisticated techniques. Full air-conditioning, air-

Below: *Budd Metroliner self-propelled high-speed club car refurbished in Amtrak colours.*

line-type catering, electrically controlled doors and a public telephone service by radio link were provided. The order included parlour cars and snack-bar coaches as well as ordinary day coaches. All had a driving cab at one end, but access between adjacent sets through a cab not in use was possible. They were marshalled semi-permanently in pairs as two-car units. An over-bold decision was taken to begin production straight from the drawing board; for once, with the Pennsylvania Railroad suffering from a terminal sickness, its officers did not insist on the usual Pennsy precaution of building and testing prototypes first. As a · result, faults galore again and again delayed entry into public service until after ill-fated Penn Central took over in 1968. A single round-trip daily began at the beginning of 1969 and even then a modification programme costing 50 per cent of the original price of the trains was needed to make them suitable for public service.

Amtrak took over in May 1971 and a year later 14 daily *Metroliner* trips were being run and start-to-stop average speeds as high as 95mph (152km/h) were scheduled. Even so, speeds as high as the announced 150mph were not run in public service, although 164mph (262km/h) was achieved on test; the work done on the permanent way was not sufficient for this, 110mph (176km/h) being the normal limit.

Since then a programme of track work has been carried out over the North East Corridor. At a cost of $2,500 million, this is 75 times as much as the original rather naive proposal, but does include the New York to Boston line. At long last this great work is drawing near to completion, and higher speeds can be envi-

saged. However, the *Metroliners*, now over 15 years old, have been displaced from the New York-Washington services by "AEM7" locomotives and trains of Amfleet coaches, which are effectively non-powered *Metroliners*. The powered *Metroliners* now work the New York-Philadelphia-Harrisburg route. The original schedule of 2½ hours for the 226 miles (362km) between New York and Washington was never achieved, but (taking 1978 as an example) hourly trains did the run in a very respectable 3 hours (or a minute or two more) with four intermediate stops, an overall average of 75mph (120km/h).

Above: *A New York to Washington train formed of four Metroliner electric cars.*

Below: *A Metroliner express train at speed on the North East Corridor main line.*

"Shao-Shan I" Co-Co
China: Railways of the People's Republic, 1969

Type: Electric freight locomotive.
Gauge: 4ft 8½in (1,435mm).
Propulsion: Alternating current at 25,000V 50Hz fed via overhead catenary, step-down transformer and solid state rectifiers to six 940hp (700kW) nose-suspended motors geared to the axles.
Weight: 304,155lb (138t).
Max. axleload: 50,695lb (23t).
Overall length: 66ft 10in (20,368mm).
Tractive effort: 119,100lb (530kN).
Max. speed: 56mph (90km/h).

The Chinese Railway authorities were fortunate in that the dc versus ac question was settled before they began an ambitious programme of electrification, appropriate to a country with ample coal and water-power but little oil. The first scheme to be put in hand was a brand new railway with some amazing engineering running north-south for 422 miles (679km) through mountain country in central China between Baoji and Chengtu. Further schemes both connected to and separate from this original one are now completed or in hand.

When the time came in the late-1950s to consider motive power, French designers had had the most experience in electrification at industrial frequency, and so with commendable good sense orders were placed in France. An early order for locomotives of conventional design was followed in 1972 by a batch of 40 mixed-traffic locomotives of 7,200hp (5,350kW), known as Class "6G". They were of advanced design with thyristor control. But in the meantime an electric locomotive works had been built at Zhouzhou and production of the "Shaoshan I" or "SS1" class had began. The class was named after the birthplace of Chairman Mao, an indication of the part electrification was expected to play in building the future of China.

The "SS1" design was based on the French locomotives supplied in 1960, except that silicon solid-state rectifiers are used instead of the ignitron type of mercury-arc rectifier. Also, in spite of an axleloading on the heavy side, the direct current traction motor drives are of the simple nose-suspended axle-hung pattern. Rheostatic rather than regenerative braking is provided, but multiple-unit capability enables trains of up to 2,400t (2,650 US tons) to be handled on 1-in-30 (3.3 per cent) grades using three "SS1" units, making almost 17,000hp (12,700kW) available. Some 250 of this class have now been built.

Class EF81 Bo-Bo
Japan: Japanese National Railways (JNR), 1968

Type: Electric mixed-traffic locomotive.
Gauge: 3ft 6in (1,067mm).
Propulsion: Direct current at 1,500V or alternating current at 25,000V 50Hz or 60Hz fed via overhead catenary to six 570hp (425kW) nose-suspended traction motors geared direct to the axles of the three bogies. The transformer for the ac current has a fixed ratio and it feeds the normal rheostatic dc control system via solid-state rectifiers.
Weight: 222,610lb (101t).
Max. axleload: 37,470lb (17t).
Overall length: 61ft 0in (18,600mm).
Tractive effort: 43,800lb (195kN) on dc, 40,200lb (179kN) on ac.
Max. speed: 72mph (115km/h).

In recent years the demands for heavy haulage on Japan's 5,270 miles (8,435km) of electrified 3ft 6in (1,067mm) gauge main lines has been met by building a series of locomotive classes of the B-B-B wheel arrangement. Single-current varieties exist for all three current systems used in Japan, that is dc, ac at 50Hz and ac at 60Hz, and also all the permutations for dual current as well as the tri-current type described here. There are also similar locomotives of the B-2-B wheel arrangement, which include a weight distribution system allowing the weight carried on the two outer motor bogies to be varied according to rail-weight limits and adhesion needs. The table sets out the different classes.

Class "EF81" is perhaps the most sophisticated design amongst this plethora of fascinating locomo-

Above: *Class EF electric locomotive at the head of a JNR container train on the Tohoku line, July 1975.*

Below: *Japanese National Railways' Class EF81 twin-current standard B-B-B mixed traffic electric locomotive.*

"SS2" and "SS3" prototypes of modernised and stretched versions of the "SS1" with thyristor control systems have appeared, and it seems that the latter is going into production to cover the demands of electrified routes that will soon exceed 1,250 miles (2,000km) in extent. Now that other than mountain lines are included in the programme, there are plans for electric locomotives capable of speeds up to 75mph (120km/h).

Right: *Chinese People's Railways' 5,640hp (4,200kW) Class SS1 or "Shao-Shan I" standard Co-Co 50Hz ac locomotive for electrified lines.*

tive variety. Complications include automatic control of wheelslip and compensation for load transfer when applying high tractive efforts, but otherwise they are very simple. They have no flexible drive system, neither rheostatic nor regenerative braking, and only the plainest of box-like bodywork. Notable is the relatively high maximum speed for the narrow gauge, although much of Japan's rail passenger traffic is handled by multiple-unit trains—including, as we shall see, overnight sleeping car expresses. Electric train heating is provided for use when passenger trains are hauled.

A total of 156 "EF81s" are in service, construction being in the hands of such well-known names as Hitachi, Mitsubishi and Toshiba. One batch of four have stainless-steel bodyshells, as much of their lives will be spent within the corrosive atmosphere of the 11.6-mile (18.7km) undersea tunnel which connects the main island of Honshu with Kyushu.

Japanese Three-Bogie Electric Locomotives

Date	Class	Type	DC 1500 V	AC 50 Hz	AC 60 Hz	Power		Weight tonnes	Speed	
						hp	kW		mph	km/h
1960	EF30	B-B-B	●		●	2,410	1,800	96	53	85
1961	EF70	B-B-B			●	3,080	2,300	96	62	100
1961	EF72	B-2-B			●	2,550	1,900	87	62	100
1962	EF63	B-B-B	●			3,420	2,550	108	62	100
1962	EF80	B-B-B	●	●		2,610	1,950	96	65	105
1964	EF64	B-B-B	●			3,420	2,550	108	72	115
1964	EF65	B-B-B	●			3,420	2,550	108	72	115
1965	EF76	B-2-B		●	●	2,550	1,900	90.5	62	100
1965	EF77	B-2-B		●		2,550	1,900	75	62	100
1966	EF66	B-B-B	●			5,230	3,900	101	75	120
1966	EF71	B-B-B		●		3,620	2,700	100.8	62	100
1966	EF78	B-2-B		●		2,550	1,900	81.5	62	100
1968	EF81	B-B-B	●	●	●	3,420	2,550	101	72	115

Class DD40AX "Centennial" D₀-D₀

USA:
Union Pacific Railroad (UP), 1969

Type: Diesel-electric locomotive for heavy freight duty.
Gauge: 4ft 8½in (1,435mm).
Propulsion: Two supercharged two-stroke General Motors 16-cylinder Type 645 engines each of 3,300hp (2,460kW) with integral alternators, feeding eight nose-suspended traction motors.
Weight: 545,270lb (247.5t).
Max. axleload: 68,324lb (31t).
Overall length: 98ft 5in (29,997mm).
Tractive effort: 133,766lb (603kN).
Max. speed: 90mph (144km/h).

If one were to choose the world's number one rail line, a fairly likely candidate would be the central section of the first United States transcontinental railroad, known now by the same name—Union Pacific—as it was when opened in 1869. In the days of steam, UP had the largest and most powerful locomotives in the world, the legendary "Big Boys", to haul the heavy and constant flow of freight across the continental divide. Going west, this began with the famous Sherman Hill (named after General Sherman who was in charge of building UP) out of Cheyenne, Wyoming; it consists of some 40 miles (64km) of 1-in-66 (1.5 per cent) grade.

When diesel traction took over, the power of a steam 4-8-8-4 could be matched or exceeded by coupling locomotive units in multiple, but UP management consistently made efforts to find a simpler solution by increasing the power of each unit. It has been described earlier how gas turbines with their increased power-to-weight ratio were used for a time, and how in the end the ability to buy off-the-shelf from diesel locomotive suppliers proved to have an over-riding advantage.

In the late-1960s, the UP operating authorities once again felt that there should be a better solution than having six or even eight locomotives on one train. General Motors had put together

a peculiar 5,000hp (3,730kW) locomotive which they called a "DD35", which was essentially a huge booster unit with the works of two standard "GP35" road-switchers mounted on it. The locomotive ran on two four-axle trucks; these were considered to be hard on the track, but being contained in a mere booster unit could not take the leading position in a train where any bad effects of the running gear would be accentuated. Even so, no one was very keen to put the matter to the test. Only a handful of "DD35s" were sold and those only to Union Pacific and Southern Pacific. UP's track was (and is) superb, however, and it was suggested to GM that a "DD35" with a normal cab hood would be useful. The result was the "DD35A", of which 27 were supplied to UP. It was not disclosed how much saving in cost, allowing for an element of custom building, there was between two "GP35s" and one "DD35A", but in length at least the former's 112ft 4in (34,240mm) compared with the latter's 88ft 2in (26,873mm).

A centenary in a new country is a great event and when during the late-1960s UP considered how to celebrate 100 years of continuous operation, they decided to do it by ordering a class of prime mover which was the

most powerful in the world on a single-unit basis. Again, virtually everything except the chassis of the locomotive came off General Motors shelves, but even so the "Centennials" (more prosaically, the "DD40AXs") are a remarkable achievement.

In the same way that the "DD35A" was a double "GP35", the "DD40AX" was a double "GP40". The 16-cylinder engines of the "GP40" (essentially a supercharged version of those fitted to the "GP35") were uprated from 3,000 to 3,300hp (2,240 to

Below: *Union Pacific DD40AX No. 6900 heads the celebratory "Golden Spike" special, marking 100 years of continuous operation across the continent.*

Above: *A pair of Union Pacific Do-Do "Centennial" diesel-electric units forming a single locomotive with 13,200hp (9,940kW) and 267,500lb (1,206kN) tractive effort.*

2,460kW), thereby producing a 6,600hp (4,925kW) single-unit locomotive. This was done by permitting an increased rpm. The result was not only the most powerful but also the longest and the largest prime-mover locomotive unit in the world. Forty-seven were built between 1969 and 1971, completion of the first (appropriately No. 6900) being pushed ahead to be ready on centenary day. The locomotives had a full-width cab and incorporated all the recent improvements which GM had introduced in the standard range of diesel locomotives. These included the new Type 645 engine, of uniflow two-stroke design like its long-lived predecessor the Type 567. The same cylinder bore and stroke is common to a 1,750hp (750kW) switcher and the 6,600hp (4,925kW) "Centennial". The generator is basically a brushless alternator, but has built-in silicon diode rectifiers to produce direct current suitable for traction motors. Naturally, the control system includes dynamic braking and wheelslip correction features.

The complex electrical system common to all diesel-electric locomotives was improved in these machines by being concentrated

Above: *Union Pacific Class DD40AX "Centennial". Its genesis as two GP40 units is clear to see from the transverse passage between the two engines.*

in a series of modules which could be isolated, tested and easily replaced if found faulty. In this way, repairs, adjustments or an overhaul could be done under factory conditions. Afterwards this arrangement became standard throughout the whole range of GM locomotives, models with it

becoming known as "Dash-2", for example "SD40-2" for an "SD40" with modular electrics.

It could be said that this development proved to be self-destructive to the future of monster diesel-electrics, for a principal advantage of combining two "GP40s" on one chassis was the saving of a lot of electrical control gear. So making the electrics less trouble-some made inroads into this advantage, and as a result these dinosaurs are not being repeated, even for Union Pacific. Another factor was the building of the

"SD45-2" series with 20-cylinder engines rated at 3,600hp (2,685kW).

After these superb "Centennials", UP once again returned to buying diesel units off-the-shelf like virt-ually all US railroads and indeed the majority of railways the world over. When a train was called, required power would be calcul-ated on a horsepower per ton basis according to the severity of the route. The most conveniently available units to make up this total horse power would then be coupled up to form the motive

power; in these circumstances large special indivisible units are more of a hindrance than a help. Thus the "Big Boys" and the turbines have been superseded, and the "Centennials" submerged by more mundane motive power; even so, the pageant of freight movement up Sherman Hill and across the Divide is still one of the great railway sights of the world.

Below: *Just out of the works. A brand new No. 6900 poses for this Union Pacific Railroad Company photograph.*

Class 92 1-Co-Co-1
East Africa:
East African Railways (EAR), 1971

Type: Diesel-electric mixed-traffic locomotive.

Gauge: 3ft 3⅜in (1,000mm).

Propulsion: Alco Type 251F 12-cylinder four-stroke 2,550hp (1,902kW) Vee-type diesel engine and generator supplying direct current to six nose-suspended traction motors geared to the main axles.

Weight: 218,200lb (99t) adhesive, 251,255lb (114.5t) total.

Max. axleload: 36,370lb (16.5t).

Overall length: 59ft 1in (18,015mm).

Tractive effort: 77,000lb (342kN).

Max. speed: 45mph (72km/h).

Construction of the so-called Uganda Railway was the start of civilisation in what is now called Kenya. Little wood-burning steam engines reached the site of the city of Nairobi in 1895, so beginning the history of a line which for most of its existence has had to struggle to move ever-increasing traffic.

Oil-burning took over from wood in the 1930s, and traffic reached a point where articulated locomotives—the legendary Beyer Garratts—were needed. The efficiency with which traffic was worked by these monsters made what was then called East African Railways a very hard nut indeed for diesel traction to crack. Various

Above: *A train of empty oil tank wagons en route from Nairobi to Mombasa, hauled by Alco Class 92 diesel-electric.*

studies over the years indicated that there was no case for change, apart from "keeping up with the Joneses", but in the 1960s the administration began to order

medium-power units from English Electric of Britain.

By 1970 some progress in dieselisation had been made on peripheral routes, but the main trunk route which climbed steadily from sea level at Mombasa to 9,131ft (2,783m) at Timboroa, en route to Uganda, was still a Garratt stronghold. To find a means of working this traffic economically with diesel traction, EAR went shopping outside Britain, almost for the first time. The result was this Class "92" diesel of Alco design, supplied by the Montreal Locomotive Works. It offered 38 per cent more power than the most powerful diesels then in Kenya.

The Class "92s" were based on the standard Alco product adapted for metre-gauge. To reduce the axleload to a value acceptable on the main line west of Nairobi, not only was it necessary to use six-wheel bogies but an idle pony wheel had to be attached to each bogie also. The arrangement was offered by MLW specially for low axleloads as their

1967 Tube Stock Four-car set
Great Britain:
London Transport (LT), 1967

Type: Electric rapid transit trainset.

Gauge: 4ft 8½in (1,435mm).

Propulsion: Direct current at 600V supplied via third and fourth rails and an automatic control system to eight 140hp (105kW) nose-suspended traction motors.

Weight: 132,250lb (60t) adhesive, 206,075lb (93.5t) total.

Max. axleload: 16,530lb (7.5t).

Overall length: 214ft 5in (65,355mm).

Max. speed: 60mph (96km/h)*.

*Design speed of train. Maximum operational speed is 55mph (88km/h).

When asked the secret of their near perfect lawns, the authorities of King's College, Cambridge, have the maddening answer that there is no problem—just roll, cut and tend them for 400 years. In the same way, London Transport, when asked their recipe for success in introducing automatic operation of a rapid transit underground railway, might suggest having a century of general experience first. The Victoria line, which began its automatic operation in 1968 and was opened throughout from Brixton to Walthamstow in 1971, was the culmination of experience gained in normal operation of underground railways

since 1863, of electrification since 1890, and of automatic working since 1963. Public operation of automatic trains began in 1964 on the shuttle service between Woodford and Hainault in east London. Experience was satisfactory, and accordingly the design of new trains needed for the Victoria line project was put in hand.

The main innovation was that once the driver/guard (who was really a 'train-person', since he did not drive) pressed the 'start' button, the train would proceed to the next station without human intervention. Two separate electric pulse systems provide the necessary messages to the control

system. There is first a medium-frequency range of pulses which are passed along the running rails and are received continuously by the trains—420 pulses/min means 'go', 270 means 'go slowly', 180 means 'power off' and no signal means 'stop'. In addition there are 'command spots' at appropriate points at which speed-related frequencies in the audio range are picked up by the trains and responded to automatically by the control system within confines of the continuously-received signal.

The cost of installing automatic control was high but there are

"African series" and EAR themselves ordered an even lighter lower-power version (Class "88") for lines with a 12 ton axleload in Tanzania on the same chassis.

In 1976, EAR was divided up among the owning nations, Kenya, Uganda and Tanzania. The Class "92s" went to Kenya, retaining the same classification. Since then a Class "93" Co-Co design of similar power has been imported from General Electric. Advances in design have enabled axleload restrictions to be met without the extra two pairs of pony wheels.

Right: *Kenya Railways' Class 92 locomotive still in the livery and lettering of its former owners, East African Railways, more than a year after the administration was divided.*

Below: *Note how additional pony wheels have been added to the three-axle trucks of this otherwise standard Alco product, in order to spread the load and provide extra guidance and support.*

considerable savings even apart from halving the number of train staff. A 20 per cent increase in average speed means corresponding savings in the number of trains needed for a given frequency of service, whilst automatic operation is also designed to minimise consumption of current for a given average speed.

A few innovations had less-direct relevance to the automatic system, although powerful headlights are there to give the trainman reference points in the tunnels in the absence of signals. In addition, there were wrap-around windscreens, hydraulic handbrakes and rheostatic braking

down to 10mph (16km/h).

The trains were arranged in four-car units with two motor cars and two trailers in each. Automatic couplers of the 'Wedgelock' pattern, which also make electrical pneumatic connections at the outer ends, facilitate making up and splitting eight-car trains. City transport under London has come a long way since those tiny locomotive-hauled windowless trains of the City & South London Railway (qv) began operation nearly a century ago.

Right: *An automatically operated tube train enters London's Seven Sisters station.*

RTG Four-car trainset
France:
French National Railways (SNCF), 1972

Type: Five-car express passenger gas turbine set.
Gauge: 4ft 8½in (1,435mm).
Propulsion: One Société Française Turbomeca Turmo IIIF 1,150hp (858kW) gas turbine in each end vehicle driving the axles of the outer bogie through Voith hydraulic transmission.
Weight: 143,040lb (64.9t). adhesive, 570,836lb (259t) total.
Max. axleload: 35,760lb (16.2t).
Overall length: 339ft 6⁵/₁₆in (128,990mm).
Tractive effort: 26,980lb (120kN).
Max. speed: 112mph (180km/h).

In 1966 SNCF, with no diesel locomotives able to run at more than 87mph (140km/h), studied the problem of designing railcars for non-electrified lines which could equal the performance then being achieved by electric traction, that is, general running at 100mph (160km/h) with speeds of 124mph (200km/h) on suitable stretches. The non-electrified routes often had more speed restrictions than the more generously laid-out electric routes, and the performance contemplated would therefore require a much higher power-to-weight ratio than was being achieved in contemporary diesel railcars to give the required acceleration and speed on gradients.

The French aero-engine industry has scored notable successes with small gas turbines for helicopters, and SNCF saw these turbines as a means of providing the high power required without a significant increase in weight over a diesel railcar. The first experiment was started in 1966. A Turmo III F engine manufactured by Société Française Turbomeca was fitted to the trailer car of a standard two-car diesel set. The output shaft of this engine was connected through reduction gears to the axles of one bogie. The engine was rated at 1,500hp (1,120kW) for aircraft use, but was de-rated to 1,150hp (858kW) for railway use, and it operated on diesel fuel, both for economy in fuel costs and greater safety.

The first trial took place on April 25, 1967, and two months later a speed of 147mph (236km/h) was recorded. The train was driven by the diesel engine below a speed of 20mph (30km/h) with the gas turbine shut down. Fuel consumption was considered acceptable, bearing in mind that there was no other way of obtaining so high a power in so small a space. This set was later designated "TGS" (*Turbine à Gaz Spéciale*).

In 1968, the next step was the ordering of 10 four-car trains for the Paris-Caen-Cherbourg service. In these a 440hp (330kW) diesel engine was fitted in one end coach and a Turmo III F in the other end coach, as in the

Above: *View of a French National Railways' gas-turbine-powered high-speed five-car train-set for non-electrified lines.*

"TGS", but the coaches were appointed to main line standards with catering facilities and warm-air ventilation. The most important technical difference was that the turbine was connected to the axles through Voith hydraulic transmission, enabling the turbine to be used from rest. These sets

Below: *The power car of an SNCF RTG train. The powerful gas turbine is accommodated in the small windowless space between the two doors at the leading end.*

Class 132 Cₒ-Cₒ
German Democratic Republic:
German State Railway (DR), 1975

Type: Diesel-electric express passenger locomotive.
Gauge: 4ft 8½in (1,435mm).
Propulsion: Energomachexport 3,000hp (2,240kW) 16-cylinder Vee-type four-stroke diesel engine with gas-turbine supercharger and alternator feeding current to six nose-suspended traction motors.
Weight: 276,600lb (125.5t).
Max. axleload: 46,285lb (21t).
Overall length: 67ft 8in (20,620mm).
Tractive effort: 146,773lb (326kN).
Max. speed: 75mph (120km/h).

The art of building successful diesel locomotives can only be learnt the hard way—that is, by long, hard and bitter experience. Russian engineers have certainly served their time in this respect ever since, in the 1920s, the legendary Professor Lomosonroff began putting experimental diesel locomotives on the road. Consequently, by the mid-1960s, with thousands of home-built diesel locomotives in service on home rails, the Russian product was good enough to sell abroad. Admittedly there have not yet been sales to administrations which have access to General Motors'

products, but it is early days yet. The Russians' adherence to the most successful principle of locomotive building—rugged simplicity—bodes very well for their future prospects.

The first export model was a 2,000hp (1,490kW) double-ended carbody unit. Sales were made to Hungary (Class "M-62"), as classes "T-679.1" and "T679.5" in Czechoslovakia, and "CT-44" in Poland. North Korea also had some and others went to the German State Railway (DR) in the German Democratic Republic, where they became Class "120". All these locomotives were built at the Voroshilovgrad

Diesel Locomotive Works and were exported via the Soviet agency Energomachexport. Experience with these modestly-powered machines led to the production of a higher-powered version with dynamic braking known as the "TE-109".

The "TE-109" prototypes were available with two gear ratios for passenger and freight traffic respectively. They used ac-dc transmission with this passenger version as well as convertor equipment to provide a 600kW output of alternating current at 16²/₃Hz for train heating. The principal customer was the German Democratic Re-

are designated "ETG" (*Élément à Turbine à Gaz*).

In 1970 the Paris-Caen and Paris-Cherbourg services were taken over by "ETGs", being the first full inter-city service in the world to be operated by gas turbine traction. Caen was reached in 109 minutes at 81.5mph (131km/h). Although the sets were designed for 112mph (180km/h), they have always been limited to 100mph (160km/h) in service.

Success of the "ETGs" created a demand for trains with still more and better accommodation. This was met by building units with longer coaches which could be run in four-coach or five-coach sets, with air-conditioning and other appointments as in the latest locomotive-hauled coaches. The diesel engine was omitted, and there was a Turmo III power unit in each end coach. An additional small Astazou turbine was installed in each power car to provide electric power at all times, the main turbines being run only when required for traction. These trains are the "RTGs" (*Rame à Turbine à Gaz*).

RTGs took over the Cherbourg services in 1972 and were later introduced on cross-country services based on Lyons. A total of 41 sets were built, of which two were later sold to Amtrak in the United States.

Gas turbine trains were a notable success for French engineers,

Above: *French RTG turbo-train at speed between Tours and Vierzon with a Nantes to Lyons cross-country express.*

Right: *Amtrak turbo-train approaching Chicago. Two sets were supplied from France and several more were built under licence in the USA by Rohr Inc.*

for not only do they perform reliably and at an acceptable cost, but they are environmentally acceptable both to the passengers and to those outside the train. Although no further extensions have been made to these services, they rank as the most successful application of gas turbines to railway passenger services.

public, which placed an order for 279 at the Leipzig Trade Fair in 1973. There are divided between the passenger Class "132", particulars given above, and Class "131" for freight traffic, the latter having a lower maximum speed of 63mph (100km/h) and a correspondingly higher tractive effort of 77,160lb (34.3kN), but is otherwise identical. Other "TE-109s" have gone to Bulgaria and Czechoslovakia where they are class "07" and "T-679.2" respectively.

Right: *Class 132 Russian-built diesel locomotive, near Halberstadt, East Germany, in 1978.*

Class 15000 B-B

France: French National Railways (SNCF), 1971

Type: Express passenger electric locomotive.
Gauge: 4ft 8½in (1,435mm).
Propulsion: Alternating current at 25,000V 50Hz from overhead wires, rectified in diodes and thyristors, supplying two 2,960hp (2,210kW) traction motors, one mounted on each bogie and connected to the axles through gearing and spring drives.
Weight: 198,360lb (90t).
Max. axleload: 49,590lb (22.5t).
Overall length: 57ft 4⅛in (17,480mm).
Tractive effort: 64,800lb (288kN).
Max. speed: 112mph (180km/h).

Early in its experiments with 25,000V 50Hz ac traction, SNCF recognised that the combination of lines electrified on the new system with its existing network of 1,500V dc lines would make essential the use of dual-voltage locomotives capable of working on both systems. Otherwise the time consumed in changing locomotives, together with the poor utilisation of locomotives which would result from this changing, would nullify much of the economy of the high-voltage system. Dual-voltage machines were therefore included in the experimental ac locomotives, and this was followed by the development of "families" of locomotives, comprising ac, dc and dual-voltage machines incorporating as many common parts as possible. The numbering of these classes was a notable manifestation of Gallic logic, for it was based on the mathematical relationship: (ac + dc) = (dual voltage). Thus the

"17000" ac class and the "8500" dc class combined to produce the "25500" dual-voltage class.

Successive phases in the post-war development of the French electric locomotive produced successive families. Thus one group comprised the first all-adhesion four-axle locomotive with individual-axle drive. The next group, one mentioned above, incorporated monomotor bogies with two gear ratios, and silicon rectifiers. The third group, "15000" + "7200" = "22200", moved into the thyristor era, and at a nominal 5,920hp (4,420kW) they are the most powerful French B-B machines. This group is also notable in reverting to a single gear ratio. Class "15000" was intended primarily for express passenger work, and a low-speed gear was unnecessary, but it was hoped that improvements in various aspects of design since the introduction of the two-speed locomotives would enable the thyristor

machines to handle freight traffic without provision of a special gear ratio.

It is SNCF's practice to apply new technology experimentally to an existing locomotive or train, retaining as much as possible of the well-proven equipment, so as to concentrate attention on the special equipment under test. Some of the first experiments with thyristors were made with one of the pioneer dual-voltage locomotives, No. 20002, which retained conventional resistance control for dc operation, and silicon diodes for ac traction, but had thyristors for ac regenerative braking. The first application of thyristors to control power circuits was on a multiple-unit train, and in 1971 there appeared the first production units equipped throughout with thyristors, a series of multiple-units, and the Class "15000" B-B locomotives.

Up to this time the standard method of controlling power on

Above: *The dc version of the Class 15000, the Class 7200, is seen at the Gare de Lyon in Paris during 1978.*

French ac locomotives had been by tap-changer on the high-tension side of the transformer. The thyristor offered an elegant alternative to the tap-changer, with the possibility of infinitely-variable control of the voltage applied to the traction motors.

Class "15000" was built to take over principal services on the former Est Railway main line from Paris to Strasbourg, now in the Eastern Region of SNCF. Their introduction followed construction of the "6500" class C-C dc locomotives and the "72000" class C-C diesel-electric locomotives; many parts were common to all three classes, including the main body structure. There is a single traction motor for each bogie, mounted rigidly on top of the bogie frame and connected to the

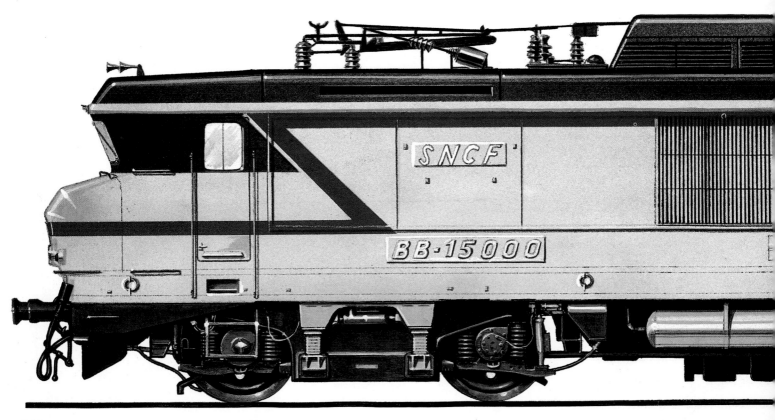

axles through gearing and Alsthom flexible drives. The body rests on four rubber springs, two at each side of the body and close together. The springs are sandwiches of steel and rubber bonded together. They resist the vertical load by compression, whilst lateral oscillations and rotation of the bogie are resisted by shearing action. This is a remarkably simple and effective suspension.

An important innovation in the "15000s" was the control system, made possible by the comparative simplicity of thyristor circuitry. The driver has two normal methods of controlling speed, constant speed or constant current. With the former the driver sets his controller to the speed required, and he also sets up the value of the current which is not to be exceeded. The control circuits accelerate the locomotive to the speed required, and then vary the current to hold it at that speed, provided that the stipulated maximum current is not exceeded. If, due to a change in gradient, the locomotive attempts to accelerate, current is reduced, and finally, if necessary, regenerative braking is set up. Alternatively the driver can isolate the speed control, and the system holds the current to the pre-selected value, observance of speed being the driver's responsibility.

The "15000s" are designed for 112½mph (180km/h), which is somewhat surprising as 124mph (200km/h) had already been permitted on some parts of SNCF when they were built, but so far on the Eastern Region the limit is 100mph (160km/h). Every effort was made to simplify the design to reduce maintenance costs, and with this in mind the traction

motor was modified to make it self-ventilating and so eliminate the need for a forced-ventilation system.

They soon established an excellent reputation, and with 74 in service they dominate the Eastern Region passenger services. Work continued on chopper control for dc locomotives, and for a time C-C locomotive No. 20002, with chopper equipment, ran coupled to standard B-B No. 9252, No. 20002 serving as a current supply to the motors of No. 9252. Next No. 15007 was converted to a dc machine, numbered 7003 to test the equipment for the "7200" class.

In 1976, delivery of the "7200" class began, followed later in the

Above: *French National Railways' Class 15000 Bo-Bo No. 15059 is seen near Pringy on the Paris-Strasbourg line with a train of "Corail" carriages.*

year by the dual-voltage "22200" locomotives. These classes differ only in that the "22200" has an additional pantograph for ac operation, and a transformer and silicon rectifier for converting the ac supply to 1,500V dc. The current is then fed into the same circuits as the dc supply, so that there is only one control system. Both classes closely resemble the "15000s", but are slightly longer in the body, and they have rheostatic braking instead of regenerative.

The "7200" and "22200" classes are allocated to the South-Eastern Region, and have displaced earlier locomotives from the principal services, apart from those worked by TGVs. Their workings include

Below: *This French locomotive design is produced as depicted for 25,000V ac (Class 15000), for 1,500V dc as Class 7200, and for both as Class 22200.*

the ac section from Marseilles to Ventimille, on which "22200s" work through from Paris to Ventimille, 695 miles (1,118km). They also work fast freight trains into northern France, a new departure in inter-regional working, which includes running 696 miles (1,120km) from Marseilles to Lille. These are the longest locomotive workings in France, and the high mileage which the locomotives can thereby build up is held to justify the small extra cost of a "22200" compared with a "7200" or "15000."

Although it had been hoped that Class "7200" would be suitable for heavy low-speed freight work, trouble was encountered with overheating of the motors, and the first 35 locomotives were temporarily fitted with bogies geared for 62mph (100km/h). All later locomotives have force-ventilated motors.

For nine months before its gear ratio was changed, No. 7233 was transferred to the South-Western Region, and worked "L' Etendard" between Paris and Bordeaux with considerable running at 125mph (200km/h). Later No. 22278 was tested similarly, thus proving that the classes were suitable for this speed, although designed for 180km/h.

By 1982, orders had been placed for 210 Class "7200" locomotives and 150 of Class "22200." All these locomotives were built by Alsthom, and in due course the firm received an order for 48 similar locomotives for Netherlands Railways. In 1982 also No. 15055 was fitted with synchronous three-phase motors, and No. 15056 was selected for another series of tests with asynchronous motors.

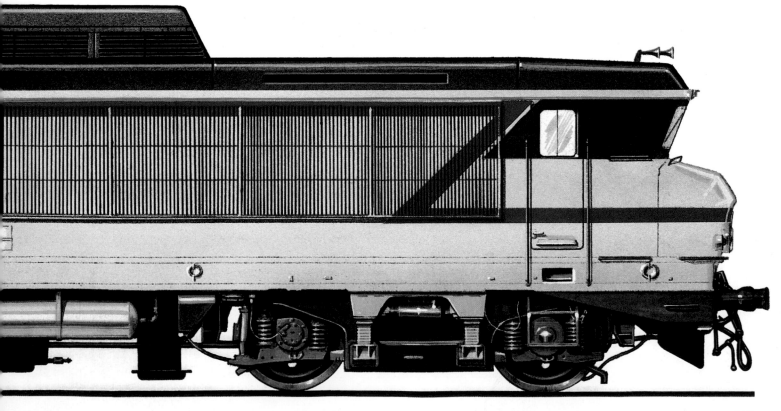

Class Re 6/6 B₀-B₀-B₀

Switzerland:
Swiss Federal Railways (SBB), 1972

Type: Heavy-duty mixed-traffic mountain locomotive.
Gauge: 4ft 8½in (1,435mm).
Propulsion: Low-frequency alternating current at 15,000V 16⅔Hz fed via overhead catenary and step-down transformer to six frame-mounted 1,740hp (1,300kW) motors each driving one axle through a flexible drive system.
Weight: 264,480lb (120t).
Max. axleload: 44,080lb (20t).
Overall length: 63ft 4½in (19,310mm).
Tractive effort: 88,700lb (395kN).
Max. speed: 87mph (140km/h).

Ten-thousand horsepower plus in a single locomotive! And no cheating either—all is contained in a single indivisible unit. The story of this Everest amongst locomotives began with the ever increasing demands of traffic on the St Gotthard main line across the Alps.

The original heavy artillery of the Gotthard line was a famous series of rod-drive 1-C-C-1 articulated 'Crocodile' locomotives, of only one-quarter the power of the "Re 6/6" engines. In all 52 were built and a few still survive. In 1931 two rather amazing experimental "Ae 8/14" 1-Bo-1-Bo-1 + 1-Bo-1-Bo-1 twin units appeared, one of which built by Oerlikon brought the power available to 8,800hp (6,560kW), combined with a drawgear-breaking maximum tractive effort of 132,240lb (588kN). The other, by Brown Boveri, was slightly less powerful. These were followed in 1939 by yet another twin locomotive of the

same unique wheel arrangement which did offer more than 10,000hp—11,400hp (8,500kW) in fact—as well as 110,200lb (490kN) of tractive effort. However, it was at the cost of a total weight twice that of the "Re 6/6". Experience with these immense machines was such that they were not repeated.

The "Re 4/4" double-bogie locomotives for express passenger work came to SBB in 1946, following the example of the Bern-Lötschberg-Simplon Railway Class "Ae 4/4" (qv) of two years earlier. With hindsight it seems extraordinary that the Swiss did not simply build a lower-geared version of the "Re 4/4" and use it in multiple on the Gotthard. The fact remains, though, that they did not and instead went on seeking a single locomotive unit that would do the job. Hence in 1952 the usual firms—this time in consort —that is Brown Boveri, Oerlikon and the Swiss Locomotive Works,

produced a locomotive with six driven axles and all but 1,000hp per axle, classified "Ae 6/6". They used all the know-how gained on the "Ae 4/4" and "Re 4/4" units, but adapting the design for six-wheel instead of four-wheel bogies.

The "Ae 6/6s" were rated at 5,750hp (4,290kW) and 120 were built between 1952 and 1966. Regenerative braking was installed and the maximum speed was 88mph (125km/h). The class ushered in the hitherto almost unheard of practice (for SBB) of naming. Naturally they began with the Swiss Cantons, but soon these ran out and it had to be important towns instead; finally, some of the much mightier successors of the "Ae 6/6s" had to make do with the names of some very small places indeed! The extra power of the "Ae 6/6s" came at the right moment, for an explosion of traffic over the line was about to occur. By the late 1960s, three times the

Above: *Swiss Federal Railways Class Re 6/6 Co-Co No. 11632 with heavy oil-tanker train on Zürich to Basle line near Effingen, May 1982.*

tonnage and over twice the number of trains were passing compared with 1950.

Amongst many measures proposed to cope with the situation was provision of still more powerful locomotives. Something was done quickly by converting existing locomotives to work in multiple —a measure that the Swiss were normally reluctant to take. But in 1972, two single-unit super-power prototypes were delivered by the same consortium. There was no point in providing for haulage of trains above 850t (935 US tons) by a single unit because European wagon couplings were not strong enough to pull heavier loads than this up the Gotthard grades. Larger trains can be hauled but a second locomotive has then to be

cut into the centre of the load.

The first two "Re 6/6s" were articulated, but later examples and the production version had the single carbody as described. The haulage capacity was nicely balanced, for an 800t (880 US tons) train could be taken up the 1-in-37 (2.7 per cent) at the line limit of 50mph (80km/h). One of the reasons for adopting the Bo-Bo-Bo wheel arrangement in place of Co-Co was that the length of rigid wheelbase is reduced. This is important on a line like the Gotthard, with almost continuous curvature as sharp as 15 chains (300m) radius. On the other hand, having a rigid body to the loco-motive greatly simplified and re-duced the cost of the centre bogie, which could align itself with the curves by being allowed sideplay. All three bogies were pivotless and each one was made to run more easily over small irregularities in track alignment by giving its axles lateral movement centralised with springs.

Now in general use on less taxing parts of the Swiss rail system, the "Ae 6/6s" are still a remarkable design, but the "Re 6/6s" are over 80 per cent more powerful within the same weight limitation. In addition to being an excellent freight-hauler for moun-tain grades, these versatile machines are also suitable for trains running at the highest speeds permitted in Switzerland.

Right: *Swiss Federal Railways Class Re 6/6 Co-Co No. 11630 below Wassen on the Gotthard line with the northbound* Barbarossa *international express on May 24, 1981.*

Below: *Swiss Federal Railways Class Re 6/6 Co-Co. A massive 10,000hp in a single unit!*

167

EMD SD40-2 C₀-C₀

United States:
Electro-Motive Division, General Motors Corporation (EMD), 1972

Type: Road switcher diesel-electric locomotive.
Gauge: 4ft 8½in (1,435mm).
Propulsion: One EMD 645E3 3,000hp (2,240kW) 16-cylinder turbocharged two-stroke Vee engine and alternator supplying current through silicon rectifiers to six nose-suspended traction motors.
Weight: 368,000lb (167.0t).
Max. axleload: 61,330lb (27.8t).
Overall length: 68ft 10in (20,980mm).
Tractive effort: 83,100lb (370kN).
Max. speed: 65mph (105km/h).

For 50 years the Electro-Motive Division of General Motors has dominated the US diesel market, taking 70 to 75 per cent of total orders. The remainder of the market has been shared between the former steam locomotive builders Alco and Baldwin/Lima, a few smaller firms, and latterly GE, but since 1969 only GE has survived. However, the effect has been that EMD has never had a monopoly, and although the company's success has been due very much to its policy of offering a limited number of off-the-shelf models, it cannot ignore specialist needs of its customers. There has thus been steady development and improvement of the EMD models over the years, directed mainly at increasing power, reducing fuel consumption and maintenance costs, and improving adhesion.

Introduction of the "hood" design "GP7" model in 1949 marked the beginning of the end for the "carbody" unit on which EMD had made its reputation. From then onwards nearly all EMD's road locomotives would be general-purpose machines. There was, however, a variant;

Right: *An Electromotive SD40-2 road-switcher diesel-electric locomotive, lettered for the Conrail system, a government-financed grouping of bankrupt railroads in eastern USA.*

the four-axle machines inevitably had a heavy axleload, and EMD therefore offered a six-axle version designated "SD", for "Special Duty". Although the axleload was reduced, the total weight of the locomotive was greater than that of a four-axle machine, and it thus appealed also to roads which had a need for maximum adhesion due to climatic conditions. The pattern thus became established of offering four-axle and six-axle variants of each model.

Elsewhere in this book the "GP" series up to "GP35" is discussed. These are the models with the original 567 engine, and corresponding six-axle "SD" models were also built. By the time this engine was pressed to 2,500hp (1,865kW) for traction, it was reaching its limit, and a new engine was produced with the same piston stroke of 10in (245mm), but with the diameter increased from 8.5in (216mm) to 9¹⁄₁₆in (230mm). The cylinder volume became 645cu in, thus giving the engine its designation "645". Like the 567 it is a two-stroke engine, and is available with or without turbocharger. A two-

Above: *Burlington Northern Railroad class SD40-2 road-switcher unit No. 7044, one of nearly 900 supplied to this line.*

stroke engine requires some degree of pressure-charging to give effective scavenging, and if there is no turbocharger, there is a Roots-type blower driven directly from the engine. There have thus been two lines of development, the turbocharged engine pressed to give successive increases in power, and the engines without turbochargers remaining at 2,000hp (1,490kW), but benefit from mechanical improvements directed at reducing fuel consumption and maintenance costs.

One of the attractions of the diesels which first replaced steam on freight work was that a number of modest-sized units working in multiple under the control of one crew could replace the largest steam engine. These diesels were little bigger than some of the diesel switchers which the roads already operated, and their maintenance was easier than that of overworked steam locomotives

which were very demanding of attention and needed good quality fuel to give of their best. The diesels could show a reduction in operating costs, even when their higher capital cost was taken into account.

However, when the possible economies from total dieselisation had been achieved, motive power officers looked for other means of effecting economies. With the problems of diesel maintenance now better understood, an attractive idea was to use a smaller number of larger units to achieve the same total power. This was found to save money both in purchase price and in operating costs. EMD's competitors were first in the field with higher horsepower as a selling point, and it was not until 1958 that EMD marketed a 2,400hp (1,790kW) engine in the "SD24" series with which to match the Fairbanks-Morse Trainmaster of 1953. In 1959 EMD produced its 2,000hp (1,490kW) four-axle model, and from then the horsepower race was on.

The 645 engine was launched in 1965 in two versions, the pressure-charged 645E and the turbocharged 645E3. The 645E was made in 8, 12 and 16 cylinder versions, and the 645E3 with 12, 16 and 20 cylinders. These engines were incorporated in a new range of nine locomotives, which included the "GP40" and "SD40" with the 16-cylinder version of the turbocharged engine, giving 3,000hp (2,240kW), and the "SD45" with the 20-cylinder engine giving 3,600hp (2,690kW). This was the first US engine with 20 cylinders, and it brought EMD firmly into the high horsepower stable, some time after Alco and GE had reached 3,000hp. All these new models incorporated a new design of traction motor,

with improved insulation, and therefore better performance at high power. The six-axle types had a new Flexicoil bogie to give improved riding, and the 3,000hp and 3,600hp engines introduced alternators, instead of generators, to the EMD range. The alternators were more compact than generators, and this assisted the designers in finding space for the larger engines.

With the railroads enthusiastic about high-powered locomotives, the "SD45" was the most popular model in the range, achieving a total of 1,260 sales in six years. The highest-powered four-axle unit in the range, the 3,000hp GP40, achieved sales of 1,201, and for roads which required a six-axle layout, 883 of the "SD40" were supplied.

These models remained standard until the beginning of 1972 when, with competition from GE still keen, a revision was made of the whole range, known as "Dash 2", from the addition which was made to the class designation, for example, "SD40-2". At this stage no further increase in power was offered, and the alterations were directed at improving fuel consumption and simplifying maintenance by eliminating some of the difficulties encountered with existing locomotives. The most important changes were in the electrical control system, which comprises largely plug-in modules of printed circuits which can be changed quickly from stock. Owners of earlier models had encountered difficult in locating electrical faults, and an annunciator was therefore developed which records and stores information about malfunctions in the system.

New high-adhesion trucks were offered in the six-axle models,

Below: *A three-unit SD40-2 combination belonging to Canadian National Railways. Note the modified "safety" cab on the second unit.*

known as "HT-C" (High Traction, three axle). Adhesion was still a major concern to the railroads, and as orders came in for the "Dash-2" range, two trends became apparent: first, that the extra maintenance costs of the 20-cylinder engine and its large turbocharger and radiators were not justified for 600hp more than the 16-cylinder engine could give, and secondly, that the 3,000hp four-axle locomotive, the "GP40", had given trouble with wheelslip and excessive maintenance of its highly-rated traction motors. The high-power model to emerge as the most popular in the range was therefore the "SD40-2", with 3,000hp transmitted through six axles. By the late-1970s this was established as virtually the standard high-power diesel in the US, with sales approaching 4,000 by the end of the decade. The railroad with the largest number was Burlington Northern with about 900, a quarter of its total locomotive stock.

Concurrently the high cost of maintaining a turbocharger compared with a Roots blower had encouraged railroads to purchase large numbers of "GP38-2" units of 2,000hp for duties for which a 3,000hp locomotive was not required, and sales of this model passed 2,000 by 1980.

EMD now tackled the problem of improving adhesion in four-axle locomotives by a wheelslip detector employing Doppler radar, which is sufficiently sensitive to allow an axle to work safely at the limit of adhesion. Engine development made it possible to offer a 3,500hp (2,610kW) 16-cylinder engine, and in 1980 the company launched the "GP50" with the 3,500hp engine on four axles, so that railroads once again had the choice of a high-power locomotive without the expense of six axles.

Class Dx C₀-C₀

New Zealand:
New Zealand Railways (NZR), 1972

Type: Diesel-electric locomotive for mixed traffic.
Gauge: 3ft 6in (1,067mm).
Propulsion: General Electric (USA) 2,750hp (2,050kW) Type 7FDL-12 twelve-cylinder diesel engine and alternator supplying current via solid-state rectifiers to six nose-suspended traction motors.
Weight: 214,890lb (97.5t).
Max. axleload: 35,925lb (16.3t).
Overall length: 55ft 6in (16,916mm).
Tractive effort: 54,225lb (241kN).
Max. speed: 65mph (103km/h).

New Zealand may be a country with a small population as well as a small-gauge railway system, but its railwaymen have always believed in big powerful locomotives. For example, the legendary New Zealand-built "K" class 4-8-4s were as powerful as anything that ran in the mother country, in spite

of an axleload limit only 71 per cent of that in Britain. Similarly, these big "Dx" diesel-electrics have a power output comparable with Britain's standard Class "47s", again within the limits of axleload in proportion as before.

Class "Dx" was the culmination of a dieselisation programme which began in the 1950s—as regards main-line traction units of, say, 750hp plus—with the 40 Class "Dg" A1A-A1A units of 1955. What was called "Commonwealth Preference" in import duties gave British manufacturers a substantial advantage in those days, and the order went to English Electric. The class was lightweight, able to

Left: *New Zealand Railways' Class Dx Co-Co diesel-electric locomotive crosses a trestle viaduct typical of the system, hauling a long freight train.*

Below: *Class Dx Co-Co diesel electric locomotive as supplied by the General Electric (USA) Co.*

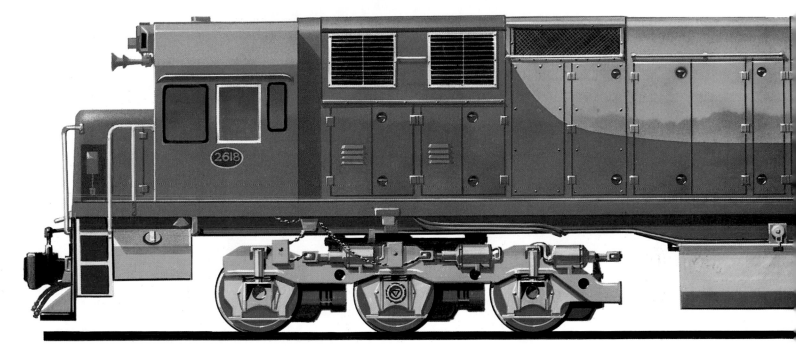

ET 403 Four-car train

West Germany:
German Federal Railway (DB), 1973

Type: High-speed four-car electric railcar set.
Gauge: 4ft 8½in (1,435mm).
Propulsion: Alternating current at 15,000V 16⅔Hz fed through transformer and thyristors to bogie-mounted traction motors driving each axle of each car, giving a total of 5,150hp. (3,840kW).
Weight: 519,480lb (235.7t).
Max. axleload: 32,400lb (14.7t).
Overall length: 358ft 4in (109,220mm).
Max. speed: 125mph (200km/h).

Following the success of the high-speed international TEE services, the German Federal Railway introduced even faster internal services under the initials "IC" for "Inter-

City". These services provided first-class accommodation only in short trains hauled by "103" class electric locomotives. However, use of multiple-unit trains on TEE services had impressed DB engineers with the advantages of this type of train, with all axles powered, both in the greater weight available for adhesion and in the lower forces imposed on the track for a given total power compared with an electric locomotive. In 1973, therefore, three high-speed emu sets were built, with a maximum speed of 125mph (200km/h). Each set normally comprises four coaches, with all axles powered. There are three types of vehicle, of which one variety has a streamlined end with a driver's cab and carries a pantograph. The others are intermediate cars, one of which

has catering facilities. From the distinctive shape of the streamlined ends, the sets earned the nickname "Donald Ducks".

The electrical equipment includes many fittings which had already been proved in the "ET420" class suburban stock. Each coach carries a transformer, a rectifier for converting the ac supply to dc, and thyristor chopper equipment both for controlling the voltage to the motors and for regenerative braking. Each coach is thus a self-contained motor coach, except that the electrical supply comes from the vehicle with the pantograph.

Main technical innovation was in the bogies, which incorporate air suspension. By variations of air pressure in the suspension bags, the body can be tilted up to

4° to improve passenger comfort on curves. The bogies have disc and magnetic track brakes. Each axle has an automatic slip-prevention device, and automatic surveillance of axlebox temperature. It was intended that the bogies should run for 600,000km without heavy maintenance, other than correction of tyre profiles.

Post-war DB coaches had been notable for a progressively lighter body weight; the "ET403" units took this reduction a stage further, large extruded aluminium profiles being used for the first time in high-speed stock. The result is an axleloading of 15t, which is much kinder to the track than the 19.5t of the Class "103" locomotives.

The sets were first introduced into regular service in May 1974 on one of the longest internal

run over the light rails of the South Island system, where there was an axleload of only 11t (12 US tons).

Between 1955 and 1967, General Motors came in in a very big way with the 74-strong 1,428hp (1,065kW) Class "Da" as the mainstay of the North Island main lines. There were also the 16 lighter GM "Db" class locomotives for North Island branch lines. In 1968 and 1969 the Japanese firm Mitsubishi delivered 60 Class "Dj" Bo-Bo-Bos for the South Island; this class offered 1,045hp (780kW) for an axleload of 10.9t (12 US tons). As a result of these deliveries the last regular steam-hauled train ran in 1972.

It then became apparent that more powerful locomotives could be used to advantage, and the result was this "Dx" class. Very surprisingly NZR went to a fourth source for these magnificent machines. General Electric of USA —not to be confused with GEC Traction of Britain or its subsidiary

Above: *The "Silver Star" express on the North Island Trunk hauled by a Class Dx.*

General Electric (Australia)—supplied 47 of these units during 1972-75. They are used on crack trains on the North Island trunk line between Wellington and Auckland, both passenger and freight.

The design is based on General Electric's standard "U26C" export model.

GEC did not capture the market, though, because subsequent deliveries were from General Motors with both A1A-A1A and Co-Co versions of a similar locomotive (classes "Dc" and "Df" of 67 and 30 units respectively). This in

spite of a debate then in full cry concerning the need for railways at all in a country with such modest transport requirements. In the end the verdict was favourable to railways but not to diesels —instead New Zealand Railways is going ahead with a major programme of electrification which will use indigenous forms of energy.

services in West Germany, from Munich to Bremen, 485 miles (781km) with six intermediate stops. These services were well patronised, and on Mondays and Fridays a fifth car was added to each set. They continued until 1979.

By 1979 the definitive pattern of DB's IC services had emerged. After several years in which the service was offered to first-class passengers only, DB had decided that a full-scale network of high-speed services could only be viable if second-class passengers were also carried. Furthermore, after experience with both emu and locomotive operation of these services, DB decided that the greater flexibility of locomotive haulage was preferable.

The "ET403" sets thus became

spare, and did not find a definite use until 1982, when the state airline, Lufthansa, sponsored a rail service to connect Düsseldorf with Frankfurt airport, with intermediate stops at Cologne and Bonn, providing a more direct city-to-airport service to connect with important flights from Frankfurt than existing airport-to-airport flights.

Originally the livery was silver grey with a brown band at window level, lined out in orange. For their new duties, they were repainted in a livery of yellow below the windows and white from the windows upwards.

Right: *German Federal Railways high-speed ET 403 train set with body-tilting capability, used now to connect the Ruhr area with Frankfurt Airport.*

Class 87 B₀-B₀

Great Britain:
British Railways (BR), 1973

Type: Mixed-traffic electric locomotive.

Gauge: 4ft 8½in (1,435mm).

Propulsion: Alternating current at 25,000V 50Hz fed via overhead catenary, step-down transformer and solid-state rectifiers to four 1,250hp (932kW) fully spring-borne traction motors, driving the axles by gearing and ASEA hollow-axle flexible drives.

Weight: 182,930lb (83t).

Max. axleload: 45,735lb (20.75t).

Overall length: 58ft 6in (17,830mm).

Tractive effort: 58,000lb (258kN).

Max. speed: 100mph (160km/h).

Although both began almost from scratch after World War II, there could be no greater contrast than between British Rail's ac electric locomotive development story and that of their diesels. Diesel developments followed each other with the consistency of successive pictures in a kaleidoscope, while ac electric locomotives moved through seven related classes all with the same appearance, maximum speed and wheel arrangement.

The first five classes were offerings on the part of five manufacturers to meet a specification for a 100mph (160km/h) locomotive capable of operation on 25,000V or 6,250V 50Hz electrification systems as shown in the table.

All had frame-mounted traction motors with flexible drive. Classes "81" to "84" originally had mercury-arc rectifiers, while Class "85" was fitted with solid-state rectifiers from the start and also had rheostatic braking. In the event, the need for 6,250V operation never arose, although provision was made for it. No steam heating boilers were provided, as electrically-heated sets were provided for all the regular trains on the electrified lines. Separate steam-heating vans were provided for occasions when stock not fitted with electric heaters was hauled by electric locomotives in the winter.

When the complete electric

Original class	Later class	Original quantity	Built by	Electrical equipment by	Present quantity
AL1	81	25	Birmingham Carriage & Wagon	AEI	22
AL2	82	10	Beyer-Peacock	Metropolitan-Vickers	0
AL3	83	15	English Electric		0
AL4	84	10	North British	General Electric	0
AL5	85	40	BR Doncaster	AEI	40

Above: *A Class 87 Bo-Bo electric locomotive at speed with an express train on the West Coast main line.*

Below: *British Railways' latest Class 87 Bo-Bo electric locomotive supplied in 1973-74 for the extension of electric working from north of Crewe to Glasgow.*

87 022

service from London to Birmingham, Manchester and Liverpool was introduced, a further 100 locomotives were supplied. These were Class "AL6", later Class "86", which had solid-state silicon rectifiers, rheostatic braking as the prime braking system and —one major simplification— nose-suspended traction motors geared direct to the axles. Not surprisingly, this simple answer was too hard on the permanent way for such dense high-speed traffic and the class is now divided up as follows:

Class "86.0" in original condition, but with multiple-unit capability added and an 80mph (130km/h) speed limit imposed. Used only for freight traffic. Total 20 locomotives.

Class "86.1", new bogies with ASEA hollow axle flexible drive. Prototypes for Class "87". Total 3 locomotives.

Classes "86.2" and "86.3" modified to permit 100mph (160 km/h) running to continue. Fitted with resilient rail wheels and (86.2 only) modified bogie springing. Total 58 of Class "86.2" and 19 of Class "86.3".

The 36 locomotives of Class "87" were supplied for the extension of electric working from Crewe to Glasgow. They were built at BR's Crewe Works with electrical equipment by GEC Traction, into which AEI, English Electric, Metropolitan Vickers and British Thompson-Houston had by now been amalgamated. Power rating had been increased 56 per cent over that of Class "81" for a 4 per cent increase of weight. The ASEA hollow-axle flexible drive, tried out on Class "86.1" was used, and multiple-

unit capability was provided. At long last it had not been thought necessary to provide an exhauster for working vacuum-braked trains. All the class carry names, mostly of distinguished people living or dead, and this pleasant practice has now spilled over on to examples of Class "86".

The latest improvement is application of thyristor control, fitted to a Class "87" locomotive redesignated Class "87.1". No. 87101 carries the honoured name of *Stephenson* and no doubt, when the present pause in British electric locomotive development is over, more will be heard of this significant step forward in traction technology.

As regards performance and reliability, it perhaps says enough that this can be entirely taken for granted with these locomotives. Ample power can be drawn from the contact wire for maintaining the maximum permitted speed with the usual loads, while the same locomotives are also suitable for heavier and slower freight trains.

Below: *British Railways' Class 87 Bo-Bo electric locomotive No. 87002, specially prepared and cleaned according to tradition, heading the Royal Train at Norton Bridge between Stafford and Crewe in June 1980.*

Class 381 Nine-car train

Japan:
Japanese National Railways (JNR), 1973

Type: Electric express passenger multiple-unit trainset with tilting mechanism.
Gauge: 3ft 6in (1,067mm).
Propulsion: Direct current at 1,500V or alternating current at 25,000V, 50 or 60Hz, fed from overhead catenary to six motor cars, each with four 160hp (100kW) traction motors geared to the axles.
Weight: 515,760lb (234t) adhesive, 753,802lb (342t) total.
Max. axleload: 21,490lb (9.75t).
Overall length: 628ft 11in (191,700mm).
Max. speed: 75mph (120km/h).

The concept of a tilting train arises from the fact that suitably designed trains can safely run round curves at much higher speeds than are normally comfortable for the passengers. This takes into account the superelevation (otherwise known as "cant" or "banking" applied to the track. The idea was born that a calculated amount of tilt could be added to the cant by servo-mechanisms on the train, and in this way trains could be run much faster, safely and comfortably, without the expensive need to build a new railway. The proposition is so attractive that many railway administrations have acquired experimental tilting trains or coaches but so far only one, Japanese National Railways, has any running in significant numbers.

The Japanese tilting trains (Class 381) are not for high-speed operation, intended to run, say, at 90mph (144km/h) where normal trains run at 75mph (120km/h), but instead to hold 60mph (96km/h) where a normal train would be limited to 50mph (80km/h). The tilt is limited to 5°, compared with the 9° of Britain's APT project, and it is applied when the cars' sensors feel a

Above: *A Japanese National Railways Class 381 electric train with tilting capability on a Hanwa line express, 1978.*

Right: *The tilting abilities of the Class 381 multiple-unit electric trains are used to advantage on mountain lines.*

Class 581 Twelve-car train

Japan:
Japanese National Railways (JNR), 1968

Type: Electric express sleeping-car train.
Gauge: 3ft 6in (1,067mm).
Propulsion: Alternating current at 25,000V 50Hz or 60Hz, or direct current at 3,000V fed via overhead catenary and conversion and control equipment in two power cars to 24 160hp (100kW) traction motors geared to the bogie axles of six of the intermediate sleeping cars in the train.
Weight: 638,720lb (290t) adhesive, 1,218,812lb (553t) total.
Max. axleload: 26,450lb (12t).
Overall length: 816ft 11in (249,000mm).
Max. speed: 100mph (160km/h)*.

*Design speed of train. The maximum permitted speed of the railway is at present 120km/h (75mph)

Above: *Sleeping car express electric multiple-unit train of Japanese National Railways.*

certain transverse acceleration. Being intended for lines with grades up to 1-in-40 (2.5 per cent), ample power is provided with two out of every three cars motored. One out of every two motor cars is a power car with pantographs and control/conversion equipment to cover operation on dc and 50 and 60Hz ac. The normal formation is nine cars, with driving trailers at each end. A nine-car train has 3,200hp (2,400kW) available and this is sufficient to produce 50mph (80km/h) up a 1-in-50 (2 per cent) gradient. Dynamic braking is available for the descent. The combination of higher uphill speeds and higher speeds on sharp curves both uphill and downhill produces worthwhile savings in overall running times. Operation of the original units has been sufficiently successful for JNR's fleet of tilting cars to have risen to over 150 during the last ten years.

The worldwide trend in modern forms of motive power towards self-contained locomotive-less trains took a hold of hitherto unconquered (but not unexplored) territory when Japanese National Railways put into service these very fine electric trains. Previous examples of the provision of sleeping cars in self-propelled trains included Union Pacific's M-10001 train (already described), various long-distance interurban electric trains in the USA and a West German set called the "Komet", which had a brief career in the 1950s. None of these examples led in any way to the idea becoming general practice on the lines concerned.

These handsome trains, however, have now taken over many long-distance overnight workings in Japan. They are also available for day use. Their scope is likely to widen considerably when the 33¾-mile (54km) Seikan tunnel connects the railway system of the Japanese main island of Honshu with that of Hokkaido.

Above: *End doors of a Class 581 train can be opened to give communication between units.*

Below: *A Class 581 driving-trailer sleeping car coupled to a motor non-driving car.*

Intended eventually for high-speed standard-gauge *Shin-Kansen* trains, the new tunnel (nearly twice as long as its nearest existing rival) is likely to carry only narrow-gauge traffic for some years.

All berths are longitudinal and separate accommodation is not provided for "green" (first) and "ordinary" class passengers. Instead, there is a higher charge for lower berths compared to that for middle and upper berths. Berth charges do, however, include night attire and washing things, as in Japanese-style hotels. With up to 45 sleeping berths in each narrow-gauge car the designers must be admired for stating that their main objective was to create an impression of spaciousness! The 12-car set includes a dining car seating 40; the remaining 11 cars can sleep 444 or seat 656. The trains are air-conditioned throughout, and it has been said that the sound-proofing is sufficient to reduce noise levels to less than that encountered in locomotive-hauled sleeping cars.

Class Rc4 B₀-B₀ Sweden:
Swedish State Railways (SJ), 1975

Type: Electric mixed-traffic locomotive.
Gauge: 4ft 8½in (1,435mm).
Propulsion: Alternating current at 15,000V 16⅔Hz, fed via overhead catenary, step-down transformer and a thyristor control system to four frame-mounted 1,206hp (900kW) traction motors, each driving one axle by gearing and ASEA hollow-axle flexible drive.
Weight: 171,910lb (78t).
Max. axleload: 42,980lb (19.5t).
Overall length: 50ft 11in (15,520mm).
Tractive effort: 65,200lb (290kN).
Max. speed: 84mph (135km/h).

The "Rc" family of electric locomotives, developed by the Allmanna Svenska Elektriska Aktiebolaget (ASEA) organisation initially for Swedish State Railways, bids fair to be the world's most successful electric locomotive design. Basically intended for mixed-traffic, the scope of the design has been developed on the one hand to cope with express passenger traffic at 100mph (160km/h), while on the other a version has been supplied for hauling heavy iron ore trains in the Arctic regions. Abroad, such widely differing customers as Austria, Norway and the USA have ordered "Rc" derivatives.

One of the reasons for this pre-eminence is that the "Rc1" was the world's first thyristor locomotive design, put into service in 1967; ingenuity on the part of other manufacturers is no substitute for years of experience in service.

In 1969, 100 "Rc2s" followed the 20 "Rc1s", and they included improvements to the thyristor control system and more sophisticated electrical filters. These are needed to prevent harmonic ripples produced by the thyristor circuits feeding back into the rails and interfering with signalling currents (which also flow in the same rails) and communication circuits generally. The 10 "Rc3s" of 1970 were "Rc2s" geared for 100mph (160km/h) while 16 units, some of which have rheostatic braking, were supplied to Austria (Class "1043") in 1971-73.

In 1975 came the "Rc4" class, the design of which included a patent system developed by ASEA for countering wheelslip, which automatically reduces the current supplied to any driving motor which begins to creep faster than the others. There are also other improvements such as solid-state instead of rotary converters for power supply to auxiliary apparatus.

A total of 150 "Rc4s" have

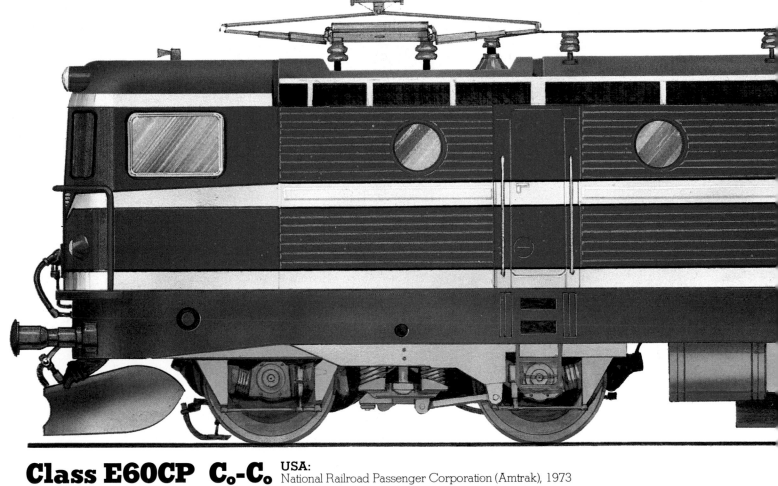

Class E60CP C₀-C₀ USA:
National Railroad Passenger Corporation (Amtrak), 1973

Type: High-speed electric express passenger locomotive.
Gauge: 4ft 8½in (1,435mm).
Propulsion: Alternating current at 12,500V 25Hz (or at 12,500V or 25,000V 60Hz) supplied via step-down transformer with thyristor control system to six 1,275hp (951kW) nose-suspended traction motors geared to the axles.
Weight: 387,905lb (176t).
Max. axleload: 48,490lb (22t).
Overall length: 71ft 3in (21,720mm).
Tractive effort: 75,000lb (334kN).
Max. speed: 85mph (137km/h)*.

*In service. Design speed was 120mph (194km/h).

In the 1970s it became urgent to seek a replacement for the legendary "GG1" electric locomotives which worked the New York to Washington express passenger route. This was not so much on account of difficulties with the "GG1s" themselves—they worked as well as ever. It was more the bad image created by having to admit reliance upon motive power almost 50 years old, plus the fact that the "GG1s" were not suitable for a then impending (but now postponed) modernisation of the power supply, involving a change from a special frequency to the normal industrial frequency.

In order to meet the requirements quickly, General Electric, who had not supplied any passenger electric locomotive to US rail-

roads since 1955, modified a coal-hauling Black Mesa & Lake Powell Railroad locomotive in 1972. The changes involved re-gearing, pro-

Above: *Amtrak E60P electric locomotive at Newark, New Jersey, with New York-Miami "Silver Star" train, June 1982.*

been supplied to Swedish State Railways, plus another 15 with modifications produced for Norway (Class "el.16"), but ASEA's greatest success occurred in the USA. The National Railroad Passenger Corporation (better known as Amtrak) had had the problem of finding motive power to replace the superb but now ageing "GG1" class of 1934 (already described). The new engines were required for use on the New York-Philadelphia-Washington main line, electrified at 12,500V 25Hz. Vari-

Below: *A Swedish Class Rc4 "universal" electric locomotive with thyristor control system.*

ous substitutes fielded by US industry (which had built very few high-speed electric locomotives since the "GG1s") and one from France were disappointing, but a modified "Rc4" sent over on trial—"our little Volvo", Amtrak's motive power men called her—proved to be just what the doctor ordered. Accordingly, a fleet of 47 was proposed.

Rather than fight the "Buy American" lobby in the USA, ASEA sensibly licensed General Motors Electro-Motive Division to build, using ASEA parts, what are now known as Class "AEM7". The "AEM7s" have stronger bodies, 25 per cent more power, and multi-current capability to cover future conversions to 25,000V 60Hz, with a certain

amount of 12,500V 60Hz in areas with close clearances. This is in addition to 12,500V 25Hz capability. Maximum speed is much higher at 125mph (200km/h), while the weight has risen by 17 per cent. This is no detriment, since very high axleloads are catered for in the USA by the use of heavy rail, closely spaced sleepers and deep ballast.

The six iron-ore haulers of 1977 (Class "Rm") had ballasting to raise the axleload to 50,700lb (23t). automatic couplers, lower gearing, rheostatic braking and multiple-unit capability, as well as better heating and more insulation in the cab.

vision for supplying auxiliary power to the train and (for some of the units) oil-fired steam-heating boilers. The 27 locomotives supplied in 1973 ran well except that the riding at high speeds left something to be desired. So, in the event, the "GG1s" had to be retained to cater for this requirement.

Some "E60CPs" were found employment on lesser duties, others were disposed of to other users; it was left for locomotives of Swedish design and possessing excellent riding qualities, to displace the old faithfuls.

Right: *The E60P locos can use either the original Pennsylvania RR supply at 25Hz, or the proposed 50Hz.*

Class X Co-Co

Australia: Victorian Railways (VicRail), 1966

Type: Diesel-electric mixed-traffic locomotive.
Gauge: 5ft 3in (1,600mm) and 4ft 8½in (1,435mm).
Propulsion: General Motors Type 16-567E 1,950hp (1,455kW) Vee 16-cylinder two-stroke diesel engine and generator supplying current to six nose-suspended traction motors geared to the axles.
Weight: 255,665lb (116t).
Max. axleload: 42,980lb (19.5t).
Overall length: 60ft 3in (18,364mm).
Tractive effort: 64,125lb (285kN).
Max. speed: 84mph (134km/h).

It is well known that Australia has a serious railway gauge problem, the various states having in the early days gone their own ways in this respect. The state of Victoria

and its neighbour South Australia were the two which opted for a 5ft 3in (1,600mm) broad gauge. In steam days this meant different designs of locomotive, but with diesels the differences can be minimal, confined almost wholly to the appropriate wheelsets.

These Class "X" diesels of Victorian Government Railways are a case in point because, now that standard-gauge has put a tentacle into the state (notably to connect Melbourne to the Trans-Australian railway as well as over the trunk route from Sydney), they provide haulage over both gauges.

The locomotives are a typical General Motors product—like virtually all VicRail's diesel locomo-

Left: *"X" class diesel-electric locomotive No. X49 arrives in Melbourne with the "Southern Aurora" express from Sydney.*

Class 2130 Co-Co

Australia: Queensland Railways (QR), 1970

Type: Diesel-electric mineral-hauling locomotive.
Gauge: 3ft 6in (1,067mm).
Propulsion: General Motors Type 16-645E 2,200hp (1,640kW) 16-cylinder Vee two-stroke diesel engine and alternator feeding via solid-state rectifiers six nose-suspended traction motors geared to the axles.
Weight: 215,050lb (98t).
Max. axleload: 35,850lb (16.3t).
Overall length: 59ft 3in (18,060mm).
Tractive effort: 64,500lb (287kN).
Max. speed: 50mph (80km/h).

Queensland's 6,206 mile (9,930km) railway system has been extended recently to serve various mining

operations, and so has rather surprisingly moved into the premier place as regards mileage amongst the Australian state and national administrations. Furthermore, in spite of being mostly laid on narrow-gauge, QR also holds the top place in load hauling. The locomotives that achieve this record are these Class "2130" diesel-electrics. The 11 machines which form the "2130" class are, like 57 per cent of the QR fleet, of General Motors design but built (or at any rate, assembled, under licence) by Clyde Engineering. They also follow US practice in being used as building blocks to form a tractive effort of the power desired.

The most heroic use for these excellent machines is their employment as two groups of three on

the newly built Goonyella line to haul 148-wagon coal trains weighing 11,140t (12,250 US tons) and carrying 8,700t (9,130 US tons) of coal. As the drawgear of the train is not strong enough to take the tractive effort of all six locomotives,

Above: *A 6,600 horsepower couplage of QR Class 2130 diesel electric units.*

Below: *Queensland Railways' Class 2130 diesel-electric locomotive, supplied in 1970.*

tives—and were assembled by GM's Australian licensee, Clyde Engineering Pty of Sydney, New South Wales. This standardisation gives an advantage in that most of the diesel fleet can be run in multiple regardless of class.

Soon after the first six "Xs" had been delivered, Clyde began offering GM's new 645 series engine and this was used for a subsequent batch of 18 supplied in 1970. The power output could thus be increased to 2,600hp (1,940kW) without weight penalty. These were then the most powerful units on the system, but subsequently axleload limits have been raised to 22.5t (24.8 US tons) on certain lines. Hence a further batch of GM Co-Co units (the "C" class) supplied with an installed power of 3,300hp (2,460kW).

One requirement for all Victorian locomotives that possibly defeated General Motors' ability to supply off-the-shelf was provision of sets of pneumatically-operated token exchange equipment. Under British-style operating rules, some physical token of authority is needed to be on any particular section of single line. The token (or staff) has to be exchanged for another when passing from one section to the next. The places where this happens often do not coincide with the train's stopping places and the exchange apparatus enables this to be done at speed. Modern electrical methods of signalling are slowly doing away with this picturesque operation, but for the moment it continues and locomotives however modern have to be equipped to cope.

Right: *Victorian Railways' Class "X" Co-Co diesel-electric locomotive No. X45* Edgar. B. Brownbill, *built in 1970.*

the second group is cut into the centre of the train. These mid-train units are remotely controlled from the lead units without any cable connections between them, by a system of US origin widely-used in North America and known as Locotrol.

The Locotrol system involves a special vehicle marshalled next to the group of units in the centre of the train. This vehicle operates on the principle of sensing the drawbar pull and applying power to the units it controls accordingly. Safety is ensured by having the brakes of the whole train under the control of the driver in the

Left: *Note the alternative of automatic couplings or link-and-screw with buffers on these Class 2130 locos.*

leading unit. Six of the locomotives (Nos. 2135 to 40) are fitted out for use as lead units, with air-conditioned cabs and Locotrol equipment.

The "2130" class is part of a group of generally similar diesel locomotives, 57 in number, all of General Motors origin and numbered in the 21xx and 22xx series, as befits their rating of 2,000hp-plus. The only non-General Motors units of this order of power on the system are the 16 Class "2350" of 2,350hp (1,735kW) supplied by English Electric and used on lines with an axleload limit of 15t. This high-power fleet may be the summit of diesel development in Queensland because plans are afoot to begin electrification of some heavily-used lines.

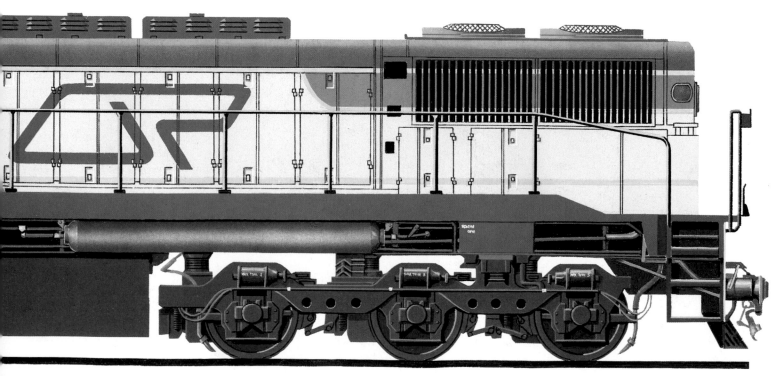

DF4 'East Wind IV' C₀-C₀ China: Railways of the People's Republic (CR), 1969

Type: General-purpose diesel-electric locomotive.
Gauge: 4ft 8½in (1,435mm).
Propulsion: 3,600hp (2,686kW) Type 16-240-Z 16-cylinder Vee-type four-stroke diesel engine and alternator supplying current via solid-state rectifiers to six traction motors geared to the axles.
Weight: 304,155lb (138t).
Max. axleload: 50,695lb (23t).
Overall length: 62ft 2½in (21,100mm).
Tractive effort: 76,038lb (338kN).
Max. speed: 75mph (120km/h).

Diesel locomotive production in China started off quite incredibly badly in the 1960s when, in response to Chairman Mao's call for a 'Great Leap Forward', the various locomotive works, 'aiming high', set out to design and build their own, unhampered by any previous experience. The result was disaster, but when sanity returned it was rightly felt important not to respond by putting the nation into the hands of some foreign country.

The immediate solution was for steam building to continue and for a slow-but-sure diesel-electric development programme to be put in hand. There were some imports of main line diesel-electric locomotives, notably 50 of 4,000hp (2,985kW) from Alsthom of France

during the early-1970s and 20 of 2,100hp (1,567kW) from Electroputere of Romania, in 1975, but home-building also began in earnest, and this is the most common type.

The DF4 is a general-purpose locomotive, of which versions exist for both passenger (numbered 2001 upwards) or freight traffic (numbered 0001 upwards). It is not often used in multiple, being the most powerful in China with a single engine and conse-

quently having adequate power to haul trains of the size normally run. Its appearance is neat and there is a cab at both ends. The engine, the ac/dc transmission and the mechanical parts are wholly Chinese-made and developed from a prototype built in 1969. Series production is now in hand at the Talien (Dairen) Works. Incidentally, the type number of the engine, 16240, indicates the number of cylinders (16) followed by their bore in millimetres

Above: *An "East Wind IV" diesel-electric locomotive of the Chinese Railways near Peking in November 1980.*

(240mm—9.45in). It is delightful to note that, with a frankness unmatched amongst the world's railway mechanical departments, the weights are officially specified as being within plus or minus 3 per cent. It is thought that about 450 had been produced by the end of 1981.

Beijing B-B China: Railways of the People's Republic (CR), 1971

Type: Diesel-hydraulic express passenger locomotive.
Gauge: 4ft 8½in (1,435mm).
Propulsion: Type 12240Z 3,300hp (2,462kW) 12-cylinder four-stroke Vee diesel engine driving the four axles through a hydraulic torque-converter system.
Weight: 202,770lb (92t).
Max. axleload: 50,695lb (23t).
Overall length: 54ft 2in (16,505mm).

Tractive effort: 52,257lb (232kN).
Max. speed: 75mph (120km/h).

In parallel with diesel-electric progress, diesel-hydraulic locomotive development has also been pursued in China. With some experience gained with 30 class "NY6" 4,300hp (3,208kW) and "NY7" 5,400hp (4,028kW) locomotives imported from Henschel

of West Germany, the February 7th Locomotive Works at Peking (Beijing) produced in 1971 some prototypes of a rather smaller locomotive for passenger work. These are known as the "BJ" or "Beijing" class. Full production began in 1975 and by the end of 1981 about 150 were in service, numbered BJ3001 upwards.

These compact-looking locomotives have more haulage capacity than would appear. The

powerful engine is matched by high tractive effort, due to the high axleloading. For example, on a really steep gradient of 1-in-30 (3.3 per cent), a load of 600t (660 US tons) can be hauled at the very respectable speed in the circumstances of 15mph (24km/h). A low-level connection to transmit tractive effort from the bogies to the body helps improve performance by reducing weight transfer from one axle to another. The hydraulic transmission incorporates two torque convertors, one for starting and one for running at normal speeds. Either can be used to drive one or both bogies and the system can also be used as a hydrokinetic brake to give dynamic braking. A twin-engine version is under development and so highly is the performance and reliability of the "BJ" class regarded that its designers now have sufficient confidence to offer it for export.

Left: *Compact Chinese Railways "Beijing" class diesel-hydraulic locomotive No. BJ3062 standing at Peking main station in October 1980.*

Right: *A "Beijing" class diesel-hydraulic locomotive of Chinese Railways at the head of the daily tourist train from Peking to the Great Wall of China.*

Class Dr 13 C-C

Finland:
Finnish State Railways (VR), 1963

Type: Diesel-electric mixed-traffic locomotive.
Gauge: 5ft 0in (1,524mm).
Propulsion: Two Tampella-MGO Type V-16 BHSR 1,400hp (1,030kW) Vee 16-cylinder diesel engines and generators supplying current to two large traction motors, one mounted on each bogie. Each motor drives the three axles of its bogie via gearing with two alternative gear ratios.
Weight: 218,200lb (99t).
Max. axleload: 36,370lb (16.5t).
Overall length: 60ft 11in (18,576mm).
Tractive effort: 62,373lb (277kN).
Max. speed: 87mph (140km/h) high gear, 62mph (100km/h) low gear.

Two prototypes of these unusual-looking locomotives were obtained in 1963 from Alsthom of France; they contained many typical features of that famous firm's products. Later a production batch of 52 was built (or certainly assembled) under licence in Finland. Lokomo and Valmet, both of Tampere, shared the order and 48 out of the original 54 are still in service.

The design was based on engines of modest power output which were available in Finland, two being used to provide the desired output. The running gear and electrical equipment, however, followed original principles, which had been adopted for both electric and diesel-electric locomotives then recently introduced in France. The bogies were of the mono-motor pattern, each with one large traction motor mounted above the wheels in the centre of the bogie. The wheels were driven by gearing which had the unusual feature of alternative ratios. The higher of these was suitable for express passenger work, while the other was appropriate for heavy freight haulage. A change-over between the two has to wait, of course, until the locomotive is stationary.

Above: *Finnish State Railways Class Dr 13 C-C diesel-electric locomotive.*

While these interesting machines have served VR well, it is clear that future diesel development in Finland is likely to be overshadowed by electrification.

Class 6E B₀-B₀

South Africa:
South African Railways (SAR), 1969

Type: Electric mixed traffic freight locomotive.
Gauge: 3ft 6in (1,067mm).
Propulsion: Direct current at 3,000V fed via overhead catenary and rheostatic controls to four 835hp (623kW) nose-suspended motors geared to the driving axles.
Weight: 195,935lb (88.9t).
Max. axleload: 49,040lb (22.25t).
Overall length: 50ft 10in (15,494mm).
Tractive effort: 70,000lb (311kN).
Max. speed: 70mph (112km/h).

The first important electrification scheme in South Africa came as early as 1925, when a steeply-graded section of the Durban to Johannesburg main line between Estcourt and Ladysmith was placed under the wires. The Class "1E" locomotives supplied—the original group came from Switzerland—were direct ancestors of Class "6E" with the same wheel arrangement and mechanical configuration. Fifty-five years of progress has resulted in increases of 77 per cent in tractive effort, 208 per cent in power output, and 180 per cent in maximum permitted speed at a cost of only 31 per cent in weight and 16 per cent in overall length. It is typical of electric traction, though, that many of the "1Es" remain in service on humble but still arduous duties after half-a-century of work.

A country that combines prosperous development and great

Left: *South African Railways' famous "Blue Train" near Fountains Pretoria, hauled by two specially painted electric locomotives.*

Class 9E C₀-C₀

South Africa:
South African Railways (SAR), 1978

Type: Electric mineral-hauling locomotive.
Gauge: 3ft 6in (1,067mm).
Propulsion: Alternating current at 50,000V 50Hz fed via overhead catenary, step-down transformer with thyristor control to six nose-suspended 910hp (680kW) traction motors geared to the wheels.
Weight: 370,270lb (168t).
Max. axleload: 61,712lb (28t).
Overall length: 69ft 4in (21,132mm).
Tractive effort: 121,000lb (538kN).
Max. speed: 56mph (90km/h).

It is said that the only work of man on Earth visible from the moon is the Great Wall of China, but a likely further candidate must be the 529-mile (846km) line from Sishen in the centre of South Africa to a new Atlantic port at Saldanha Bay. Not only would it have been noticed by a moon-bound earth-watcher on account of the rapidity with which it appeared, but its conspicuousness would have been enhanced by the featureless semi-desert nature of the most of the route.

Although built by the South African government's Iron & Steel Industrial Corporation (ISCOR) for moving iron ore for shipment, South African Railways operate the line, and the scale of operations is such that some unprecedented equipment has been needed. In virtually uninhabited country, electric power supplies are far apart and hence a nominal voltage twice that normally used nowadays was specified. The result is that there are only six substations for the entire route, the contact wire itself acting as a main transmission line. The 25 locomotives built for the railway (after a period of diesel operation) were designed by GEC Traction in Great Britain but built in South Africa by Union Carriage & Wagon. They normally operate in threes, so making up a 16,350hp (12,200kW) unit capable of starting as well as hauling a 20,000t (22,000 US tons) load on the ruling gradient—against loaded trains—of 1-in-250 (0.4 per cent). They can also operate (but at reduced speed) when the voltage drops as low as 25,000, which can happen in certain conditions, say 45 miles (70km) from the nearest substation.

One delightful feature of a harsh operation in the harshest of environments is the motor scooter provided in a special cabinet below the locomotive running board. This enables someone to inspect both sides of a 200-wagon train almost 1½ miles (2.3km)

Right: *South African Railways' Class 9E 50,000V electric locomotive, as used on the Sishen to Saldanha Bay line.*

mineral riches with non-existent oil supplies is well-suited to electrification. Both the scale of electric operation and its rate of development in South Africa are indicated by the fact that the "6E/6E1" fleet already approaches 1,000 in number, while 850 of their very similar immediate predecessors, classes "5E" and "5E1," were built between 1955 and 1969. South Africa's growing industrial capability is also shown by the fact that while the 172 "1Es" (and the similar "2Es") were wholly built in Europe, only the earlier examples of Class "5E" and none of the "6Es" were built abroad.

All the classes mentioned, and this is especially impressive for half-a-century ago, are capable not only of regenerative braking but also of working in multiple. This whole concept of railroading, using exclusively tractors with the

same two bogies as most other vehicles but coupling up as many of them as are needed to haul the train was far ahead of its time. Five or six locomotives running in multiple can often be seen.

Below: *South African Railways' standard 5E/6E series Bo-Bo locomotives, depicted here in the special "Blue Train" colours, are now fast approaching the amazing total of 2,000 in number.*

Above: *The striking matching livery of the locomotive and carriages of the prestigious and luxurious "Blue Train", running three times a week between Johannesburg and Cape Town.*

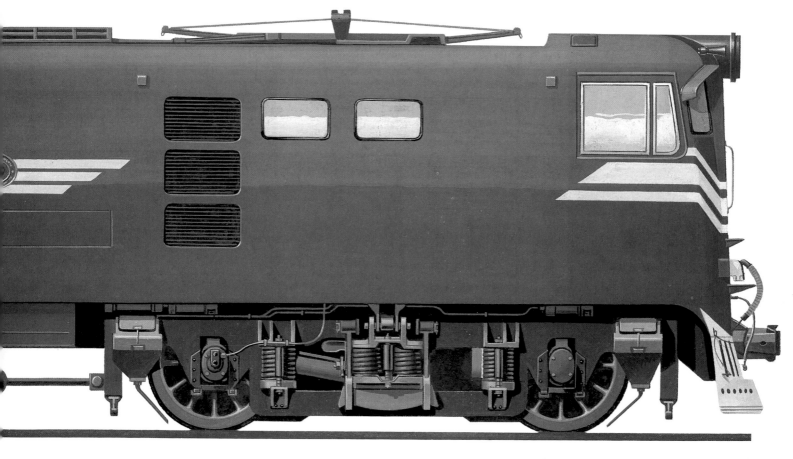

long, returning reasonably quickly to the locomotive after the round trip. Other comforts provided for the crew include full air-conditioning, a toilet and a refrigerator, as well as a hotplate for cooking. The unusual appearance is due to the roof having to be lowered to accommodate the large insulators and switchgear needed for the high voltage.

The control system is of advanced design, using thyristors. The position of the driver's main control lever is arranged to determine not external physical things such as resistance values or transformer tapping, but instead the actual value of the traction motor currents and therefore the individual torque

applied to each pair of wheels. This gives a much more direct control over the movement of the train. There are five systems of braking: straight air on the locomotive, normal air braking for the train, vacuum brakes (on some units) for occasional haulage of ordinary SAR rolling stock, a handbrake and electrical braking. The latter, which is rheostatic rather than regenerative, can hold a full 20,000t (22,000 US tons) train to 34mph (55km/h) on a 1-in-167 (0.6 per cent) downgrade. It is thought that this operation is the only one in the world where trains of this weight are operated using other than North American designs of equipment.

F40PH B₀-B₀

Type: Diesel-electric passenger locomotive.
Gauge: 4ft 8½in (1,435mm).
Propulsion: One EMD 645E3 3,000hp (2,240kW) 16-cylinder turbocharged two-stroke Vee engine and alternator supplying current through silicon rectifiers to four nose-suspended traction motors geared to the axles.
Weight: 232,000lb (105.2t).
Max. axleload: 58,000lb (26.3t).
Overall length: 52ft 0in (15,850mm).
Tractive effort: 68,440lb (304kN).
Max. speed: 103mph (166km/h).

The last of the EMD passenger "carbody" diesels was built at the end of 1963, and with passenger traffic declining rapidly, the need for special passenger locomotives seemed to have disappeared. Both EMD and its competitors offered a train-heating steam generator as an optional extra on certain "hood" units, and this met the needs of the railroads which required replacements for ageing "E" or "F" series units.

In 1968, with the railroads' enthusiasm for high-power diesels at its climax, the Atchison, Topeka & Santa Fe Railway proposed to buy from EMD some 20-cylinder 3,600hp (2,690kW) Co-Co locomotives geared for high speed to operate its premier passenger services. The railroad asked that the locomotives should be given a more acceptable appearance for passenger work, and that the body should have less air resistance at speed than a normal hood unit. The outcome was the "cowl", a casing shaped like an angular version of the old carbody, but differing from it in that the casing does not carry any load. The cowl extends ahead of the cab, giving the front of the cab more protection against the weather than a normal hood.

The model was designated "FP45", and was very similar in its equipment to the "SD45" road switcher. Another variant had a shorter frame resulting from the omission of the steam generator; it was designated "F45".

In 1971 the National Railroad Passenger Corporation (Amtrak) took over most of the non-commuter passenger services in the US, and in 1973 took delivery of its first new locomotives to replace the old "E" and "F" series. By this

Above: *A push-pull commuter train hauled by F40PH No. 4120 of New Jersey Transit passes Harrison, New Jersey.*

Below: *An F40PH belonging to Ontario's GO Transit brings a rake of striking double-deck cars through Scarborough, Ont.*

time, enthusiasm for engines above 3,000hp had declined, so the Amtrak units were similar to the "FP45" but with a 16-cylinder 3,000hp (2,240kW) engine. A total of 150 were delivered in 1973-74. They were equipped with two steam generators mounted on skids, which could easily be replaced by two diesel-alternators when steam-heated stock was replaced by electrically-heated vehicles. In view of the similarity to the "SD40s", these locomotives were classified "SDP40".

For a time all was well, but then an alarming series of derailments occurred to the trailing bogies of "SDP40s" whilst negotiating curves. No explanation could be found, but it was clear that the track had been spread or rails turned over by excessive lateral forces. The bogies were only slightly different from those of other EMD "Dash-2" three-axle bogies, but it was the only part of the locomotive on which suspicion could fall.

In the meantime, for shorter-distance routes on which the coaches were already electrically-heated, Amtrak had ordered a four-axle 3,000hp (2,240kW) locomotive, with an alternator for

Below: *Amtrak's standard passenger locomotive is this F40PH "Cowl" Bo-Bo unit built by General Motors' Electro-Motive Division. The F40PHs displaced most of the vintage "F" and "E" series locomotives from Amtrak's principal long-distance trains in the late 1970s.*

supplying three-phase current at 60Hz for train services driven by gearing from the engine crankshaft. This model is designated "F40PH", and deliveries began in March 1976 when the problem of the "SDP40" derailments was acute. As the well-tried Blomberg truck fitted to the "F40PH" had given no cause for criticism, Amtrak decided that the Co-Co locomotives should be rebuilt as "F40PHs". The frame could be shortened by 16ft, as the steam generator was no longer needed. The "F40PHs" built new had a 500kW alternator, which drew a maximum of 710hp from the engine, but for the transcontinental "Superliner" trains an

800kW alternator and larger fuel tanks were needed, so that the "F40PHs" obtained by rebuilding are 4ft longer than the others.

In the fact the rebuilding was nominal, for it cost nearly 70 per cent of the price of a new locomotive, and in effect the "SDP40s" were scrapped when only four to five years old. Amtrak now has a fleet of 191 "F40PH" locomotives.

Many US commuter services are the responsibility of transit authorities, some of whom operate their own trains. A number of these operators bought a shortened version of the unhappy "SD40F", in which the steam generator was replaced by an

alternator. This is the "F40C", and in this application the engine is uprated to 3,200hp (2,390kW). At the moderate speeds of commuter services, no trouble has been experienced with derailments, but nevertheless when further locomotives were required the transit authorities ordered the four-axle "F40PH", in some cases with the engine uprated to 3,200hp.

Below: *An F40PH Bo-Bo diesel-electric locomotive belonging to Amtrak arrives at Chicago Union Station with a short train composed of "Amfleet" passenger cars.*

Class 1044 B₀-B₀

Austria:
Austrian Federal Railways (OBB), 1974

Type: Electric express passenger locomotive.

Gauge: 4ft 8½in (1,435mm).

Propulsion: Low-frequency alternating current at 15,000V 16⅔Hz fed via overhead catenary, step-down transformer with thyristor control system to four 1,765hp (1,317kW) traction motors driving the axles through Brown Boveri spring drives and gearing.

Weight: 185,140lb (84t).

Max. axleload: 46,285lb (21t).

Overall length: 52ft 6in (16,000mm).

Tractive effort: 70,600lb (314kN).

Max. speed: 100mph (160km/h).

Austrian locomotives were in the past distinctive almost to the point of quaintness, whether steam or electric. But since the German occupation, during which standard German types were imposed, the Federal Railways locomotives have been capable but otherwise as conventional as could be. Only 62 out of 406 electric locomotives supplied since the war were not Bo-Bos, and of these 50 were Co-Cos and the others rod-drive switchers.

Most of the 406 also came from the Austrian state-owned locomotive-building firm of Simmering-Graz-Pauker (SGP) of Vienna and Graz, but an exception was a batch of 10 thyristor-controlled locomotives (Class "1043") imported from Sweden between 1971 and 1973. Satisfactory experience with these led to the thought that Austrians had been

Above: *Austrian Federal Railways class 1044 electric locomotive No. 1044.83 leaving Seefeld, Tirol, in September 1982.*

building electric locomotives a lot longer than these northerners. The result was this Class "1044", of which two prototypes were completed by SGP in 1974. Orders for a further 96 have followed.

Their high-speed capability is only relevant to a tiny proportion of the Austrian rail network, but high tractive effort and surefootedness, the key to operations in the mountains, are special features. Accordingly, the new locomotives were designed to complement

Left: *Innsbruck locomotive depot in foreground; note Class 1020 Co-Co locos on siding. A Class 1044 Bo-Bo locomotive is leaving the station.*

No. 12 B-B

Great Britain:
Romney, Hythe & Dymchurch Railway (RH&DR), 1983

Type: Locomotive for local passenger haulage.

Gauge: 1ft 3in (381mm).

Propulsion: Perkins Type 6.3544 120hp (90kW) diesel engine driving all four axles direct via two-speed bidirectional gearbox and torque converter, drop-down gearbox, longitudinal cardan shafts and gearing.

Weight: 13,225lb (6t).

Max. axleload: 3,310lb (1.5t).

Overall length: 21ft 0in (6,400mm).

Tractive effort: 6,000lb (27kN).

Max. speed: 25mph (40km/h).

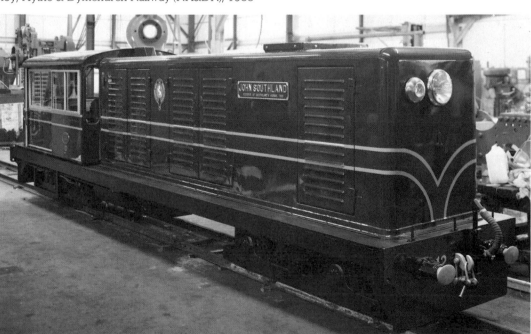

This minute locomotive already plays a vital role in local light rail transport and may well play a bigger one in the future. Ever since it was opened in 1927, the 13 mile (21km) Romney, Hythe & Dymchurch Railway has claimed the title of "Smallest Public Railway in the World". A few years ago the claim became a degree firmer when a contract was obtained from local government to carry some 200 pupils to and from school each day.

Steam traction—however attractive as part of the RH&DR's

normal tourist-railway operations —was quite uneconomic for the school train. Accordingly, with the assistance of a local government grant, a diesel locomotive was designed and built for the railway by the firm of TMA Engineering of Birmingham.

Sufficient tractive effort to handle a 200-passenger train was required and to obtain this a major ingredient was the Twin-Disc transmission. This was based on that used for many years on British

Above: *Romney, Hythe & Dymchurch Railway B-B diesel mechanical locomotive in the maker's works, 1983. The machine is named after the founder of the school whose pupils travel daily behind the locomotive.*

the stepless thyristor control with other measures, to bring adhesion up to values that only a very few years ago were thought beyond the bounds of possibility.

One measure taken is to provide linkage so that the tractive effort from each bogie is transmitted to the body as near to rail level as possible. This avoids weight transfer from one wheelset to another when either bogie applies tractive force to the body. Transverse forces imposed on the bogies by constant changes of curvature in the mountains are ameliorated by giving the axles spring-controlled sideplay.

Although some problems have arisen, leading to a temporary cessation of production, their effectiveness means that one of these locomotives (and they are often employed in pairs) can, for example, be rostered to take 550t (605US tons) up the 1-in-32½ (3.1 per cent) ascent to the Arlberg tunnel on the trunk route from Switzerland to Salzberg and Vienna. The amazing one-hour output of 7,075hp (5,278kW) that makes such feats possible shows how far ac traction using double-bogie four-axle locomotives has come since the New York, New Haven & Hartford Railroad put their first Baldwin-Westinghouse Bo-Bo on the rails in 1905, with a rated power output of 1,420hp (1,060kW).

Right: *Head-on view of Austrian Federal Railways Class 1044 Bo-Bo locomotive at Innsbruck station with Vienna-Basle Trans-Alpine express, Autumn 1980.*

Railways' diesel-mechanical trains and therefore, hopefully, the long build-up of experience so gained will lead to reliability. The shape of the locomotive has been designed to give the driver a good look-out both ways as well as protection in the event of a level-crossing collision. The cab is heated, sound-proofed, equipped with radio for signalling purposes, and has reversible seats with duplicate instrumentation for each direction. Vacuum brake equipment is provided to work the train brakes, using an off-the-shelf exhauster and other fittings of automotive origin.

To some, of course, the introduction of diesel traction to this famous piece of railway showbiz is as if the *Folies Bergére* decided to dress its equally famous girls in denim overalls. So to that extent a question mark must stand over the use of this acquisition. But perhaps the most interesting thing about it is that a combination of this locomotive and a rake of standard RH&DR light-alloy passenger carriages could now offer a way of providing a low-key rapid-transit system.

Such a system might bear a similar relationship to what is now

called LRT (Light Rapid Transit) as LRT does to a full metro system. An LRT—effectively what used to be called trams, but mainly, or wholly confined to reserved tracks —has perhaps one-third the capacity of a hypothetical metro and achieves half the average speed, but only costs one-seventh of its grander rival. A Romney-style VLRT (Very Light Rail Transit) might provide half the capacity, and a very little lower speed, all for one-quarter the cost of LRT.

Above: *The cab end of RH&DR locomotive No. 12. Within an axleload limit of 1.5t and an overall height of 6ft 6in (2m), haulage capability has been provided for handling trains with a load of 200 passengers.*

Class Ge 4/4 B₀-B₀

Type: Electric mixed-traffic mountain locomotive.
Gauge: 3ft 3⅜in (1,000mm).
Propulsion: Low-frequency alternating current at 11,000V 16⅔Hz fed via overhead catenary and step-down transformer with thyristor control to four 570hp (425kW) traction motors with both series and independent field windings. Connection to the wheels is through gearing and Brown Boveri spring drives.
Weight: 110,220lb (50t).
Max. axleload: 27,550lb (12.5t).
Overall length: 42ft 6½in (12,960mm).
Tractive effort: 40,050lb (178kN).
Max. speed: 56mph (90km/h).

'To The Clouds By Rail' wrote Cecil J. Allen, King of railway journalists, referring to Switzerland's remarkable mountain railways. Nearer the clouds than most of those which crossed Alpine passes was the Furka-Oberalp Railway reaching, with rack-and-pinion assistance on 1-in-9 (11 per cent) gradients, 7,085ft (2,160m) at the Furka tunnel and 6,668ft (2,033m) at Oberalp Passhoehe. The ascents to the former were a little too close to the clouds in winter. Which leads to these neat locomotives with such remarkable properties for their size, which were acquired in connection with an amazing project to convert the line into an all-weather route open all year.

The project was construction of a 9¾ mile (15.5km) Furka base tunnel running from Oberwald (4,480ft—1,366m) to Realp (5,045ft —1,538m) to avoid the difficult section. These stations were the termini of the winter shuttle services from Brig and Andermatt respectively. Work started in 1973 and traffic began to pass on June 25, 1982; the estimates were overun by three times in cost and one-and-a-half times in contruction time.

There were to be motor-car shuttle trains through the tunnel as well as additional trains coming up from Brig. To work this traffic the FO management wondered whether the extra expense of rack-equipped motive power could be avoided, by working with adhesion on the rack sections concerned which had a lesser gradient of 1-in-11 (9 per cent). They were encouraged in this by the performance of four-axle locomotives (Class "Ge 4/4 II") recently supplied to the connecting Rhaetian Railway. On test they had produced 50 per cent adhesion, that is a drawbar pull of 25t, and in addition they could manage the equally unprecedented speed for the Swiss metre-gauge of 56mph (90km/h). This would be useful now that the FO at last had acquired straight track in the tunnel—the only possible place for high speed on its 62½ miles (100km) of route. Hence Nos. 81 *Uri* and 82 *Wallis*, supplied in 1979, and lent to the Rhaetian Railway when acquired until the tunnel was ready.

Above: *Furka-Oberalp rack-and-adhesion motor luggage vans, Class De 4/4, used for working trains on 1-in-9 (11 per cent) grades.*

Adhesion, that all important quantity for a rack-less mountain railway, was maximised on these locomotives by step-less thyristor control and low-level traction bars connecting the bogies to the body, as in the Austrian Class "1044". In addition, to minimise the effect of drawbar pull causing weight transfer from the front to the rear bogie, there is an electrically-con-

Below: *Class Ge 4/4 adhesion-only Bo-Bo locomotive used for working car-carrying trains through the new Furka tunnel.*

trolled compensation system with two stages of adjustment. Wheel-creep, indicating the imminence of slipping, is also detected automatically and the appropriate motor current adjusted to correct the situation. Friction (and wear) is reduced by a flange-lubricating system and, in addition, rheostatic braking is provided. Finally, it is a pleasure to find accompanying all this superb technology provision of rectractable rail brushes for clearing and cleaning the rail heads of leaves and other detritus.

The locomotives can haul loaded car trains weighing 350t (385 US tons) on the 1-in-37 (2.7 per cent) grade in the tunnel. On 1-in-11 (9 per cent) grades, on which other motive power uses the rack for traction, some 75t (88 US tons) could in principle be hauled by adhesion alone. This does not sound a lot, but lightweight FO carriages weigh a mere 12t empty although carrying up to 48 passengers.

Although trains are worked by adhesion alone on gradients as steep as 1-in-11 (9 per cent) on other mountain railways in Switzerland, for the moment it seems that this will not occur on the Furka-Oberalp. The fleet of De4/4 rack-and-adhesion motor luggage vans has been increased to cater for the increase in regular traffic anticipated as a result of opening the new tunnel.

Right: *End view of FO rack-and-adhesion motor luggage van. Note the central buffer with screw couplings on each side.*

HST 125 ten-car train

Great Britain:
British Railways (BR), 1978

Type: Diesel-electric high-speed train.

Gauge: 4ft 8½in (1,435mm).

Propulsion: One supercharged two-stroke Paxman Valenta 12RP200L Vee-type 12-cylinder engine of 2,250hp (1,680kW) with integral alternator in each of two driving motor luggage vans, each engine feeding current to sets of four traction motors mounted in the bogie frames.

Weight: 308,560lb (140t) adhesive, 844,132lb (383t) total.

Max. axleload: 38,570lb (17.5t).

Overall length: 720ft 5in (219,584mm).

Max. speed: 125mph (200km/h).

These superb diesel-electric trains, the fastest in the world with that system of propulsion, marked a great step forward in the long history of the British express passenger train and, in addition, represent the first real original and countrywide success story of Britain's nationalised rail system in the passenger field.

As with most other success stories, the main ingredient of this triumph was the technical restraint of the trains involved, representing as they did a development of existing equipment rather than the result of beginning with a clean sheet of paper. The disastrous experiences at the time of writing with the Advanced Passenger Train—a clean-sheet-of-paper design if ever there was one—are a case in point.

If, then, the technology of the HST was just an update—except possibly for bogie suspension

Below: One of these power car-luggage vans at each end of an HST 125 set provides a total of 4,500hp for high-speed operation.

—then so much more impressive is the somersault in operational thinking. Ever since Liverpool & Manchester days, long distance trains had had detachable locomotives, not only because the locomotives were liable to need more frequent (and messier) attention than the carriages, but also because they could then haul more than one type of train at different times of the day. The argument was that if the obvious disadvantages of self-propelled

Above: *British Rail's prototype High Speed Train. This unit still holds the world's speed record for diesel traction at 143mph (230km/h).*

trains with fixed formation could be accepted, then the problems of giving them the ability to run at 125mph (200km/h) were much reduced. The power units themselves were simplified, since the need to haul other types of trains was non-existent. Things like

vacuum brake equipment, slow running gear and much else was just not required and their space, cost and weight would all be saved.

As well as disadvantages, self-propelled trains have advantages. For example, HSTs can run into a London terminus and leave again after a minimum interval for servicing (in 1983 as little as 18 minutes). At the same time there is no question of trapping its locomotive against the buffer stops until another locomotive is attached at the opposite end. Annual mileages in the quarter-million region can be the rule rather than the exception. And to counter the argument that the locomotives that handled the day trains would be needed for sleeping car expresses at night, there is still the point that, for example, now that Newcastle to London is only a 3-hour ride, the need for sleeping car accommodation is much reduced.

The plan was originally for 132 HST trains intended to cover the principal non-electrified routes of British Railways with a network of 125mph (200km/h) trains. The routes in question were those between London (Paddington and King's Cross) and the West of England, South Wales, Yorkshire, the North East, Edinburgh and Aberdeen, as well as the North-East to South-West cross-country axis via Sheffield, Derby and Birmingham. Modifications to the plan since it was first drawn up have reduced this number to 95, providing a dense and comprehensive service of high speed diesel trains which has no precedent nor as yet any imitators worldwide.

The improvement in running time over routes where there is an adequate mileage available for running at maximum speed can approach as much as 20 per

Above: *An HST 125 train set, made up temporarily to eleven cars, raises a dust of powdery snow on an East Coast main line express working.*

cent. For example, the shortest journey time for the 268 miles (428km) from King's Cross to Newcastle is 2hr 54min (in 1983) compared with the 3hr 35min applicable during 1977 for trains hauled by the celebrated "Deltic" diesel locomotives. Coupled with a substantial improvement in passenger comfort, this acceleration has led to a gratifyingly increased level of patronage. A particular point is that the HSTs are not first-class only, or extra-fare trains, but available to all at the standard fare.

The design of the train was based on a pair of lightweight Paxman Valenta V-12 diesel engines each rated at 2,260hp (1,680kW) and located in a motor-baggage car at each end of the train. The specific weight of these engines is about half that of other conventional diesel engines in use on BR and the design is very compact. This led to the motor cars of the units being built within 154,000lb (70t) overall weight, and it was also possible to provide baggage accommodation within the vehicle's 58ft 4in (17,792mm) length. Compare this with the "Peak" (Class "44") diesel locomotives of 20 years earlier (already described), where a unit of similar power output was so heavy it

needed *eight* axles to carry it. The lower axleloads of the HST trains were also important because raising the speed of trains has a progressively destructive effect on the track.

The MkIII carriages of the trains were the result of some 10 years development from British Railways' Mk1 stock, standard since the 1950s. In spite of the addition of air-conditioning, sophisticated bogies, soundproofing, automatic corridor doors, and a degree of luxury hardly ever before offered to second-class passengers, the weight per seat *fell* by around 40 per cent. One factor was adoption of open plan seating—allowing four comfortable seats across the coach instead of three—and

another was the increase in length from a standard of around 64ft (19,507mm) to 75ft 6in (23,000mm). This represented two additional bays of seating.

Particularly noticeable to the passenger is the superb ride at very high speeds over track whose quality is inevitably sometimes only fair. This is the result of the application of some sophisticated hardware evolved for the APT train, using air suspension. Including refreshment vehicles, some of the HST trains have seven passenger cars and others eight. For a period some of those on the East Coast route had nine, but this was only a temporary expedient, as maintenance installations had been designed round the standard formations.

The concept of the HST was to provide a super train service on the existing railway, without rebuilding, replacing or even electrifying it. This meant being able to stop when required at signals within the warning distances which were implicit in the existing signalling system and, accordingly, the braking system—with disc brakes on all wheels—includes sophisticated wheelslip correction.

A complete prototype train was built and tested; this train reached 143mph (230km/h) on one occasion, a world record for diesel traction. Even so, there were aggravating problems with minor details of the production trains when they first went into service. Two things, however, mitigated the effects; first, a failure of one power car still left the other to drive the train at a more modest but still respectable pace. The second factor was the will to win through at all levels on the part of the staff, engendered by the possession of a tool which was not only a world-beater in railway terms but capable of beating airliners and motor cars as well.

Class 120 B₀-B₀

West Germany:
German Federal Railway (DB), 1979

Type: Mixed-traffic electric locomotive.
Gauge: 4ft 8½in (1,435mm).
Propulsion: Alternating current at 15,000V 16⅔Hz from overhead wires rectified by thyristors and then inverted by thyristors to variable-frequency three-phase ac for supply to four 1,880hp (1,400kW) induction traction motors with spring drive.
Weight: 185,140lb (84t).
Max. axleload: 46,280lb (21t).
Overall length: 63ft 0in (19,200mm).
Tractive effort: 76,440lb (340kN).
Max. speed: 100mph (160km/h).

The relative merits of the three types of traction motors, dc, single-phase ac and three-phase ac, were well understood at the turn of the century, but the choice of motor in early electrification schemes was determined more by considerations of supply and control than by the characteristics of the motors. The commutator motors (dc and single-phase ac) proved to be the most adaptable to the control equipment available, and three-phase motors were little used. Recently, however, new control systems using thyristors have revived the three-phase motor, because it is now possible to exploit efficiently and economically its inherent qualities.

Three-phase motors are of two types: synchronous, in which the frequency is directly tied to the supply frequency, and asynchronous or induction motors. It is the latter which have excellent traction

Below: *German Federal Railway's Class 120 Co-Co prototype electric locomotive with advanced three-phase transmission system.*

characteristics. In this motor, three-phase current is supplied to poles located round the inside of the stator, producing a "rotating" magnetic field. The rotor carries closed turns of conductors, and as the magnetic field rotates relative to the rotor, currents are induced in the rotor conductors. Due to these currents, forces act on the conductors (the normal "motor" effect), and these cause the rotor to turn. The torque thereby exerted on the rotor shaft depends upon the difference between the rotor speed and the speed of rotation of the field. This difference is expressed as the "slip" (not to be confused with normal wheelslip).

It can be shown that the speed of the rotor is proportional to the frequency of the current supplied to the motor, to the slip, and inversely to the number of poles. Under steady running conditions, slip is only one or two per cent of the speed, so varying the slip does not offer much scope for speed control. In early three-phase systems, the frequency of the supply to the motor was the

frequency of the mains supply, and was fixed. The only way of varying the speed of the motor was thus by changing the number of poles. Even by regrouping the poles by different connections, it was only possible to get three or four steady running speeds. It was this limitation on speed control which hindered development of three-phase traction.

It was only possible to vary the frequency of the current supplied to the motors by the use of rotating machinery. This was done in several installations by a rotary converter, but the advantages of the three-phase motor were then offset by the disadvantages of an additional heavy rotating machine.

The development of thyristors opened up a new future for the induction motor. By their ability to switch current on and off quickly and very precisely, thyristors can be used to "invert" dc to ac by interrupting a dc supply. By inverting three circuits with an interval of one third of a "cycle" between each, a three-phase ac supply can be produced, and it is relatively simple to vary the frequency of

Above: *The stylish lines of the Class 120 German Federal Railway electric locomotive is matched by its equally advanced electric circuits.*

this supply within wide limits. This is the key to controlling the speed of an induction motor by varying the frequency of the current supplied to it. Furthermore, this variation can be "stepless', that is, it can be varied gradually without any discontinuities.

In any motor control system the effects of "steps" or sudden changes in motor current are important because they can institute wheelslip. With thyristor control, three-phase motors can be worked much nearer to the limit of adhesion than can other types because not only is wheelslip less likely to develop, but also it is self-correcting. If a pair of wheels loses its grip on the rails, it accelerates slightly, thereby reducing the slip, and, in turn, reducing the torque which it transmits. This reduces the tendency for the wheels to lose their grip, so that wheelslip is self-correcting.

If the train begins to accelerate on a down gradient, the rotor accelerates, and "overtakes" the speed of the rotating field. Motor slip changes direction, and the motor exerts a braking rather than a driving torque, that is, the motor becomes a three-phase alternator. If provision is made for the current generated to be fed back into the overhead line, or to resistances, the induction motor provides electric braking quite simply.

Various experiments with induction motors were made in Europe in the 1960s and 1970s, both for electric locomotives and for diesel-electrics. Although all the systems had the common aim of supplying variable-frequency three-phase current to the traction motors by the use of thyristors, the circuitry varies between manufacturers.

In 1971, the West German locomotive manufacturer Henschel built, as a private venture, three 2,500hp (1,865kW) diesel locomotives with induction motors, using an electrical system produced by Brown Boveri (BBC). The basis of the BBC system is that the incoming supply is first changed to direct current at 2,800V, this voltage being closely controlled. This dc supply is fed into the inverter circuits, which feed variable-frequency three-phase ac to the traction motors. Deutsche Bundesbahn acquired the locomotives, and they were extensively tested and then put into regular service. In 1974 one of them had its diesel engine removed and replaced by ballast, and the locomotive was coupled permanently to an electric test coach equipped with pantograph, transformer and rectifier, from which direct current at 2,800V was supplied to the inverters on the locomotive.

Experience with this experi-

Above: *An end of DB No. 120.001-3. The last number is a check digit, used when entering locomotive identities into a computer.*

mental unit encouraged DB to order five four-axle locomotives using equipment developed from the experimental work, and they appeared in 1979. The specification called for the locomotive to haul passenger trains of 700t at 100mph (160km/h), fast freights of 1,500t at 62mph (100km/h), and heavy freights of 2,700t at 50mph (80km/h); this performance was achieved in a locomotive weighing only 84t. Full advantage was taken of the good adhesion of the induction motors, for the continuous rating is 7,500hp (5,600kW), making them the most powerful four-axle locomotives in the world. The omission of commutators and brushes from the motors enables their weight to be reduced, and in these locomotives the motors are 65 per cent lighter than corresponding DB single-phase motors. Maintenance is also simplified. The single-phase supply

from the overhead is rectified to dc at 2,800V, and is then inverted to three-phase ac at a frequency which can vary from zero to 125Hz.

Early testing revealed a number of problems, and particular attention had to be given to the effect of the inverter circuits on signalling and telephone systems, and the general effect of thyristor control on the overhead supply (technically, the "harmonics" caused). Extensive tuning of the circuitry was necessary. The body suspension is by Flexicoil springing, as in other modern DB types, and it was necessary to reduce the stiffness of this springing to control bogie oscillations.

With these problems under control, the locomotives were tested on trains of various loads, and one of them was also subjected to high-speed trials hauling one test coach. It reached 143.5mph (231km/h), thus beating the previous world record for induction motor traction set up in 1903 in the Zossen-Marienfelde trials in Germany with high speed motor coaches. Another remarkable feat was to accelerate from rest to 124mph (200km/h) in 30 seconds. One of the locomotives was tested on the Lötschberg route in Switzerland where, in severe weather conditions, it performed almost as well on the 1-in-37 (2.7 per cent) gradients as a lower-speed BLS locomotive designed specifically for work on heavy gradients.

These results are promising, but three-phase traction is not cheap, and some time will elapse before DB can assess whether it offers economic advantages over its well-tried and highly standardised single-phase equipment. Nevertheless, the induction motor is the most promising new development in electric traction.

Type: High-speed diesel-electric locomotive for matching train with tilting mechanism.
Gauge: 4ft 8½in (1,435mm).
Propulsion: Alco Type 251 16-cylinder 3,900hp (2,910kW) turbocharged four-stroke diesel engine and alternator feeding via rectifiers four nose-suspended direct current traction motors geared to the axles.
Weight: 185,135lb (84t).
Max. axleload: 46,285lb (21t).
Overall length: 66ft 5in (202,692mm).
Max. speed: 125mph (200km/h)*.

*Design speed of train; track limitations at present reduce this to 80mph (128km/h).

Having as its designation carefully chosen letters that read the same in English or French—Light, Rapid, Comfortable or *Leger, Rapide, Confortable* respectively —the designers had to have pointed out to them the letter L might in French just as well stand for *Lourd* or 'heavy'. The fact that an LRC passenger car weighs "only" 57 per cent more than, for example, an HST car of the same capacity in Britain does lend some sharpness to the point made. Similarly the LRC locomotive weighs 20 per cent more than the HST power car. Even so, LRC is an impressive creation, although the many years which have passed in development have seen as many (or more) setbacks and premature entries into service as Britain's APT. Even so, the new trains were due to go into service between Montreal and Toronto in September 1981. A scheduled time of 3hr 40min was originally intended for the 337 miles (539km), 45 minutes better than that offered

Below: *The LRC diesel-electric locomotive, production version, decked out in the handsome livery of VIA Rail Canada.*

by their best predecessors, the lightweight "Turbo-trains" in the late-1970s. But by July 1982 the best offered in the timetable was 4hr 25min, with an ominous note "Timings subject to alterations, journeys may be extended by up to 55 minutes", indicating a possible need to substitute conventional equipment.

This note reflects the fact that the LRC trains had to be withdrawn during the Canadian winter of 1981-82, having suffered from fine dry powdery snow getting inside sophisticated equipment. That the improvement in timings has been so relatively modest is due to the effects of heavy freight traffic on the existing track and the speed limits consequently imposed on the LRC. Two sets

leased by the USA operator Amtrak have also not given satisfaction, and they have recently been returned to the makers.

Even so, LRC is a well thought out concept with a fourteen-year period of development behind it. An "active" tilting system allowing 8½° of tilt, ½° less than BR's APT, is combined with an advanced level of comfort of passengers. Ample power is available from the locomotives (which, incidentally, do not tilt) for both traction and substantial heating/air-conditioning requirements. One unique detail is the provision of outside loudspeakers so that announcements can be made to intending passengers on station platforms. The current order for Via Rail Canada provides for 22

locomotives and 50 cars. At the present time, however, problems with the cars have led to a surplus of motive power; LRC locomotives have been noted coupled to non-tilting stock on the Toronto to Chicago "International Limited".

Right: *The Canadian LRC train developed by Bombardier is shown under test in prototype form with a single coach during 1978, and (below) as a series-production unit in full Via Rail Canada livery in 1982. The train attains its objective by having sophisticated tilting capability —up to 8½°—a low profile and a low centre of gravity. Propulsion is conventional diesel-electric.*

XPT Eight-car train
Australia:
New South Wales Public Transport Commission, 1981

Type: High-speed diesel-electric passenger train.
Gauge: 4ft 8½in (1,435mm).
Propulsion: Paxman 2,000hp (1,490kW) "Valenta" 12-cylinder Vee diesel engine and alternator supplying through solid-state rectifiers to four dc traction motors geared to the axles with hollow-axle flexible drive.
Weight: 156,485lb (71t) adhesive, 826,500lb (375t) total.
Max. axleload: 39,675lb (18t).
Overall length: 590ft 2in (179,870mm).
Max. speed: 100mph (160km/h).

The HST125 development in Britain (already described) is so successful and remarkable that one wonders whether others might not consider adopting it. One organisation that has done just this is the railway administration of the Australian State of New South Wales. Their Express Passenger Train or "XPT", however, has certain differences to take account of conditions met 'down-under'. First, there are only five passenger cars per train instead of seven, eight or even nine in Britain. Although the Paxman Valenta engines are down-rated by 10 per cent, the overall power-to-weight ratio is increased and this, combined with lower gearing (a 125mph maximum speed would be meaningless on Australian alignments), gives increased acceleration to recover from stops and slacks. Preliminary experiments led to bogie modifications to suit rather different permanent way and there are improvements to the ventilation systems to cater for a hotter and dustier external environment. The passenger cars are built of corrugated stainless steel, matching other modern Australian passenger stock, notably that of the "Indian-Pacific" Trans-Australian Sydney to Perth express.

The new train silenced many critics by pulverising the Australian rail speed record with 144mph (183km/h) attained near Wagga-Wagga in August 1981. Early in 1982, the XPTs went into service with a daily trip on three routes out of Sydney. Best time-saving achieved was that of 1hr 46min over the 315 miles (504km) between Sydney and Kempsey.

It says enough of the experience gained that an inital order for 10 power cars and 20 trailers to make up four seven-car trains (with two spare power cars) was augmented in April 1982 by an order for four power cars and 16 trailers to form six eight-car trains. In addition, Victorian Railways decided in February 1982 to purchase three "XPT" sets for the Melbourne-Sydney service.

Above and below: *The Australian version of the British HST 125 high-speed diesel-electric train. These sets, built for the New South Wales Public Transport Commission in 1981 by Clyde Engineering of Sydney, for rail passenger services within the state, will shortly extend their activities to include Sydney to Melbourne inter-state expresses.*

ER 200 Fourteen-car train
USSR:
Soviet Railways (SZD), 1975

Type: High-speed electric train.
Gauge: 5ft 0in (1,524mm).
Propulsion: Direct current at 3,000V fed via overhead catenary to forty-eight 288hp (215kW) traction motors driving the axles of the 12 intermediate cars of the train with gearing and flexible drives.
Weight: 1,586,880lb (720t) adhesive, 1,829,320lb (830t) total.
Max. axleload: 33,060lb (15t).
Overall length: 1,220ft 6in (372,000mm).
Max. speed: 125mph (200km/h).

This, Soviet Railways' first high-speed electric self-propelled train, was built in 1975 at the Riga Carriage Works. The intention was to provide high-speed service over the 406 miles (650km) between Moscow and Leningrad. This was the line for which the Czar, when asked to choose a route, picked up (so legend has it) a ruler and ruled a line. Hence there was no need for tilting, just adequate power—in this case 13,834hp (10,320kW). In addition, adequate braking, rheostatic above 22mph (35km/h) and electromechanical disc brakes below that speed. An electromagnetic rail brake is provided for emergency use.

Electrically, the 14 cars of the train are divided into six two-car powered units, each with 128 seats, plus, at each end, a driving

trailer car. Each of these has seats for 24, a buffet section and luggage space. An 'Autodriver' system automatically responds to transponder units at track level which set the speed to be maintained between particular points.

It has been reported that "ER 200" travelled between Moscow and Leningrad in 3hr 50min (an average speed of 106mph (170km/h) on a test carried out in 1980, but entry into public service at anything like these speeds has not yet taken place. No doubt Soviet Railways is not yet convinced—in an uncompetitive situation—of either the need or the

Above: *The leading driving trailer car of the Soviet Railways' high-speed experimental 14-coach ER 200 electric passenger train.*

desirability for high-speed trains. In the meantime SZD customers have to accept times on this route of 7 hours or more.

Fairlie B-B
Wales:
Festiniog Railway (FR), 1979

Type: Steam locomotive for tourist railway.
Gauge: 1ft 11¾in (600mm).
Propulsion: Atomised oil fuel burnt in two fireboxes within a single boiler shell, generating steam at 1,600psi (10.6kg/cm²) which is fed to twin 9in bore × 14in stoke (229 × 356mm) cylinders on each of two bogies, the wheels of which are driven directly by connecting and coupling rods.
Weight: 88,640lb (40t).
Max. axleload: 22,040lb (10t).
Overall length: 30ft 6in (9,297mm).
Tractive effort: 9,140lb (41kN).
Max. speed: 25mph (40km/h).

The majority of railway power units in the world (and in this book) run on two four-wheel bogies with all four axles driven. No exception to this rule is this Fairlie steam locomotive built in 1979 for and by an historic narrow-gauge tourist line in North Wales, called the Festiniog Railway. In fact, back in the mid-nineteenth century Fairlie steam locomotives were the first to use this now almost universal B-B wheel arrangement. Also very unusual nowadays is the fact that the locomotive was built "in-house" at the railway's own Boston Lodge Works. The end result is a modern-

ised version of the last one built there in 1879, 100 years before.

Although the line is operated for pleasure travellers rather than for serious customers, the specification is a severe one. Trains of up to 12 cars seating up to 500 passengers need to be hauled up gradients up to 1-in-80 (1.25 per cent), with curves as sharp as 2¼ chains (45m) radius and all within a 22,040lb (10t) axleload limitation.

The use of oil as fuel for a steam locomotive might seem an extravagance, but a high proportion of that used is obtained cheaply as waste and residues. There were problems with coal-burning because of setting fire to forest plantations, while the use of steam propulsion in this day and age is essential because of the customer-drawing qualities of steam locomotives. The waste oil happily gives the authentic "coaly" smell demanded by the public.

The Fairlie design involves raising steam in a patent double boiler with twin fire-boxes and smokeboxes at both ends. The steam is then fed via two throttles —arranged so that the two handles can be moved either together or singly—and two main steam pipes complete with flexible joints to the two motor bogies. The driver and fireman have to stand in restricted space, one each side of the boiler.

A drawback of the Fairlie design

is the complexity of the boiler. But once this is accepted the advantages of being able to run out the power bogies easily from under the locomotive for repair or attention are considerable. Some concession is made on *Iarll Merionnydd (Earl of Merioneth)*—one of the titles of the Duke of Edinburgh—to the approaching 21st

Above: *Fairlie B-B steam locomotive on Porthmadog train near Blaenau Ffestiniog. Note vintage carriages and slate tip in the background.*

century with an electronic speedometer in the cab. An electric headlamp at each end is also a welcome innovation.

Class 26 2-D-2

Type: Mixed-traffic steam locomotive.
Gauge: 3ft 6in (1,067mm).
Propulsion: Coal-fired gas-producer firebox with grate area of 70sq ft (6.5m²) generating superheated steam at 225psi (15.75kg/cm²) in a fire-tube boiler and supplying it to two 24x28in (610x711mm) cylinders, driving the four main axles direct by means of connecting and coupling rods.
Weight: 167,505lb (76t) adhesive, 506,920lb (230t) total.
Max. axleload: 43,640lb (19.8t).
Overall length: 91ft 6½in (27,904mm).
Tractive effort: 47,025lb (209kN).
Max. speed: 60mph (96km/h).

Many people regard steam locomotives as the only proper motive power, any other kind being *ersatz* to some degree. Yet at the same time we are aware of steam's drawbacks—its low thermal efficiency, its labour-intensiveness and its dirtiness. Of course, the low thermal efficiency can be countered by use of less costly fuels—in some countries oil costs four (or more) times coal for the same heat content and this more than cancels out the better efficiency of diesel vis-a-vis steam. At the same time the amount of fuel wasted by a steam locomotive can be reduced by relatively small improvements, and since the dirt connected with steam operation represents waste, less waste auto-

Above and below: *Views of the rebuilt South African Railways Class 25 steam locomotive, now known variously as Class 26. Red Devil after its colour, or L.D. Porta after the Argentinian who evolved the proposal.*

Class 20 2-D-1+1-D-2

Type: Beyer-Garratt steam freight locomotive.
Gauge: 3ft 6in (1,067mm).
Propulsion: Coal fire with a grate area of 63.1sq ft (5.9m²) in a fire-tube boiler generating steam at 200psi (14kg/cm²) which is supplied to two pairs of 20in bore by 26in stroke (508 × 600mm) cylinders, each pair driving the main wheels of its respective unit directly by connecting and coupling rods.
Weight: 369,170lb (167.5t) adhesive, 503,614lb (228.5t) total.
Max. axleload: 38,019lb (17.25t).
Overall length: 95ft 0½in (28,969mm).
Tractive effort: 69,330lb (308kN).
Max. speed: 35mph (56km/h).

Most railways in Africa were built to open up newly-developed colonies. Traffic expectations were not great, and the lines were often constructed cheaply to a narrow gauge, with light rails, and with severe curvature. As the colonies developed, and particularly when their mineral resources became important, the railways faced the problem of acquiring larger locomotives which would be suited to existing gauge and curvature. The solution for many lay in articulated or hinged locomotives, particularly if there was a limited axleload.

The type of articulated locomotive most popular in Africa was the Garratt, a British design which originated in 1907, and which reached its highest state of development in the 1950s. In this design the boiler is mounted on a frame suspended by pivots from two rigid units which carry the fuel bunker and water tanks. As there are no wheels under the boiler, it can have a large diameter and deep firebox, and the whole boiler unit is more accessible than in a normal rigid locomotive. Each end unit can have as many axles as the curvature of the line permits, six or eight driving axles being the norm.

The largest user of Garratts was South African Railways with 400, but Rhodesia Railways, now the National Railways of Zimbabwe, came second. This system bought 250 of them between 1926 and 1958 from Beyer Peacock of Manchester, 200 of them coming after World War II. They constituted half the total steam locomotives built for the railway. The last and largest were 61 4-8-2+ 2-8-4 machines built between 1954 and 1958. The engines have an axleload of 17t, made possible by installation of heavy rail on parts of the system, and their total weight put them near the top of the Garratt league table. They are equipped with every device for reducing maintenance costs and fuel consumption, and for increasing availability. They are notable in being the only Rhodesian Garratts to be stoker fired.

As with other African railways, Rhodesia Railways succumbed to the charms of the diesel salesmen, who could offer not only machines which were much more economical in fuel than steam engines, but also low-interest loans, which some Western governments would make available to third-world countries to assist their own diesel manufacturers. 1980 was thus set as the date for the dieselisation of the whole Rhodesian system.

However, the combination of the tremendous increase in the cost of oil from 1973 onwards with the difficulties caused by imposition of sanctions against Rhodesia following UDI, made the railway authorities review their policy. The country had large supplies of coal but no oil, so that imported oil cost thirty times as much as coal. Even though the diesel had three times the efficiency of a steam engine, this still left fuel costs for the diesel ten times as great as for steam. Furthermore, whereas many wearing parts of the steam engines could be manufactured locally, the diesels required specialised parts which only the makers could supply, and sanctions had cut these supplies. Plans for dieselisation were therefore halted, and replaced by a long-term target of electrification. In the meantime, in

matically means less pollution too.

This "Red Devil" (named *L.D. Porta* after the Argentinian engineer who was responsible for the basics of the system) is an attempt to produce a steam locomotive for the 21st century by rebuilding a "25NC" 4-8-4, a class built by Henschel and North British in 1953. The principal change is in the method of burning the coal, which is now gasified before being burnt; the other alterations are more in the nature of the fine tuning. All were carried out in South African Railways' Salt River Workshops at Cape Town, at very modest cost.

The first big change is that now less than half the air needed for combustion enters the firebox through the fire itself, the amount of reduction being set by smaller and exactly calculated openings between the bars of the grate. This change cuts down waste by eliminating fire-throwing when the locomotive is working hard.

Steam is also fed into the hot firebed from the sides. This comes from the auxiliaries and from the exhaust side of the main cylinders. It reacts chemically with the hot coal to produce cleanly combustible water gas, while at the same time the reaction is one which absorbs rather than produces heat. So the temperature of the firebed does not reach the level at which fusion takes place and clinker forms. The air passing through the hot (but not too hot) firebed makes producer gas and it is this mixture of gases which burns cleanly, using the air entering through openings in the side of the firebox. The existing mechanical stoker is retained; the hard labour of running steam power is reduced both when putting the fuel in and when taking the residues out.

Other improvements made include increased superheat (with consequent provision of improved cylinder lubrication), better draughting and a feed-water heater, all of which contribute to a further improvement in thermel efficiency. Adding this to the contribution made by the avoidance of unburnt fuel in the residues of combustion gives the startling result of one-third less fuel burnt for a given output. The maximum power output is increased, whilst both the quantity and the difficulty of disposal of the residues is considerably reduced. The result is a machine that can really look its diesel brethren in the eye in respect of such important matters as availability and cleanliness, and really wipe the floor with them when it comes to fuel costs in South African conditions.

Below: *The* Red Devil *ready to go forth and re-conquer the rails of South Africa.*

Above: *For a country with ample coal supplies and no oil it makes sense to continue with steam traction. Many of the Beyer-Garratt locomotives of National Railways of Zimbabwe such as this Class 20 2-D-1 + 1-D-2 machine have been rebuilt and fully modernised.*

1978, a scheme was initiated for rehabilitating 87 of the remaining Garratts, many of which had already been laid aside.

Although locomotives had never been built in the country, there was an engineering firm which could undertake major work on locomotive parts, beyond the capacity of the railway workshops. The work included renewal of fireboxes and, surprisingly, replacement of friction bearings by roller bearings, together with a thorough overhaul of all other working parts.

The locomotives concerned were 18 light branch line 2-6-2+ 2-6-2s of Class "14A," 35 4-6-4+ 4-6-4s of classes "15" and "15A" (these had been the principal passenger engines before dieselisation), 15 heavy 2-8-2+ 2-8-2 of Class "16A," and 19 of the largest 4-8-2+2-8-4s of classes "20" and "20A." As a symbol of their revivification, many of the locomotives were given names. The first rehabilitated engines emerged in June 1979 and the scheme was completed in 1982.

The locomotives are largely employed in the south-western part of the country near the coalfields, and they work between Gwelo, Bulawayo and Victoria Falls. They are intended to have a life of at least 15 years, but whether electrification will be sufficiently advanced by that time for them to be released remains to be seen. In the meantime, Zimbabwe has the largest steam locomotives still in operation in the world, many of which are as good as new. There must be other African countries which have coal but no oil wondering if their hasty replacement of steam was really wise.

TGV Ten-car trainset

France:
French National Railways (SNCF), 1981

Type: High-speed articulated multiple-unit electric train.
Gauge: 4ft 8½in (1,435mm).
Propulsion: In each of two motor coaches, current taken from overhead wires at either 1,500V dc or 25,000V 50Hz (or, in a few cases 15,000V 16⅔Hz) supplied through rectifiers and/or chopper control to six 704hp (525kW) traction motors mounted on the coach body and geared to the axles through spring drive; two motors on each bogie of the power car and two on the adjoining end bogie of the articulated set.
Weight: 427,575lb (194t) adhesive, 841,465lb (381.8t) total.
Max. axleload: 35,480lb (16.1t).
Overall length: 656ft 9½in (200,190mm).
Max. speed: 162mph (260km/h) initially, 186mph (300km/h) ultimately.

When, in 1955, two French electric locomotives separately established a world record of 205.7mph (331km/h) in the course of tests to measure various parameters on the locomotive and track, it seemed an esoteric exercise, far removed from everyday train running, which at that time was limited in France to 87mph (140km/h). But 21 years later two French test trains had between them exceeded 186mph (300km/h) on 223 test runs, and construction had commenced of 236 miles (380km) of new railway laid out for 300km/h running.

The main line of the former PLM railway connects the three largest cities in France, and has the heaviest long-distance passenger traffic in the country. Post-war electrification increased traffic still further, and by the 1960s congestion was severe. In an effort to overcome the problem of interleaving fast passenger trains and slower freights, traffic was arranged in "flights", with a succession of passenger trains at certain times of day and a succession of freights at others. The case for additional line capacity was very strong, and in 1966 serious study of a possible new route began. This line would not only relieve the existing route, but by taking advantage of French research into higher speeds, it would win traffic from air and road.

It was clear that a great advantage would accrue if the line could be dedicated solely to passenger traffic. The canting of curves on a line carrying mixed traffic at different speeds is always a compromise, and technology had reached a stage at which considerable increases in passenger train speeds were possible, but not those of freight trains. The axleloads of freight vehicles reach 20t and those of electric locomotives 23t, but if the axleloading on the new line could be limited to about 17t, it would be much easier to maintain the track in a suitable condition for very high speeds.

One outcome of the 1955 test running was that in 1967 limited running at 124mph (200km/h) was introduced on the Paris-Bordeaux line of the South Western Region, but further testing beyond that speed was made by railcar sets. The first experimental gas turbine train was run up to 147mph (236km/h), and one of the production gas turbine sets made 10 runs above 155mph (250km/h), but it was the experimental very-high-speed gas turbine set which pointed the way ahead. Designated at first TGV001 (but later changed to TGS when TGV was applied to the electric version) this was the first French train specifically designed to run at 186mph (300km/h), and it made 175 runs in which 300km/h was exceeded, with a maximum of 197mph (317km/h). A special high-speed electric motor coach was also built, and this reached 192mph (309km/h).

The project for a new line to relieve traffic on the Paris-Lyons section was initially based on using gas turbine trains similar to TGV001. To avoid the tremendous expense of a new entry into Paris, the existing route from Paris Gare de Lyon would be used for

Above: *French National Railways' (TGV) holds the world speed record of 236mph (380km/h) for a conventional train.*

18.6 miles (30km), and from there to the outskirts of Lyons there would be a completely new line, connected to existing lines at two intermediate points to give access to Dijon and to routes to Lausanne and Geneva in Switzerland. Substantial state aid would be needed to finance the project, but it was predicted that both SNCF and the State would reap a satisfactory return on the investment.

Before the project received ministerial approval, the oil crisis of 1973 caused a radical change of plan, and gas turbine propulsion was abandoned in favour of electrification at 25,000V 50Hz. As the new route would be used solely by very fast passenger trains, it was possible to have much steeper gradients than on a conventional railway. The "kinetic energy" or energy of movement of a vehicle depends on the *square* of the speed, and the

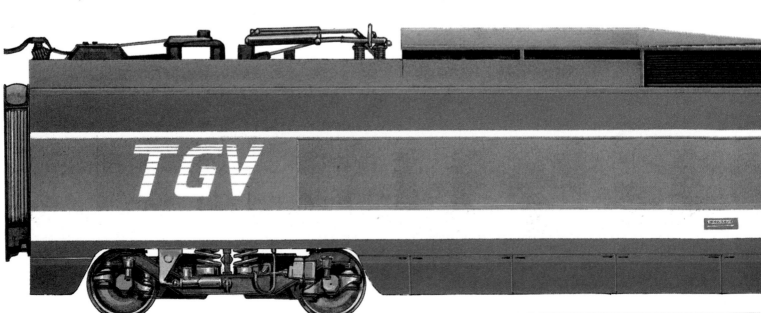

faster a train is travelling, the smaller is the loss of speed due to "rushing" a given gradient. On the new line, maximum gradient is 1-in-28.5 (3.5 per cent), or four times as steep as the gradients on the existing route. By adoption of steep gradients the cost of the line has been reduced by about 30 per cent compared with a conventional railway. The longest gradient on the new line will reduce speed from 162mph (260km/h) to 137mph (220km/h).

Orders for the electric version of the TGV (*Train à Grande Vitesse*) were placed in 1976, and delivery began two years later. Although the design of the train follows that of the gas turbine version, the equipment is completely different, but it incorporates well-proven parts wherever possible. Each train comprises two end power cars flanking an eight-car articulated rake of trailers; that is, the adjoining ends of coaches are carried on a common bogie. To transmit the maximum power of 8,450hp (6,300kW) requires 12 motored axles, so in addition to the four axles of the motor coach, the end bogie of the articulated set also has motors. As the existing lines on which the trains work are electrified at 1,500V dc, the sets can operate on this system also, and six are equipped to work on 15,000V 16⅔Hz in Switzerland. For ac working there is one transformer in each motor coach, with a separate thyristor rectifier for each motor, to reduce the risk of more than one motor being out of action at once. The same thyristors work as choppers for control of the motor voltage on dc.

The sets have a new type of bogie developed directly from the gas turbine train. As the new line is used only by "TGVs", the curves are canted to suit these trains, and no tilting of the coach bodies on curves is needed. The traction motors are mounted on the body of the motor coach, with a flexible drive to the axles. By this means the unsprung mass of the

bogie is unusually low, and the forces exerted on the track at 300km/h are less than with an electric locomotive at 200km/h.

There are no lineside signals on the new line, the driver receiving signal indications in the cab. The permitted speed is displayed continuously in front of the driver, and he sets his controller to the speed required. The control system maintains speed automatically. There are three braking systems, all of which are controlled by the one driver's brake valve:

Above: *The TGV trains can run on lines electrified at 1,500V dc as well as on the 25,000V ac Paris to Lyons high-speed line. This TGV is speeding across the plain of Alsace.*

dynamic, disc and wheel tread. The dynamic brake uses the traction motors as generators, feeding energy into resistances. During braking the motors are excited from a battery, so that failure of the overhead supply does not affect the braking. The dynamic

brake is effective from full speed down to 3km/h. In normal service applications the disc brakes are half applied, and wheel tread brakes are applied lightly to clean the wheel treads. For emergency braking all systems are used fully. The braking distance from 162mph (260km/h) is 3,500m. Most of the 87 trains have first and second-class accommodation; six are first-class only and three others are exclusively mail carriers.

The trains were built by Alsthom, the motor coaches at Belfort and the trailers at La Rochelle. Initial testing was done on the Strasbourg-Belfort line, where 260km/h was possible over a distance. As soon as the first part of the new line was ready, testing was transferred, and one of the sets was fitted with larger wheels than standard to allow tests above the normal speeds. On February 26, 1981 a new world record of 236mph (380km/h) was established.

Services over the southern section of the new line began in September 1981, and passenger carryings soon showed an increase of 70 per cent. The northern section was due for opening in September 1983, with a scheduled time of 2 hours for the 266 miles (426km) from Paris to Lyons. In 1983 also the maximum speed was due to be raised from 260km/h to 270km/h (168mph).

Apart from some trouble with damage to the overhead wires at maximum speed, which necessitated a restriction to 124mph (200km/h) for a period, the new trains have worked very well. Riding on the new line is very good, but the sets are not so smooth when running on conventional lines.

The Paris-Sud-Est line is a remarkable achievement, for which the detailed planning and construction required only 10 years, and was completed to schedule. It seems also likely to become a financial success earlier than expected. Other new high-speed routes are being planned.

Below left: *A power-car of the French National Railways' TGV. All wheels, as well as those of the adjacent bogie of the next coach, are powered.*

ETR 401 Pendolino Four-car train
Italy: Fiat Ferroviaria Savigliano SpA (Fiat), 1976

Type: High-speed electric train with body-tilting mechanisms.
Gauge: 4ft 8½in (1,435mm).
Propulsion: Direct current at 3,000V fed via overhead catenary to eight 335hp (250kW) motors, two on each car, each driving one axle with longitudinal cardan shafts and gearing.
Weight: 177,422lb (80.5t) adhesive, 354,845lb (161t) total.
Max. axleload: 23,145lb (10.5t).
Overall length: 340ft 2½in (103,700mm).
Max. speed: 156mph (250km/h).

Italy was the second country to put tilting trains into service, Japan being the first with the Class "381" trains described elsewhere in this book. The project was financed by Fiat. High-speed is provided for with ample power in relation to the train's weight, plus three independent systems of braking. Dynamic braking, using the motors as dynamos is for normal use, with conventional electro-pneumatic air brakes for application at low speeds. In addition there is an electro-magnetic rail brake which, of course, acts independently of the adhesion between wheel and rail. Because of the effects of high speed vehicles on the track, the axleload has been limited to the low figure given above.

But most of the interest arises out of the high tilting capability of the train, which seats 170 passengers and permits a tilt of up to 9°. The tilt is positively actuated and is controlled by a combination of accelerometers and gyroscopes. The pantograph current collector is mounted on a framework attached to one of the bogie bolsters, so that it is not affected by the tilting.

Operation has been successful up to a point. The train has gone into regular service over the 185 mile (298km) Trans-Appennine route between Rome and Ancona. Only over a short length of the journey is its speed capability utilised, but the tilting mechanism is used to full effect on the sharp curves of the line in the mountains.

Below: *The 15.20 Ancona express ready to depart from Rome on April 19, 1978. It is formed of the impressive looking experimental ETR 401 tilting high-speed train.*

An acceleration of 45 minutes (or 25 per cent) over the best previous time for the journey was theoretically possible, but prudence has dictated that the actual improvement should be half that. However, lingering doubts would appear to have precluded any further adoption of the tilting principle, and the Fiat train remained until recently (when some similar *Basculante* trainsets based on the Fiat example were supplied to Spanish National Railways) the sole example of this principle in public service outside Japan.

Right: *The Fiat "Pendolino" train demonstrates its undoubted agility in tilting (up to 9° is possible). This train is currently in commercial service on Italian State Railways.*

Class 58 Cₒ-Cₒ
Great Britain: British Railways (BR), 1982

Type: Diesel-electric freight locomotive.
Gauge: 4ft 8½in (1,435mm).
Propulsion: One GE (Ruston) RK3ACT 3,300hp (2,460kW) 12-cylinder four-stroke turbocharged Vee engine and alternator, generating three-phase current which is supplied through rectifiers to six nose-suspended traction motors geared to the axles.
Weight: 286,520lb (130t).
Max. axleload: 47,750lb (21.7t).
Overall length: 62ft 9in (19,130mm).
Tractive effort: 59,100lb (263kN).
Max. speed: 80mph (129km/h).

Dieselisation of non-electrified lines of British Railways was completed in 1968, and from then onwards no new diesel locomotives were needed until, in 1973, BR was warned to expect a large increase in coal traffic due to the oil crisis. Work began forthwith on designing a new class of locomotive, to be more powerful than the existing 2,580hp (1,925kW) Class "47", and with a maximum speed of 80mph (129km/h) to give much better performance on heavy freight trains at low speeds than the 95mph (153km/h) Class "47."

The most common diesel engines on BR are the family derived from the pre-war English Electric shunter. This engine first appeared as a main line unit in 1947, developing 1,600hp (1,190kW) from 16 cylinders. By 1973 the engine had been uprated to 3,520hp (2,625kW), although for reliability BR decided to rate it at 3,250hp (2,425kW).

As BR could not produce a new design from its own resources in the time available, a contract was placed with Brush Electrical Machines to design a locomotive based on that builder's Class "47," but incorporating the English Electric-type engine and ac transmission. This work was done jointly by Brush and Electroputere of Romania, with whom Brush had an agreement for technical co-operation. As Electroputere could deliver the locomotives sooner than BR's Doncaster Works, the first 30 were ordered from Romania.

The first of these locomotives, designated Class "56," appeared in 1976. BR regarded them as an interim design, produced with the minimum of new design work to meet an urgent need, and it was soon decided that only 135 would be built. Further construction would be to a completely new design, Class "58," to be capable of hauling 1,000t on the level at 80mph (129km/h).

Class "58" was much influenced by design work which had been done by BR on a 2,500hp (1,865kW) locomotive which BR's workshop subsidiary, British Rail Engineering, hoped to sell abroad. Great emphasis had been laid on reducing the cost of this locomotive, and in its severely restricted financial condition BR was glad to have a locomotive cheaper than a Class "56."

The most obvious change in Class "58" is that it is a "hood" unit, with the structural strength in the underframe (Class "56" has a stressed bodyshell inherited from Class "47"). The massive underframe should have an indefinite life, whereas the thin panels of the stressed bodies corrode easily. The hood construction gives easier access to equipment and simplifies

Right: *British Railways' new Class 58 freight locomotive.*

the division of the body into airtight compartments. Most of the equipment is in sub-assemblies which are bolted to the underframe, and can be replaced from stock. The cabs are self-contained, and can be disconnected, unbolted, and replaced in a few days, whereas on earlier BR diesels repairs to a damaged cab can take months. Access is from a cross-passage between the cab and the machinery compartments, so that the cab has no outside door to admit draughts. The layout of the controls is new for BR, and they can be operated whilst the driver is leaning out of the cab window.

The engine is a new model in the long line descended from the English Electric units of 1947. Compared with the engine in Class "56," the speed has been increased from 900rpm to 1,000rpm, and a new and simpler turbocharger is fitted. As a result

it has been possible to reduce the number of cylinders from 16 to 12, and yet to rate the engine 50hp higher than the Class "56" engine, at 3,300hp (2,460kW).

Amongst other duties, these locomotives will be used on "merry-go-round" coal trains which discharge their loads at power stations whilst in motion, and for this purpose they are fitted with an automatic slow-speed control to hold the speed accurately at 1mph (1.6km/h).

Simplification in the design has produced a reduction of about 13 per cent in the cost of a Class "58" compared with a Class "56," and further economies will result from reduced maintenance costs. An initial order for 30 was placed with BREL's Doncaster Works, and the first was delivered in December 1982, wearing new colours based on the current livery of BR "Speedlink" freight wagons.

Class 370 "APT-P" Train
Great Britain:
British Railways (BR)

Type: High-speed electric passenger train.
Gauge: 4ft 8½in (1,435mm).
Propulsion: Alternating current at 25,000V 50Hz fed via overhead catenary, step-down transformer and thyristor-based control system to four body-mounted 1,000hp motors in two power cars, driving the wheels through longitudinal shafts and gearing.
Weight: 297,540lb (135t) adhesive, 1,014,942lb (460.6t) total.
Max. axleload: 37,248lb (16.9t).
Overall length: 963ft 6in (293,675mm).
Max. speed: 150mph (240km/h).

Although the final outcome of this project, one of the most far-sighted and ambitious passenger train developments ever begun, is still in the future, it is fair to say that up to now it has also been one of the most painful. The saga began in the 1960s when British Railways set its much-enlarged Research Department at Derby to do a thorough study of their most fundamental problem, the riding of flanged wheels on rails. Out of this emerged the possiblity of designing vehicles which could run smoothly at higher speeds than previously permitted over sharply-curved track with the usual imperfections. To keep the passengers comfortable, the trains would tilt automatically when negotiating curves which would have to stay canted or banked only for normal speeds

Several railways have done or are doing this, notably those of Japan, Italy and Canada. The Canadian LRC train (described previously) is the only one which approaches the ambitiousness of the British scheme—in the others the body tilt is purely a passive response to the sideways forces encountered. In the APT, body-tilting is achieved in a much more sophisticated and positive manner, each coach adjusting its tilt response to curvature by sensing movement of the coach ahead. The amount of body tilt can rise to as much as 9°, which means that at full tilt one side of the car can be 16in (400mm) higher than the other. The result would be a train which could provide the high average speeds that the future would seem to demand if railways are to remain in business for

journeys over 200 miles, without the hugh capital investment involved in building new lines for them. For example, 105mph (167km/h) or 3h 50min between London and Glasgow is very close to 103mph (165km/h) envisaged in France over a similar distance from Paris to Marseilles, using the new purpose-built railway between Paris and Lyons. Put another way, the British solution—if it had succeeded—would have equalled the French for a cost of only one-fifth.

At this point one must say that the body-tilting is only part of this advanced concept—a new and fundamentally improved suspension system with a self-steering feature in the bogies contributed even more to a package which looked like being a winner. A formal submission for funds to

Above: *The driving end of British Railways' Advanced Passenger Train, production-prototype version, "APT-P". The power cars were situated in mid-train and also had tilting capability.*

develop the project was made in December 1967. In 1973 after some delay, a four-car experimental prototype powered by a gas turbine was authorised and in 1975 was brought out into the world after early testing in secret on BR's test track near Nottingham. APT-E as it was called managed 151mph (242km/h) run-

Below: *The futuristic lines of British Railways' Advanced Passenger Train did not, alas, presage a successful future for these magnificent examples of carriage-building skills.*